THE LION BECOMES MAN

SOCIETY
OF BIBLICAL
LITERATURE

DISSERTATION SERIES

Charles Talbert, New Testament Editor
J. J. M. Roberts, Old Testament Editor

Number 81
THE LION BECOMES MAN
The Gnostic Leontomorphic Creator
and the Platonic Tradition
by
Howard M. Jackson

Howard M. Jackson

THE LION BECOMES MAN
The Gnostic Leontomorphic Creator and the Platonic Tradition

Scholars Press
Atlanta, Georgia

THE LION BECOMES MAN
The Gnostic Leontomorphic Creator and the Platonic Tradition

Howard M. Jackson

Ph.D., 1983
Claremont Graduate School

Advisor:
James M. Robinson

©1985
Society of Biblical Literature

Library of Congress Cataloging in Publication Data

Jackson, Howard M.
  The lion becomes man.

  (Dissertation series / Society of Biblical Literature ;
81)
  Originally presented as the author's thesis (Ph. D.)—
Claremont Graduate School.
  Includes bibliographies.
  1. Lions—Religious aspects—History. 2. Gnosticism.
I. Title. II. Series: Dissertation series (Society of Biblical
Literature) ; 81.
BL443.L56J33   1985   299'.932   85-10914
ISBN 0-89130-872-5 (alk. paper)
ISBN 0-89130-873-3 (pbk. : alk. paper)

Printed in the United States of America
on acid-free paper

To Beth
non iam uxori sed etiamnum
aeternumque mihi
carissimae

οὐκ ἔστι λέουσι καὶ ἀνδράσιν ὅρκια πιστά

Iliad 22.262

ma non sì che paura non mi desse
la vista che m'apparve d'un leone.
    Questi parea che contra me venisse
con la test' alta e con rabbiosa fame
sì che parea che l'aere ne tremesse.

La Commedia. Inferno 1.44-48

Contents

Abbreviations

ANET[3]	James B. Pritchard, ed.; *Ancient Near Eastern Texts Relating to the Old Testament*; 3rd ed. with Supplement
AOAT	Alter Orient und Altes Testament
AOF	*Archiv für Orientforschung*
APF	*Archiv für Papyrusforschung*
APOT	R. H. Charles, ed.; *Apocrypha and Pseudepigrapha of the Old Testament* I and II
ArOr	*Archiv orientální*
ARW	*Archiv für Religionswissenschaft*
ASAE	*Annales du Service des antiquités de l'Égypte*
ASAK	*Anzeiger für schweizerische Altertumskunde*
ASC	Analecta Sacra et Classica
ATD	Das Alte Testament Deutsch
ATDan	Acta Theologica Danica
BAO	Beihefte zum Alten Orient
BAT	Die Botschaft des Alten Testaments
BBM	*Bulletin of the Brooklyn Museum*
BCH	*Bulletin de correspondance hellénique*
BCTH	*Bulletin archéologique du Comité des travaux historiques et scientifiques*
BDB	Francis Brown, S. R. Driver, and Charles A. Briggs, eds.; *A Hebrew and English Lexicon of the Old Testament*
Bib	*Biblica*
BibOr	Biblica et Orientalia
BIE	*Bulletin de l'Institut d'Égypte*
BIHBR	*Bulletin de l'Institut historique belge de Rome*

BIFAO	*Bulletin de l'Institut français d'archéologie orientale*
BJbb	*Bonner Jahrbücher*
BJRL	*Bulletin of the John Rylands University Library of Manchester*
BKAT	Biblischer Kommentar: Altes Testament
BMB	*Bulletin du Musée de Beyrouth*
BMHBA	*Bulletin du Musée hongrois des beaux-arts*
BMMA	*Bulletin of the Metropolitan Museum of Art*
BollS	Bollingen Series
BSOAS	*Bulletin of the School of Oriental and African Studies*
BZAW	Beihefte zur *Zeitschrift für die alttestamentliche Wissenschaft*
CAH	*The Cambridge Ancient History*
CAT	Commentaire de l'Ancien Testament
CBQ	*Catholic Biblical Quarterly*
CChr	Corpus Christianorum
CEg	*Chronique d'Égypte*
CG	Codex Cairensis Gnosticus
CII	Jean-Baptiste Frey, ed.; *Corpus Inscriptionum Iudiacarum*
CIMRM	M. J. Vermaseren, ed.; *Corpus Inscriptionum et Monumentorum Religionis Mithriacae* I and II
ColLat	Collection Latomus
CPJ	Victor A. Tcherikover and Alexander Fuks, eds.; *Corpus Papyrorum Judaicarum*
CQ	*Classical Quarterly*
CRAI	*Comptes rendus des séances de l'Académie des inscriptions et belles-lettres*

OBO	Orbis Biblicus et Orientalis
OLZ	*Orientalische Literaturzeitung*
OMRO	*Oudheidkundige mededelingen uit het Rijkmuseum van Oudheden te Leiden*
OrAnt	*Oriens Antiquus*
OrChr	*Oriens Christianus*
OTS	*Oudtestamentische studiën*
PAeg	Probleme der Ägyptologie
PG	J. Migne, ed.; *Patrologia Graeca*
PGM	Karl Preisendanz, *Papyri Graecae Magicae* I and II
PL	J. Migne, ed.; *Patrologia Latina*
POxy	Oxyrhynchus papyrus/papyri
PP	*La parola del passato*
PSBA	*Proceedings of the Society of Biblical Archaeology*
PW	Pauly-Wissowa, eds.; *Real-Encyclopädie der classischen Altertumswissenschaft*
PWSup	Supplements to Pauly-Wissowa
RAAO	*Revue d'assyriologie et d'archéologie orientale*
RÄRG	Hans Bonnet, ed.; *Reallexikon der ägyptischen Religionsgeschichte*
RB	*Revue biblique*
RBPH	*Revue belge de philologie et d'histoire*
RdQ	*Revue de Qumran*
REA	*Revue des études anciennes*
REG	*Revue des études grecques*
RGVV	Religionsgeschichtliche Versuche und Vorarbeiten

RHR	*Revue de l'histoire des religions*
RNT	Regensburger Neues Testament
RNum	*Revue numismatique*
Roscher	W. H. Roscher, ed.; *Ausführliches Lexikon der griechischen und römischen Mythologie*
RPh	*Revue de philologie, de littérature et d'histoire anciennes*
RSR	*Recherches de science religieuse*
RTPE	*Receuil de travaux relatifs à la philologie et à l'archéologie égyptiennes et assyriennes*
SBLDS	Society of Biblical Literature. Dissertation Series
SBLTT	Society of Biblical Literature. Texts and Translations
SBM	Stuttgarter biblische Monographien
SBT	Studies in Biblical Theology
Sem	*Semitica*
SHR	Studies in the History of Religions
SJ	Studia Judaica
SMSR	*Studi e materiali di storia delle religioni*
SO	*Symbolae Osloenses*
SÖAW.PH	*Sitzungsberichte der österreichische Akademie der Wissenschaften, Philosophisch-historische Klasse*
SPAW.PH	*Sitzungsberichte der preussischen Akademie der Wissenschaften, Berlin, Philosophisch-historische Klasse*
STDJ	Studies on the Texts of the Desert of Judah
StGen	*Studium Generale*
SVF	Joannes von Arnim, ed.; *Stoicorum Veterum Fragmenta*

TDNT	G. Kittel and G. Friedrich, eds.; *Theological Dictionary of the New Testament*
TextsS	Texts and Studies
ThF	*Theologische Forschung*
THKNT	Theologischer Handkommentar zum Neuen Testament
ThLZ	*Theologische Literaturzeitung*
ThR	*Theologische Rundschau*
TMMM	Franz Cumont, ed.; *Textes et monuments figurés relatifs aux mystères de Mithra* I and II
TS	*Theological Studies*
TU	Texte und Untersuchungen
UF	*Ugarit Forschungen*
VBW	*Vorträge der Bibliothek Warburg*
VC	*Vigiliae Christianae*
VTSup	Supplements to *Vetus Testamentum*
WS	*Wiener Studien*
WUNT	Wissenschaftliche Untersuchungen zum Neuen Testament
WZ(L).GS	*Wissenschaftliche Zeitschrift der Karl-Marx-Universität, Leipzig, Gesellschafts- und Sprachwissenschaftliche Reihe*
ZA	*Zeitschrift für Assyriologie*
ZÄS	*Zeitschrift für ägyptische Sprache und Altertumskunde*
ZAW	*Zeitschrift für die alttestamentliche Wissenschaft*
ZDMG	*Zeitschrift der deutschen morgenländischen Gesellschaft*

List of Plates

8f-g   Alexandrian coins of Traianic date depicting the sphinx "pantheos" (in g as the γρύψ of Nemesis) (after Ch. Picard, "La sphinge tricéphale, dite 'panthée,' d'Amphipolis et la démonologie égypto-alexandrienne," *MMFP* 50 [1958] p. 83, fig. 16)

9a   Alexandrian coin of Hadrianic date depicting the sphinx "pantheos" with the γρύψ of Nemesis astride its back (after J. Leibovitch, "Le Griffon d'Erez et le sens mythologique de Némésis," *IEJ* 8 [1958] pl. 29F)

9b   Stele from Coptos depicting *Twtw* as a sphinx "pantheos" with the γρύψ of Nemesis astride his back (after Ch. Picard, "La sphinge tricéphale" p. 71, fig. 6)

9c   Stele depicting *Twtw* as a sphinx "pantheos" dispatching an enemy (after Ch. Picard, "La sphinge tricéphale" p. 69, fig. 5)

10a   *Twtw* as a polycephalic man and as a sphinx (after Ch. Picard, "La sphinge tricéphale" p. 63, fig. 3)

10b   Stele from Luxor depicting *Twtw* as a sphinx "pantheos" (after Ch. Picard, "La sphinge tricéphale" p. 73, fig. 7)

11a   *Twtw* as a sphinx, accompanied by the seven "messengers," facing a knife-wielding Bes (after Serge Sauneron, "Le nouveau sphinx composite du Brooklyn Museum et le rôle du dieu Toutou-Tithoès," *JNES* 19 [1960] pl. 14)

11b-c   The seven groups of "messengers" at Dendera (after Auguste Mariette, *Dendérah. Description générale du grande temple de cette ville* IV; Paris: Franck, 1873; pls. 78, 79 respectively)

12a-f   Amulets depicting leontocephalic human figures (a-d after Campbell Bonner, *Studies in Magical Amulets* ##234, 236, 235, 149 respectively; e-f after A. Delatte and Ph. Derchain, *Les intailles gréco-égyptiennes* ##303, 304 respectively)

12g   The Abbott gem (obverse) (after Paul Perdrizet, "Antiquités de Léontopolis," *MMFP* 25 [1921-1922] p. 357, fig. 2)

12h   Map of the two cities Leontopolis and their environs (after *DBSup* 5; Paris: Letouzey et Ané, 1957; p. 362, fig. 507)

1

The Gospel of Thomas

1.1   A Puzzling Logion of Jesus

Among the hardest of "hard sayings" that the Coptic *Gospel of Thomas* from Nag Hammadi (CG II, 2) sets upon the lips of Jesus is the seventh,[1] which reads as follows:

1.   пехе ⲓⲥ
2a. ⲟⲩ/ⲙⲁⲕⲁⲣⲓⲟⲥ ⲡⲉ ⲡⲙⲟⲩⲉⲓ
2b. ⲡⲁⲉⲓ ⲉⲧⲉ / ⲡⲣⲱⲙⲉ ⲛⲁⲟⲩⲟⲙϥ
2c. ⲁⲩⲱ ⲛⲧⲉⲡⲙⲟⲩⲉⲓ / ϣⲱⲡⲉ ⲣ̄ⲣⲱⲙⲉ
3a. ⲁⲩⲱ ϥⲃⲏⲧ ⲛ̄ϭⲓ ⲡⲣⲱⲙⲉ
3b. ⲡⲁⲉⲓ ⲉⲧⲉ ⲡⲙⲟⲩⲉⲓ ⲛⲁⲟⲩⲟⲙϥ
3c. ⲁⲩ/ⲱ ⲡⲙⲟⲩⲉⲓ ⲛⲁϣⲱⲡⲉ ⲣ̄ⲣⲱⲙⲉ[2]

A literal translation might run:

1.   Jesus said:
2a.   Blessed is the lion

---

[1]Logion 7 in the *editio princeps* (A. Guillaumont, H.-Ch. Puech, G. Quispel, W. Till and Yassah ʿAbd Al Masīḥ, *The Gospel according to Thomas*; Leiden: Brill and New York: Harper & Row, 1959), but number 6 in Johannes Leipoldt's translation ("Ein neues Evangelium? Das koptische Thomasevangelium übersetzt und besprochen," *ThLZ* 83 [1958] 481-496), which understands the subject of ⲡⲉⲭⲁϥ in 32[60].12 to be Thomas, not Jesus, and so makes the statement it introduces part of the prologue, not the first logion. Some follow his scheme.

[2]CG II, 2; 33[81].23-28. I have rearranged the Coptic to suit the structure of the saying; slash marks indicate where lines end in the original.

2b.   whom the man shall eat
2c.   and the lion becomes man;
3a.   but foul is the man
3b.   whom the lion shall eat
3c.   and the lion shall become man.[3]

The "ἑρμηνεία of these words" that at the outset of *Gos. Thom.*
(32 [80].13) Jesus (or Thomas) bids the reader seek for the logia has in this
instance failed even the most enlightened and persistent researchers. "Ich
habe nicht alles in unserem Texte verstanden," Johannes Leipoldt admits
in his remarks at the end of the first published translation, and in this
context he cites logion 7 (his 6) as an example of sayings "mit völlig
klarem, sicher übersetzbarem Texte, die uns sozusagen Widerstand lei-
sten. Es fehlt der ursprüngliche Zusammenhang oder der Schlüssel der
Allegorie."[4] The key indeed! What, or whom, do the man and the lion
represent? What does it mean for the lion to devour the man, and even
more, for the man to devour the lion? Why is the *lion* blessed when the
man consumes him, and not the man, as one might justifiably expect? How
exactly does the lion *become* man, and why is it invariably the lion, both
as eater and as eaten, who is made to undergo the transformation? Obvious and satisfactory answers to these questions do not leap to the tongue.

Answers might perhaps more readily have done so had this enigmatic
oracle of "Jesus" any parallel whatsoever—excluding, of course, the
simple formulas of macarism and curse—either in any of the dominical
sayings preserved in the canonical Gospels and other books of the New
Testament or in the "Agrapha" to be culled from patristic and Gnostic
sources. But there are none. Not even an "echo" is registered for the
logion in the list of scriptural parallels compiled for the *editio princeps*.[5]
Although this vacuum is somewhat misleading and the leonine metaphor
recurs in two passages of the New Testament that I intend to demonstrate
are intimately connected with one of the strands of tradition underlying
the logion, the fact remains that as a whole it is quite unique.

It is understandable, then, that scholars should evade wrestling with
this dark pronouncement. Few so much as make passing reference to it,
even in works whose scope or subject matter invite anticipation of its

---

[3]All translations in this dissertation, unless otherwise explicitly noted
to the contrary, are my own.
[4]"Ein neues Evangelium?" 496.
[5]*Gospel according to Thomas* 59.

exegesis.[6] Only the commentators offer anything like an attempt at exposition, and they preface their remarks with discomforting disclaimers. To Rudolphe Kasser, for example, the logion is "l'une des sentences les plus obscures du recueil."[7] Even with the correction he now cautiously accepts in 3c (this matter will be taken up momentarily), in a later edition of his earlier work Leipoldt concedes that the text "auch so lässt sich keine sichere Deutung geben."[8]

The purpose of this study is to uncover the background of the Gnostic mythologem of a leontomorphic demiurge and its implications for the structure and operation of the human psyche. A firm grasp of this background is essential for an adequate understanding of the logion.[9] Many

---

[6]R. McL. Wilson in *Studies in the Gospel of Thomas* (London: Mowbray, 1960) and Ernst Haenchen in "Die Anthropologie des Thomas-Evangeliums," *Neues Testament und Christliche Existenz. Festschrift für Herbert Braun* (ed. H.D. Betz and L. Schottroff; Tübingen: Mohr, 1973; 207-227) omit any mention of the saying whatsoever. Haenchen twice adduces the logion in *Die Botschaft des Thomas-Evangeliums* (Berlin: Töpelmann, 1961) 12-13, but only for an example of catchword connection as a compositional feature of the document. Given his broad knowledge of the field, it is especially regrettable that Henri-Charles Puech does not include the logion in his series of discussions on "Doctrines ésotériques et thèmes gnostiques dans l'"Évangile selon Thomas' (Later l'*Évangile selon Thomas*)" in *ACF* (1962) 195-203; (1963) 199-213; (1964) 209-217; (1965) 247-256; (1966) 259-262; (1967) 253-260; (1968) 285-297; (1969) 269-283; (1970) 273-288; (1971) 251-268; (1972) 287-322.

[7]*L'Évangile selon Thomas. Présentation et commentaire théologique* (Neuchâtel: Delachaux & Nestlé, 1961) 38.

[8]*Das Evangelium nach Thomas, koptisch und deutsch* (TU 101; Berlin: Akademie-Verlag, 1967) 57. Others voice similar sentiments. Robert M. Grant and David Noel Freedman (*The Secret Sayings of Jesus;* Garden City, NY: Doubleday, 1960; 126) agree with Jean Doresse (*Les livres secrets des gnostiques d'Égypte* II: "L'Évangile selon Thomas ou Les paroles secrètes de Jésus"; Paris: Plon, 1959; 134) in pronouncing it "extremely obscure." So too George W. MacRae ("The Gospel of Thomas— Logia Iesou?" *CBQ* 22 [1960] 68: "extremely difficult to understand") and R. Schippers, who concludes some rather lengthy remarks with the statement: "Maar het geheel blijft raadselachtig" (with T. Baarda, *Het evangelie van Thomas. Apocriefe woorden van Jezus;* Kampen: Kok, 1960; 67).

[9]So Oscar Cullmann, "Das Thomasevangelium und die Frage nach dem Alter der in ihm enthaltenen Tradition," *ThLZ* 85 (1960) 334. The English translation of this article, "The Gospel of Thomas and the Problem of the Age of the Tradition Contained Therein," *Int* 16 (1962) 418-438, is misleading here.

commentators have taken this hypothesis for granted by providing patchy references to the tradition and brief sketches of their significance,[10] but no concerted effort has ever been made to explore it fully. The interpretation of *Gos. Thom.*'s seventh logion is thus only the occasion for a far more wide-ranging investigation of theriomorphic imagery in Gnosticism. In the discussion that follows I intend to trace the mythological, philosophical and social origins of this facet of Gnostic speculation by an examination of pertinent traditions in antiquity and by the endeavor to assess the time and context in which, if at all, they made their individual contributions to the development of the Gnostic amalgam.[11] The amalgam is undeniably complex, and I have exerted myself to leave no promising stone unturned. If the journey leads far afield and, in many cases, into the darker corners of ancient religiosity—from classical Greek myth, Egyptian religion, Plato and Judaism to Hellenistic bestiaries, Mithraism, magic and astrology—I trust that what may be learned about Gnosticism and about the late antique world in general makes the venture worth the undertaking.

1.2   The Text-Critical Issue

The interpretation of the seventh logion of *Gos. Thom.* is complicated by the possibility of textual corruption in 3c. Ostensibly, at least, one expects for this line ⲁⲩⲱ ⲡⲣⲱⲙⲉ ⲛⲁϣⲱⲡⲉ ⲙ̄ⲙⲟⲩⲉⲓ "and the man shall become the lion" to counterbalance 2c, since 3b reverses the situation in 2b. The text as the manuscript has it poses the last of the questions raised a moment ago: Why should it be that it is invariably the lion who is made to undergo the transformation? If the lion turns into man when eaten, then the man ought to turn into lion when their consumptive roles are exchanged.

Indeed, though they did not alter the text, in notes to the Coptic and

---

[10]Kasser, *L'Évangile selon Thomas* 38-39; Doresse, "L'Évangile selon Thomas" 134; Grant and Freedman, *Secret Sayings* 126; and others. Bertil Gärtner, *The Theology of the Gospel according to Thomas* (trans. E. Sharpe; New York: Harper & Bros., 1961) 162-163, gives the fullest account.

[11]This work does not pretend to have found the key that unlocks all the mysteries of Gnosticism, but its attempt to trace the theriomorphic tradition to its roots may be of heuristic value in suggesting where to look for answers about the origin of other aspects of Gnosticism.

the English translation at 33[81].28 the editors of the *editio princeps* instruct the reader to adopt the correction. Doresse eventually took the step of assuming the alteration into his translation, claiming great probability that this yields the correct meaning,[12] and others, among them Jacques-É. Ménard[13] and, conjecturally, Haenchen,[14] followed suit. Leipoldt is a bit more cautious, but he still regards the correction as plausible.[15]

The error has regularly been held to be either transcriptional or translational in origin. Haenchen favors the former alternative, positing a copyist's oversight as the source of the mistake. He adduces the repetition of 2c in 3c as evidence that CG II, *2 Gos. Thom.* is not a translation directly from a Greek *Vorlage*, but the occasionally faulty copy of a Coptic manuscript.[16] He evidently means to argue that the nature of the mistake—simple repetition where in 3c the inverse word order is required—is such that it precludes the likelihood of an error in translation. H. E. W. Turner sides with Haenchen in attributing the mistake to a transcriber but

[12] *The Secret Books of the Egyptian Gnostics* (London: Hollis & Carter, 1960) 356 and 371. In emending the text this English edition, "revised and augmented by the author," dared what the French original ("L'Évangile selon Thomas" 91) had not.

[13] *L'Évangile selon Thomas* (NHS 5; Leiden: Brill, 1975) 56-57, 87-88.

[14] *Synopsis Quattuor Evangeliorum* (8th ed.; Stuttgart: Württembergische Bibelanstalt, 1973) 518, which follows the translation offered in *Botschaft* 15. B. M. Metzger's English translation for the *Synopsis* contents itself with remarking in parenthesis *"sic; perhaps an errror for"* the correction; G. Garitte's Latin renders the text as it stands without comment.

[15] *Evangelium nach Thomas* 26-27, 57. "Ein neues Evangelium?" 483 appends "(sic!)" to a translation of the unaltered text. This earlier translation appeared later as an independent reprint, with the coauthorship of Hans-Martin Schenke, under the title *Koptisch-gnostische Schriften aus den Papyrus-Codices von Nag-Hamadi* (*ThF* 20; Hamburg-Bergstedt: Reich, 1960).

[16] "Literatur zum Thomasevangelium," *ThR* 27 (1961) 160. He refers to Søren Giversen (*Thomasevangeliet. Indledning, oversaettelse og kommentarer*; Copenhagen: Gad, 1959; 38, 39), who similarly sets the matter down to scribal error. In Giversen's view it is an "obvious" and "typical" transcriber's mistake which may be taken as evidence that CG II, *2 Gos. Thom.* is a copy of another Coptic manuscript: "Den i linie 27-28 åbenbare fejl i teksten er en typisk afskriverfejl, der kan tages som et af beviserne for at den foreliggende koptiske tekst er skrevet af efter en anden tekst" (*Thomasevangeliet* 39).

replaces the inadvertent repetition that Haenchen posits as the specific reason for the error by referring vaguely to homoioteleuton "or similar causes."[17] How exactly the error is to be explained by homoioteleuton (ⲙⲟⲩⲉ ⲓ and ⲣⲱⲙⲉ?) and what precisely the "similar causes" might have been he does not say.

But even inadvertent repetition is not an adequate explanation. The matter is not so simple as Haenchen suggests, for in fact 2c and 3c are not identical; only the order of the nouns in the lines is identical. The Coptic verbal elements in the two clauses show a subtle variation in grammatical construction: whereas 2c uses the Conjunctive to continue the tense of 2b, 3c repeats the I Future. There is, to be sure, little to choose between them, but that little is of sufficient *stylistic* importance to nuance the meaning in a delicate fashion that translators, whether they alter the word order or not, do not always reflect.[18]

In Coptic the Conjunctive often has a subordinating function[19] and, in spite of the additional presence of a coordinating ⲁⲩⲱ, that is how it functions in 2c. In other words, as many translators suggest, 2c is virtually a dependent result clause. The clause 3c, on the other hand, is simply coordinated with its antecedent circumstances and hence is fully independent. The net effect is that it is much more loosely bound to what precedes it than 2c is to its setting.

The divergence in form between the two clauses is not likely to be accidental, then, but rather a rhetorical device intentionally employed to a specific end. That end may be no other than to enhance the surprise

---

[17]"The Theology of the Gospel of Thomas" in *Thomas and the Evangelists* (SBT 35; Naperville, Ill.: Allenson, 1962) 94.

[18]Exceptions: Hans Quecke (whose translation appears as an "Anhang" in Willem Cornelis van Unnik, ed.; *Evangelien aus dem Nilsand*; Frankfurt am Main: Scheffler, 1960; 162); Leipoldt ("Ein neues Evangelium? 483 and *Evangelium nach Thomas* 27); WIlliam R. Schoedel's translation for Grant and Freedman's volume (*Secret Sayings* 125); and Thomas O. Lambdin's translation for *The Nag Hammadi Library in English* (ed. James M. Robinson; San Francisco: Harper & Row, 1977; 118) soon to be included in a revised form in the critical edition of the tractates of Codex II (excluding CG II, *1 Apoc. John*) *Nag Hammadi Tractates II, 2-II, 7 together with XIII, 2, Brit. Lib. Or. 4926(1) and P. Oxy. 1, 654, 655* (ed. Bentley Layton; NHS 11 [probably]; Leiden: Brill). The Coptic text for this volume, established by Bentley Layton, leaves logion 7 unaltered, though the critical note *ad loc.* refers to the emendation proposed by the *editio princeps*.

[19]Walter C. Till, *Koptische Grammatik* (3d ed.; Leipzig: VEB Verlag Enzyklopädie, 1965) §323.

effect of the unexpected word order of the nouns in 3c by setting off that clause much more strongly from its context than 2c was from its own. The logia frequently offer such mysterious, unpredictable "punch lines," and there are other examples where ⲁⲩⲱ with the I Future, in some cases preceded by the use of the Conjunctive, marks a surprising climax, e.g., logion 68 (45[93].21-24), similarly a macarism, where the sequence is Conditional, Conjunctive, ⲁⲩⲱ I Future. Another example is logion 18, where the climax (36[84].14-17), also a macarism, runs Relative I Future, ⲁⲩⲱ I Future, ⲁⲩⲱ I Future.

These examples from the *Gospel of Thomas* show that the text may be correct as it stands. There are further grounds for thinking so. The primary scribe of Codex II (a second scribe copied only the first eight lines of page 47[95]) was a particularly careful worker, and, though he made his share of mistakes, corrections in his own hand are numerous.[20] This fact does not, of course, guarantee that in 3c an error did not slip by him, but it makes it less likely that one of such magnitude should have escaped his notice here. The errors that did escape his notice are distinctly minor by comparison.

Yet another argument for leaving the text unaltered is hermeneutical. The problem lies not so much with the text as with its interpretation, for once the background and the full significance of the imagery of the logion is grasped it becomes clear why the text does not say "and the man shall become lion" in 3c. It is who *consumes* whom—2b and 3b, upon which the blessing and the curse depend—that is the key issue for the saying, not so much what results. What results as the saying now stands is consistent with the tradition upon which the logion is here ultimately dependent, as this study will demonstrate.

1.3 Oxyrhynchus Papyrus 654

In such an uncertain state of affairs over the text of 3c, however, it is most unfortunate that the mid- to late third century verso side of the scrap of Oxyrhynchus papyrus #654,[21] which preserves a Greek version of

---

[20]Bentley Layton's Introduction to Codex II in *Nag Hammadi Tractates* discusses and illustrates the scribe's varied methods of correction.

[21]B. P. Grenfell and A. S. Hunt, *The Oxyrhynchus Papyri* IV (Oxford: Horace Hart, 1904) 1-22, especially 3, 9-10, and pl. 1. An abridged version of this edition was published by Grenfell and Hunt as the first half of *New Sayings of Jesus and Fragment of a Lost Gospel from Oxyrhynchus* (London: Froude, 1904); their commentary on the section of the papyrus of

what corresponds to the prologue and the first six logia of CG II, *2 Gos. Thom.*, peters out precisely at the beginning of logion 7; a few letters (lines 40-42 of the papyrus) are all that remain.[22] Grenfell and Hunt read them thus:[23]

```
40  [ . . . . . . . .]ΚΑΡΙ[. .]ΕΣΤΙΝ[
    [ . . . . . . . . . . . .]Ω ΕΣΤ[
    [ . . . . . . . . . . . . . .] ΙΝ[
```

On the basis (so it seems) of a professed "general parallelism" between their fifth saying and Matt 19:16-22//Luke 18:18-22 the original editors made lines 40-42 part of the foregoing saying and not the beginning of a new one, though the μα[κάρι[ος] that, to judge from the Coptic version, they correctly restore in line 40 might equally well have suggested comparison with the canonical Beatitudes and hence the inception of a new logion. Be that as it may, so fragmentary is the papyrus at this point that Grenfell and Hunt attempted no restoration of what is left of lines 40-42 beyond the macarism in line 40 and the suggestion in the notes that the blessing "very likely" ran "'Blessed is he who doeth these things.'"[24] Even those braver hearts who, before the discovery of the Coptic *Gos. Thom.*, hazarded further reconstruction of the text acquiesce in the original editors' view of the coherence of these lines with what precedes.[25]

---

interest here represents part of the abridgment (see *New Sayings of Jesus* 19).

[22] The discovery that POxy 1, 654 and 655 represent (a) Greek version(s) of the Coptic *Gospel of Thomas* was made by H.-Ch. Puech in 1952. On the relationship between the Greek and the Coptic versions good general summaries are those provided by W. Schneemelcher and J. Jeremias in Edgar Hennecke, *New Testament Apocrypha* I (ed. W. Schneemelcher; trans. R. McL. Wilson; Philadelphia: Westminster, 1963) 97-113, and by Harold W. Attridge in the Introduction to his edition of the Oxyrhynchus fragments forthcoming in *Nag Hammadi Tractates.*

[23] *Oxyrhynchus Papyri* IV 3.

[24] *Oxyrhynchus Papyri* IV 9.

[25] Hugh G. Evelyn White (*The Sayings of Jesus from Oxyrhynchus*; Cambridge: University Press, 1920; 21-25) sees the Sermon on the Mount in Grenfell and Hunt's fifth saying and restores lines 40-42 after Matt 6:1 and 4 with help for the macarism (essentially as Grenfell and Hunt suggested it) from Isa 56:2 LXX. Erich Klostermann (*Apocrypha* II: *Evangelien*; KlT 8; 3d ed; Berlin: de Gruyter, 1929) prints Evelyn White's text largely (except for minor alternations) unchanged. Proposals by other

That *they* should do so is understandable. But even with CG II, *2 Gos. Thom.* before him Joseph Fitzmyer could not see Coptic logion 7 reflected in the Greek remains.[26] He continues to attach lines 40-42 to the preceding saying and restores them along lines very similar to those suggested by Evelyn White. Fitzmyer's reasons are two: (1) If μαＩχάριＩοςＩ begins a new logion either the restoration of the last sentence of the preceding saying must be shortened or one must suppose the omission of the usual introductory formula "Jesus says." (2) The letters of lines 41-42 do not seem capable of being supplemented in such a way as to conform to any possible Greek version of the Coptic.

Fitzmyer remarks of the two alternatives in his first objection that "neither seems possible." There is little doubt that this statement is true for the first alternative, for the remains of line 39 are sufficient to demand a restoration in accordance with the Coptic of 33[81].21-22 and the restoration can scarcely be much different from that which Fitzmyer proposes. But of the impossibility of the second alternative one is justified in feeling some uncertainty. The Greek fragments are well known to represent a different recension of the *Gospel of Thomas* that deviates, often considerably, from the document's Coptic form,[27] and, though in no case do the Greek fragments demonstrate the omission of an introductory ΛΕΓΕＩ ＩＨＳ (or ＩＳ) attested by the Coptic, the inverse situation obtains in the case of Coptic logion 27 (38[86].17) and POxy 1,

---

scholars are conveniently cited by Charles Wessely, "Les plus anciens monuments du Christianisme écrits sur papyrus," *Patrologia Orientalis* 4.2 (Paris: Firmin-Didot, 1946 [1906]) 168-169.

[26]"The Oxyrhynchus *logoi* of Jesus and the Coptic Gospel according to Thomas," *TS* 20 (1959) 505-560, reprinted in *Essays on the Semitic Background of the New Testament* (Missoula, MT: Scholars Press, 1974) 355-433. The discussion pertaining to the end of POxy 654 appears on pp. 384-87 in *Essays*. A useful but not fully dependable summary of some of the arguments is presented by T. Akagi, *The Literary Development of the Coptic Gospel of Thomas*; Ph.D. dissertation, Western Reserve University, 1965 (Ann Arbor, MI: University Microfilms) 280-283. Akagi's interpretation of logion 7 will be summarized later; suffice it to note at this point that he uses it (unsuccessfully, it seems to me, though I agree with his conclusion) to defend retention of the text in 3c without emendation.

[27]In his Introduction to the Oxyrhynchus fragments for *Nag Hammadi Tractates* Attridge handily prints a list of the variations between the Greek and Coptic attestations to the *Gospel of Thomas*.

lines 4-5.[28] Moreover, generally speaking such redactional elements are notoriously subject to arbitrary modification, and all the more is this likely to have been so in the present circumstances where settings for the sayings, especially such a clearly dispensable feature as "Jesus says," are strictly of secondary importance.

Fitzmyer's second objection is weightier. The problem is that (disregarding the additional problem of fitting line 42's remains into the scheme) to match the Coptic for 2c of logion 7 one would certainly need to restore the extant portion of line 41 of the papyrus with ὁ λέων ἔσται ἄνθρωπος but the lack of ν after ω makes this impossible. Scholars who side with Doresse[29] in maintaining the inception of a new saying in line 40 and who are for that reason committed to the essential identity of what POxy 654 once read with the Coptic logion, circumvent this difficulty by resorting to a variety of expedients. Kasser, for example, simply inserts the missing letter, as though the scribe had accidentally omitted it.[30] M. Marcovich—without an acknowledged recollation of the papyrus—quietly replaces Grenfell and Hunt's ω̣ with γ.[31] Ménard follows his lead and goes so far as to drop the mark of uncertainty under the letter.[32]

In fact, what for Marcovich and Ménard appears to have been only conjecture may, if Attridge is correct, be the true reading. Attridge, who carried out a fresh examination of the papyrus for the new critical edition of tractates from Codex II, read lines 40-42 in the following way:

40   [. . . μα]κ̣άρι[ός] ἐστιν [. . .]
      [. . . . . . λέ]ων ἔστα̣[ι . . .]
      [. . . . .]ο̣ν [. . . . . .]

and proposes as a restoration, by way of example:

40   [. . . μα]κ̣άρι[ός] ἐστιν [ὁ λέων ὃν ἄνθρωπος]
      [ἐσθίει καὶ ὁ λέ]ων ἔστα̣[ι ἄνθρωπος καὶ ἀνά-]
      [θεμα ὁ ἄνθρωπος] ὃν [λέων ἐσθίει and so on].

---

[28] See Fitzmyer himself, "Oxyrhynchus logoi" in Essays 390.

[29] "L'Évangile selon Thomas" 91; Secret Books 356.

[30] L'Evangile selon Thomas 38. His suggestions to fill out the text as it stands are, by his own admission, difficult.

[31] "Textual Criticism on the Gospel of Thomas," JTS 20 (1969) 66.

[32] L'Évangile selon Thomas 87-88. He restores line 42 without any regard for the original editors']Ν in this line.

With the provision that Attridge's reading for lines 41 and 42 is sound Fitzmyer's second objection disappears.

It is reasonable to conclude, then, that there is a high degree of probability that with μα]χάρι[ος] in line 40 of the papyrus (presuming the lack of space for the introductory formula) begins a new saying which corresponded to Coptic logion 7. So little is left of the last three lines of the Greek, however, and so often do the two recensions diverge from each other in the text they present that no safe reconstitution of the Greek can be made from the Coptic.

The meager remains of lines 40-42 of POxy 654 extend at best to 3b of the Coptic logion; reconstructions of a Greek *Vorlage* for 3c are thus the merest guesswork. Among others who invert the order of the nouns in 3c Kasser at least—for whom "le contexte demande l'expression inverse"— holds out an error in translation as the source of the difficulty in the Coptic line. He makes the proposal that the ambiguity inherent in his own restoration of the Greek for line 41 of the papyrus, καὶ λέων ἔσται ἄνθρωπος with no article to mark the subject, would account for the Coptic translator's mistake in rendering what must have been the same Greek text identically in the second section (3c) as in the first (2c).[33] While this is an interesting suggestion and in itself within the realm of possibility, it is vitiated by the fact, as I have already pointed out, that 2c and 3c are not identical, and the nature of their variance is such as to suggest that, all the more as the work of the translator, the wording of 3c is intentional. It is equally possible that the Greek original underscored the surprise effect of the identical order of nouns in 3c by the use of particles with this force—καὶ δὴ καὶ for example—and the Coptic translator, sensitive to this nuance, rendered it in his native tongue as best he could.

Yet other scholars simply restore the Greek text of 3c as they see fit and offer no explanation for how the error arose. Marcovich regards the necessity for transposition of the nouns in Coptic 3c as "obvious" and remarks that "there is really no need to insist on the transmitted text." Naturally, then, he restores the Greek original for this line with [καὶ ὁ ἄνθρωπος ἔσται λέων].[34] Ménard does the same.[35]

Most bizarre is the view of Otfried Hofius. So uncertain is the text of the Coptic logion for him that not only is he unwilling to risk a

---

[33] *L'Évangile selon Thomas* 38.
[34] "Textual Criticism" 66-67.
[35] *L'Évangile selon Thomas* 88.

reconstruction of the Greek papyrus on its basis but, even with the transposition of nouns in 3c (which as they stand he attributed to scribal error)
carried out, he deems more radical measures necessary to wring sense
from it. With a view to harmonizing logion 7 with logia 11 and 60 where
the devouring of dead things is deprecated, Hofius avers that ⲙⲟⲩⲉⲓ,
wherever it occurs in the logion, does not mean "lion," but "corpse"[36]—
even in 3b! Hofius evidently intended a nominal formation from the Coptic verb ⲙⲟⲩ "die,"[37] but unfortunately no such word exists. Haenchen
wisely rejects this proposal.[38]

1.4 Summary

In sum, lines 40-42 of POxy 654, which contain the remnants of what
was all but certainly a Greek version of Coptic logion 7, are of no help
either in interpreting the saying or in proving or disproving an error of
whatever sort in the Coptic text at 3c. Scholars who restore the Greek for
this line in such a way as to demonstrate a translational mistake in the
Coptic version do so with a predisposition to read it there.

There may actually be no mistake. Scholars who posit an error in
transcription rely upon the supposed identity of lines 2c and 3c to bolster
their claim. These lines show a subtle variation in construction, however,
that suffices to cast some doubt on this hypothesis and to suggest the
possibility that the identical order of the nouns in the two clauses is
intentional.

Furthermore, there are hermeneutical reasons for holding that the
Coptic text is correct as it stands. Once the complex mix of tradition that
underlies the saying is fully undertood it becomes comprehensible why 3c
could not be worded inversely. It is to the task of uncovering that complex
tradition that attention will now be turned.

---

[36]"Das koptische Thomasevangelium und die Oxyrhynchus-Papyri Nr. 1,
654 und 655," *EvTh* 20 (1960) 41 and n. 72. Schippers and Baarda (*Het
evangelie van Thomas* 67) find Hofius' idea attractive.
[37]"Das koptische Thomasevangelium" 35 n. 54.
[38]"Literatur zum Thomasevangelium" 160.

2

The Gnostic
Leontomorphic Demiurge

2.1 The Old Testament

As I have already pointed out, the logion as a whole bears no similarity whatsoever to any of the canonical or extra-canonical sayings of Jesus. It is actually the oracle of Balaam, in particular Num 24:9, that furnishes the closest biblical parallel to the logion, not only in terms of formal structure (blessing followed by curse) but of content as well. In that verse Balaam compares Israel to a ravening lion that springs upon its prey and devours it. Similarly in 23:24.

In fact, it is the Old Testament, not the New, that provides the *biblical* background of the leonine imagery of the logion, and the reason is Gnosticism's antipathy to the demiurge in the person of Yahweh. Israel is not the only individual to be compared to a lion in the Old Testament; Yahweh himself often is too, and in language equally—and, for Gnosticism, appropriately—savage as that in Numbers. Job, for example, in his desperation complains that Yahweh is hunting him relentlessly down like a lion (10:16-17); Hosea in the heat of his anger at corruption in the land prophesies that Yahweh will act like a lion toward the people, maul them and carry them off with none to rescue (5:14; 13:7-8); a stricken Hezekiah moans that like a lion his god is breaking all his bones (Isa 38:13). Yahweh even roars like a lion (Jer 25:30; Hos 11:10; Joel 3[4 Hebr]:16; Amos 1:2; 3:8; and so in the New Testament Rev 10:3).

If Yahweh can behave like a lion it is because, for obvious reasons, the lion had acquired proverbial status as a symbol for strength, boldness and ferocity (Judg 14:18; 2 Sam 1:23; Prov 28:1; 30:30). So much was this the case that not only are powerful armies frequently compared to ravening lions (Jer 4:7; 5:6; Nah 2:11-13; and Hosea's thinly veiled reference to the Assyrians), but the animal, especially in the Hebrew term כְּפִיר, also became, along with other animal names in archaic times, a titular designation for men possessed of lion-like characters—warriors and other individuals of courage and power.[1] It was perfectly natural, then, for Yahweh to be endowed with leonine attributes.

In all the passages just cited, alike as the threat is directed against his people or against his enemies, the lion is simply a theriomorphic metaphor for Yahweh's anger (explicitly so in Jer 25:37-38; cp. Prov 19:12; 20:2). At other times it is the animal in the flesh that carries out his sentence: individual punishment for disobeying his word (1 Kgs 13:24-26; 20:36) or collective imposition of the curse of bestial plague promised for covenant transgression by Lev 26:22 and Deut 32:24 (2 Kgs 17:25-26). According to this last passage Yahweh sent lions to devour the Eastern peoples whom the Assyrians had planted in Samaria because they did not "fear" him. In the case of the Cuthites, at least, the punishment particularly suited the crime, for the Nergal whom they worshipped (2 Kgs 17:30), at first in Yahweh's stead and later in addition to (conjunction with?) him (17:29, 32-34), was among other things a god of slaughter, famine and plague, and the lord of the kingdom of death. What is more, Nergal is sometimes likened to a lion and is regularly represented by a double (and single? or both?) lion-headed staff, or club, especially on the *kudurru* (pl. 1a, second register, second figure from the right; pl. 1b, fourth register, third figure from the right).[2]

Two facets of the subsequent history of 2 Kgs' account of the new settlers in the Northern Kingdom are of sufficient interest to warrant a brief digression. Both significantly concern the Samaritan sect, whose

---

[1]Patrick D. Miler, Jr., "Animal Names as Designations in Ugaritic and Hebrew," *UF* 2 (1970) 177-186, specifically pp. 183-184, 185-186.

[2]See Édouard Dhorme, *Les religions de Babylonie et d'Assyrie* (Paris: Presses Universitaires de France, 1949) 38-44, 51-52; Hans Wilhelm Haussig, *Götter und Mythen im vorderen Orient* (Wörterbuch der Mythologie I.1; Stuttgart: Klett, 1965) 109-110 with p. 35 (#17); Egbert von Weiher, *Der babylonische Gott Nergal* (AOAT 11; Neukirchen-Vluyn: Butzon & Bercker Kevelaer, 1971) 19 n. 5, 29 n. 3, 45-46 with pls. 1.1-4, 2.5-8, and 3.9; Alfred Jeremias, "Nergal," Roscher III.1, 250-271; William Hayes Ward, *The Seal Cylinders of Western Asia* (Washington, D.C.: Carnegie Institution, 1910) 389-394, 402-403 (##14, 16); F. Pomponio, "'Löwenstab' e 'Doppellöwenkeule.' Studio su due simboli dell' iconografia mesopotamica," *OrAnt* 12 (1973) 183-208. Nergal, like Yahweh, was also a god of retribution; he figures, for example, among the deities who mete out punishment for refusal to obey Hammurabi's code of laws, where he is called upon to "burn his people . . . like raging fire" (Theophile J. Meek in *ANET*[3] 180).

origin the Rabbis held the passage to delineate, and both—the second admittedly much less certainly than the first—entail its disparagement by allusion to the leonine references involved in that account. First: To invalidate the Samaritans' self-professed status as adherents to Judaism the Jews derived from 2 Kgs 17:25-28 the custom of referring to them as גרי אריות "proselytes of lions" (b. Ḥul. 3b; Qidd. 75b; Sanh. 85b). That is, in the eyes of the Jews, the original conversion of the "Samaritans"— actually, of course, the foreigners whom the Assyrians imported, with whom the later Samaritan sect may have nothing whatsoever to do—was not a genuine conversion because it was based on fear and did not consti- tute a free-will choice.

More tenuously connected with the leonine associations of 2 Kgs' account, but certainly within the realm of possibility, is the fact that the Rabbis should choose precisely כּוּתִים as a slanderous name for their hated co-religionists.[3] Josephus (Ant. 9.14.3 §290) assures an early date for the practice; as a consequence of its existence as established usage for him he gathers the five different peoples of 2 Kgs 17:24 and 30-31 under the single umbrella Χουθαῖοι (§288) from a locality Χοῦθος (9.14.1 §279). But why exactly the כּוּתִים should have been selected from among the five by the Jews of a later epoch to brand the Samaritan sect as idolatrous is unknown. There is certainly no evidence that the cult of Nergal lasted in Israel into the post-Exilic period or that it influenced emerging Samari- tanism in any way. It may, however, be a case of guilt by association. The cult of Nergal is the only one of the five mentioned by 2 Kgs 17:30-31 that lasted into Seleucid times, and by then it had spread far beyond the city in which it was anciently centered. A bilingual inscription of the third century B.C. from the Piraeus[4] proves Nergal to have been well endowed with a priesthood at the Sidon of that time, and it is interesting to note that Josephus (Ant. 11.8.6 §340-344 and 12.5.5 §257-264) reports the Sam- aritans of Shechem, hard by their sacred Mount Gerizim, proudly pro- claimed themselves Sidonians (and not Judeans) to Alexander the Great

---

[3]Primary references are provided by Marcus Jastrow, A Dictionary of the Targumim, the Talmud Babli and Yerushalmi, and the Midrashic Lit- erature, s.v. כּוּתִי. See further James D. Purvis, The Samaritan Penta- teuch and the Origin of the Samaritan Sect (Cambridge: Harvard Univer- sity Press, 1968) 95-97, 119 with n. 4; Hans Gerhard Kippenberg, Garizim und Synagoge. Traditionsgeschichtliche Untersuchungen zur samarita- nischen Religion der aramäischen Periode (RGVV 30; Berlin: de Gruyter, 1971) 33 n. 1, 35 n. 8.

[4]KAI #59; text: I, p. 3, translation and commentary: II, pp. 72-73.

and later to Antiochus IV Epiphanes, in the latter case denying that the god whom they worshiped was Yahweh. What better patronymic for the Samaritans could the Jews have picked from 2 Kgs 17 than the Cuthites and their hellish lion-god Nergal, a choice made singularly appropriate by the punishment meted out to them by 2 Kgs 17:25-26? It is wise not to belabor this argument, however, for Rabbinic texts betray no knowledge of Nergal and his leonine representations,[5] though given their general silence on such matters this is in itself hardly surprising.

To return to the bestowal of Yahweh with leonine characteristics: Rabbinic homiletics did not scruple to continue the analogy; the lion remained for it a powerfully evocative symbol of Yahweh's strength and power. One aspect of this continued tradition is especially interesting because it also crops up in Gnosticism. The Nag Hammadi tract *On the Origin of the World* maintains that Yahweh/Yaldabaoth, who had the appearance of a lion, took his name from a command given him by Pistis Sophia; "die Vollkommenen aber nennen ihn Ariael (ⲀⲢⲒⲀⲎⲀ), weil er löwengestaltig war."[6] Following the analogy of a multitude of similarly formed angelic names and in perfect accord with the Gnostic view of Yahweh as an inferior, merely angelic deity (and the angel of Yahweh is repeatedly the equivalent of Yahweh himself in the Old Testament, in particular in Exod 23:20-21, around which so much Jewish esoteric speculation centered), this etymology assumes an interpretation of biblical אֲרִיאֵל to mean either "lion-god" or perhaps, less perversely, "lion of God," a lion, that is, born of the pleromatic realm beyond him.

In a note *ad loc.* to his translation of *Orig. World*, Hans-Martin Schenke refers to passages in the Septuagint where 'Αριηλ is a proper name possessed by human beings,[7] but it is far more likely that Isa 29:1-7 is in the background because it is far from obvious in this passage to what or whom the name belongs, and a mysterious meaning can therefore more easily be

---

[5]In the light of Nergal's solar associations it is odd, though, that a tradition ascribed by y. ʿAbod. Zar. 3.42d to the second century B.C. should substitute בית שמש for כות in 2 Kgs 17:30.

[6]The translation is that of Alexander Böhlig and Pahor Labib, *Die koptisch-gnostische Schrift ohne Titel aus Codex II von Nag Hammadi* (Berlin: Akademie-Verlag, 1962) 42-43, with "Ariael" substituted for their "Ariel." The passage is CG II, 5, 100[148].24-26, which should be read with lines 1-11 on Yaldabaoth's origin.

[7]"Vom Ursprung der Welt. Eine titellose gnostische Abhandlung aus dem Funde von Nag Hamadi," *ThLZ* 84 (1959) 250 n. 23.

read into it. Scholars still debate its reference.[8] Regardless of what the actual significance of "Ariel" may have been in its original Isaianic context, however, Rabbinic exegetes, at least, understood אֲרִי in אֲרִיאֵל to mean "lion" just as CG II, 5 *Orig. World* does (and many moderns do as well). They, for the most part, quite naturally apply the expression to the Temple (*Ex. Rab.* 29.9; *Pesiq. Rab Kah.* 116a; *Pesiq. R.* 133b)[9]—though *Pesiq. R.* (at least in Friedmann's edition) actually goes so far as to use אֲרִיאֵל of Yahweh himself—but Gnostics in search of hidden names could, even more freely than their Jewish counterparts, wrench whatever they desired from its context and put it to good use in their own interest. Their adoption of the name Ariel as a secret designation for a leonine Yahweh/ Yaldabaoth could very possibly, indeed, have been encouraged by Rabbinic enthusiasm for the metaphor; Gnostics show themselves in other cases familiar enough with Jewish haggadah for their own polemical purposes.[10]

---

[8]For a variety of opinions see BDB s.vv. אֲרִיאֵל and אֲרִאֵיל and, more currently, Walther Eichrodt, *Der Herr der Geschichte: Jesaja 13-23 und 28-39* (BAT 17.2; Stuttgart: Calwer, 1967) 142; Edward J. Young, *The Book of Isaiah* II (NICOT; Grand Rapids: Eerdmans, 1969) 304 and n. 1; Otto Kaiser, *Der Prophet Jesaja, Kapitel 13-39* (ATD 18; Göttingen: Vandenhoeck & Ruprecht, 1973) 212-213; William Henry Irwin, *Isaiah 28-33* (BibOr 30; Rome: Biblical Institute, 1977) 47 with n. 3, 48.

[9]The latter two passages, incidentally, are not blind to the nice astrological happenstance that the Temple, Ariel, the "lion of God," was destroyed in the fifth month (Ab), the month when the sun is in Leo. *Pesiq. Rab Kah.* refers to Jer 1:3 and 31:13 for justification. Such astrological sensitivity is not surprising, given, for example, the prominence of zodiacal mosaics in ancient synagogues at Beth Alpha, Naaran, and Isfiya (no earlier than the fifth century A.D., though the practice itself seems to have originated in the first half of the fourth). See E. L. Sukenik, *Ancient Synagogues in Palestine and Greece* (Schweich Lectures 1930; London: The British Academy, 1934) 27-35, 85-86; Erwin R. Goodenough, *Jewish Symbols in the Greco-Roman Period* I (BollS 37; New York: Pantheon, 1953) 248-249, 255, and *Jewish Symbols* III (1953) figs 631-632, 640, 644 and 658. On the use of the lion in other contexts in Jewish iconography see *Jewish Symbols* IV (1954) 14-15; XII (1965) 133-136; and especially VII (1958) 29-86.

[10]Despite the negative appraisal of the situation by Ithamar Gruenwald, "Jewish Sources for the Gnostic Texts from Nag Hammadi?" *Proceedings of the Sixth World Congress of Jewish Studies* III (Jerusalem, 1977) 45-56. See, for example, Birger A. Pearson, "Jewish Haggadic Traditions in *The Testimony of Truth* from Nag Hammadi (CG IX, 3)," *Religious Syncretism in Antiquity* (ed. Birger A. Pearson; Missoula: Scholars Press,

In many Psalms (7:1-2[2-3 LXX]; 10:9 [9:30]; 17[16]:12; 22:13, 16 [Hebr. only], 21 [21:14, 22] ; 35 [34] :17; 57:4[56:5]; 58:6[57:7]) the lion is an image for vengeful, boastful, blasphemous persecutors mercilessly hounding the helpless soul of the righteous with curses and oppression. If one couples with this the Old Testament's repeated portrayal of Yahweh as a ferocious lion and the Rabbis' perpetuation of the metaphor, it is easy to see how enemies of Yahweh might receive support from this quarter in the depiction of him as a leontomorphic god. As far as the Gnostics were concerned the leonine figures of the Psalms fit Yahweh/Yaldabaoth's personality to a tee; they are enough to satisfy any Marcion.[11] As will become clearer later, if Yaldabaoth is himself vengeful, boastful and blasphemous it was at least in part from the "lions" of the Psalms that he acquired these nasty traits.

Once again, as with Isaiah's Ariel, it is irrelevant to point to the original setting of the Psalmists' imagery. It is useless to insist that the "lions" of the Psalms are either human enemies,[12] as they are in Job 4:9-11—though for David, as 1 Sam 17:34-37 shows, the imagery had a real-life basis in a shepherd's struggle to fend off predators—or perhaps, as Hans-Joachim Kraus suggests for Ps 22:13, infernal demons of disease, which in Mesopotamian texts are given, like Nergal their lord, the heads and the gaping jaws of lions, and the fangs of serpents (pl. 2a-b).[13] It is irrelevant

---

1975) 205-222, with further references p. 205 n. 2. What Alexander Altmann in "Gnostic Themes in Rabbinic Cosmology," *Essays in honour of the Very Rev. Dr. J. H. Hertz* (ed. I. Epstein, E. Levine and C. Roth; London: Goldston, 1942) 19-32, and in "The Gnostic Background of the Rabbinic Adam Legends," *JQR* 35 (1945) 371-391, regards as the inverse relationship is in fact influence in the same direction.

[11] Compare the texts cited and discussed by Adolf von Harnack, *Marcion: das Evangelium vom fremden Gott* (2nd ed.; Leipzig: Hinrichs, 1924) 262-265, 271-274, 278-282.

[12] So, for example, Bernhard Duhm, *Die Psalmen* (KHKAT 14; 2nd ed.; Tübingen: Mohr, 1922) 94-95, 227.

[13] *Psalmen* I (BKAT 15.1; Neukirchen: Neukirchener Verlag, 1960) 180-181. Kraus cites an exorcism dating to the Third Dynasty of Ur (A. Falkenstein and W. von Soden, *Sumerische und akkadische Hymnen und Gebete;* Zürich/Stuttgart: Artemis, 1953; 214-215, 377-378) against the demon Samana, "der mit dem Löwenmaul, der mit dem Drachenzahn, . . . der wilde Löwe Enlils, der Löwe Enkis, der den Hals abschneidet, der Löwe Nininsinnas mit dem bluttriefenden Maul, der Löwe der Götter, der das Maul aufsperrt." Other horrific lion-monsters of the Mesopotamian Netherworld are described in the mid-seventh century text entitled by

because by the Roman period Hellenized Judaism had learned most expertly to wield the powerful weapon of allegorical exegesis, and the New Testament already attests its application to the "lions" of the Psalms, themselves, after all, already patently metaphorical. There is more to be said about the mythological content of the Psalms' lion-imagery and its subsequent development in the New Testament and elsewhere, and it will be taken up later.

Exegetes of the *Gospel of Thomas* have not sufficiently grasped the relevance of these passages from the Old Testament (and examples could be multiplied) to the lion of logion 7. Most do not cite the Old Testament at all.[14] Kasser speaks simply of "vagues parallelismes bibliques" and

---

Erich Ebeling (*Tod und Leben nach den Vorstellungen der Babylonier*; Berlin and Leipzig: de Gruyter, 1931; 1-9) "Höllenfahrt eines assyrischen Königs"; see further Wolfram von Soden, "Die Unterweltsvision eines assyrischen Kronprinzen," *ZA* 43 (1936) 1-31; and the English translation by E. A. Speiser for *ANET*[3] 109-110. For other representations of such demons (particularly Pazuzu and Lamashtu) see, for example, H. W. F. Saggs, *The Greatness that was Babylon* (New York: Hawthorn, 1962) pls. 54B and 55 with pp. 302-318; G. Contenau, *La magie chez les Assyriens et les Babyloniens* (Paris: Payot, 1947) pls. 2a-b, 4a, and especially 8 (my pl. 3, the most famous of the many stone and bronze exorcism plaques, with Pazuzu peering over the top and Lamashtu departing astride an ass with Pazuzu behind her in the bottom register) with pp. 97-100, 227-230; David W. Myhrman, "Die Labartu-Texte. Babylonische Beschwörungsformeln nebst Zauberverfahren gegen die Dämonin Labartu," *ZA* 16 (1902) 180-181 lines 38-42; F. Thureau-Dangin, "Rituel et amulettes contre Labartu," *RA* 18 (1921) pl. 1 ##1-3 obverse, with pp. 161-199, publishing an exorcism tablet against Lamashtu, of Seleucid date; Carl (or Karl) Frank, *Babylonische Beschwörungsreliefs. Ein Beitrag zur Erklärung der sog. Hadesreliefs* (Leipzig: Hinrichs, 1908) figs. 1-5 (pp. 26, 46, 74, 80, 87) and pls. 1-4; *Lamastu, Pazuzu und andere Dämonen. Ein Beitrag zur babylonisch-assyrischen Dämonologie* (Leipzig: Harrassowitz, 1941) p. 1 ##1, 3 and pl. 3; "Köpfe babylonischer Dämonen," *RAAO* 7 (1910) 21-23 with the plate; Ward, *Seal Cylinders* 48-52, 280-283, 384 (#54); H. Frankfort, *Cylinder Seals. A Documentary Essay on the Art and Religion of the Ancient Near East* (London: Gregg, 1965 [1939]) 174-177 "The Lion-headed Demon" with pls. 27.1 (brandishing the "dagger of pestilence"), 28.c, 29.g, i (holding a man upside down); Stephen Herbert Langdon, *The Mythology of All Races* V. *Semitic* (Boston: Jones, 1931) figs. 44, 98-102 with pp. 84, 352-374.

[14]In an article wholly devoted to the subject ("Das Thomasevangelium und das Alte Testament," *Neotestamentica et Patristica*; NovTSup 6;

refers to Judg 14:8-9 (Samson); 1 Kgs 13:11-32; 21[20]:36 (punishment by lions for disobeying Yahweh's word) as well as to 1 Pet 5:8 and Rev 4:7— both adaptations of Old Testament themes, the former of the "lions" of the Psalms and the latter of Ezekiel's נ׳ ׳ה (more on this, too, later)—"et passim."[15] Schippers also realizes the pertinence of Ps 22:21 as reflected in 1 Pet 5:8,[16] but like Kasser he makes no effort to account for the parallelism. Akagi, for his part, adduces a spate of Old Testament *loci*, but it is only in a misguided effort to refute the scattered attempts that have been made to explain the logion from Gnostic sources, and so they are neither those passages in which Yahweh assumes leonine characteristics nor the "lions" of the Psalms.[17]

Surely off the track is the proposal, originally made by Doresse[18] and reproduced with some reservation by Turner,[19] that the lion of the logion may be a Christological title appropriated from Rev 5:5 ("the Lion of the tribe of Judah"), itself based upon Gen 49:9. The lion was understandably a popular Messianic image in Jewish apocaylptic circles in these troubled times (4 Ezra 11:37 with 12:31-32), and also with their Christian successors, as a result of which the animal as a symbol of a victorious Christ made an attractive subject for medieval Christian art.[20] But that this is

---

Leiden: Brill, 1962; 243-248) Gilles Quispel has no entry for logion 7 in his list of sayings containing Old Testament allusions (p. 247).

[15] *L'Évangile selon Thomas* 38 n. 3.

[16] *Het evangelie van Thomas* 66-67.

[17] *Literary Development* 284-287. Akagi does not appreciate the continuity of the tradition. Reference to Gnostic texts is to him "neither necessary nor desirable"; the logion may be understood strictly "in keeping with the rich contents of human experience that are sufficiently illustrated in the Bible." In his view "the logion may be interpreted as referring to: (1) the individual believer's inner struggle; (2) the church's effort to attain its true unity; or (3) the Roman persecution which the early Christians had to undergo, as reflected in the Apocalypse of John." No detailed explanation of how these interpretations follow from the logion is provided; (2) and (3) founder on the rocks of 2a in the logion, much as Akagi maneuvers to avoid it. His (1) is correct, but unfortunately it requires Gnostic sources for its elucidation.

[18] "L'Évangile selon Thomas" 134.

[19] "Theology of the Gospel of Thomas" 94.

[20] See Bertram in Michaelis' entry "λέων" for *TDNT* 4 (1967) 253 n. 21 with references, and further P. Bloch's article "Löwe" for the *Lexikon der christlichen Ikonographie* III (Rome-Freiburg-Basel-Wein: Herder, 1971), section II.C: "Der Löwe als Christus u. Messias," pp. 116-117.

the referent for the lion in logion 7 of *Gos. Thom.* is out of the question.[21] The implicit antagonism between man and lion there makes it impossible, for Christ "devours" no one.

The bridge between the Old Testament's lion-imagery as applied to Yahweh and to the persecutors of the Psalms, on the one hand, and the lion of *Gos. Thom.*'s seventh logion, on the other, is the Gnostic mythologem of a leontomorphic demiurge. I turn now to consideration of the relevant texts.

2.2   Origen, Against Celsus

Ariel proved to be a fashionable archontic name for Gnostic mythographers; it emerges in decadent contexts in which its original leonine associations seem either to have been neglected or forgotten altogether. For the Peratae, for example, Ariel is a ruler of the winds (Hippolytus, *Refutation of all Heresies* 5.14.5; 109.14-15 Wendland); in the *Pistis Sophia* he is the dog-faced ruler (Anubis, no less!) of Amente, the Egyptian hell.[22] He also surfaces in magic texts.[23]

These passages may evince no knowledge of the leonine associations that CG II, 5 *Orig. World* explicitly attaches to the name Ariel, but that is not the case with a green jasper amulet (as usual with such objects it is not closely datable), originally of the Joseph Brummer collection (pl. 4a-b).[24] The obverse shows an imposing lion-headed male figure dressed in

---

[21] So Schippers, *Het evangelie van Thomas* 66, rightly.

[22] *Pistis Sophia* 3.102 (256.20; 257.22; 258.2 in the new edition which prints Carl Schmidt's text and offers a translation by Violet MacDermot; NHS 9; Leiden: Brill, 1978); 4.144 (375.7), 146 (377.25; 378.26; 379.3).

[23] Angelicus M. Kropp, *Ausgewählte Koptische Zaubertexte* II (Brussels: Fondation Égyptologique Reine Élisabeth, 1931) #36, line 1 [ⲁ] ⲡ ⲓ ⲏ ⲁ ⲙⲁ ⲣ ⲙⲁ ⲣ ⲓ ⲱ ; A. Delatte and Ph. Derchain, *Les intailles magiques gréco-égyptiennes* (Paris: Bibliothèque nationale, 1964) #519, p. 339; *PGM* II P 14.2, where it is interpreted to mean φῶς μου θεοῦ, as though 'Aρ-derived from ⲁⲟⲣ. For אֲרִיאֵל in Mediaeval Jewish Kabbalistic speculation (specifically the *Sepher Raziel*) see Moïse Schwab, "Vocabulaire de l'angélologie d'après les manuscrits hébreux de la bibliothèque nationale," *MAI* 1.10 (1897) 185.

[24] Pictured and discussed by Campbell Bonner, "An Amulet of the Ophite Gnostics," *Commemorative Studies in Honour of Theodore Leslie Shear* (HespSup 8; Athens, 1949) 43-46 with pl. 8.1; and subsequently in *Studies in Magical Amulets, chiefly Graeco-Egyptian* (Ann Arbor: University of Michigan Press, 1950) #188 (pl. 9, p. 284) with pp. 135-138.

the common Egyptian loincloth and holding in his right hand the equally common Egyptian *situla* (pail). In his left hand he grasps a tall staff. Inscribed to the right and left are the figure's names: ΙΑΛΔΑΒΑϢΘ and ΑΑΡΙΗΛ, [25] respectively. The reverse is fully covered by the following eight lines: ΙΑ / ΙΑϢ / ΣΑΒΑϢΘ / ΑΔϢΝΑΙ / ΕΛϢΑΙ / ϢΡΕΟΣ / ΑΣΤΑ / ΦΕΟΣ.

The name Yaldabaoth together with the series of names that cover the reverse (the first name ΙΑ evidently represents a transcription of יה and might be intended as a shortened form of ΙΑΛΔΑΒΑϢΘ, perhaps for lack of space) suffice to point to an ultimate origin—for the names if not for the gem as a whole—in the primitive[26] Gnostic systems to which the labels "Ophite" and "Sethian" were attached by the heresiologists, for Gnostic archon-lists of this affiliation bear close comparison with that provided by the stone (e.g., Irenaeus, *Refutation and Overthrow of the so-called Gnosis* 1.28.3; I, 230 Harvey). What Egyptian deity served the engraver as an exemplar for his lion-headed Yaldabaoth, and why, are related questions that will be addressed in the next chapter, but there is no doubt in any case that the engraver was guided by a tradition somehow delineating Yaldabaoth in leonine form. Though they differ in important details, a variety of Gnostic texts attest to this tradition.

The oldest as actually preserved is Celsus' source (at the latest mid-second century A.D.) as epitomized by Origen in book six of his work *Against Celsus*.[27] According to the group known to Celsus, the chief of the seven ἄρχοντες δαίμονες, the creator of this world, the god of the Jews, an accursed god (6.27), is ἰδέᾳ λέοντος μεμορφωμένον (6.30; 100.4-

---

[25] The doubled Α is likely to represent another example of vocalic obfuscation common in magical texts, not carelessness or an effort to correct the placement of the first Α too close to the tip of the staff (so Bonner, "Amulet of the Ophite Gnostics" 46). Its placement may be intentional, as it could be intended to turn the staff into a spear. The same explanation applies to the second Α in CG II, 5 *Orig. World*'s ΑΡΙΑΗΛ, though it might conceivably reflect Aramaic אַרְיֵא.

[26] The Valentinian system presupposes them. See, for example, Ferdinand Christian Baur, *Die christliche Gnosis oder die christliche Religions-Philosophie in ihrer geschichtlichen Entwicklung* (Tübingen: Osiander, 1835) 171; Hans Jonas, *Gnosis und spätantiker Geist* I. *Die mythologische Gnosis* (3rd ed.; Göttingen: Vandenhoeck & Ruprecht, 1964) 358-362.

[27] On Celsus' identity and date see Henry Chadwick's full discussion in his *Origen: Contra Celsum* (Cambridge: University Press, 1965) xxiv-xxviii. For the latter problem he inclines to a solution A.D. 177-180 (p. xxviii).

5 Koetschau). His cohorts have the forms of a bull, a partially serpentine double being of some sort (ἀμφίβιόν τινα καὶ φρικῶδες ἐπισυρίζοντα 6.30; 100.11-12 Koetschau), an eagle, and other animals. To judge from the purely facial descriptions of the last three, by ἰδέᾳ . . . μεμορφω- μένον it is the first archon's face alone that is meant; the rest of his body was presumably human.

Though the fact that Celsus offers a name for his source's seventh archon suggests that it may have contained one,[28] he failed to record a name for the troop's lion-shaped ruler. Origen fills the lack from what he claims (6.24) to be the same "diagram," but it is far from certain that the document he obtained was indeed identical with that possessed by Celsus nigh on a century before.[29] Adolf Hilgenfeld opines that Origen's was a more recent version of Celsus', to which the archontic names had now been added (but see n. 28);[30] Wilhelm Bousset, conversely, holds that Origen seems to have preserved the tradition in its more primitive form,[31] but he submits no grounds for thinking so. There is no way to decide the question either way, but as an element common to both tradi- tions, the depiction of Yahweh/Yaldabaoth as a lion-headed god is safely attested for at least the mid-second century and is likely, as I shall argue, to be much older than that.

With the Alexandrian Father, at any rate, it is a case of *embarras de richesses*. In the list of names that he sets beside his description of Celsus' archons in 6.30 the figure λεοντοειδής is Michael, but in the litany of password incantations that he proceeds to cite in 6.31 it is Yaldabaoth who has the leonine form. Theodor Hopfner offers what appears to me a reasonable solution to the problem, namely that the second group of names represents the "true," secret names of the archons, the former group the "common" ones.[32] Such a double system of nomenclature is

---

[28]Chadwick (*Origen: Contra Celsum* 345 n. 6) cites a passage from 7.40 which he plausibly ascribes to Celsus and which may be taken to imply that his source offered a complete list of names.

[29]See, for example, Eugène de Faye, *Gnostiques et Gnosticisme. Étude critique des documents du Gnosticisme chrétien aux IIe et IIIe siècles* (2nd ed.; Paris: Geuthner, 1925) 358-359.

[30]*Die Ketzergeschichte des Urchristentums urkundlich dargestellt* (Darmstadt: Wissenschaftliche Buchgesellschaft, 1963 [1884]) 280-281.

[31]*Hauptprobleme der Gnosis* (Göttingen: Vandenhoeck & Ruprecht, 1907) 10.

[32]"Das Diagramm der Ophiten," *Charisteria Alois Rzach zum achtzigsten Geburtstag dargebracht* (Reichenberg: Stiepel, 1930) 89: "Dass

frequent in magical texts obsessed with knowing the "true" names of gods[33]—circles whence, according to Origen (6.32), certain of his archontic names, including the name "Yaldabaoth," derive. Furthermore, Michael is not an inapposite choice as another name for Yahweh/Yaldabaoth since (1) Dan 10:21 makes him the especial angelic prince of the Jews (so too *Test. Levi* 5:6 and elsewhere), and a passage like Deut 32:8-9 LXX would then invite his identification with Yahweh; (2) the Ophite system as described by Irenaeus makes the serpent of Gen 3 the son of Yaldabaoth (*Refutation* 1.28.3; I, 232 Harvey, together with 1.28.4; I, 234 Harvey; similarly Epiphanius, *Medicine Chest* 37.4.4; 56.7-8 Holl; and Pseudo-Tertullian, *Against all Heresies* 2.4; 1404.4-8 Kroymann), enough like his dad to form himself his own personal Hebdomad (Irenaeus, *Refutation* 1.28.4; I, 235 Harvey), and names him Michael and Samael (1.28.5; I, 236 Harvey), which latter is a name for Yaldabaoth himself in the Sethian tracts CG II, *1 Apoc. John* 11[59].15-18; II, *4 Hyp. Arch.* 87[135].3; 94[142].25; II. 5 *Orig. World* 103[151].18; and XIII, *1 Trim. Prot.* 39.26-27; and (3) the archangel was understandably a popular figure in magic texts for his role as dragon-slayer,[34] a role attributed to him by Rev 12:7-9 where Michael fights against "the ancient serpent"—the serpent of Gen 3—and casts him out of heaven, a fate which Yaldabaoth is likewise made by Ophite myth to impose upon his ophidian son (Irenaeus, *Refutation* 1.28.4; I, 235 Harvey; Epiphanius, *Medicine Chest* 37.5.4; 57.8-9 Holl).

Origen offers the additional piece of interesting information that Celsus reported his group as holding ὥς τινων εἰς τὰς ἀρχοντικὰς μορφὰς ἐπανερχομένων, so that some become lions, others bulls, yet

---

Origenes die Planetendämonen einmal mit den Namen der Erzengel, dann aber Jaldabaoth usw. nennt, erklärt sich daraus, dass die Namen der zweiten Gruppe die 'wahren' und sicherlich auch geheimen Namen der Dämonen waren, die nur in den liturgischen Sterbegebeten der Gläubigen ausgesprochen werden durften und denen magische Kräfte innewohnten . . . ."

[33]Compare, for example, the distinction between the κύριον and the προσηγορικὸν ὄνομα of the primal inner Man of spirit in the Nikotheos-source used by the alchemist Zosimos of Panopolis (early fourth century A.D.) in his tract *On the Letter Omega* as cited by R. Reitzenstein, *Poimandres. Studien zur griechisch-ägyptischen und frühchristlichen Literatur* (Leipzig: Teubner, 1904) 104.

[34]*PGM* I P 4.2768-2771, on which see Albrecht Dieterich, *Abraxas. Studien zur Religionsgeschichte des spätern Altertums* (Leipzig: Teubner, 1891) 122-126.

others dragons or one of the other animals represented by the powers (6.33; 102.27-29 Koetschau). Chadwick[35] proposes as a probable explanation that "the Ophite initiates wore masks shaped according to the animal forms of the Archons." He points to the existence of theriomorphic grades in Mithraism and to the possibility that initiates at times wore masks corresponding to their grade.[36] I shall have more to say about Mithraism and its grade *leo* later. Chadwick is almost certainly mistaken in this proposition, however, in part because no such performance is attested for any Gnostic group—though admittedly little enough exact is known about cultic practice in Gnostic sectarianism—but particularly because the verb ἐπανέρχεσθαι, which Chadwick correctly translates by "return," is unsuited to such a context. In fact Hopfner's reasoning again seems sound to me in referring the passage to a belief in the transmigration of souls. The idea is that ascending souls which cannot succeed in passing through any one of the "gates" of the archons because they do not know the proper password (as, e.g., Origen records them in 6.31) are forced to return to earthly embodiment in the animal shape of that particular power.[37] The doctrine of the transmigration of souls is, after all, as Hopfner intimates, of frequent occurrence in a variety of Gnostic systems,[38] derived, whether directly or indirectly, from the pre-Socratics and from Plato.

---

[35] *Origen: Contra Celsum* 349 n. 4.

[36] Though Porphyry *On Abstinence from Animal Food* 4.16 (for the text see *TMMM* II, 42), to which Chadwick refers, does not say so in so many words (and the text is at points corrupt), the reverse of a Mithraic relief from Dalmatia (Konjica), for example, shows Sol and Mithras (or their human representatives, men of the grades *heliodromus* and *pater*) at banquet with four persons approaching, and two of them wear animal masks—raven and lion—to represent their grade (*CIMRM* #1896 with fig. 491; my pl. 4c). "Ambrosiaster" (text in *TMMM* II, 7-8) maintains, furthermore, that they imitated their animals to the point of flapping wings and crowing like birds, and roaring like a lion.

[37] "Diagramm der Ophiten" 89: "Jene Seelen, die nicht die nötige Zauberkraft besassen und des weiteren Aufstiegs noch nicht würdig waren, wurden in irgend einem 'Tor der Archonten' zurückgehalten und 'mussten,' wie Celsus (VI 33) sagt, 'zu Löwen, Stieren, Schlangen, Adlern, Bären oder Hunden werden,' d.h., sie mussten auf die Erde zurück um dort in diesen Tieren wiedergeboren zu werden, denn 'den engen Wiederhinabsteig' erwähnt Celsus selbst (VI 34)."

[38] Hopfner refers to Hans Leisegang, *Die Gnosis* (4th ed.; Stuttgart: Kröner, 1955), where see pp. 207, 236-238 (Basilides), and 261, 265-270 (Carpocratians).

Celsus' description of the "Persian mysteries" in 6.22 hints in this same direction.

Evidently on the basis of this evidence some researchers have maintained that logion 7 of *Gos. Thom.* is to be interpreted in the light of this doctrine.[39] Giversen is rightly critical of this view, arguing that it is totally without support either from the logion itself or from *Gos. Thom.* as a whole. But he goes too far when he states that he knows of no text which allows such a conjecture.[40] However inapplicable to the logion, the Gnostic texts which expound the transmigration of souls do indeed allow precisely this conjecture, and although, so far as I know, none of them—with the exception of the text presently under consideration—refers explicitly to reincarnation as a lion, classical and late antique texts often do: Empedocles in his *Purifications* (D-K 31 [21] B 127 from Aelian); Plato, *Republic* X, 620B, where the great warrior Ajax, son of Telamon, chooses the life of a lion; the Hermetic tract *Kore Kosmou* 42 (14.1-4 Festugière); and Philostratus, *Life of Apollonius of Tyana* 5.42, where Apollonius informs his audience that a tame lion is possessed of the soul of Pharaoh Amasis and has him taken away and fittingly ensconced in the temple at Leontopolis.

2.3 The Pistis Sophia

The *Pistis Sophia* and the *Apocryphon of John*—the latter at least in the redactions in which it now exists—both represent developed forms of the tradition of the leonine Yaldabaoth. The *Pistis Sophia* involves its expansion into bewildering complexity with a multifarious array of new detail, the most important of which here is the *Verdoppelung* of the leonine Yaldabaoth into a predecessor in the shape of a power of Authades with similarly feline features. If the development from relative simplicity toward greater complexity is a secure guide, the *Apocryphon of John* is

---

[39]In his earlier publications ("Ein neues Evangelium?" 483 n. 10; *Koptisch-gnostische Schriften* 11 n. 8) and perhaps with implicit endorsement, Leipoldt offers this as the view of S. Morenz, who evidently saw in logion 11 reference to the same idea. Subsequently, however, Leipoldt (*Evangelium nach Thomas* 57) chose to follow another track altogether, one that will be taken up later. R. Arthur (*The Gospel of Thomas and the Coptic New Testament*; ThD dissertation, Graduate Theological Union, Berkeley, 1976; 4) still sides with Morenz and includes logion 60 with the other two in providing "a hint of [this] doctrine."

[40]*Thomasevangeliet* 38.

likely to form an intermediate stage. The development which it evinces is that, unlike the texts available to Celsus and to Origen, as well as the kindred system known to Irenaeus, Yaldabaoth is no longer merely the first member of the seven that make up the planetary Hebdomad, but an eighth apart from it.[41] Let me summarize both of these accounts before I comment on them, as they will prove useful in other respects as well later on.

The *Pistis Sophia* recounts how Authades—"the Arrogant One," "the Remorseless One"—and his Watchers hated Pistis Sophia and how he emanated from himself "a great power with the face of a lion" together with a group of more material emanations, and sent them to dwell in Chaos to seduce her into coming down to dwell there herself, to persecute her and deprive her of the light, her power. Mistaking the radiance of the lion-faced power for the pleromatic Light, Sophia descended in order to swallow him up, but was instead surrounded by Authades and all his powers and had her own light devoured. Her material element, thrust down

---

[41]See Jonas, *Gnosis und spätantiker Geist* I, 229 n. 4 and the additional texts (relating to the Basilides and Saturninus) cited there, with Simone Petrement, "Le mythe des sept archontes créateurs peut-il s'expliquer à partir du christianisme?" *Le origini dello gnosticismo. Colloquio di Messina 13-18 Aprile 1966* (SHR [NumenSup] 12; ed. U. Bianchi; Leiden: Brill, 1970) 460-487, for the background. Jonas believes that this process of distinction was accompanied by the acquisition by Yaldabaoth of the traits of Yahweh, traits which were not originally his. Bousset (*Hauptprobleme der Gnosis* 351) is of the same opinion. Jonas' position is prompted by his well-known (and well-justified) rejection of theories postulating alleged Jewish origins for Gnosticism; for a concise statement of his views see his "Response to G. Quispel's 'Gnosticism and the New Testament'" in *The Bible in Modern Scholarship*; ed. J. Philip Hyatt; Nashville, Tenn.; Abingdon, 1965; 286-293. While I concur in dismissing the possibility of origination by Jews, I hold to the hypothesis, somewhat grudgingly admitted by Jonas as plausible ("Response" 289), that "Gnosticism *originated* out of a reaction (that is, *as* a reaction) to Judaism." If that is so then there is no reason why Yaldabaoth, like his cohorts, should not have been an hypostasis of Yahweh from the beginning. R. van den Broek, "The Creation of Adam's Psychic Body in the Apocryphon of John," *Studies in Gnosticism and Hellenistic Religions presented to Gilles Quispel on the Occasion of his 65th Birthday* (EPRO 91; ed. R. van den Broek and M. J. Vermaseren; Leiden: Brill, 1981) 42, also appreciates the fact of Yaldabaoth's promotion, but makes no effort to account for it.

into Chaos, became Yaldabaoth, himself a lion-faced power, whose one part is fire and the other part darkness.[42]

Thereafter Sophia cries out in one ΜΕΤΑΝΟΙΑ after another to the true Light, confessing her error in being led astray by the lion-faced power and begging rescue from oppression at his hands. She prays the Light to deprive the lion-faced power surreptitiously of the light he has devoured and to have his counterfeit light, the light which ensnared her, removed from her. In answer to her prayers Jesus secretly descends to lead her up out of Chaos. The lion-faced power sees him, however, is furious, and emanates further powers to do her violence; Authades tries to help his offspring by dispatching to their aid another emanation himself; the lion-faced power's fellows turn themselves into a giant serpent, a basilisk-snake with seven heads, a dragon. But all to no avail, for Jesus succeeds in depriving the lion-faced power and his cohorts of their light and enables Sophia to trample the lion-faced power and his snaky comrades under foot as she ascends.[43]

This account is peculiar in a number of interesting ways. I have already mentioned the creation of a double for the leonine Yaldabaoth. That the old arch-villain of the drama should be remolded into an emanation of Authades is not surprising since αὐθάδεια is a regular—indeed, the essential—feature of Yaldabaoth's character: repeatedly so, for example, in CG II, *4 Hyp. Arch.* 86 [134].29; 90 [138].29-30; 92 [140].27; 94 [142].21; and especially 94 [142].16-17 where it is related that Sophia's misbegotten offspring "became an arrogant (ΑΥΘΑΛΗΣ) beast in the form of a lion."[44]

---

[42] *Pistis Sophia* 1.30-31 (43.25-46.22 MacDermot). For Sophia's persecution by the lion-faced power see also 1.32 (47.7-14); 39 (63.2-6); 47 (85.14-17); 48 (86.14-18); 52 (98.13-14). MacDermot mistranslates ΑϹϢΠΕ ΠΟΥΑΡΧϢΝ Π2Ο ΠΜΟΥΪ in 46.14, which I paraphrased above by "*became . . . a lion-faced power*," with "*There existed . . .*" (italics mine), as though Yaldabaoth were not born of Sophia's dregs, which is a consistent feature of the myth. Carl Schmidt (*Koptisch-gnostische Schrifen* I. *Die Pistis Sophia. Die beiden Bücher des Jeû. Unbekanntes altgnostisches Werk*; GCS 45 [13]; 3rd ed.; Berlin: Akademie-Verlag, 1962; 28.17) had it right.

[43] *Pistis Sophia* 1.50 (91.13-20); 52 (98.19-99.7); 54 (101.12-16); 55(104.3-14); 2.66 (136.17-138.7; 141.4-142.7).

[44] See Bentley Layton's edition of this document in *HTR* 67 (1974) 351-425 and 69 (1976) 31-101. The passage just cited may be found in *HTR* 67 (1974) under the page and lines of the Coptic manuscript. From the broken context *Hyp. Arch* 87 [135].27-29 it is at least apparent that here too Yaldabaoth's comrades also have the faces of beasts.

In Irenaeus' "Barbeloite" account, moreover, Protarchon mates with his own hypostasized *Authadia* to produce a variety of passions (*Refutation* 1.27.2; I, 226 Harvey).

Why the doubling? The natural surmise is that it was in order to paint a pathetic picture of Sophia as a misguided and repentant sinner ruthlessly persecuted by the archontic powers and rescued by her Savior. The guiding spirit behind this depiction can only have been a community whose soteriology was served by such a projection of their own lot into the sufferings of a pleromatic being at the hands of the lords of this material, passionate world of ours.

What makes this conclusion all the more reasonable is that in its *mise en scène* the text repeatedly presents Jesus' disciples offering Old Testament Psalms of the Persecuted Righteous as "interpretations" of Sophia's hymns of repentance, and twice specifically has James refer Sophia's cry for deliverance from the lion-faced power (1.50[93.5-6] and 2.77 [173.8-9]) to passages from the Psalms where the persecutors are compared to lions (Ps 35 [34] :17 in 1.51 [96.15-16] and Ps 7:2 [3] in 2.78 [174.11]). Of course, it is actually Sophia's (viz. the *Pistis Sophia's* author's and readers') hymns of repentance and supplication that are interpretations of the Psalms that the disciples recite in exposition, not the reverse; the former are gnosticizing paraphrases of the latter.[45] As I intimated earlier

---

[45]See Adolf Harnack, *Über das gnostische Buch Pistis-Sophia* (TU 7.2; Leipzig: Hinrichs, 1891) 31-49: "Die Pistis-Sophia und das Alte Testament." Jean Carmignac, "Le genre littéraire du 'péshèr' dans la Pistis Sophia," *RdQ* 4 (1964) 497-522, sums up the author's method succinctly (p. 500): "il invente un récit qui s'inspire des principales expressions du texte biblique et qui les transpose en d'imaginaires péripéties, puis il fait intervenir un personnage du Nouveau Testament qui montre comment cette description est en somme la réalisation de l'oracle contenu dans la Bible. En somme, il crée des mythes, en les justifiant par les textes mêmes dont ils sont la projection." Note further Herman L. Jansen, "Gnostic Interpretation in Pistis Sophia," *Proceedings of the IXth International Congress for the History of Religions, Tokyo and Kyoto 1958* (Tokyo: Maruzen, 1960) 106-111; and especially Alv Kragerud, *Die Hymnen der Pistis Sophia* (Oslo: Universitetsforlaget, 1967), in particular pp. 16-17 on the choice of Psalms, 90-95 on the origin of the Gnostic paraphrases (his conclusion, pp. 94-95: "Die Paraphrasen sind sämtlich zum vorliegenden Rahmen gebildet, aber ihre Art an und für sich, d.h., interpretierende Umschreibung von at.lichen Texten, hat ihren Ursprung im Kultus"), 101-115 on the *Pistis Sophia's* view of the Old Testament as a body of enigmatic, oracular texts requiring interpretation, 116-158 on the

and will demonstrate more fully later, by the time the *Pistis Sophia*'s
myth of Sophia was written[46] a long-standing and well-established Gnostic tradition existed which saw in the Old Testament Psalms of the above-
mentioned type the paradigm and the prefiguration of the Gnostic soul
suffering persecution in the clutches of bestial archons bent on engulfing
it in the oblivion of Matter.[47] The author of the *Pistis Sophia* used this
time-honored hermeneutical tradition to create a new myth, a Sophia in
his own image, replete with hymns of repentance.[48] He endowed her with
a lion-headed persecutor cloned from his own ancient enemy the lion-
headed Yaldabaoth, whose additional presence the myth still required, and
justified the clone's existence by the discovery of his foreshadowing in the
"lions" of those Davidic Psalms, just as earlier generations of Gnostics had
done.

---

paraphrases' exegetical form and method, and 159-220 on the relationship
between the Gnostic exegesis of the Psalms and the mythological frame-
work in which they are set; and lastly, supplementary to the work just
cited, Geo Widengren, "Die Hymnen der Pistis Sophia und die gnostische
Schriftauslegung," *Liber Amicorum. Studies in Honour of Professor Dr.
C. J. Bleeker* (SHR [NumenSup] 17; Leiden: Brill, 1969) 269-281.

[46]Carl Schmidt sides with the view which places the Codex
Askewianus in the second half of the fourth century and dates the
composition of the sections of the *Pistis Sophia* under consideration to the
second half of the third (*Pistis Sophia neu herausgegeben mit Einleitung
nebst grieschischem und koptischem Wort- und Namenregister*; Haune:
Gyldendalske Boghandel—Nordisk Forlag, 1925; xviii and xxxiii).

[47]Epiphanius' "Gnostics"—a group not only contemporary but sharing
many similarities, if it is not identical, with that which produced the part
of the *Pistis Sophia* under consideration—are said to have allegorized the
Old Testament (*Medicine Chest* 26.6.1-2; 282.25-283.4 Holl). Epiphanus
later cites a specific example of their method and the text interpreted
comes precisely from the Psalms; Ps 1:3a-c is programmatically paraphrased (the passage is actually, according to the sect, περὶ τῆς αἰσχρό-
τητος τοῦ ἀνδρός, and τὴν ἔξοδον τῶν ὑδάτων means τὴν
τῆς ἡδονῆς ἀπόρροιαν) just as are those adduced by the disciples in the
Pistis Sophia.

[48]Walter C. Till, "Die Gnosis in Aegypten," (*PP* 4 (1949) 248: "Der
eindrucksvolle Stoff vom Schicksal der Sophia wurde . . . eingehend aus-
gearbeitet und als ein Mythos gestaltet, dessen ursprünglicher Sinn längst
verloren war, der aber nun wohl als symbolisch für das Schicksal des
ganzen Menschengeschlechtes aufgefasst wurde."

Another interesting feature of the *Pistis Sophia*'s account is the addition of several fully new villainous characters to the drama. The serpent, the basilisk and the dragon that persecute Sophia, and her trampling them under foot as well, are adapted directly from Ps 91 [90] :13 (ἐπ' ἀσπίδα καὶ βασιλίσκον ἐπιβήσῃ καὶ καταπατήσεις λέοντα καὶ δράκοντα LXX), possibly with some help from Luke 10:18-19 (δέδωκα ὑμῖν τὴν ἐξουσίαν τοῦ πατεῖν ἐπάνω ὄφεων . . . καὶ ἐπὶ πᾶσαν τὴν δύναμιν τοῦ ἐχθροῦ), itself at least partially inspired by the same verse of this Psalm. The "interpretation" of these beasts by reference to the verse of this Psalm in 2.67 (148.20-149.4 with 143.15-16 in the continuous citation of the Psalm that precedes the "interpretation") shows that the Old Testament text is their source. That the verse should be used in this way by the *Pistis Sophia* is not surprising given the fact that the interpretation of the verse's beasts as personifications of sin and of evil or as demonic powers—already suggested, after all, by the whole original context of the Psalm itself[49]—

---

[49]Hans-Joachim Kraus (see p. 18 and n. 13 for his views on Ps 22:13) is on surer ground in referring Ps 91:5-6 and 13 to demonic powers that cause disease and death (*Psalmen* II, 638-639). See, for example, Artur Weiser, *Die Psalmen* II (ATD 15; 5th ed.; Göttingen: Vandenhoeck & Ruprecht, 1959) 415-416, 418; Hans Schmidt, *Die Psalmen* (HAT 1.15; Tübingen: Mohr, 1934) 192; Mitchell Dahood, *Psalms* II (AB; Garden City, NY: Doubleday, 1968) 331-333; and the fine article by André Caquot, "Le psaume XCI," *Sem* 8 (1958) 21-37, in particular 29-31 on vv 5-6 and 34-35 on v 13. דֶּבֶר and קֶטֶב in v 6 are especially likely to be personified demonic powers: see A. Caquot, "Sur quelques démons de l'Ancien Testament (Reshep, Qeteb, Deber)," *Sem* 6 (1956) 53-68. The LXX's translator thought so; he renders v 6b by ἀπὸ συμπτώματος καὶ δαιμονίου μεσημβρινοῦ. So did Aquila, who translates the verse with ἀπὸ δηγμοῦ δαιμονίζοντος μεσημβρίας, and Symmachus, with οὐ συγκύρημα δαιμονιῶδες μεσημβρίας (Fridericus Field, *Origenis Hexaplorum quae supersunt* II; Hildesheim: Olms, 1964; 249); so too does *b. Pesaḥ* 111b. The same may apply to the lions (שַׁחַל and כְּפִיר) and serpents of v 13: so W. O. E. Oesterly, *The Psalms* (London: SPCK, 1953) 410 (the whole of his treatment, pp. 407-411, is edifying); Sigmund Mowinckel, *Psalmenstudien* III. *Kultprophetie und prophetische Psalmen* (Amsterdam: Schippers, 1961) 103; and Hermann Gunkel, *Die Psalmen* (5th ed.; Göttingen: Vandenhoeck & Ruprecht, 1929) 405, who thinks the Psalmist had the ancient Near Eastern motif of a hero's triumph over fierce beasts in mind and the fact that such representations were used as amulets to ward off harmful animals of this kind (the references of vv 5-6 are in his view certainly to demonic powers: *Die Psalmen* 404). As a general theory for the identity of the persecutors in those Psalms where they are distinctly human, sor-

had long before been explicitly carried out, for example by Irenaeus

---

cerers who send demons of disease have—and justly—not found universal acceptance (see Harris Birkeland's concise summary of the prevailing views in *The Evildoers in the Book of Psalms*; Oslo: Dybwad, 1955; 9-11, though Ps 91 is not included in the discussion). But the hypothesis that the "lions" of Ps 91 [90] :13 are, like דֶּבֶר and קֶטֶב in v 6, demonic is strengthened by the circumstance that the Babylonians, and the Assyrians after them, associated the lion with Nergal, as I have already pointed out, and frequently cast their demons in leonine and serpentine images. Furthermore, it is precisely against the calamities caused by such agents that Ps 91 guarantees protection. In fact Ps 91 may originally have been composed as an apotropaic incantation against such nefarious influences, a theory initiated by Julius Wellhausen (*The Book of Psalms*; New York: Dodd, Mead, and Co.; London: James Clarke and Co.; Stuttgart: Deutsche Verlags-Anstalt, 1898; 201 in a note on Ps 91) and followed by many others (references in Caquot, "Le psaume XCI" 22 n. 2; add a cautious Mowinckel, *Psalmenstudien* III, 102-103). Nicolaj Nicolsky's commentary in support of this hypothesis (*Spuren magischer Formeln in den Psalmen*; BZAW 46; Giessen: Töpelmann, 1927; 14-29) is especially full; in his remarks on v 13 (pp. 24-25 and notes), whose beasts he too holds to be ciphers for demons, he cites Babylonian parallels of the lion-headed type I have already referred to from Morris Jastrow, *Die Religion Babyloniens und Assyriens* I (Giessen: Ricker, 1905) 281 and particularly 335: "Die Hauptfigur in den Darstellungen ist ein monströses Weib mit Löwenkopf, von deren Brüsten je ein Schwein und ein Hund herabhängen, und das in jeder Hand eine Schlange hält" (cp. again pl. 2a). Nicolsky also adduces the demon in leonine form, appositely named Λεοντοφόρος, evoked by Solomon in the *Testament of Solomon* 11.1-4 (39*-40* McCown; so also the demon Ornias in 2.3, p. 14* McCown). As for Ps 91's amuletic character there is no doubt that it was so employed in late antiquity; *b Šebu.* 15b, *y. ʿErub.* 10:26c, and *y. Šabb.* 6:8b testify to its general use for recitation over the demon-possessed, and Satan is being especially crafty in citing vv 11a and 12 to Jesus during the Temptation in the Wilderness (Matt 4:6//Luke 4:10-11). To judge from the special position accorded it and from what is left of the contents of the recension in which it occurs, the Psalm seems to have been similarly so used at Qumran where it has been discovered to conclude a very badly damaged scroll collection of otherwise apocryphal psalms: see J. van der Ploeg, "Le psaume XCI dans une recension de Qumran," *RB* 72 (1965) 210-217 with pls. 8-9; "Un petit rouleau de psaumes apocryphes," *Tradition und Glaube: Das frühe Christentum in seiner Umwelt. Festgabe für Karl Georg Kuhn zum 65. Geburtstag* (Göttingen: Vandenhoeck & Ruprecht, 1971) 128-139; Otto Eissfeldt, "Eine Qumran-Textform des 91. Psalms," *Bibel und Qumran. Beiträge zur*

(*Refutation* 3.23.7) and by Origen (*On Prayer* 13.4; *Against Celsus* 7.70). The additional endowment of the basilisk with seven heads may stem, as Kragerud argues,[50] from *Odes Sol.* 22.5 (22.4 in Schmidt's Coptic text), for this text is cited somewhat later in the *Pistis Sophia* (2.71; 157.21-23) as a "prefiguration" of the corresponding verse in Sophia's hymn of thanksgiving in 2.70 (156.1-4) and then interpreted as such still further on in 2.71 (159.14-21). The serpent's seven-headedness, in turn, derives perhaps from Rev 12:3, as James Charlesworth proposes,[51] or, since the *Odes of Solomon* may conceivably be as old (or nearly so) as Rev itself, from some common tradition ultimately dependent on ancient Semitic myth.[52] He rears his ugly heads in *Apoc. John* too, as we shall see.

It needs to be stressed, however, that while the ophidian villains are elements newly introduced by the *Pistis Sophia* into the traditional Gnostic mythological complex surrounding the figure of Sophia, the same does not apply equally to her lion-faced persecutor. He may be a double of the leonine Yaldabaoth—and that is a new development—but the character he mirrors is not drawn from Old Testament Psalms that "prefigure" the mythology, but rather from far earlier strata of the Gnostic myth, strata for which handy concordance could be found—and had already been found—-in the "lions" of Pss 7, 22 [21] , 35 [34] and the others. Kragerud's methodological remarks are to the point here; though made of a single test case, they apply equally to all the episodes of the *Pistis Sophia*: "Es wird Grund für die Annahme vorliegen, dass der mythische Rahman aus dem

---

Erforschung der Beziehungen zwischen Bibel- und Qumranwissenschaft (Berlin: Evangelische Haupt-Bibelgesellschaft, 1968) 82-85.

[50] *Hymnen* 192.

[51] James Hamilton Charlesworth, *The Odes of Solomon. The Syriac Texts* (SBLTT 13, Pseudepigrapha series 7; Missoula: Scholars Press, 1977) 91 in his note ad loc. J. H. Bernard's comments on the verse (*The Odes of Solomon*; TextsS 8.3; Cambridge: the University Press, 1912; 94-95) offer a wealth of early Christian baptismal references to overthrowing the dragon (i.e., Satan), many by way of allusion to Ps 74 [73] :13 or 14 (σὺ συνέτριψας τὰς κεφαλὰς τῶν δρακόντων ἐπὶ τοῦ ὕδατος / σὺ συνέθλασας τὰς κεφαλὰς τοῦ δράκοντος LXX). Rendel Harris and Alphonse Mingana, *The Odes and Psalms of Solomon* II (Manchester: the University Press, and London: Longmans, Green & Co. and Bernard Quaritch, 1920) 327-332 offer equally valuable commentary on the Ode.

[52] Reference to a primeval serpent *dšbʿt rʾašm* "with seven heads" in the Ugaritic Baal-cycle (see, for example, G. R. Driver, *Canaanite Myths and Legends*; Edinburgh: T. & T. Clark, 1956; Baal V iii 57, pp. 86-87). The seven-headed Lernaean Hydra that Heracles battled is of similar ancestry.

Psalm (or *Ode Sol.*, as the case may be) hervorgewachsen ist, wenn die Übereinstimmung zwischen Psalm (or *Ode Sol.*) und Mythus sehr nahe ist," and this applies to the serpent, the basilisk, and the dragon of Ps 91 [90]:13; "Umgekehrt muss mann M (the mythological episode) für ursprünglich halten, wenn a) der Stoff anderswo bekannt ist, oder b) unbedeutende Übereinstimmung mit dem Psalm vorliegen,"[53] which is true of Sophia's lion-headed persecutor insofar as he represents a clone of the old leonine Yaldabaoth. It is merely nice corroboration, then, that Ps 91 [90]:13 also mentions a lion and, similarly, that earlier in the *Pistis Sophia* the references to "lions" in Pss 7 and 35 [34] can be adduced as prefigurations of the lion-faced power's activities.

One other feature of the *Pistis Sophia*'s account deserves mention: the bizarre detail that Sophia's intent in descending into Chaos was to devour the lion-faced light-power (1.31; 46.9 ⲭⲉ ⲉⲥⲉⲟⲙⲉⲕⲧ̅). Such an effort on Sophia's part is, so far as I know, unique, but it is likely to be no more than a rather crass reformulation of Sophia's continuous labor to recapture from her abortive offspring Yaldabaoth the light which he inherited through her from the perfect world beyond him (as in Irenaeus, *Refutation* 1.28.3; I, 232-233 Harvey, for example). On the face of it her attempt offers an interesting mythological parallel to 2b of logion 7 from *Gos. Thom.*, especially as the result of Sophia's encounter with the leonine power corresponds to 3b of the saying: she is herself somehow devoured. The parallel is not coincidental for, as I intend to show in greater detail later, the engulfment of pleromatic life by cosmic powers and the struggle to reabsorb it form the mythological backdrop to the logion. As 2a and 3a of the logion make plain, however, the battlefield for the logion is not the cosmos, but rather the soul of man. The anthropological dimension of the struggle must first be understood, then, before the logion can be fully explained, and that subject will be explored in due time.

2.4   The Apocryphon of John

Let us turn now to the *Apocryphon of John*.[54] Here the relevant

---

[53] *Psalmen* 162.

[54] I follow the account of the long recension as represented by CG II, *1*; variations in the two representatives of the short recension (CG III, *1* and BG 8502, *2*) crucial for my purposes will be taken up later. For the text of CG II, *1* see Søren Giversen, *Apocryphon Johannis* (ATDan 5; Copenhagen: Prostant apud Munksgaard, 1963); and Martin Krause and Pahor Labib, *Die drei Versionen des Apokryphon des Johannes im*

portion of the story is as follows: From Sophia's forbidden desire is born a monstrous being whom she casts away and sequesters outside the pleromatic realm. Yaltabaoth, as she calls him, has the form of a dragon with the face of a lion; his eyes coruscate lightning. Deriving great power from his mother's light, he creates for himself aeons out of fire (cp. Ps 104 [103]:4), authorities and kings to whom he parcels out his fire, and powers and angels with the faces of a variety of animals. Yaltabaoth himself actually has a multitude of faces upon which he sits, so that he is able to present whatever face he may desire to his ministers.[55]

Armed with his mother's light, Authades Yaltabaoth creates his cosmos and crows his ignorant blasphemy; Sophia, realizing her error, repents. Unlike the *Pistis Sophia*, however, in *Apoc. John* it is through the purely psychic man plagued by passions, which the archons fashion in imitation of the heavenly Man, that Yaltabaoth is deprived of the light. At the instigation of Sophia Yaltabaoth blows into his man's face and unwittingly transmits to him the Spirit, the light that he had taken from his mother. But jealous now of their creation's luminosity and superior knowledge, the archons banish the soul to the lowest regions of Chaos, create a mortal body out of fire, water, earth and fiery winds in which to imprison him, and give him their counterfeit spirit to lead him into darkness and desire.[56]

The most interesting characteristic of this account for our study is the form with which Yaldabaoth (Yaltabaoth is a variant spelling attested elsewhere) is here invested. He is now no longer simply a lion-headed deity (i.e., a lion-headed *man*), as he is in Celsus' and Origen's sources' portrait, but a *serpent* with the face of a lion. What is more, even the two

---

koptischen Museum zu Alt-Kairo (ADAI.K 1; Wiesbaden: Harrassowitz, 1962) 109-199. Krause-Labib register variants from the other examples of *Apoc. John* in their critical apparatus, but for the full text see *Die drei Versionen* 55-108 (CG III, *1*); 201-255 (CG IV, *1*—long recension, very fragmentary); Walter C. Till and Hans-Martin Schenke, *Die gnostischen Schriften des koptischen Papyrus Berolinensis 8502* (TU 60[2]; 2nd ed.; Berlin: Akademie-Verlag, 1972) 78-195 (BG 8502, *2*).

[55]CG II, *1*; 9 [57].25-12 [60].8 (Giversen 62-69; Krause-Labib 134-142); III, *1*; 14.9-18.19 (Krause-Labib 68-74); IV, *1*; 15.1-19.6 (Krause-Labib 212-215); BG 8502, *2*; 36.16-43.2 (Till-Schenke 112-127).

[56]CG II, *1*; 12 [60].33-21 [69].14 (Giversen 68-87; Krause-Labib 144-166); III, *1*; 21.2-27.1 (Krause-Labib 74-84); IV, *1*; 20.10-32.27 (Krause-Labib 216-231); BG 8502, *2*; 44.9-55.15 (Till-Schenke 128-151).

recensions of *Apoc. John* do not fully agree in this description; the short recension offers a significantly different picture. The long recension (CG, II *1*; 10 [58].8-9; CG IV, *1* is here totally in lacuna) has:

ⲁϥϣⲱⲡⲉ   ⲛ̄ⲟⲩⲧⲩⲡⲟⲥ   ⲉϥϣⲃⲃ ⲓ ⲁⲉ ⲓ ⲧ
ⲛ̄ⲁⲣⲁⲕⲱⲛ   ⲛ̄₂ⲟ   ⲙ̄ⲙⲟⲩⲉ ⲓ

he assumed a deviant (or, composite) shape,
(the shape of) a dragon with the face of a lion.

But the texts of the short recension, which themselves are not identical, read as follows: CG, III, *1*; 15.10-11:

ⲁϥϣⲱⲡⲉ ⲛ̄ⲕⲉⲙⲟⲣ ⲫ ⲏ ⲛ̄₂ⲁ ⲛ̄ⲙⲟⲩⲉ ⲓ
ⲛ̄₂ⲁ   ⲛ̄₂ⲁϥ

he assumed a different form, with the face
of a lion with the face of a serpent,

and BG 8502, *2*; 37.19-21:

ⲉⲁϥϣⲱⲡⲉ ⲙ̄ⲡⲧⲩⲡⲟⲥ ⲛ̄ⲕⲉⲉⲓⲛⲉ ⲉϥⲟ
ⲛ̄₂ⲁ ⲛ₂ⲟϥ ⲁⲩⲱ ⲛ̄₂ⲟ ⲙⲙⲟⲩⲉ ⲓ

he assumed the shape of a different form,
having the face of a serpent and the
face of a lion.

The short recension's portrait is very awkwardly worded (especially CG III, *1*) and looks derivative. Its intent is certainly to endow Yaldabaoth with more than one face. The reason for this is not far to seek; the short recension has attempted to reconcile the second description of Yaldabaoth as possessing a multitude of faces—it follows directly upon that which describes him as a lion-headed serpent and represents a tradition obviously quite different from the other—by altering both of them in the interest of giving Yaldabaoth a plurality of faces. It did so with the long recension's lion-headed serpent by making it the two faces of a lion and a serpent; the following extracts will make clear how it did the same with the second tradition. The long recension (CG II, *1*; 11 [59].35-12 [60].3, strictly parallel to CG IV, *1*; 18.26-19.1) has:

but Yaltabaoth had a multitude of faces upon all of which he sat, so that he could present whatever face he wished to them all (i.e., to his cohorts), a description which, as the incongruous reference to the Seraphim in what immediately follows nevertheless makes quite plain, stems ultimately from Ezekiel's חַיּוֹת and which is still faithful to the prophet's vision in ascribing the multiplicity of countenance to them, not to Yahweh/Yaldabaoth. But the short recension (BG 8502, 2; 42.10-13, essentially identical with CG III, 1; 18.9-12), on the other hand, has:

> but Yaltabaoth Salkas, who possessed the multitude of forms, so that he could manifest himself in every face that he willed, etc.,

which, by replacing "faces" with "forms" and omitting the phrase "upon all of which he sat," subtly but effectively transfers this facial shiftiness to Yaldabaoth himself.

Besides, the change had the additional advantage of bringing Yaldabaoth into line with the rest of his comrades, whose animal forms are restricted to their faces, not their bodies. The description of the animal-faced powers of the archons in each of the texts (omitting CG IV, 1; 18.18-24, which is almost totally destroyed) is as follows:

II, 1; 11 [59].26-34	III, 1; 17.20-18.7	BG 8502 1; 41.16-42.7
Athōth : sheep-face	Aōth : lion-face	Iaōth : lion-face
Elōaiou : Typhon-face	Elōaios : ass-face	Elōaios : ass-face
Astaphaios : :[hyen]a-fa[ce]	Astophaios : hyena-face	Astaphaios : hyena-face
Iaō : seven-headed [drago]n-fa[ce]	Iazō : dragon-face with lion-face	Iaō : seven-headed serpent-face
Sabaōth : dragon-face	Adōnaios : dragon-face	Adōnaios : dragon-face
Adōnin : ape-face	Adōnin : monkey-face	Adōni : monkey-face
Sabbede : shining fire-face	Sabbadaios : shining fire-face	Sabbataios : shining flame-of-fire-face

It is interesting that CG III, 1 has performed the same facial operation on Iaō (Iazō) that it has on Yaldabaoth. The long recension has Iaō in the form of our old archontic friend the seven-headed serpent; indeed, it may equally have been from *Apoc. John* that the *Pistis Sophia* derived the beast and then, in normal fashion, demonstrated him "prefigured" in *Ode Sol.* 22.5. But CG III, *1* has stripped him of his body and made him (as he actually is) a virtual duplicate of Yaldabaoth, except that with the latter the lion-face is the primary element (Ⲛ₂Ⲁ ⲚⲘⲞⲨⲈ Ⲓ Ⲛ₂Ⲁ Ⲛ₂Ⲁϥ 15.11 cited above), whereas with Iazō the serpent-face remains primary (ⲡ₂Ⲁ ⲚⲀⲢⲀⲔⲰⲚ Ⲛ₂Ⲁ ⲚⲘⲞⲨⲈ Ⲓ 18.2). BG 8502, *2* has seen fit to leave the long recension's Iaō alone.

Just as it is truer to Ezekiel in its description of Yaldabaoth as "seated upon" his faces, so the long recension's portrait of the archon as a serpent with the one head of a lion is likely to be primary also. This is so for another, more important reason than simply that the short recension's version looks derivative. By "primary" I do not mean, of course, that this was necessarily the form that Yaldabaoth had in *Apoc. John* in its original, Greek, early to mid-second century form. All four manuscripts of the document belong to the fourth century, and neither recension they offer need by any means reproduce the autograph. It is unfortunate that in his woefully curt paraphrase of the system either closely kindred to that represented by *Apoc. John* or possibly identical with it, Irenaeus, (*Refutation* 1.27) neglects to mention what his Protarchon looked like.[57] The same is true of the related "Ophite" or "Sethian" system summarized in

---

[57] See Carl Schmidt, "Irenäus und seine Quelle in adv. haer. I, 29," *Philotesia Paul Kleinert zum LXX. Geburtstag dargebracht* (Berlin: Trowitzsch & Sohn, 1907) 315-336. (Schmidt followed a chapter-division different from that of Harvey.) The divergences between Irenaeus and *Apoc. John* as we have it (Schmidt, of course, used only BG 8502, *2*) are often very great, and so it is uncertain what exactly lay before Irenaeus. Because he finds in it confirmation of an earlier guess, Schmidt is convinced that Irenaeus had an original Gnostic document to hand, not, as Adolf Hilgenfeld (*Ketzergeschichte* 230 and *passim* of other heresies in Irenaeus' catalogue) opined, an (already bowdlerized) heresiological tract (Justin's *Syntagma*). But even Schmidt must concede that the bishop possessed only "ein unvollkommener Auszug" of *Apoc. John* ("Irenäus und seine Quelle" 317). His comparison of the section of Irenaeus' extract with that in BG 8502, *2* which contains the portrait of Yaldabaoth may be found on pp. 329-331; of the two he remarks (p. 330): "Bei oberflächlicher Vergleichung dieser beiden Berichte könnte man an eine Identität der von Irenäus benutzten Quellenschrift mit unserm koptischen Werke zweifeln." It is far from certain, then, that just because Irenaeus' report fails to record a form for the chief archon the source which ultimately underlies his account lacked one.

1.28.[58] If he had, we would assuredly be closer to the original. But in relation to the short recension's portrait, that offered by the long recension is likely to be the earlier because the lion-headed serpent was an extremely popular figure in the late Egyptian pantheon, and, in one of his guises at least, had been identified with Yahweh/Iao. This whole matter will be taken up in exhaustive detail in the following chapter, but for the moment I want only to suggest that it was this figure and this identification which led the long recension of *Apoc. John* to adopt the lion-headed serpent as an alternate form for its Yahweh/Yaldabaoth. The short recension then secondarily altered this portrait in the interest of reconciling this picture with that derived from Ezekiel and, at the same time, of granting its Yaldabaoth more than one face. Why it should want to do this will be studied later.

If, as I proposed earlier, *Apoc. John* in both extant recensions represents a more developed stage of the tradition than that known to Celsus, Origen and Irenaeus, it is because in the latter group Yaldabaoth is still a member of the planetary Hebdomad, while in the former he has been elevated out of it. His special position as supplier of soul to the human body fashioned by the other archons (Irenaeus, *Refutation* 1.28.2; I, 232-233 Harvey), and generally his increasing prominence in the evolution of the Gnostic myth, could not suffer him to remain merely *primus inter pares*. But it is interesting to note that the first archon of the short recension's maleficent seven is lion-faced. This portrait may, in effect, be a concession to the original tradition, in which the first of the seven was lion-headed; the short recension's attempt to make its first archon's name (Aōth, Iaōth) more closely approximate Iaō points in the same direction. The long recension's earlier Athōth, with which it replaced Yaldabaoth, who had now been kicked upstairs, was taken over, it seems, from the similarly named first in the list of "authorities" in CG II, *I*; 10 [58].29. It betrays its intrusive character by not being a name stemming either from the common Old Testament appellatives of Yahweh or from older Jewish tradition.[59] Yaldabaoth's promotion naturally required (or was required by) his change in looks.

---

[58] This system, as Schmidt correctly remarks, ("Irenäus und seine Quelle" 334), "nur eine Abart der in Kap. 29 (that is, 1.27 Harvey) geschilderten gnostischen Sekte repräsentiert, darum auch Irenäus diese mit den Worten einfuhrt: *Alii autem rursus portentuosa loquuntur.*"

[59] On these and other archon-lists and the problems they present see further Giversen's commentary, *Apocryphon Johannis* 218-223, and particularly A. J. Welburn, "The Identity of the Archons in the 'Apocryphon Johannis,'" *VC* 32 (1978) 241-254.

2.5   Mandaean and Manichaean Texts

Not surprisingly—given their dependence on old Gnostic mythology—
Mandaean and Manichaean sources have similar tales to tell. The Mandaean *Ginza* (Rechter Teil, 12.6; 277.31-280.7 Lidzbarski) gives the King
of Darkness the face of a lion,[60] the body of a dragon, the wings of an
eagle, the flanks of a tortoise, and the hands and feet of a demon; he
pounces upon the world of Light like a ravenous lion upon its prey to
infect it with his horde of fiends embodying every hideous passion conceivable.

The Mandaean cosmos, the domain of the King of Darkness, is itself a
den of lions and dragons, the dwelling place of demons; in the Mandaean
Book of John 66 (222.16-20 Lidzbarski) the Father sends his son, the
primal Man, into Chaos with the words "Geh in die Welt der Finsternis, in
die Finsternis, in der es keinen Lichtstrahl gibt, an den Ort der Löwen, an
den Sitz der verwünschten Leoparden, an den Ort der Drachen, an den Sitz
der verderblichen Dämonen," a world peopled, with help from the bestial
enemies of the Psalms, by lion- and serpent-demons in good Babylonian
fashion. The primal Man is justifiably terrified, and his worst fears are
realized; the lions, dragons, and other beastly demons surround him,
threatening him. In answer to his prayer of complaint the Father grants
his son a staff and commands him to slay his enemies with it. Fortified by
this aid from the world of Light, his mission a success, the primal Man
strikes down the Darkness and its powers and reascends.

The Manichaean portrait of the King of Darkness closely resembles the
Mandaean for having served as its source.[61] *Kephalaion* 27, entitled "On

---

[60]Lidzbarski's "des Adlers" is an error: see Kurt Rudolph, *Theogonie,
Kosmogonie und Anthropogonie in den mandäischen Schriften* (Göttingen:
Vandenhoeck & Ruprecht, 1965) 92 and n. 5.

[61]Lately Kurt Rudolph, in his work *Die Mandäer I. Prolegomena. Das
Mandäerproblem* (Göttingen: Vandenhoeck & Ruprecht, 1960) §4.8, pp.
176-195, especially p. 182, suggests, as others have done, the priority of
the Mandaean system, but in the case of the Prince of Darkness' looks the
remarks of Hanri-Charles Puech, "Le Prince des Ténèbres en son
royaume," reprinted with additional notes in *Sur le manichéisme et autres
essais* (Paris: Flammarion, 1979) 114-116, seem to me decisive in establishing Manichaeism as the source of the Mandaean description. The
Cologne Mani-Codex has now revealed that the Babylonian Jewish-
Christian baptismal sect in which Mani spent his early life was Elchasaite,
not Mandaean: see A. Henrichs and L. Koenen, "Ein griechischer Mani-

the five forms which the Ruler of the Darkness possesses," appropriately gives the prince of demons animal parts corresponding to the bestial representatives of the five dark worlds over which he rules:

> his head has the face of a lion from the world of Fire; his wings and shoulders have the look (face!) of (those of) an eagle, in conformity with the sons of Wind; his hands and feet are (those of) demons, in conformity with the sons of the world of Smoke; his belly has the look (face) of a dragon, in conformity with the sons of the world of Darkness; and his tail has the form of a fish, which is peculiar to the world of the sons of Water

(77.22-78.3 Polotsky-Böhlig, restorations, all but certain, left unindicated). *Kephalaion* 6 offers a similar description, specifying further that the individual kings of the four elemental worlds that have animals to represent them each has the form or "face" of his particular beast, the lord of them all being logically enough a composite of all of them (30.17-31.2; 33.9-10, 18, 25, 33).[62] Regardless of whether, in addition to earlier Gnostic theriomorphic archons, Mesopotamian or any other ancient Near Eastern *Mischwesen* had a hand in his creation, the pentamorphic

---

Codex," *ZPE* 5 (1970) 133-160; Albert Henrichs, "Mani and the Babylonian Baptists: A Historical Confrontation," *HSCP* 77 (1973) 23-59, but this new source, insofar as it has been published, does not shed any light on origins and prototypes for the Manichaean and Mandaean prince of devils.

[62]For the Manichaean description of the Prince of Darkness as preserved by Ibn al-Nadim note the translation by Bayard Dodge, *The Fihrist of al-Nadim* II (New York: Columbia University Press, 1970) 778: "From this land of Darkness there was Satan . . . , who is not eternal in his own person, but the elements of his ingredients are eternal. These elements of his ingredients became compounded and brought Satan into existence. His head is the head of a lion and his body like the body of a dragon (great serpent). His wing is like the wing of a bird, his tail like the tail of a great fish, and his four feet like the feet of a beast of burden"; true to his lion-head he "swallowed, gulped down, and corrupted" whatever opposed him. This description differs somewhat from that offered by the Coptic *Kephalaia*; the overly immaterial and non-theriomorphic demons have been replaced by quadrupeds.

Manichaean world-ruler has the form he has in order to suggest his derivation from and lordship over the five elements on the Manichaean cosmos.
Unlike the Mandaean, the Manichaean accounts (Ibn al-Nadim's included)
make this quite plain, a fact which further suggests the priority of the
latter system over the former. Each of the five beings which compose him
were well known as the consummate products of the realm they represent;
the odd Mandaean substitution of a tortoise for the Manichaean fish has
disturbed this symmetry. The lion as a quintessentially fiery beast is a
subject I will discuss in detail later.

A passage from the Coptic *Psalm-Book* indicates, however, that the
Manichaeans in Egypt were also quite familiar with the earlier portrait
tradition represented by the long recension of *Apoc. John*, for *Psalm to
Jesus* 248 (57.16-18 Allberry) speaks of "the ογcιλ of the Enemy . . . the
body of death, the son of the great [. . .], this dragon with the face of a
lion"—from what precedes it is obvious that he is the god of the Old
Testament—"and his mother Matter also." The passage affirms the likelihood that one of the direct models for the developed portrait of the
Manichaean (and Mandaean) cosmocrator was the lion-headed serpent of
Apoc. John, who dutifully sprouted wings, legs, arms, and a tail. As the
Turfan text M 2 Recto I, 1-33 shows,[63] Egypt was a prime target for
evangelization by the Manichaeans, and, given the Manichaean practice of
grafting itself onto the local traditions of the regions it chose to pene-
trate, it stands to reason that the invaders should favor a document whose
popularity is attested by the plurality of recensions and copies in which it
has survived there.

Passages from the *Psalm-Book* recount Manichaean versions of Man's
primeval encounter with the cosmic rulers. In a simile *Psalm of the Bema*
223 (9.31-10.19 Allberry) compares the powers of the Kingdom of Darkness to a lion[64] with mouth agape in their desire to devour the Maiden,

---

[63]F.C. Andreas and Walter Henning, "Mitteliranische Manichaica aus
Chinesisch-Turkestan II," *SPAW.PH* (1933) 301-302.   Further   Geo
Widengren, *Mani and Manichaeism* (trans. C. Kessler; London: Weidenfeld
and Nicolson, 1965) 34.

[64]It is interesting that Middle Persian Manichaean texts give a
certain class of demon the form of lions: F. C. Andreas and Walter
Henning, "Mitteliranische Manichaica aus Chinesisch-Turkestan I,"
SPAW.PH (1932) 193-194 (e I Verso I, 21-31): "Darauf zog die *Āz* von allen
jenen Sprösslingen der Dämonen, die vom Himmel auf die Erde gefallen
waren, an jenen männlichen *Āsrēštār* und jene weibliche *Āsrēštār*,
(welche) löwengestaltig, . . . zornig, sündig und räuberisch waren, diese

the soul of the primal Man, whom the Father uses as bait with which to catch them. The son dutifully exhibits his soul to the beasts, and "she wormed her way into them and bound them all without their knowledge." *Psalm of Thomas* [11] (216.14-217.17 Allberry) provides the mythological basis for the simile. In deference to Gnostic allegorization of the "lions" of the Old Testament Psalms as figures for the archons and specifically of the "lion and dragon" of Ps 91[90]:13, as in the *Pistis Sophia* and the derivative Mandaean account from its *Book of John,* the dragon is not the lion's body here, but his consort. The two beasts seize the soul of the primal Man and drag her into their lair, roaring and hissing frightfully; "indeed, they and all their powers as well roar out everywhere, but they do not reveal themselves to my (the primal Man's) daughter lest their power be diminished." The Man cries out to the Father for rescue, pleading that if his soul has done wrong to either of the beasts, they may swallow her. Vindicated, she is released from their den and set high above them all in her bridal chamber. Together with her father she destroys the traps they had laid for her, and the two overthrow their "wheel" (of γένε-σις, birth and death: cp. Jas 3:6 τὸν τροχὸν τῆς γενέσεως; *Acts of Thomas* 55).

2.6 Summary

The biblical background for the leonine imagery of Jesus' seventh logion in *Gos. Thom.* is not the New Testament but rather the Old, and the relevant passages are those in which Yahweh himself is compared to a lion. Gnostic enemies of the creator in the form of the god of the Jews found such metaphors suitably savage and evolved in addition a tradition which allegorized the "lions" and other beasts of many Psalms, where they are already symbols for human or demonic persecutors of the righteous (now the Gnostics), as figurative references to Yahweh and his ministers.

This exegetical tradition was used to support a depiction of the god of the Jews as a leontomorphic deity. One facet of this development was the use of Isaiah's cryptic allusion to an Ariel as a secret name for the Gnostic Yahweh because its prefix element could—perhaps rightly—be interpreted to mean "lion."

Two strands of tradition exist which picture the Gnostic creator and ruler of the cosmos as lion-formed. The earliest extant, actually illus-

---

(beiden zog sie an)." Similarly c Recto I, 1-16 (p. 195) and c Verso I, 27-34 (p. 197). The description of these demons is doubtless of Babylonian origin, though set in the context of the myth of the Fallen Angels.

trated on the Brummer gem, makes him a lion-headed man. This strand emerges in the mid-second century with the primitive "Sethian" or "Ophite" system known to Celsus and crops up in CG II, *4 Hyp. Arch.* (probably) and in the *Pistis Sophia* as well as in the document which lay before Origen. With the long recension of *Apoc. John* a new strand comes to light in which the chief archon is a lion-headed serpent. The short recension's double-headed figure is derivative. The new strand is also attested in a developed form by Manichaean sources and by the Mandaean *Ginza* dependent upon them. The new Manichaean portrait, in turn, is likely to have been at least in part dependent upon *Apoc. John*'s description, since there is evidence that the new movement was familiar with that tradition. Manichaean and Mandaean myth both evince knowledge of the Gnostic exegesis of the Psalms' "lions" as figures for demonic archontic powers.

3

The Making of
the Gnostic Synthesis

3.1 The Old Testament and Early Christianity

The task now at hand is to identify the different cultural ingredients which went to produce the Gnostic mythological amalgam, and, so far as possible, to mark out the stages of their individual development and the sequence of their entry into Gnostic tradition. The place to begin is once again with the Old Testament, since trajectories can be clearly traced from its leonine imagery into intertestamental Judaism and through early Christianity into the full-blown Gnostic systems of the second century and beyond.

I have already touched more than once upon the "lions" of the Psalms. As I showed, there is reason to suspect that, in the case of Ps 91[90]:13 at least, in its original setting the "lion" is a figure, not for human enemies, but, as Babylonian and Assyrian texts suggest, for demonic powers of possession, disease and death. Even when the enemies of the Psalmist are most obviously human, however, their description is still often couched in mythological categories that freely lent themselves to the more figurative interpretation for being ultimately rooted in that soil. These mythological forms were inherited by Israel from ancient Canaanite portraits of Death. The gaping, insatiable gullet of Mot is graphically depicted by the Ugaritic Baal-cycle,[1] and the lion was a natural

---

[1] For instance, G. R. Driver, *Canaanite Myths and Legends* 104-105: Baal I* ii 1-6; and the passage I* i 6-8 and 12-22 as translated by John Gray, *The Legacy of Canaan* (VTSup 5; Leiden: Brill, 1957) 56-57, where Mot is also likened to a lioness for savagery. See further Ulf Oldenburg, *The Conflict between El and Ba ͨal in Canaanite Religion* (Leiden: Brill, 1969) 36, with parallels as applied to מָוֶת and שְׁאוֹל in the Old Testament offered on p. 35.

theriomorphic metaphor for this image of the Underworld, all the more as
its rulers and agents (Nergal and his death-dealing demons), partially for
the same reason, were lion-mouthed. Thus in Ps 35 [34], where in v 17
the Psalmist's enemies are compared to lions, v 21 portrays them pro-
ceeding with mouths agape against him (ἐπλάτυναν ἐπ' ἐμὲ τὸ στόμα
αὐτῶν LXX) and v 25 as gloating that they have swallowed him up
(κατεπίομεν αὐτόν); in Ps 22:13, 21 [21:14, 22], similarly, in being likened
to lions the persecutors open their mouths to devour their hapless victim
(ἤνοιξαν ἐπ' ἐμὲ τὸ στόμα αὐτῶν ὡς λέων ὁ ἁρπάζων καὶ ὠρυόμενος
. . . σῶσόν με ἐκ στόματος λέοντος).[2] As we have seen, this voracious
attribute of the lion-figure is one which runs through the whole Gnostic
mythological tradition (including logion 7 of *Gos. Thom.*), and it stems,
with general help from the lion's well-deserved reputation for a ravenous
appetite, from these passages in the Psalms, as the following discussion
will make clear.[3]

Under the inspiration of these same verses from Pss 35 [34] and
22 [21] the lion continued to be a popular symbol for Death and the grave,
which devour the flesh of the dead, in Christian art of the Middle Ages.
As σαρκοφάγος the lion adorns cathedrals and the tombs of men; the dead
and the damned are shown, half-engulfed, protruding from his yawning
throat. His jaws are the jaws of Hell; the Devil sits astride his back.
Medieval liturgies for the dead and for those *in extremis* pray deliverance
from his maw with citations from precisely those Psalms where the righteous beseech their Lord for rescue from the mouths of the "lions."[4]

---

[2]On the theme of the voracity of Death see Nicholas J. Tromp, *Primitive Conceptions of Death and the Nether World in the Old Testament*
(BibOr 21; Rome: Pontifical Biblical Institute, 1969) 112-113, 213.

[3]The jaws of the Lion formed a distinct astrological constellation:
Franz Boll, *Sphaera. Neue griechische Texte und Untersuchungen zur
Geschichte der Sternbilder* (Leipzig: Teubner, 1903) 129.

[4]See W. Deonna's erudite study "'Salve me de ore leonis.' A propos de
quelques chapiteaux romans de la cathédrale Saint-Pierre à Genève,"
RBPH 28 (1950) 479-511; Bertram in Michaelis, "λέων" 253 n. 21; Bloch,
"Löwe" section II.A: "Der Dämon," pp. 115-116; Louis Charbonneau-
Lassay, *La bestiaire du Christ* (Milano: Archè, 1940) chapter 5.12: "Le
lion, emblème de Satan, des vices et de l'hérésie," pp. 50-51; W. Deonna,
"Les lions attachés à la colonne," *Mélanges d'archéologie et d'histoire
offerts à Charles Picard à l'occasion de son 65ᵉ anniversaire* I (Paris:
Presses Universitaires de France, 1949) 289-308, in particular pp. 293-296.
The same symbology was popular in late Roman sepulchral art, wherein
the lion is shown devouring an animal; it was from this source that the

The impetus for this Medieval pictorial tradition of the lion as an image of the Devil (but not as an image of Death, which is far more ancient) came perhaps in part from Rev 9:17 and 13:2, where diabolic beasts have leonine attributes, but in particular from the warning given by (pseudo-)Peter: ὁ ἀντίδικος ὑμῶν διάβολος ὡς λέων ὠρυόμενος περιπατεῖ ζητῶν τινα καταπιεῖν (1 Pet 5:8); allusions to it in descriptions of the Devil in the humble Christian hagiographical literature of late antiquity attest to its popularity (for example, the *Confession of Saint Cyprian of Antioch* 8).[5] Commentators are in general accord in holding 1 Pet inspired by Ps 22:13 [21:14];[6] Ezek 22:25 (ὡς λέοντες ὠρυόμενοι ἁρπάζοντες ἁρπάγματα, ψυχὰς κατεσθίοντες LXX), alternatively suggested by Rud. Knopf,[7] is not as likely a source (1) because there the lions are not in their context metaphors with no specified referent, as they are in Ps 22 [21]; (2) because 1 Pet's verb καταπιεῖν (v. l. καταπίῃ) is used of the lion-persecutors in Ps 35 [34]:25; and, most importantly, (3) because by the time 1 Pet was written (mid-90s at the earliest, if the persecution assumed by the document is the Domitianic) a well-established Christian tradition existed which interpreted Ps 22 [21] of Jesus and his Passion; the Gospels leave no room for doubt in this matter, for they weave allusions to it and proof-text citations from it into the very fabric of their accounts of his death.[8]

Christians derived the iconography, though they injected it with new meaning: see Franz De Ruyt, "Etudes de symbolisme funéraire. A propos d'un nouveau sarcophage romain aux Musées Royaux d'Art et d'Histoire, à Bruxelles," *BIHBR* 17 (1936) 143-185 with pls. 1-10, especially pp. 169-175: "Les lions ravisseurs," and, for earlier Greek prototypes, A. B. Cook, "Animal Worship in the Mycenaean Age," *JHS* 14 (1894) 103-20 ("The Cult of the Lion"), especially pp. 109-112.

[5]Text in *Acta Sanctorum* 47, Septembris, Tomus Septimus (editio novissima; Paris and Rome: Palme, 1867) 211A.

[6]For example, Norbert Brox, *Der erste Petrusbrief* (EKK 21; Zürich, Einsiedeln, Köln: Benziger Verlag, and Neukirchen-Vluyn: Neukirchener Verlag, 1979) 237; Leonhard Goppelt, *Der Erste Petrusbrief* (KEKNT 12.1; Göttingen: Vandenhoeck & Ruprecht, 1978) 339 n. 11; Hans Windisch and Herbert Preisker, *Die katholischen Briefe* (HNT 15; 3rd ed; Tübingen, Mohr, 1951) 80.

[7]*Die Briefe Petri und Judä* (KEKNT 12; Göttingen: Vandenhoeck & Ruprecht, 1912) 194.

[8]See C. H. Dodd, *According to the Scripture. The Substructure of New Testament Theology* (London: Nisbet, 1961) 97-98; Barnabas Lindars, *New Testament Apologetic: The Doctrinal Significance of the Old Testament*

Behind 1 Pet's application of the "lions" of Ps 22 [21] and 35 [34] to the persecutor of his community (cp. 1 Pet 5:9-10) lies a long martyrological tradition. It was along this line of exegetical tradition that the "lions" of the Psalms, themselves originally metaphors for the Psalmist's oppressors, were reapplied to new situations. The first is the book of Daniel, composed to console and to strengthen the faithful in the face of persecution at the hands of Antiochus IV Epiphanes. Whatever one may think of Aage Bentzen's theory that behind the story of Daniel in the lion's den lies the ancient Near Eastern myth of a hero's descent into the Underworld,[9] the possibility remains strong nevertheless that Bentzen is correct in answering in the affirmative his question "Kann man also das Schema der Martyrerlegenden aus den Leidenspsalmen ableiten?" and in referring to the leonine oppressors of Pss 57:4-6 and 91:13 for the models upon which Daniel among the lions was based.[10] He could just as well have added the

---

Quotations (Philadelphia: Westminster, 1961) 89-93; Harmut Gese, "Psalm 22 und das Neue Testament. Der älteste Bericht vom Tode Jesu und die Entstehung des Herrenmahles," ZThK 65 (1968) 1-22; André Rose, "L'influence des psaumes sur les annonces et les récits de la Passion et de la Résurrection dans les Evangiles," Le Psautier. Ses origines, ses problèmes littéraires, son influence (OBL 4; Louvain-Leuven: Publications Universitaires, 1962) 297-356; J.R. Scheifler, "El Salmo 22 y la Crucifixión del Señor," EstB 24 (1965) 5-83, with further bibliography p. 5 n. 1; and most recently Fritz Stolz, "Psalm 22: Alttestamentliches Reden vom Menschen und neutestamentliches Reden von Jesus," ZThK 77 (1980) 129-148.

[9]See, for example, "Daniel 6. Ein Versuch zur Vorgeschichte der Märtyrerlegende," Festschrift Alfred Bertholet zum 80. Geburtstag gewidmet von Kollegen und Freunden (Tübingen: Mohr, 1950) 58-64; Daniel (HAT 19; 2nd ed.; Tübingen: Mohr, 1952) 55. Werner Kessler, Zwischen Gott und Weltmacht. Der Prophet Daniel (BAT 22; Stuttgart: Calwer Verlag, 1950) 84 implies endorsement; André Lacocque, Le livre de Daniel (CAT 15b; Neuchatel and Paris: Delachaux & Niestlé, 1976) 89 is sternly (and rightly, in my opinion) critical. To fit his theory, at any rate. Bentzen must incline to the view that the "lions" of the Psalms are demons: "Daniel 6" 61.

[10]"Daniel 6" 62. I concur with Otto Plöger's judgment (Das Buch Daniel; KAT 18; Gütersloh: Mohn, 1965; 98): "So wenig ansprechend der von Bentzen mehrfach geäusserte Deutungsversuch ist, die Löwengrube symbolisiere die Unterwelt, so wird man ihm darin zustimmen können, dass gewisse Metaphern in den Psalmen (22,14; 57,4; 91,13) hier in Form einer Erzählung ausgestaltet sein können, zumal da auch in der prophetischen Literatur Jahwe selbst in seinem Verhalten gegenüber Israel mit

relevant verses of Pss 22, 35 and the others to the list. It is a logical deduction. Certain elements of the narrative Dan 6:17-28 (Aram.) distinctly echo prototypes in the Psalms, specifically the king's question v 20, Daniel's answer v 22, and the king's hymn of praise v 27 (ὁ θεὸς τοῦ Δανιηλ . . . ἀπέκλεισε τὰ στόματα τῶν λεόντων . . . · σέσωκέ με ὁ θεὸς ἀπὸ τῶν λεόντων vv 19, 23 LXX; εἰ ἠδυνήθη ἐξελέσθαι σε ἐκ στόματος τῶν λεόντων; . . . ἐνέφραξεν τὰ στόματα τῶν λεόντων vv 21, 23 θ').

Daniel in the lions' den became, in turn, the paradigmatic illustration of miraculous deliverance from a tyrant's clutches. Early embellishments like Bel and the Dragon 30-42 testify to the importance of Daniel 6 for Jews suffering later Seleucid persecution: there are now seven lions; Daniel must pass six days in the den (one night Dan 6:20); with angelic assistance Habakkuk sees to it that Daniel does not suffer overmuch from hunger during his confinement. With his dying breath Mattathias, literally the father of the Maccabean revolt, offers Daniel's successful bout with the lions as encouragement to continue the resistance (1 Macc 2:60); Eleazar's wife offers the same example to her seven sons, martyrs about to be horribly tortured by Antiochus (4 Macc 16:21; 18:13). The Greek Addition to Esther C has Esther pray before her audience with Artaxerxes δὸς λόγον εὔρυθμον εἰς τὸ στόμα μου ἐνώπιον τοῦ λέοντος (Esth 4:17s LXX; APOT I, 677; C, 24). Qumran scrolls, finally, attest the application of the same tradition to their own community's circumstances. The Psalmist of 1QH (the Righteous Teacher?) in V, 9-19 casts his persecutors in leonine imagery borrowed from Daniel and from the Psalms of the Persecuted Righteous;[11] 4QpNah I, 4-5 and 4QpHos a, 1 discover in the

---

einem Löwen verglichen wird (Hos 5,14) oder sich des Löwen als eines Strafwerkzeuges bedient (1 Reg 13)." Norman W. Porteous, *Das Danielbuch* (ATD 23; Göttingen: Vandenhoeck & Ruprecht, 1962) 70, agrees.

[11]For example, וּתְחֹגוּר פִּי כְּפִירִים V, 9 recalls Dan 6:23 פֻּם וּפַגָּר אֲרְיָוָתָא and וֹולָא פָּצוּ עָלַי פִּיהֶם V, 10-11 recalls Ps 22:14 פָּצוּ עָלַי פִּיהֶם. The "lions of 1QH V, 6-7 stand either for wicked oppressors, as in what follows, or for God's instruments for punishing them, which has precedents in the Old Testament (the passages from 1 and 2 Kgs cited earlier). On these passages from Qumran see Menahem Mansoor, *The Thanksgiving Hymns* (STDJ 3; Leiden: Brill, 1961) 132-134 with notes; J. Carmignac and P. Guilbert, *Les textes de Qumran* I (Paris: Letouzey et Ané, 1961) 213-215 with notes; M. Delcor, *Les hymnes de Qumran* (*Hodayot*) (Paris: Letouzey et Ané, 1962) 156-161 with notes; Svend Holm-Nielsen, *Hodayot. Psalms from Qumran* (ATDan 2: Aarhus: Universitetsforlaget, 1960) 90-99; Alfred

mention of lions in Nah 2:13 and Hos 5:14, respectively, reference to an
oppressor whom the commentator brands "the Furious Lion."[12]

And so from Judaism into early Christianity. The author of the Epistle
to the Hebrews, his community likewise the object of persecution (clearly
so in 10:32-39), offers Daniel's escape as an example of steadfastness in
faith (ἔφραξαν στόματα λεόντων 11:33). So too 1 Clem 45:6. In 2 Tim
4:16-18 (pseudo-)Paul characterizes the reprieve he earned at his hearing
before the imperial authorities by saying ἐρρύσθην ἐκ στόματος λέοντος
and by affirming his rescue from all evil and preservation for his Lord's
heavenly kingdom. The reference to the "lion" is directly in line with the
martyrological tradition we have been discussing; Ps 21:22 LXX or Daniel
6 or 1 Macc 2:60 (Δανιηλ . . . ἐρρύσθη ἐκ στόματος λεόντων) or Addition C to Esther—or all alike—may have been in the author's mind. For
that reason it is pointless to center the exegesis of this passage, as the
Church Fathers did and many still do, around the search to discover any
particular identity for its "lion"; it is enough to know that for generations
of martyrs the "lions" of the Psalms had been the standard symbol for a
despot's persecution and his instruments of torture.[13] To say the least,
the whole tradition acquired still greater significance for Christians when
Christianos ad leonem (Tertullian, *Apology* 40.2) became a common hue
and cry; it is not for nothing that Daniel among the lions is one of the
most common scenes in the Christian art of the catacombs and elsewhere.[14] Small wonder that for 1 Pet systematic persecution ended up

---

Mertens, *Das Buch Daniel im Lichte der Texte vom Toten Meer* (SBM 12;
Würzburg: Echter Verlag, and Stuttgart: Katholische Bibelwerk, 1971) 52-
53.

[12]J. Carmignac, É. Cothenet and H. Lignée, *Les textes de Qumran* II
(Paris: Letouzey et Ané, 1963) 80 with n. 2 and 86 with n. 12.

[13]See Michaelis, "λέων" 252-253 and n. 20: G. Wohlenberg, *Die Pastoralbriefe* (KNT 13; 3rd ed.; Leipzig and Erlangen: Deichert, 1923) 346;
Jeremias in Joachim Jeremias and August Strobel, *Die Briefe an Timo-
theus und Titus. Der Brief an die Hebräer* (NTD 9; Göttingen: Vanden-
hoeck & Ruprecht, 1975) 66; Gottfried Holtz, *Die Pastoralbriefe* (THKNT
13; Berlin: Evangelische Verlagsanstalt, 1965) 198; Martin Dibelius and
Hans Conzelmann, *The Pastoral Epistles* (trans. P. Buttolph and A.
Yarbro; Hermeneia; Philadelphia: Fortress, 1972) 124; Norbert Brox, *Die
Pastoralbriefe* (RNT 7.2; 4th ed.; Regensburg: Pustet, 1969) 276; Walter
Lock, *A Critical and Exegetical Commentary on the Pastoral Epistles*
(ICC; Edinburgh: T. & T. Clark, 1924) 119; Alfred Plummer, *The Pastoral
Epistles* (EB; 4th ed.; London: Hodder and Stoughton, 1894) 418-429, espe-
cially his remarks pp. 426-427 which seem quite apposite to me.

transforming the "lion" from a merely human tyrant into the Devil himself!

In the second century the Christian compilation of maxims ascribed to Sextus attests the interesting but natural development of a coalescence of the Judaeo-Christian lion-persecutor with the long Stoic and Cynic tradition of the philosopher's resistance to a tyrant's coercion. The second half of maxim 363b σοφοῦ σώματος καὶ λέων ἄρχει, τούτου δὴ μόνου καὶ τύραννος clearly assumes (as do maxims 364 and 387 also) the Stoic commonplace that a sage's true possessions are not his body and its goods, to which he remains indifferent, but rather his behavior and his beliefs, which cannot be influenced or affected by calamity. The lion of the first half of the maxim is sufficient for a Christian to evoke the martyrological tradition that I have been at pains to trace.[15]

---

[14]See H. Leclerq, "Daniel," *DACL* 4.1 (1920) 221-248 with many illustrations; Walter Lowrie, *Art in the Early Church* (New York, N.Y.: Pantheon, 1947) pls. 19a, 25b, 28, 105 bottom, 107a, 148c with pp. 59, 83, 88-89, 182-183; Giuseppe Wilpert, *I sarcofagi cristiani antichi* II.1: Testo (Roma: Pontificio Istituto di archeologia cristiana, 1932) 256-258; Oskar Beyer, *Die Katakombenwelt. Grundriss, Ursprung und Idee der Kunst in der römischen Christengemeinde* (Tübingen: Mohr, 1927) 77; Antonio Ferrua, *Le pitture della nuova catacomba di via Latina* (Vatican City: Pontificio Istituto di archeologia cristiana, 1960) pls. 10, 116 and 117 with pp. 43 and 83. In evident commemoration of the martyrs Constantine I adorned Constantinople with bronze statues of Daniel and the lions (Eusebius, *Life of Constantine* 49). Samson slaying the lion appears in early Christian art for the same reason: Ferrua, *Le pitture della nuova catacomba* pl. 109 with p. 73.

[15]Henry Chadwick, *The Sentences of Sextus. A Contribution to the History of Early Christian Ethics* (TextsS 5; Cambridge: University Press, 1959) 52-53. Chadwick (*Sentences of Sextus* 103) appreciates the connection with the Stoic philosophical stance. A fragmentary Coptic version of a portion of the *Sentences* has turned up in the Nag Hammadi library (CG XII, 1 SentSextus); Frederik Wisse provides an English translation in *The Nag Hammadi Library in English* 454-459. For the marriage of Greek philosophy and Christianity as exemplified by the *Sentences of Sextus* see Robert L. Wilken, "Wisdom and Philosophy in Early Christianity," *Aspects of Wisdom in Judaism and Early Christianity* (ed. Robert L. Wilken; Notre Dame and London: University of Notre Dame Press, 1975) 143-168; Gerhard Delling, "Zur Hellenisierung des Christentums in den 'Sprüchen des Sextus,'" *Studien zum Neuen Testament und zur Patristik Erich Klostermann zum 90. Geburtstag dargebracht* (TU 77; Berlin: Akademie-Verlag, 1961) 208-241, especially p. 239 of Stoicism.

What did Gnosticism do with this tradition? Its sectarians considered themselves a spiritual elite whose salvation guaranteed them insulation from all mere earthly disturbance, and—perhaps with help from a radical interpretation of the Stoic and Cynic stance—they generally held denial of their faith before the Roman inquisitorial authorities a matter of indifference. The tradition consequently took a different turn in their hands. For them the true enemies were astral powers (Eph 6:10-13), the creator Yahweh and his archontic hypostases, not worldly ones. Paul himself shows how ambivalent for those with a strongly dualistic orientation the distinction between earthly and heavenly authority is, how easily (cp. 1 Cor 2:8, for instance) human judges such as those of 2 Tim 4:16-18 could be mythologized into cosmic ones and translated to the sky. Jewish animosity toward its rival the fledgling Christian movement can, then, only have fueled Christian Gnostics who, like Marcion, were enemies of Yahweh as creator and as god of the Jews to feel justified in their identification of *him* as the lion-persecutor of the martyrological tradition. They had the passages of the Old Testament in which Yahweh behaves like a lion to back them up. Moreover, 1 Pet sees Satan in the "lions" of the Psalms, and this is already a sinister new development translating what was earlier a strictly human drama to the cosmic plane, though Sirach's simile in 21:2 (and cp. 27:10) comparing sin to a lion in slaying the souls of men—and here the influence of Ezek 22:25 LXX is evident—points in this direction. If 1 Pet can see Satan in the "lions" of the Psalms, then Gnostics could appeal, as the Peratae actually did (Hippolytus, *Refutation* 5.17.7; 115.9-10 Wendland), to John 8:44 for proof that to Jesus the god of the Jews was the Devil himself. Furthermore, given the fact that earliest Christianity read Jesus' persecution and death at the hands of the Jews into Ps 22 [21] and wove that reading into their accounts of his life, it should occasion no surprise that Christian Gnostics (or just plain Christians, for that matter) might accept the invitation to identify Jesus' persecutors with the "lions" of that Psalm, especially when a well-established martyrological tradition existed to make it yet easier. Justin accepted the invitation, and so did Augustine.[16]

---

[16]Justin offers Trypho a lengthy disquisition on how the events of Jesus' life and Passion are prefigured in every verse of Ps 22[21] (*Dialogue with Trypho* 97-106). The calves and bulls of v 13 LXX are the Pharisees, the Scribes and their agents; the lion of v 14 LXX is either Herod Antipas (the lion is king of beasts) or the Devil—perhaps, though he does not explicitly say so, on the basis of 1 Pet 5:8 (*Dialogue* 103). Justin sees an evil angel in the "lion" of v 22 LXX (*Dialogue* 105), neatly attesting a

In sum, there were many forces operant—and another was a complex of still older traditions, yet to be discussed, that linked the lion and the god of the Jews—which prompted Gnosticism to see Yahweh in the leonine oppressor of a hallowed exegetical pattern whose ultimate dependence on the "lions" of the Psalms was never forgotten. The evidence shows that this is exactly what occurred. It is interesting to find the Naassenes (Hippolytus, *Refutation* 5.8.15; 92.4-6 Wendland) putting the leonine imagery of the Psalms into the mouth of the incorporeal Man trapped in the archons' world of γένεσις. With a text stitched together from desirable elements of Pss 34:17 LXX and 21:21-22 LXX he prays salvation for his soul: ῥῦσαι . . . ἀπὸ λεόντων τὴν μονογενῆ μου. His "only-begotten" is, of course, that part of him imprisoned by embodiment in the material cosmos tyrannized by the powers—the "lions"—that rule it. So, too, Theodotus in Clement of Alexandria's *Extracts from Theodotus* 83-84 attributes the necessity of self-abnegating rituals before baptism to the tendency of ἀκάθαρτα πνεύματα to attach themselves to the neophyte. His explanation is: ὅτι ψυχὴ ἐκ κόσμου καὶ ἐκ στόματος λεόντων ἀνασῴζεται, juxtaposing salvation "from the world" (John 17:14) with that "from the mouth of lions" (Pss 21:22 and 34:17 LXX again? Daniel 6?), here clearly and quite appropriately demonic agencies. Direct application of the "lions" of the martyrological tradition to the cosmocrator and his lackeys, already made by the Naassenes and by the *Pistis Sophia,* as I have shown, surfaces again in CG VII, *2 Second Treatise of the Great Seth* 55:9-10 wherein the Savior, descending into their realm, says of their plot to seize him: "I was in the mouths of lions."[17] It is from such earlier Gnostic adaptations of the leonine persecutorial tradition of the Psalms that Manichaeism in Egypt acquired its picture of the virginal soul of the primal Man swallowed up by "lions" who are ciphers for cosmic rulers.

---

somewhat more orthodox version of the contemporary Gnostic view of the "lions" of the Psalms as ciphers for the archons, as I am about to show. Augustine is equally direct. His *Commentary on Psalm 21* 2.14 (on v 13 [14]) reads: Aperuerunt super me os suum, sicut leo rapiens et rugiens. *Audiamus rugitum ipsorum in evangelio:* Crucifige! Crucifige! (citing John 19:6); 2.22 (on v 21 [22]): Saluum me fac de ore leonis. *Leo rugiens nostis quis sit,* circumiens et quaerens quem devoret (citing 1 Pet 5:8) (CChr, *series latina,* 38; 126.1-3 and 128.1-2). In the earlier verse the "lion" is the Jews, in the second the Devil.

[17]See M. Krause's edition and translation in *Christentum am Roten Meer* II (ed. F. Altheim and R. Stiehl; Berlin: de Gruyter, 1973) 118-119 or Roger A. Bullard's translation in *The Nag Hammadi Library in English* 332.

The date of the sources indicates that the Gnostic adaptation of this martyrological tradition is a second century phenomenon. That the adaptation presupposes the tradition's Christianization is confirmation that this must be so.

3.2   Ezekiel's חַיּוֹת and the Merkabah

There can be no doubt that Ezekiel's visions of the "living creatures" that Yahweh rides (1:4-28; 10:1-22) played a role in some stages of the Gnostic investment of Yahweh's archontic hypostases with animal shapes. In the prophet's visions the creatures are mostly human, but each has four faces: those of a man, a lion, a bull, and an eagle.[18] There is one exceptional passage: the restored Temple is to have Cherubim adorning its walls, and they are to have two faces only, those of a man and of a lion (41:17-20), perhaps because here it is a matter of two-dimensional representation and the first two of the four have been selected.

Gnostic interest in the prophet's visions is readily accounted for; they were of intense interest to later generations of Jews who shared (albeit for different reasons) with their Gnostic contemporaries the attitudes that sparked that interest in the first place. Ezekiel's visions, already purposely obscure and possibly extensively marred by harmonization, interpolation, and attempts to temper their gross anthropomorphism,[19] were further embroidered upon as a result of their subsumption, firmly rooted as they already were in Chaldean (Perso-Babylonian) astrological ground, into the ouranological speculations of inter-testamental Jewish and early Christian devotees of apocalypticism. The privileged position of the Cherubim in these speculations was guaranteed by their role as the

---

[18]Ezekiel's חַיּוֹת (they are never called כְּרוּבִים in chapter 1) are based in part (the astrological connections of their four faces will be discussed later) on more ancient Near Eastern prototypes, intercessory and tutelary genii, themselves invariably *Mischwesen,* but never precisely of the sort seen by Ezekiel. For depictions and discussions see particularly P. Dhorme and L. H. Vincent, "Les chérubins," *RB* 35 (1926) 328-358 and 481-495 with plates; Georg Fohrer, *Ezekiel* (HAT 13; Tübingen: Mohr, 1955) 8-10; and the excellent summary article "Kerub, Kerubim" by J. Trinquet in *DBSup* 5 (1957) 161-186.

[19]See, for example, Walther Zimmerli, *Ezekiel 1. A Commentary on the Book of the Prophet Ezekiel, Chapters 1-24* (trans. R. Clements; Hermenia; Philadelphia: Fortress, 1979) 101-104.

central mystery of ascensional mystics who gave the vision of Yahweh's מֶרְכָּבָה pride of place in the "Himmelsreise der Seele." Jews who shared with Ezekiel sight of God's Chariot—like the Gnostic visionaries, elitists, revelationists—may already have existed at Qumran, and Paul, whom many Gnostics held in high regard, was of their number (indeed, 2 Cor 12:1-4 was prompted by spiritualists who, if not Gnostics, were their next of visionary kin).[20]

In CG II, 4 *Hyp. Arch.* and CG II, 5 *Orig. World,* which, as I have already pointed out in the last chapter, both make Yaldabaoth out to be a lion, the Merkabah is bestowed upon the chief archon's son Sabaoth (CG II, 4; 95 [143] .26-30 and CG II, 5; 104 [152] .35-105 [153] .20).[21] In both accounts the chariot itself is called ⲭⲉⲣⲟⲩⲃⲓⲛ and itself has four faces; only *Orig. World* offers a fuller description: the chariot's four corners each have eight forms—lion-, bull-, man-, and eagle-forms in this order—so that somehow the total number of forms is sixty-four.[22]

Although, as I noted earlier, in a very fragmentary section *Hyp. Arch.,* at least, gives Yaldabaoth's henchmen bestial forms, from these two documents it is not apparent that Ezekiel's Cherubim provided the archons with any of their animal faces, for the Merkabah tradition is here somewhat radically detached from them by the myth in which it is set. That is

---

[20]On Merkabah mysticism see Fohrer, *Ezekiel* 6 n. 1; Wilhelm Bousset and Hugo Gressmann, *Die Religion des Judentums im späthellenistischen Zeitalter* (HNT 21; 3rd ed.; Tübingen: Mohr, 1966) 355-357 and 500; Hans Bietenhard, *Die himmlische Welt im Urchristentum und Spätjudentum* (WUNT 2; Tübingen: Mohr, 1951) 53-56 and 86-95; Gershom Scholem, *Jewish Gnosticism, Merkabah Mysticism, and Talmudic Tradition* (New York: Jewish Theological Seminary of America, 1965), especially chapter 9; *Ursprung und Anfänge der Kabbala* (SJ 3; Berlin: de Gruyter, 1962) 15-20; *Kabbalah* (New York: Quadrangle, 1974) 10-14 and 373-376; Ithamar Gruenwald, *Apocalyptic and Merkavah Mysticism* (AGJU 14; Leiden and Köln: Brill, 1980), in particular 29-97; J. W. Bowker, "'Merkabah' Visions and the Visions of Paul," *JSS* 16 (1971) 157-173; Jacob Neusner, "The Development of the *Merkavah* Tradition," *JSJ* 2 (1971) 149-160.

[21]On these pericopes in the two documents, which share a common tradition here, see Francis T. Fallon, *The Enthronement of Sabaoth. Jewish Elements in Gnostic Creation Myths* (NHS 10; Leiden: Brill, 1978).

[22]Fallon (*Enthronement of Sabaoth* 102-103) sides with Böhlig and Labib (*Schrift ohne Titel* 52) in making each of the forms bisexual; 2 sexes x 8 forms x 4 corners gives the appropriate total. Schenke ("Vom Ursprung der Welt" 252 n. 45) suggests as an alternate solution a double-decker plan of the vehicle.

not the case with the system known to Celsus (and to Origen) and with *Apoc. John* in both of its recensions. Celsus' source knew Yahweh/Yaldabaoth, chief of the seven archons, as a lion, the next three archons being, successively, a bull, the serpentine ἀμφίβιον, and an eagle. The faces of this primary quartet match those of Ezekiel's חַיּוֹת—with one notable exception: Ezekiel's "man" has been replaced by a serpent. The reason is obvious: in a Gnostic system the rulers of the cosmos *cannot* have a fully human form, for Man is utterly alien to their world; the man whom they create is a woefully botched image of an image of the primal Man, whom they had never seen or known before they caught their first glimpse of him. The remaining three archontic forms of Celsus' system—bear, dog, and ass—are added to Ezekiel's four to produce the astrologically obligatory tally of a Hebdomad.

What is equally interesting is that the *order* of Celsus' archons precisely matches that of *Orig. World* except, of course, that the latter has preserved Ezekiel's "man"-face where Celsus' Gnostics have substituted their serpent. And, furthermore, this common order of theirs deviates from that of Ezek 1:10 (as well as from that of 10:14, which differs somewhat from the earlier passage's but which is an interpolation lacking in the LXX and which must have been unknown to most, if not to all). It is natural that the lion must come first if Yahweh/Yaldabaoth, a leader of the group, is to be leonine, but the rest follow in identical sequence. It is tempting to attribute this equivalence, which is hardly coincidental, to a shared source within the developed Merkabah tradition. It cannot be an accident that the visionary who penned the Johannine Apocalypse saw the creatures about the throne in exactly this same order (Rev 4:7).[23] Moreover, the *Apocalypse of Abraham* 18, a Merkabah text roughly contemporary with Rev, also gives the lion first place, though its order—lion, man, bull, eagle—otherwise differs slightly from that of Rev, Celsus and *Orig. World*.[24] If, for whatever reason, the lion's position as first on the

---

[23]Rev's deviation from Ezekiel's order has often been remarked: R. H. Charles, *A Critical and Exegetical Commentary on the Revelation of St. John* I (ICC; Edinburgh: T. & T. Clark, 1920) 124; Franz Boll, *Aus der Offenbarung Johannis. Hellenistische Studien zum Weltbild der Apokalypse* (Leipzig and Berlin: Teubner, 1914) 37; Wilhelm Bousset, *Die Offenbarung Johannis* (KEKNT 16; 5th ed.; Göttingen: Vandenhoeck & Ruprecht, 1906) 250.

[24]G. H. Box and J. I. Landsman, *The Apocalypse of Abraham* (London: Society for Promoting Christian Knowledge, and New York: Macmillan, 1919) 62. Box (p. x) dates the document to the end of the first or beginning of the second century A.D.

cherubic list was an established feature in some visionary circles, then Gnostics who were familiar with this order and took it up into their archontic portraiture can only have found support in it for their chief archon to be a lion.

One element of Rev 4:7's adaptations of Ezekiel's vision, widely noted by the commentators for its astonishing deviation from Ezekiel, particularly favored Gnostic assimilation of the Cherubim's faces to their theriomorphic archons. Ezekiel's חַיּוֹת *each* have four faces, and so they are all identical; the Johannine Apocalypse, however, has taken the step of distributing the four faces among the four ζῷα so that each has but a single face. This move effectively endows each with its own individual personality, a *sine qua non* for the Gnostic system, in which Yahweh's titles have become separate beings. All the more did the rulers of the cosmic spheres need different animal faces as the Cherubim's transformation into theriomorphic Gnostic archons took place, in all likelihood, on Egyptian soil. The direct models for that transformation were, as I shall argue later, one of the groups of frightening animal-headed judges with which classical Egyptian descriptions of the afterlife peopled the Netherworld in the sky. As one can see from the passage Origen, *Against Celsus* 6.31, for example, the Gnostic archons and the celestial magistrates of the Egyptians shared performance of an important duty: they both stood watch at the gates through which the soul of the deceased or of an ascending mystic (and here the Merkabah tradition enters the arena) had to travel, and they both required knowledge of the appropriate password before they would allow the soul to pass.[25]

---

[25]Generally see J. Zandee, *Death as an Enemy according to Ancient Egyptian Conceptions* (SHR [NumenSup] 5; Leiden: Brill, 1960) 114-125 on the gates, and 200-208 on the demonic powers that guard them. Examples of the classical Egyptian literature are the *Book of the Two Ways*; the texts of the *Quererts* (both in Alexandre Piankoff and Helen Jacquet-Gordon, *The Wandering of the Soul*; BollS 40.6; Princeton: Princeton University Press, 1974; 3-37 and 41-114, respectively); the *Book of Caverns*; the *Book of Gates*; the *Book of Am-Duat* or *What is in the Netherworld* (all in Alexandre Piankoff, *The Tomb of Ramesses VI*; BollS 40.14; New York: Pantheon, 1954; I: Texts; 45-135, 137-224, and 227-318, respectively). Hermann Kees, *Totenglauben und Jenseitsvorstellungen der alten Ägypter* (2nd ed.; Berlin: Akademie-Verlag, 1956) is a good general introduction to the subject for the earlier period of Egyptian civilization. The impact of the soul's *Himmelsreise* in late Egyptian religion upon similar conceptions in Gnostic thought has long been appreciated: see L. Kákosy, "Gnosis und ägyptische Religion," *Le origini dello gnosticismo*

I have already obliquely dealt with what becomes of the Cherubim in *Apoc. John*; the two recensions illustrate a process of their integration into the system they represent. The long recension, for which Yaldabaoth is a dragon with the one face of a lion, preserves the integrity of the חיות as distinct entities, even if they are only "faces" upon which the chief archon sits; as in *Hyp. Arch.* and *Orig. World* the Merkabah tradition coexists uneasily with that which gave the seven archons animal faces. The short recension, on the other hand, whose Yaldabaoth has the face of a lion *and* the face of a serpent, has altered his portrait because it seeks to reconcile the two traditions by assimilating the Cherubim to Yahweh/ Yaldabaoth himself, and their faces become faces of his own. The resulting plurality of faces had other motivations that will be taken up later.

What is obvious about the archon-lists in the redactions of *Apoc. John* as we have it is that Ezekiel's חיות did not, as they did for the system known to Celsus (and that known to Origen, if it is not the same), provide this Gnostic system with animal faces for its rulers, however Jewish their names may be. While the ubiquitous lion is present here also, he is either only the head on a serpent, a gargoyle that I will later demonstrate to be of strictly native Egyptian lineage, or he has, in the short recension, replaced an originally leonine Yaldabaoth who has been promoted from leadership of the seven to an eighth in a class by himself. Ezekiel's bull, eagle, and, naturally, man are conspicuous for their absence. The animals (and the one inanimate entity) that *have* provided the archons of *Apoc. John* with their beastly countenances loudly betray the Egyptian landscape that I just proposed for the whole mythologem of theriomorphic celestial authorities. Here, instead of bear, dog, and eagle we encounter hyena, ape, and flame of fire, all three attested for classical Egyptian tradition, as perusal of the literature cited just now will confirm.

If the archons of *Apoc. John* inherited their heads from native Egyptian religious traditions and Yahweh/Yaldabaoth derived from the same source the leontocephalic serpent in which the long recension of that document embodies him, then it is unlikely that the chief archon should have gotten from Ezekiel's Cherubim the lion-headed human form that Celsus, Origen, and the others grant him. This is so despite the lion's preeminence in

---

240-244; "Probleme der ägyptischen Jenseitsvorstellungen in der Ptole-mäer- und Kaiserzeit," *Religions en Égypte hellénistique et romaine. Colloque de Strasbourg 16-18 mai 1967* (Paris: Presses Universitaires de France, 1969) 64-65; Siegfried Morenz, "Fortwirken altägyptischer Elemente in christlicher Zeit," *Koptische Kunst. Christentum am Nil* (Essen-Bredeney: Villa Hügel, 1963 [?]) 58.

certain developed forms of Jewish mysticism, and despite the fact that Ezekiel's חַיּוֹת in their revised order were in various ways integrated into the scheme of seven theriomorphic archons. Rather, as his dress on the Brummer gem suggests and as I shall argue in detail later, this purely leonine form of his is to be traced to the same Egyptian milieu. The lion of the Merkabah tradition, like other Jewish traditions—viz., the Old Testament's use of lion-metaphor as applied to Yahweh, the "lions" of the Psalms, and Isaiah's Ariel—which, however perversely, were pressed into service by Gnostics bent on linking Yahweh with the lion, can only have served to corroborate a depiction already in existence, not to create it.

This classical and Hellenistic Egyptian milieu must now be more fully explored.

3.3   The Zodiacal Leo

The contribution of astrology and astral mysticism to the thought of the Hellenistic and Roman periods is immeasurably great, and Gnostic systems, as products of their age, reflect—some to a greater extent than others, of course—the all-pervasive influence of this development. Judaism was, as I have already mentioned, itself not immune; the ouranological speculations of Jewish apocalyptic are grounded in this "Chaldean" science which, in combination with Iranian ideas, penetrated Judaism of the post-Exilic period exhilarated by the liberation it owed its Achaemenid masters. Disgruntled Epicureans might deplore it all as gross superstition, but Stoics and Platonists yielded gracefully to a *force majeure*; in Stoicism an astrologically based cosmology acquired apodictic incontestability, and the lesser demiurges of Plato's *Timaeus* unabashedly transform themselves into planetary powers. It was no act of scoundrelly legerdemain, then, that Gnosticism should have its world-creator Yahweh/Yaldabaoth and his several hypostases a planetary Hebdomad and should hold the zodiacal constellations to be soul-creating numina. There was no other choice. To understand the leonine Yaldabaoth, then, one must first know the celestial Leo.

Franz Boll's expert work on the Revelation of John glaringly illustrates just how much that document, and by extension Jewish apocalyptic in general and, *mutatis mutandis,* Gnosticism, owes to astrological ideas. A particularly instructive example is again Rev's adaptation of Ezekiel's חַיּוֹת; Boll and many other scholars have traced them, in their original context in Ezekiel as well as in Rev, back to Babylonian and Egyptian astral figures. (In Rev certain new features—e.g., Rev 4:6: the creatures themselves, not the wheels, are "full of eyes," i.e., of stars—are held to enhance the connection.) The four beasts represent, on this line of interpretation, the four quarters of heaven embodied in appropriately quadrangular, seasonally critical constellations, each of which contained a particularly bright, "royal" star. If in Rev (and other traditions) the lion comes first in order it is because its "royal" star was king of them all (more on this below), and for this reason many stellar catalogues begin with the stars of Leo.[26]

In their celestial lion, at any rate, the peoples of the Mediterranean catasterized all the folklore which popular fabulists and the writers of hackneyed Hellenistic bestiaries retailed about the animal. The most widespread motif is the enthronement of the lion as king of beasts (a position which he still enjoys) because he was the beast of kings. His regal demeanor, his fearsomeness and his might ensured his popularity, universal and ancient, as a royal symbol and the prey of royal sport.[27] If Yahweh is repeatedly likened to a lion, this is in part the reason. The celestial Leo declares his primeval connection with kingship by the presence on his breast of a star of the first magnitude (α Leonis), the brightest star of the whole ecliptic, which already the Sumerians named [mul]LUGAL, the Babylonians called *šarru,* the "Chaldeans," their Hellenistic successors, translated with βασιλίσκος, Pliny with *stella regia* (*Natural History*

---

[26]Boll, *Aus der Offenbarung Johannis* 36-39; H. Zimmern in Eberhard Schrader, *Die Keilinschriften und das Alte Testament* (3rd ed. "mit Ausdehnung auf die Apokryphen, Pseudepigraphen und das Neue Testament" by H. Zimmern and H. Winckler; Berlin: Reuther & Reichard, 1903) 626-635, specifically pp. 631-632 on the Cherubim; Carl Clemen, *Religionsgeschichtliche Erklärung des Neuen Testaments. Die Abhängigkeit des ältesten Christentums von nichtjüdischen Religionen und philosophischen Systemen* (Giessen: Töpelmann, 1909) 74-77, and (2nd ed.; Giessen: Töpelmann, 1924) 377-381; Hermann Gunkel, *Zum religionsgeschichtlichen Verständnis des Neuen Testaments* (FRLANT 1; 3rd ed.; Göttingen: Vandenhoeck & Ruprecht, 1930) 43-47; Bousset, *Die Offenbarung Johannis* 251-252; and lately Heinrich Kraft, *Die Offenbarung des Johannes* (HNT 16a; Tübingen: Mohr, 1974) 99.

[27]H. Lesêtre, "lion," *DB* 4 (1912) 267-280 with many illustrations from ancient Near Eastern reliefs; Charbonneau-Lassay, *La bestiaire du Christ* 35-37: "Le lion dans la symbolique des cultes préchrétiens;" Otto Keller, *Die antike Tierwelt* I (Leipzig: Engelmann, 1909) 24-61 passim, with many illustrations; J. Wiesner, "Löwe," *Lexikon der alten Welt* (Zürich and Stuttgart: Artemis, 1965) 1757-1758; Steier, "Löwe" PW 13.968-990, in particular sections f, g, i, k, l, and m; Hermann Grapow, *Die bildlichen Ausdrücke des Aegyptischen* (Leipzig: Hinrichs, 1924) 69-71.

18.26.64), and we with Regulus. It was the "royal" star *par excellence,* and its influence read out the fate of monarchs and kingdoms.[28] According to

---

[28]Felix Gössmann, *Planetarium Babylonicum oder die sumerisch-babylonischen Stern-Namen* (Roma: Päpstl. Bibelinstitut, 1950; vol. 4.2 of Anton Deimel's *Šumerisches Lexikon*) #240, pp. 89-91, in particular sections I.B; II.2; IV.A and B; V; Franz Boll, "Die Entwicklung des astronomischen Weltbildes in Zusammenhang mit Religion und Philosophie" in *Kleine Schriften zur Sternkunde des Altertums* (Leipzig: Koehler & Amelang, 1950) 241; *Aus der Offenbarung Johannis* 37, 91-92; Franz Boll, Carl Bezold, Wilhelm Gundel and Hans Georg Gundel, *Sternglaube und Sterndeutung. Die Geschichte und das Wesen der Astrologie* (5th ed.; Stuttgart: Teubner, 1966) 56, 147; Firmicus Maternus, *Instruction* 8.23.1-2; 8.31.4, cited and discussed by Franz Cumont, *L'Égypte des astrologues* (Bruxelles: Fondation Égyptologique Reine Élisabeth, 1937) 213-214; (W.) Gundel, "Leo," PW 12.1975.63.-65 and 1976.59-1977.5; (H.) Gundel, "Zodiakos," PW 10.A.473.12-19; 480.7-8; F. Boll and W. Gundel, "Sternbilder, Sternglaube und Sternsymbolik bei Griechen und Römern," Roscher 6.954.46-51 and 955.35-44; A. Jeremias, "Sterne (bei den Babyloniern)," Roscher 4.1452.58-1453.2; A. Bouché-Leclercq, *L'astrologie grecque* (Bruxelles: Culture et Civilisation, 1963 [1899]) 139, 438. Gundel is wrong when ("Sternbilder, Sternglaube und Sternsymbolik" 954.53-64; identical arguments in his "Leo" 1977.7-44) he criticizes the astronomer Geminos' (first century B.C.) explanation that the star is called βασιλίσκος because δοκοῦσιν οἱ περὶ τὸν τόπον τοῦτον γεννώμενοι βασιλικὸν ἔχειν τὸ γενέθλιον by saying: "Das ist sicher eine der zahlreichen falschen Erklärungen ägyptischer Namen von seiten später hellenistischer Interpreten; es handelt sich um den Stern oder die Sterne, welche die im ägyptischen Himmelsbild unter dem Löwen liegende Uraeusschlange (= βασιλίσκος) zum Ausdruck bringen. ... Ubrigens ist das Wort βασιλίσκος in dem von *Geminos* gebrauchten Sinne sonst im Griechischen nicht nachweisbar." In fact, as Gössman's references show and Boll in the same article argues (955.40-44), the star's kingly name is of Sumerian and Babylonian origin, and Geminos is simply correctly translating that name into Greek. It is true that the Egyptian Leo is often (but not always) depicted treading on a serpent (as on the famous Dendera zodiac: Boll, *Sphaera* 171, 236; my pl. 4d) but, aside from the fact that the serpent upon which the lion treads is not likely to have been the royal uraeus in an Egyptian context, the serpent too may possibly have been inherited from Babylonia: Jeremias, "Sterne (bei den Babyloniern)" fig 51; Gössmann, *Planetarium Babylonicum* 66; B. L. van der Waerden, "Babylonian Astronomy II. The Thirty-Six Stars," *JNES* 8 (1949) 14, fig. 2 (*muš* = Hydra); older Egyptian representations show him on a crocodile: Ernst Zinner, "Die Sternbilder der alten Aegypter," *Isis* 16 (1931) 94. The word βασιλίσκος here has nothing to do

a scholium on Aratus the Chaldeans considered the star ἄρχειν τῶν

---

with the Egyptian uraeus, as I said, and Gundel is wrong again in saying that the adjective is not attested in the sense Geminos attributed to it; Polybius (3.44.5) shows that it is (Arno Mauersberger, *Polybios-Lexikon* I; Berlin: Akademie-Verlag, 1956; 323). The Greek use of βασιλίσκος for the uraeus stemmed precisely from the word's meaning "royal," as the uraeus was the royal serpent *par excellence*. The curious stellar shoulder-ornament that appears on representations of lions at all times throughout the ancient Near East (see my pl. 5a) is exactly the star Regulus as the star of kings, and so every lion so depicted is in some sense thereby made an embodiment of the zodiacal Leo: see Willy Hartner, "The Earliest History of the Constellations in the Near East and the Motif of the Lion-Bull Combat," *JNES* 24 (1965) 1-16 with pls. 1-16, especially p. 3 n. 11; Willy Hartner and Richard Ettinghausen, "The Conquering Lion, the Life Cycle of a Symbol," *Oriens* 17 (1964) 161-171 with pls. 1-8. The article that Helene J. Kantor devotes to the subject in "The Shoulder Ornament of Near Eastern Lions," *JNES* 6 (1947) 250-274 with many illustrations, misses the point. The zoological fact that young male lions actually do often bear hair whorls in the same spot (A. J. Arkell, "The Shoulder Ornament of Near Eastern Lions," *JNES* 7 [1948] 52; Dorothea M. A. Bate, "The 'Shoulder Ornament' of Near Eastern Lions," *JNES* 9 [1950] 53-54 with pl. 2) is not likely in itself to have caused its presence as an artistic motif on so many depictions of lions in so many different cultural settings over so long a period of time; rather, if anything, it may have served to fix the spot where Regulus would be set on the breast of earthly pictures of Leo. E. Douglas van Buren, "An Additional Note on the Hair Whirl," *JNES* 9 (1950) 54-55, demonstrates that the motif occurs much earlier in Near Eastern art than Kantor had supposed; note Kantor's response, "A Further Comment on the Shoulder Ornament," *JNES* 9 (1950) 55-56. Jean Sainte Fare Garnot, "Le lion dans l'art égyptien," *BIFAO* 37 (1937) 75-91 with pls. 1-5, is of no help with this whole question. I should add, finally, that it is not absolutely certain that the Sumerian constellation UR.GU.LA was a lion and not a dog; its Akkadian successor was certainly leonine, however, no doubt because it contained the royal star Regulus and the lion was the royal animal: see Jeremias, "Sterne (bei den Babyloniern)" 1452.19-28; (W.) Gundel, "Leo" 1975.19-22; B. L. van der Waerden, "History of the Zodiac," *AOF* 16 (1952-53) 219-220; "The Thirty-Six Stars" 14; Gössmann, *Planetarium Babylonicum* #160, p. 64; Wolfram von Soden, *Akkadisches Handwörterbuch* III (Wiesbaden: Harrassowitz, 1981) 1429 s.v. *urgulû*; Arthur Ungnad, "Besprechungskunst und Astrologie in Babylonien," *AOF* 14 (1941-1944) 257 and n. 44; Albert Schott, "Das Werden der babylonisch-assyrischen Positions-Astronomie und einige seiner Bedingungen," *ZDMG* 88 (1934) 319-320 with n. 4 and pls. 3-4. The

οὐρανίων, and it is partially for this reason that in some zodiacal lists (though not all) the series begins with Leo.[29] Later the whole

---

lion as "king of beasts" in the folklore of the Greco-Roman period: Steier, "Löwe" 985.47-53; Keller, *Die antike Tierwelt* I, 24, 27.

[29]The scholium on Aratus: (W.) Gundel, "Leo" 1977.5-7; Boll and (W.) Gundel, "Sternbilder, Sternglaube und Sternsymbolik," 954.51-53; Leo's initial position: Jeremias, "Sterne (bei den Babyloniern)" 1452.29-38; Boll, Bezold, (W.) Gundel and (H.) Gundel, *Sternglaube und Sterndeutung* 51; and Wilhelm Gundel and Hans Georg Gundel, *Astrologumena. Die astrologische Literatur in der Antike und ihre Geschichte* (Wiesbaden: Steiner, 1966) 117 on a text ascribed to Zoroaster (Joseph Bidez and Franz Cumont, *Les mages hellénisés* II; Paris: "Belles Lettres," 1938; #0 40; pp. 178-181) where the prospects for the new year, marked by the appearance of the Dog-star Sothis-Sirius, are predicted from the position of the moon, and a sketch of the significance of the moon's presence in each of the zodiacal constellations is offered. Leo begins the series precisely because Regulus in Leo shares a simultaneous heliacal rise with Sirius, which marked the opening of the Egyptian New Year because its appearance heralded the flooding of the Nile: *Astrologumena* 111; (W.) Gundel, "Leo" 1982.25-40; Keller, *Die antike Tierwelt* I, 47-48. The flood actually began in late June and early July when the sun was still in Cancer: "The Nile begins to rise at the new moon which follows the (summer) solstice, gradually and moderately while the sun traverses Cancer, but most abundantly when it is in Leo" (Pliny, *Natural History* 5.10.57; also 5.10.56). Plutarch's remark (*Table-Talk* 4.5.2 [*Moralia* 670C]; similarly *On Isis and Osiris* 38 [*Moralia* 365F-366A], quoting Aratus, *Phaenomena* 151) that in Egypt, "it is from the gaping jaws of lions that the spouts of fountains gush jets of water, because the Nile brings new water to the fields of Egypt when the sun is traversing Leo" is loosely based on native Egyptian practice. The reason he gives for their leonine shape was not, however, the original one: see Jean Hani, *La religion égyptienne dans la pensée de Plutarque* (Paris: "Belles Lettres," 1976) 404-406 on the two passages in Plutarch; Constant de Wit, *Le rôle et le sens du lion dans l'Égypte ancienne* (Leiden: Brill, 1951) 84-90, and "Les inscriptions des lions-gargouilles du temple d'Edfou," *CEg* 29 (1954) 29-45, for actual examples; Danielle Bonneau, *La crue du Nil, divinité égyptienne, à travers mille ans d'histoire (332 av. - 641 ap. J.-C.) d'après les auteurs grecs et latins, et les documents des époques ptolémaïque, romaine et byzantine* (Paris: Klincksieck, 1964) 303-305, on this and the other traditions linking the flooding of the Nile with the lion; and generally Theodor Hopfner, "Die Tierkult der alten Ägypter nach den griechisch-römischen Berichten und den wichtigeren Denkmälern," *DAWW.PH* 57.2 (1913) 44-45; Ursula Schweitzer, *Löwe und Sphinx im alten Ägypten* (AeF 15; Glückstadt and Hamburg: Augustin, 1948) 25-

constellation became the astral sign of choice for the horoscope of kings, as for example on the famous relief of Antiochus I of Commagene at Nemrud-Dagh, and in the nativities of Alexander the Great and Julius Caesar, according to some traditions. In merer mortals Leo sired men possessed of regal natures, forcible, magnanimous, bold.[30] Visionary beasts which represent tyrants with worldwide dominion are naturally, then, regularly at least part lion (Dan 7:4; Rev 13:2).

---

26 and 26-27 with pl. 5.2-3, 38 with pl. 8.4, 48, 68-69. Horapollo (*Hieroglyphics* 1.21; pp. 54-56 Sbordone, with notes; B. van de Walle and J. Vergote, *CEg* 35 [1943] 60, with notes pp. 61, 63) attests the same nexus of tradition. Similarly, though of course not for the Egyptian reason, the month which began the Attic calendar year roughly corresponded to the month during which the sun is in Leo. For lion-spouts in Greek settings, see Cook, "Animal Worship in the Mycenaean Age" 112.

[30] Antiochus I of Commagene's relief at Nemrud-Dagh: (W.) Gundel, "Leo" 1988.14-18; Boll, Bezold, (W.) Gundel and (H.) Gundel, *Sternglaube und Sterndeutung* 56; *Astrologumena* 48 n. 16 with pl. 4.5; Bouché-Leclercq, *L'astrologie grecque* 373 n. 2, 438-439; Jean Gagé, *"Basiléia." Les Césars, les rois d'Orient et les "mages"* (Paris: "Belles lettres," 1968) 143-148; Hugo Gressmann, *Die hellenistische Gestirnreligion* (BAO 5; Leipzig: Hinrichs, 1925) 22-23; Helmut Waldmann, *Die kommagenischen Kultreformen unter König Mithradates I. Kallinikos und seinem Sohne Antiochos I* (EPRO 34; Leiden: Brill, 1973) 150-152, 169-170, 197-198 with pl. 15.2. Waldmann sees in the astral lion an additional reference to Antiochus' patron deity Helios-Mithras (p. 170); note too his remark (pp. 151-152): "Näherhin werden wir in ihm (the lion as Leo) den Stern Regulus zu sehen haben, unter dessen Gestalt Antiochos auf dem Löwenhoroskop die Planetengötter begrüsst," Regulus being, of course, the star of kings. Alexander the Great: (W.) Gundel and (H.) Gundel, *Astrologumena* 89 n. 43; (W.) Gundel, "Leo" 1983.60-1984.1. Julius Caesar: (W.) Gundel and (H.) Gundel, *Astrologumena* 127 n. 14. As for humans born under Leo, note Bouché-Leclercq, *L'astrologie grecque* 438: "Comme on ne pouvait pas déclarer candidats à la royauté tous les enfants nés sous le Lion, il y avait lieu d'exiger soit que l'Horoscope tombât exactement sur—élimination encore insuffisante,—soit qu'il y eût dans ce signe réunion des planètes apportant l'idée symbolique de puissance, de force, de primauté ...." Failing these conditions even ordinary men born under Leo might possess kingly qualities: (W.) Gundel, "Leo" 1986.51-1987.11; "Individualschicksal, Menschentypen und Berufe in der antiken Astrologie," *JCh* 4 (1927) 133-193, in particular p. 160: "(Those born under Leo) sind gewalttätig, jähzornig, kühn .... In ihren Unternehmungen sind sie führende Naturen, eigenmächtig, tatkräftig, berühmt und reich"; similarly pp. 163, 164-65.

The catasterization in the celestial Leo of folklore about the lion and, by the reverse process, the endowment of the earthly animal with traits derived from astrological theory as to the nature of the heavenly lion combined with the Hellenistic transformation of Yahweh and his angelic hypostases into planetary powers to help guarantee that he could be naturally portrayed as a lion-god. What the bestiaries of late antiquity have to say about the nature of the lion admirably suited Yahweh's character and must have had a hand in fixing a leonine portrait for him in Gnostic tradition. Consider but one, Aelian (circa A.D. 170-235) *On the Characteristics of Animals*, a work contemporary with the flowering of Gnosticism in the second and third centuries. I have shown that ancient Sumerian and Akkadian astrological ideas surrounding the star Regulus in Leo, nurtured as they were in the bosom of a royal ideology, already served to connect the constellation with kingship, and the Hellenistic Leo merely continued this tradition. If the lion is king of beasts (Aelian 3.1; 15.17) then Yahweh/Yaldabaoth as king of the universe (Ps 47:2, 7 [46:3, 8], for example) and as lord of the planetary powers must be leonine if bestial at all. The Manichaean *Kephalaion* 6 cited earlier merely states explicitly what is already implicit in the Gnostic tradition. Similarly, if the lion, like a good monarch, is δίκαιος (like Marcion's Yahweh) and gives tit for tat (Aelian 5.39; cp. 7.23), so does Yahweh (Exod 20:5-6; 34:7). And if, again like a good monarch, the lion is always vigilant and never sleeps (Aelian 5.39; note too Philo, *Life of Moses* I, §284; the Hermetic tract *Kore Kosmou* 42; Plutarch, *Table-Talk* 4.5.2 [*Moralia* 670B-C]; Horapollo, *Hieroglyphics* 1.19—a very popular folklore motif[31]),

---

[31]Francesco Sbordone provides enlightening commentary (with further references) in his edition of Horapollo, pp. 52-53. A good translation of this document with similarly excellent Egyptological notes (already referred to in n. 29) is provided by B. van de Walle and J. Vergote, "Traduction des *Hieroglyphica* d'Horapollon," *CEg* 35 (1943) 39-89 and 36 (1943) 199-239; the section just cited appears at 35 (1943) 58-59. Aelian (5.39) claims this piece of folklore for a native Egyptian tradition, and the sources—both those I have cited for it and earlier Egyptian ones—bear him out. Horapollo shows whence the tradition derives: the apotropaic use of lions as guardians of temples. The Ptolemaic temple of Horus at Edfu, for instance, offers excellent examples, both literary and iconographic: de Wit, "Les inscriptions des lions-gargouilles" 29-45 and generally *Le rôle et le sens du lion* 71-82: "Le lion, gardien de portes et de temples." Horapollo's statement that Egyptian locks are shaped in the form of lions (to symbolize their guardian function) is also borne out by actual discovery, and his contention that the Egyptian language conveys the idea "guardian"

neither does Yahweh (Ps 121 [120]:3-4). Leo's intimate connection with
kingship ensured that when the inevitable coordination of the twelve chief
divinities of the Graeco-Roman pantheon (first in Plato, *Phaedrus* 246E-
247A, already astrologically motivated?) with the twelve zodiacal
constellations was made the celestial lion was assigned to Zeus/Jupiter.[32]
And here again the lion suited Yahweh because the earliest *interpretatio
graeca* of the god of the Jews for obvious reasons centered on the same
deity, the principal texts being *Ep. Arist.* 15-16//Josephus, *Ant.* 12.2.2
§22; Varro in Augustine, *On the Agreement of the Evangelists* 1.22.30, and
On the City of God 4.9.3 (frgs. 47 and 48 Condemi), dependent upon
earlier Stoic sources who, in turn, may have been influenced by Antiochus
IV Epiphanes' campaign to convert the temple of Yahweh in Jerusalem to
the worship of Zeus Olympios and that of the Samaritans on Mount Gerizim to the worship of Zeus Xenios [2 Macc 6:1-2]).[33]

Besides, the animal marvelously well suited Yahweh/Yaldabaoth's
personality not only because it was a royal beast and because, as I have
already said, its voracious ferocity exemplified the Gnostic view of the
god of the Old Testament, but also for another important reason: its
astrological counterpart, as a mid-summer sign when the sun's force
culminated in intensity, was naturally accorded fire in the correlation of
the zodiacal constellations with the four elemental principles of the
Empedoclean universe.[34] The terrestrial lion was therefore a beast the

---

with the hieroglyphic head of a lion has some basis in fact. See on all this
Hopfner, "Der Tierkult der alten Ägypter" 44; Schweitzer, *Löwe und
Sphinx* 25 with pl. 16.4, 49-50, 69-70; "Löwe," *RÄRG* 429; de Wit, *Le rôle
et le sens du lion* 83: "Le lion-verrou ou barrière mobile." Hopfner offers
other examples of the lion's role as guardian in Egyptian settings, and so
does de Wit; for this practice throughout the ancient Near East see
Keller, *Die antike Tierwelt* I, 54. Yet other references to the lion's wake-
fulness are registered by Steier, "Löwe" 976.48-53; its continuance in the
medieval tradition by Charbonneau-Lassay, *La bestiaire du Christ* 41-42:
"Le lion, emblème de la vigilance du Christ."

   [32]O. Weinreich, "Zwölfgötter," Roscher 6.823-825 in context; Bouché-
Leclercq, *L'astrologie grecque* 183-184; (W.) Gundel, "Leo" 1985.28-30, all
on Manilius 2.433-452.

   [33]On Zeus/Jupiter = Yahweh see Marcel Simon, "Jupiter-Yahvé. Sur un
essai de théologie pagano-juive," *Numen* 23 (1976) 40-66.

   [34](W.) Gundel, "Leo" 1974.50-60; 1981.40-1982.25; Boll, *Sphaera* 226;
Bouché-Leclercq, *L'astrologie grecque* 138, 185; Keller, *Die antike Tierwelt* I, 45-46, 52-53; Gagé, *"Basiléia"* 345-346; and A. Delatte, "Études sur
la magie grecque I. Sphère magique du Musée d'Athènes," *BCH* 37 (1913)

very marrow of whose bones is fire (from its bones, when broken, fire erupts, according to Aelian 4.34; and cp. 12.7 where he puts the cart before the horse in claiming: "Since the lion is of such an exceedingly fiery nature, they [the Egyptians] say that Leo is the house of the sun"). Hence the pseudo-Heracleitean allegorist (*Homeric Questions* 66) can inform us that διὰ τοῦ λέοντος ἐμπύρου ζῴου Homer actually meant the empyrean αἰθήρ in his references to the animal; hence the visionary John can see that the frightful horses in the army of Yahweh's destroying angels have the heads of lions whose mouths belch fire (Rev 9:17-18); and hence the great Egyptian magical papyrus of Paris can invoke the sun as a lion (together with his seemingly inseparable Egyptian companion the serpent, a partnership which has an astrological basis there) with χαῖρε, δράκων ἀκμαῖέ τε λέων, φυσικαὶ πυρὸς ἀρχαί (*PGM* I P 4.939).[35]

What does this have to do with Yahweh? Leo and the terrestrial lion's intimate connection with fire provided further impetus for the Gnostic association of the animal with the god of the Jews because fire is a natural expression of Yahweh's zealous rage, as Korah, Dathan and Abiram discovered much to their chagrin (Num 16:35). Hebrew poets and prophets do not hesitate to describe the pyrotechnic aspects of Yahweh's fury in the most lurid and monstrous detail (Deut 32:22; Ps 18:8 [17:9]; Isa 30:27, 30; Jer 15:14, for example). No wonder that the Deuteronomist (4:24; so too 9:3; taken up by the New Testament at Heb 12:29) may confess Yahweh an אֵשׁ אֹכְלָה!

Gnostics did not have to reach very far, then, for this support in their portrait of Yahweh/Yaldabaoth as a leonine god; like the lion Yahweh's very essence was "a fire which devours." This was all precious grist for the Gnostic mill. What is more, fire, already a cosmogonic principle for the Stoics and for Heracleitus before them, was taken up long before from classical and Hellenistic Greek philosophy into Gnosticism and suitably

---

257-258, in the course of his explanation of the significance of the lion on the sphere (pl. 3).

[35]On the passage from *PGM* and other connections between the lion, serpent, and sun in late antique tradition, some of which will be taken up later, see Delatte, "Sphère magique" 259-263; Albrecht Dieterich, *Abraxas* 51-54; 2 Enoch 12:1-2 where the Chalkydrai that accompany the sun are part lion and, evidently, as their name implies, part serpent.

embodied in the demiurge.[36] Hence many of the texts cited and summarized in the last chapter repeatedly connect the leonine Yaldabaoth and his ministers with fire. Other Gnostic sources state the matter even more baldly. With some justification Hippolytus accuses Simon, for example, of actually plagiarizing Heracleitus (*Refutation* 6.9.3; 136.14 Wendland) when the bishop's Simonian source justifies its claim πῦρ εἶναι τῶν ὅλων . . . τὴν ἀρχήν by the fact Μωσέως γὰρ λέγοντος ὅτι ὁ θεὸς πῦρ φλέγον ἐστὶ καὶ καταναλίσκον (*Refutation* 6.9.3; 136.9-12 Wendland), referring precisely to Deut 4:24 and Exod 24:17; the Simonian source identifies this fire with its "Great Power," the ῥίζα τῶν ὅλων (*Refutation* 6.9.5; 136.20-22 Wendland). Apelles, the disciple of Marcion, held the creator, the god of Israel, to be an *angelus igneus* (Tertullian, *On the Soul* 23; similarly Hippolytus, *Refutation* 7.38.1; 224.3-4 Wendland); similar views are held by Hippolytus' Docetae (*Refutation* 8.9.7; 228.27-28 Wendland and 8.10.1; 229.8-13 Wendland) and "Ophitic" Naassenes (τῷ ταύτης τῆς κτίσεως δημιουργῷ 'Ησαλδαίῳ, θεῷ πυρίνῳ 5.7.30-31; 86.9-10 Wendland). This early, widespread Gnostic tradition about the fiery nature of the demiurge, a tradition inherited from the Stoics, had equally widespread astrological ties—themselves popularized by the Stoics, for whom Fate was a hotly debated issue—to warrant coalescence with the tradition of a leontomorphic Yaldabaoth whose anger is so fiery. The Manichaean author of *Kephalaion* 69 (167.26-27 Polotsky-Böhlig) demonstrates how well he knows his stuff when he remarks in an astrological context that "Leo belongs to the world of fire," because elsewhere, as I noted in the last chapter, he explains the ruler of the world of darkness' lion-face by reference to the "world of fire" as his domain.

Equally seminal in the lion's astrological suitability for Yahweh/Yaldabaoth's role as demiurge is the widely publicized position of Leo as that single zodiacal constellation whose natural ruler is the sun (Pliny, *Natural*

---

[36]Hans Jonas, *The Gnostic Religion. The Message of the Alien God and the Beginnings of Christianity* (2nd ed.; Boston: Beacon, 1963) 197-199; *Gnosis und spätantike Geist* II.1. *Von der Mythologie zur mystischen Philosophie* (Göttingen: Vandenhoeck & Ruprecht, 1954) 160 n. 3. Lucan (*Pharsalia* 1.655-657) cites Nigidius Figulus for the astrologically sound theory that the Stoic ἐκπύρωσις will occur when the sun is in Leo—a fire sign whose lord is the sun, the hottest time of the year: "Were your rays, Phoebus, now upon the ferocious Nemean/Lion to strike, then would the world be engulfed by fire,/And, kindled by your chariot's wheels, the empyrean burst into flame." On this passage see Boll, Bezold, (W.) Gundel and (H.) Gundel, *Sternglaube und Sterndeutung* 201; Boll, *Sphaera* 362.

History 24.17.162; Macrobius, *Saturnalia* 1.21.16, for example), because Helios' prominence as creator in late antiquity can only have further encouraged Gnostic association of the god of the Jews with Leo's earthly counterpart.[37] It is particularly, though not exclusively in Syria that the lion as Leo is conjoined with the sun; here the influence of the "Chaldeans" was supreme. In Phoenicia, where contact with Egypt existed from remote antiquity and the debt to Egyptian culture was heavy, the lion's association with the sun is to be traced in part as well to an Egyptian context,[38] but in the interior the cultural ties were traditionally exclusively eastward. It is at the Syrian Heliopolis and at Emesa that the sun is intimately connected with the cult carried on there,[39] and in the former city the appearance of lion-masks on cult images and altars is doubtless to be regarded as a symbol for the heavenly body which ruled the animal's stellar equivalent.[40] The sponsorship accorded these solarized Syrian cults

---

[37]On Helios-'Ιάω see, for example, Ganschinietz, "Iao," PW 10.708.1-50; Theodor Hopfner, "Orientalisch-Religionsgeschichtliches aus den griechischen Zauberpapyri Aegyptens," *ArOr* 3 (1931) 340-342; Erik Peterson, Εἷς θεός. *Epigraphische, formgeschichtliche und religionsgeschichtliche Untersuchungen* (Göttingen: Vandenhoeck & Ruprecht, 1926) 265-266, 305-308.

[38]Robert du Mesnil du Buisson, *Études sur les dieux phéniciens hérités par l'empire romain* (EPRO 14; Leiden: Brill, 1970) 7-29 and passim, with many illustrations; *Nouvelles études sur les dieux et les mythes de Canaan* (EPRO 33; Leiden: Brill, 1973) passim, with many illustrations. For Egyptian influence in Canaan generally see, for example, Raphael Giveon, *The Impact of Egypt on Canaan* (OBO 20; Freiburg, Switzerland: Universitätsverlag, and Göttingen: Vandenhoeck & Ruprecht, 1978).

[39]See lately René Mouterde, "L'astrologie à Héliopolis Baᶜalbek. *Jupiter Heliopolitanus Rex* et *Regulus*," *BMB* 13 (1956) 7-21; Henri Seyrig, "Antiquités syriennes 95. Le culte du Soleil en Syrie à l'époque romaine," *Syria* 48 (1971) 337-373, particularly 340-345 on Emesa and 345-348 on Heliopolis. The classic exposition is that of Franz Cumont, *Les religions orientales dans le paganisme romain* (3rd ed.; Paris: Leroux, 1929) 160-210.

[40]Franz Cumont, "Le Jupiter héliopolitain et les divinités des planètes," *Syria* 2 (1921) 45 with n. 3; Mouterde, "L'astrologie à Héliopolis-Baᶜalbek" 11-12 commenting on an inscription in which Jupiter Heliopolitanus is identified with Regulus as the star in Leo most intimately connected with kingship, 13-16 on the lion-masks, and 20-21; Youssef Hajjar, *La triade d'Héliopolis-Baalbek. Son culte et sa diffusion à travers les textes littéraires et les documents iconographiques et épigraphiques* I (EPRO 59; Leiden: Brill, 1977) 294-295.

by the Severi and later emperors spread their astrological symbology far
and wide.

Beyond an arid symbology, however, useful for cults that made conces-
sions to astrology, in Semitic pantheons the lion figures profusely in
conjunction with—often as the mount of—a whole host both of male and
especially of female divinities—to name but a few of the latter: Hierapol-
itan Atargatis (the "Dea Syria"), Cybele, Ishtar-Astarte, and Qadesh, the
last two adopted by the Egyptians at an early date (pl. 5b).[41] The most
famous and most interesting text which relates to the Syrian tradition is
one which Photius (*Library* 348a-s) cites from Damascius' *Life of Isidorus*.
It runs as follows:

> "I saw," he (Damascius) says, "the betyl flying through the air,
> and at other times I saw it hidden in the vestments or cradled
> in the hands of its minister. The name of the betyl's minister
> was Eusebius. He said that one day the strange desire had
> suddenly come over him to leave Emesa in the middle of the
> night and to journey a great distance to a mountain where a
> venerable temple of Athena stood. He made his way as
> quickly as he could to the foot of the mountain and sat down
> there to rest, as one does on a journey, when suddenly he saw
> a fiery sphere that shot down from the sky, and a huge lion
> standing beside the sphere. The lion immediately disappeared,
> however, and so Eusebius ran to the sphere, the fire having
> now extinguished itself, and seized it. The sphere was the
> betyl. Eusebius took it up and asked it to which of the gods it
> belonged, and it answered that it belonged to Gennaios.—
> Gennaios (is a god whom) the Heliopolitans revere, and they
> present his image in the temple of Zeus in a particular leo-
> nine form (ἐν Διὸς ἱδρυσάμενοι μορφήν τινα λέοντος).—
> And Eusebius took it back home that very night, traveling
> without stopping, even though, as he said, the distance was
> not less than two hundred stadia."

Some scholars have uncritically taken this story, in whole or in part,

---

[41]See, for example, R. V. Lanzone, *Dizionario di mitologia egizia*
(Torino: Doyen, 1881 and 1886; 3 vols. consecutively paginated) 146-147
with pls. 47, 191-192; Rainer Stadelmann, *Syrisch-palästinensische Gottheiten in Ägypten* (PAeg 5; Leiden: Brill, 1967) passim; Henri Seyrig,
"Antiquités syriennes. Héraclès-Nergal," *Syria* 24 (1944-1945) 62-80 with
pls. 1-4, especially 69, 72, 73 with n. 1, 74; René Dussaud, "Melqart,"
Syria 25 (1946-1948) 205-230, especially 222-225.

too much at face value, despite the fact that the story itself came from
the betyl's minister who, as Damascius goes on to relate, used the stone,
the surface of which was covered with symbols only he could explain, for
divinatory purposes and whose only interest may therefore have been to
arouse awe in his audience by whatever concocted tale he could muster.
Other details of the passage have caused difficulty. In the first place
γενναῖος is only an epithet of an otherwise unnamed divinity; it is not to
be equated with the equestrian god Genneas, who is not a solar deity and
with whose cult the lion is never associated. Furthermore, Damascius'
aside is an attempt to explain Eusebius' story from the Heliopolitan cult,
in which Jupiter Heliopolitanus was called γενναῖος and represented, for
astrological (solar) reasons, by lion-masks (Leo was assigned to Jupiter, as
I noted just now). But his remark does not posit a lion-cult at Heliopolis,
for which there is otherwise no evidence. The lion of Eusebius' tale is
either intended for a livelier than normal symbol of Jupiter Heliopolitanus
or his equivalent at Emesa, or perhaps was originally the paredros of the
goddess to whose sacred mountain-shrine Eusebius claimed to have trav-
eled—Athena-Allāt, who, like the other goddesses just enumerated, is
regularly in league with the ferocious feline that suits her character.[42]

---

[42]Henri Seyrig, "La triade héliopolitaine et les temples de Baalbek,"
Syria 10 (1929) 335-338; Henri Seyrig and Jean Starcky, "Genneas," *Syria*
26 (1949) 230-257 with pls. 11-12; with a somewhat revised position, Henri
Seyrig, "Antiquités syriennes 57. Questions héliopolitaines," *Syria* 31
(1954) 94 with n. 2, 95; René Dussaud, "Temples et cultes de la triade
héliopolitaine à Baᶜalbeck," *Syria* 23 (1942-1943) 43-45; Mouterde, "L'
astrologie à Héliopolis-Baᶜalbek" 18-20; J. T. Milik, "Les papyrus araméens d'Hermoupolis et les cultes syro-phéniciens en Égypte perse," *Bib* 48
(1967) 602-603; Daniel Schlumberger, "Le prétendu dieu Gennéas," *MUSJ*
46 (1970-1971) 209-222; Hajjar, *La triade d'Héliopolis-Baalbek* I, 154-56,
288-295 with pl. 95. Hajjar prints the text and a translation of the passage
from Photius in *La triade d'Héliopolis-Baalbek* II (Leiden: Brill, 1977) 426-
427. Milik, "Les papyrus araméens d'Hermoupolis" 604-605, observes that
the lion appears with the betyl and then disappears "comme pour assurer
l'origine céleste de l'objet," that "on ne peut guère cependant parler . . .
d'un dieu-lion," and concludes: "le lion est bien un animal-attribut du
'Maître du Ciel' comme il l'était pour plusieurs dieux et déesses phén. et
aram.," referring to the Leontopolis near Sidon, on which see Beer-
Honigmann, "Λεόντων πόλις," PW 12.2053.50-2054.2. A. Delatte, "Études
sur la magie grecque VI. Notes complémentaires," *MB* 26 (1922) 253-255,
uses the passage from Photius and the oracular powers which the context
ascribes to the betyl to deduce the function of the magic sphere from

In addition, moreover, to its cosmogonic connection as the fiery sign ruled by the sun and, in Egypt, as that sign whose heliacal rising brought with it the world-renewing waters of the Nile, Leo plays a very interesting psychogenetic role in the secret teachings of late antique Neo-Pythagoreans. According to this doctrine souls descend into embodiment from and reascend out of it back to their natural home in the Milky Way through two gates located at the tropic extremities of the sun's yearly course, at the zodiacal constellations Cancer and Capricorn, respectively. The earliest source for this tradition is Varro (first century B.C.) as cited by Servius in his *Commentary on Vergil's Georgics* 1.34 (141.13-18 Thilo). Varro generally followed Nigidius Figulus in these matters, hence its Neo-Pythagorean associations. The passage runs:

> Varro says that he read of a man from Syracuse named Empedotimus that his mortal form was stripped away by some divine power and that he saw, among other things, three gates and three roads. One led to the constellation Scorpio, the road by which Hercules is said to have traveled to the gods; another led along the border between Leo and Cancer, and the third along that between Aquarius and Pisces.

Nothing is said here of the descent or ascent of average souls through the latter two of the celestial gates, though it is doubtless implied. Far more explicit (and normal in identification of the winter gate) are Porphyry, *On the Cave of the Nymphs in the Odyssey* 21-24 (70.25-73.2 Nauck), and Proclus, *Commentary on Plato's Republic* II, 128.26-129.24 Kroll, both of whom present the myth as a mystical exegesis of Homer's description of the cave of the nymphs in *Od.* 13.109-112 and both of whom are citing Numenius (frs 31 and 35 des Places)—another Neo-Pythagorean, a Syrian from Apamea (second half of the second century A.D.)—who must be dependent upon Varro or his source.

Common to these accounts, at any rate, is the idea that souls descend into embodiment through the celestial gate between Cancer and Leo. Macrobius, in his *Commentary on the Dream of Scipio* 1.12.4-5 (probably eventually dependent upon the same account of Numenius—the passage is

---

Athens on which the lion is a prominent figure (see n. 34 above). For Allāt and her lions, see H. J. W. Drijvers, "*De matre inter leones sedente.* Iconography and character of the Arab goddess Allât," *Hommages à Maarten J. Vermaseren* I (ed. Margaret B. de Boer and T. A. Edridge; EPRO 68; Leiden: Brill, 1978) 331-351 with pls. 63-75.

fr 34 des Places), after offering basically the same story as Varro, Porphyry and Proclus (1.12.1-3; 47.30-48.18 Willis), goes on to add the following additional information (48.18-22, 27-31 Willis):

> So while the souls which are about to descend are yet in Cancer they are still in the company of the gods because in that constellation they have not yet left the Milky Way. But when in their fall they reach Leo they enter into the primary form of their future condition. . . . From there—that is, from the borderland where the Zodiac and the Milky Way intersect —the descending soul is drawn out in its downward rush from a sphere, which is the only divine shape, into a cone, just as a line is born of a point and passes from an indivisible state into dimensionality.

At Leo, then, the realm of γένεσις, the dimensional, phenomenal cosmos begins; at Leo souls take their first step toward birth in this world.[43] Once again Hellenistic and late antique tradition discloses that there was no more fitting bestial shape for the creator and ruler of this world than a lion's. All the more is that so in the present case as in Gnostic myth the cosmocrator is himself strictly a soul-entity (not πνευματικός), is only capable of animation, of (in the Gnostic view) a comparatively low level of life-endowment because soul is constantly threatened by passion, is not fully spiritual. No matter that soul is of depreciated value in Gnosticism, however; in both myths the intermediary between the perfect immaterial state and the material world, the transitional agent— Leo in the Neo-Pythagorean myth and Yaldabaoth in the Gnostic—is involved in the subjugation of an inherently superior element to a new state of being which obscures or obliterates its original form. Given Numenius' extreme dualism and other doctrinal affinities with Gnosticism, it would not be a shock to find that along with the other astrological traditions this piece of Neo-Pythagorean mysticism influenced his

---

[43]On these passages and the astral mysticism they represent see, for example, (W.) Gundel, "Leo" 1987.65-1988.10; (H.) Gundel, "Zodiakos" 546.30-52; J. Kroll, *Die Himmelfahrt der Seele in der Antike* (Köln: Müller, 1931) 13-14; Pierre Boyancé, *Études sur le Songe de Scipion* (Bordeaux: Feret & Fils, and Paris: de Boccard and Klincksieck, 1936) 133-137; Franz Cumont, *Lux Perpetua* (Paris: Geuthner, 1949) 280-281, 344-345; A. J. Festugière, *Proclus, Commentaire sur la République, traduction et notes* III (Paris: Vrin, 1970) 72-74.

contemporaries the great Gnostic masters of the second century. If so here was yet another reason for their creator to be leonine.

3.4   Chnoumis

Cumulatively considered, all of the evidence so far examined sets the Gnostic leontomorphic demiurge deeply in a variety of milieux that provided motivation both diverse and compelling for Yaldabaoth to be compared with the lion, but, as I have repeatedly affirmed, the evidence cannot account for the *creation* of the portrait in either of its forms. However much the Hellenistic and late antique congeries of leonine associations may have contributed color to the portraits, there must still have existed a specific model or models for each of them to begin with, deities from whose likenesses the Gnostic (or proto-Gnostic) portraits were directly drawn. Who were they?

I have already given reason to suspect that Egypt was the place where the sittings were held. Certain Syrian cults, particularly that centered at Heliopolis, may have become seedbeds of astrological associations and thus proved instrumental in the dissemination of the lion as a solar emblem, but no cult of a male divinity in a leonine form matching either of those we are interested in existed there to furnish the primary motivation for the transformation of Yahweh/Yaldabaoth into a lion-shaped god. Only Egypt provides an exemplar for *Apoc. John*'s (in the long recension) and the Egyptian Manichaean texts' lion-headed serpent, and, as I will seek to demonstrate in the next section, only Egypt furnishes a geographical and a historical as well as a religious setting in which the evolution of a portrayal of Yahweh as a god in lion-headed human form may be clearly explained.

First the serpentine form. Two scholars (and there may be others whose work I have overlooked) have already sniffed out the truth here, but their accounts are both deficient in important respects. The earlier of the two, printed over thirty years ago, is unfortunately only a brief résumé of a paper which was never, so far as I know, subsequently published in its full form, and aside from constituting a necessarily superficial treatment it suffers from being burdened with inaccuracies.[44] The second merely

---

[44] J. Doresse, "Images de dieux gnostiques," *BIE* 32 (1949-1950) 364-65, among its "Procès-verbaux des séances." Doresse alludes to the same (?) paper in *The Secret Books of the Egyptian Gnostics* 93 and n. 65, 260 and n. 15, but without providing any further discussion of its content. The

makes passing reference to the appearance of lion-headed serpents on Graeco-Egyptian magical gems and immediately abandons the subject in pursuit of the attempt to prove its central thesis: the long recension of *Apoc. John* owed the form it bestowed upon Yaldabaoth to the Phanes of some late Orphic tradition.[45] I will take up that subject later.

The magical gems which depict a serpent with radiate lion's head (at times additionally with nimbus or solar disk) belong to an extremely common type, examples of which have been unearthed in locales spanning the Graeco-Roman world. The creature is regularly accompanied (usually on the reverse) by a symbol—a (normally vertical) stroke crossed by three broken or wavy lines, thus: ⚡ or ⚡ —and an inscription, evincing many variants, which identifies it (with the orthography normalized) as XNOYMIΣ, XNOYBIΣ, or XNOYΦIΣ (pl. 5c-m).[46]

---

provincial coins of Elagabalus, Septimius Severus, and Caracalla to which Doresse refers are likely to be the coins of Nicopolis struck under these and other emperors listed by Wilhelm Drexler, *Der Cultus der aegyptischen Gottheiten in den Donauländern* (Mythologische Beiträge I; Leipzig: Teubner, 1890) 66-67, that show a serpent with solar rays, but they are not identified as Chnoumis. Doresse might also have meant the coins discussed by Drexler on pp. 62-66 in connection with the description of certain coins from Thrace and Moesia Inferior minted under Caracalla, Julia Domna, Septimius Severus and Geta represented by Barclay V. Head, Percy Gardner, Reginald Stuart Poole, *A Catalogue of the Greek Coins in the British Museum. The Tauric Chersonese, Sarmatia, Dacia, Moesia, Thrace* (Bologna: Forni, 1963 [1877]) 31, 84, 117, 146, 178, as showing a coiled serpent with lion's head surrounded by radiate nimbus and a fish's tail. Drexler is, however, skeptical of the accuracy of this description and writes: "In anderen Münzbeschreibungen finde ich nirgends den Löwenkopf angegeben (my experience also); auch schreibt mir Imhoof-Blumer: 'Schlangen mit Löwenkopf gibt es keine unter den vielen Münzen und Abdrücken, die ich gesammelt.'" Doresse may have been able to prove the *Catalogue*'s description accurate.

[45]Gilles Quispel, "The Demiurge in the Apocryphon of John," *Nag Hammadi and Gnosis. Papers read at the First International Congress of Coptology (Cairo, December 1976)* (ed. R. McL. Wilson; NHS 14; Leiden: Brill, 1978) 6, 10-23.

[46]Bonner, *Studies in Magical Amulets* ##81-93 (pl. 4, pp. 266-268), 97-98 (pl. 5, pp. 268-269), 296 (pl. 6, p. 302—symbol only, on the reverse of an example of the Solomonic type, with the inscription σφραγὶς θεοῦ see p. 209), 393 (p. 321, no illustration); "Amulets chiefly in the British Museum. A Supplementary Article," *Hesp* 20 (1951) ##20-22 (pls. 96-97, pp. 325-326); "A Miscellany of Engraved Stones," *Hesp* 23 (1954) ##35-36

The amazing popularity and widespread distribution of these gems are readily accounted for. The reasons are two, widely divergent but equally interesting. The first is eminently practical: the gems were designed to be worn as amulets by clients with dyspeptic complaints. Incisive phrases (for example, πέσσε πέσσε "digest! digest!") cut on many of the Chnoumis gems leave no room for doubt that this was their function.[47] Indeed, the occurrence of the word γιγαντορηκτα "giant-slayer"(pl. 5k)—along with others more obscure—on these amulets would logically be in effect an invocation of Chnoumis' power to repel disease-causing demons by way of mythological reference to some primordial gigantomachy.[48]

(pl. 36, p. 149); Delatte-Derchain, *Les intailles magiques* ##52-81, pp. 58-67; 83-86, pp. 69-70; 89, p. 72; Dierk Wortmann, "Neue magische Gemmen," *BJbb* 175 (1975) #6, pp. 67-68; S. Eitrem, "Die magischen Gemmen und ihre Weihe," *SO* 19 (1939) 74; and among older works note, for example, W. Deonna, "Notes d'archéologie suisse VII. Amulette des Fins d'Annecy," *ASAK* 22 (1922) 173-175; René Mouterde, "Le Glaive de Dardanos. Objets et inscriptions magiques de Syrie," *MUSJ* 15.3 (1930) 74-76; C. W. King, *The Gnostics and their Remains, Ancient and Mediaeval* (Minneapolis: Wizards Bookshelf, 1973 [1888]) fig. 15 with p. 434, pl. D1-4 with pp. 437-438; A. Delatte, "Études sur la magie grecque IV. Amulettes inédites des Musées d'Athènes," *MB* 18 (1914) #A30, pp. 69-70; Adolf Jacoby, "Ein Berliner Chnubisamulett," *ARW* 28 (1930) 269-285; Wilhelm Drexler, *Der Cultus der aegyptischen Gottheiten* 61-67; "Knuphis," Roscher 2.1258.54-1260.13.

[47] Bonner, *Studies in Magical Amulets* #83 (pl. 4, p. 267; for this type's digestive application see pp. 25, 51-60, with further examples); "A Miscellany of Engraved Stones" #36 (pl. 36, p. 149); "Amulets chiefly in the British Museum" ##22 (pl. 97, p. 326, with Imhotep-Asklepios facing Hygieia on the obverse) and 44 (pl. 98, p. 332, inscribed στόμαχε πέπτε); Delatte-Derchain, *Les intailles magiques* ##80, p. 67; 89, p. 72; Mouterde, "Le Glaive de Dardanos" 74-76. The appearance of the Chnoumis-serpent with other gods on the uterine type of amulet (my pl. 5g; Bonner, *Studies in Magical Amulets* ##126, 130, 132, 136, 140 [pl. 6, pp. 273-275, and generally pp. 57, 79, 89]; "Amulets chiefly in the British Museum" ##26 [pl. 97, p. 327] and 38 [pl. 97, p. 330, probably uterine]; Delatte-Derchain, *Les intailles magiques* ##189-191, pp. 147-148; 343-348 and 350-358, pp. 248-255) is for the same curative purposes; after all, the womb and the stomach are both in the "belly," and, more exactly, as A. A. Barb points out ("Seth or Anubis," *JWCI* 22 [1959] 368 n. 14, and elsewhere) the word στόμαχος is used of the womb as well as of the stomach.

[48] Bonner, *Studies in Magical Amulets* ##86, 88 (pl. 4, p. 267) and 393 (p. 321, no illustration) with pp. 168-169; "Amulets chiefly in the British

Physicians of every stripe, from Galen to the humblest writer on the healing properties of stones, fully believed in the effectiveness of the Chnoumis-gem and prescribed its use to cure maladies of precisely those organs depicted or alluded to on the extant amulets. The passage in Galen (*On the Composition and Specificity of Simple Remedies* 10.19; XII, 207 Kühn) runs as follows:

> Some authorities ascribe special properties to particular varieties of stone—special properties of the sort that the green jasper, for example, actually does possess. Worn (about the neck) it heals the stomach and the mouth of the womb.

Museum" ##21 (pl. 97, pp. 325-326, inscribed γιγαντοφοντα πανταρηκτωρ among other things), 23 (pl. 97, p. 326); Delatte-Derchain, *Les intailles magiques* ##71-72, pp. 63-64; Delatte, "Amulettes inédites" 32—note especially his conclusion: "Ces épithètes se rapportent à un rôle qu'on attribuait au dieu Abraxas (from whom Chnoumis has borrowed them) dans une gigantomachie gnostique où se mêlaient les récits des deux mythologies grecque et orientale, comme dans les légendes des mystères de Mithra. La valeur magique et religieuse de ces épithètes, qui s'appliquent bien aux représentations d'un dieu armé, réside dans l'identification des Géants avec les mauvais esprits qui rôdent autour des hommes." The "oriental" element in this gigantomachy, an element which Delatte-Derchain despair of having found (*Les intailles magiques* 29 n. 1), is likely to have been Jewish; the identification of Yahweh with Zeus, mentioned earlier, paved the way for the fusion of the two gods' war against their respective gigantic foes. The interpretation of Gen 6:1-7 in the light of the Greek gigantomachy, aided or even already attested by the LXX (הַנְּפִלִים Gen 6:4 = οἱ γίγαντες LXX), meant that now the giants were corrupters of the earth, and 1 Enoch 15:8-16:1 makes the spirits of the dead giants, killed by Yahweh in the Flood, demons that oppress men with all sorts of affliction. The commonality of function for Chnoumis and Abraxas as repellers of demons resulted in Abraxas'—normally a rooster-headed anguipede—acquisition of Chnoumis' lion-head: Bonner, *Studies in Magical Amulets* #181 double snake-legged (pl. 9, pp. 283 and 128-129, 169) fittingly labeled ΙΑΩ as the god who overcame the demonic giants of Gen 6 and 1 Enoch 15-16 and, on the reverse, λεοντορηκτα, lion-god against lion-demon, and ##99-101 single snake-legged (pl. 5, pp. 269 and 55-58; my pl. 5j-l), #99 inscribed Χνουβις and γιγαντορηκτα and the rest; Delatte-Derchain, *Les intailles magiques* #35, p. 38, similarly labeled ιλω ; further, Max Pieper, "Die Abraxasgemmen," *MDAI.K* 5 (1934) 127, 142 with pl. 22b. For the explanation of these epithets offered here see further Drexler, "Knuphis" 1263.15-60.

Some people also set the stone in a ring and inscribe on it the radiate serpent, precisely as king Nechepso prescribes in his fourteenth book. I have myself, in fact, put this stone to experimental test. I strung together a little necklace of stones of this type and hung it around the neck (of a patient) at just such a length that the stones touched the mouth of the womb. They proved to be no less effective even when they lacked the design that Nechepso prescribes.

Galen is obviously not so convinced of the necessity of the engraving as he is the curative power of the stone itself—so much so that one cannot be absolutely certain that the serpent he knew about was lion-headed, for some Chnoumis gems are simply radiate serpents with normal serpent heads. But more superstitious souls stuck closer to what (as we shall see) was surely the original lion-headed design that Nechepso prescribed, a work with which Galen was obviously intimately familiar.[49]

---

[49]On the passage from Galen and other ancient writers see Bonner, *Studies in Magical Amulets* 53-55 (Bonner, who offers a rendering of Galen's witness, twice mistranslates στόμα τῆς γαστρός, once with "oesophagus" and later with "cardiac orifice"; he also assumes that Galen hung the necklace around his neck); King, *The Gnostics and their Remains* 218-220; Drexler, "Knuphis" 1262.56-1263.15. Of the two passages in Marcellus (a physician of Theodosius' time) the one (20.98; 208.22-24 Helmreich) follows Galen closely, adding only that the serpent is to have seven rays (as many, though by no means all, Chnoumis serpents do on the surviving amulets), and the other (24.7; 244.26-28 Helmreich) recommends inscription of what is recognizable as the Chnoumis symbol. Important though it obviously was, the doctors and the lapidaries do not seem to agree on the type or the hue of the stone to be employed (although our knowledge of what minerals and colors they meant by the terms they use is inadequate), and the extant amulets themselves comprise a great variety of minerals (see Bonner, *Studies in Magical Amulets* 59-60 on this). For the work of Socrates and Dionysius *On Stones* consult the edition of Josef Mesk, "Ein unedierter Tractat ΠΕΡΙ ΛΙΘΩΝ, *WS* 20 (1898) 309-321. The passage of interest (320.30-321.7) offers two prescriptions, one using λίθος ὀνυχίτης . . . λευκὸς καὶ διαυγὴς δι' ὅλου καθάπερ ἀήρ, upon which is to be chiseled "a coiling serpent with the forepart or the head of a lion, and rays" and which aids the digestion, the other using λίθος ὀνυχίτης . . . μέλας τῇ ὄψει δι' ὅλου requiring a "Χνούβιος with three heads" and beneficial to pregnant or nursing women. The three-headed serpent will emerge later when the Orphic tradition is examined, whence the serpent here.

The second reason for Chnoumis' popularity presupposes the first. At some point, probably in the first half of the third century A.D., though perhaps earlier, Chnoumis underwent assimilation with the serpent Glycon, whose oracle was founded by one Alexander late in the reign of Antoninus Pius (mid-second century) and situated at Abonouteichos in Paphlagonia on the southern shore of the Black Sea. The cult met with astonishing success, in part through the conversion of gullible and high-placed Roman officials like Rutilianus; Lucian of Samosata, whose stinging invective *Alexander, or, The False Prophet* is our chief source for the whole business, ruefully admits that the cult swept the entire Roman world (*Alexander* 2 generally, with specifics in 24, 30-31, 36-37 on an oracle sent "everywhere in the Roman Empire" during the Great Plague, and 48 for its influence even with Marcus Aurelius). Inscriptions from the Danube area show that Lucian is not exaggerating here.

Now Chnoumis and Glycon were kindred spirits. In the first place they somewhat resembled one another, for Glycon was, as I said, an enormous serpent for whose oracular consultations Alexander had rigged up a contraption to make its head look vaguely human (ἀνθρωπόμορφόν τι *Alexander* 12). Coins of Abonouteichos—and of Nicomedia as well, where Glycon was identified with a local serpent of similar function—confirm the accuracy of this information. Gems showing human-headed serpents could with greater confidence be avowed portraits of Glycon were such forms for deities not already a long-standing tradition in Egypt.[50] But more

---

[50]Human-headed serpents on gems: Adolf Furtwängler, *Die antiken Gemmen. Geschichte der Steinschneidekunst im klassischen Altertum* I (Amsterdam: Hakkert and Osnabroeck: Zeller, 1964 [1900]) pl. 64 #24 with II (1965 [1900]) 291; Bonner, *Studies in Magical Amulets* ##95-96 (pl. 5, p. 268), especially the latter where the humanness of its head is certain and the reverse bears the remains of the Chnoumis symbol. In Ptolemaic times Isis and Sarapis came to be represented with the bodies of cobras: see, for example, W. Drexler, "Isis," Roscher 2.536.61-537.15 with the illustration; G. J. K. Kater-Sibbes, *Preliminary Catalogue of Sarapis Monuments* (EPRO 36; Leiden: Brill, 1973) mon. 456 (p. 80 with pl. 14); Wilhelm Hornbostel, *Sarapis. Studien zur Überlieferungsgeschichte, den Erscheinungsformen und Wandlungen der Gestalt eines Gottes* (EPRO 32; Leiden: Brill, 1973) 296-298 with pl. 191; Françoise Dunand, *Le culte d'Isis dans le bassin oriental de la Méditerranée* I. *Le culte d'Isis et les Ptolémées* (EPRO 26; Leiden: Brill, 1973) pls. 26-28 with pp. 90-92 on Isis-Thermouthis. One can see at work here the influence of Agathodaimon, the city god of Alexandria, that serpentine embodiment of good fortune which, shaped by the Machiavellian hands of the Ptolemies, cleverly fused

important is the fact that both gods were healers. On numismatic evidence Abonouteichos seems to have been a center of worship of Asclepius even before Alexander's arrival with Glycon (and recall that Chnoumis appears on the reverse of a gem showing Asclepius and Hygieia); Glycon is naturally then a new incarnation of the god of healing (*Alexander* 10, 13-14, 43) and frequently prescribes medical treatments for the ailing (*Alexander* 22, 24, 28, 53). In one case, moreover, it is specifically for a man complaining of stomach pain that Glycon suggests a regimen (*Alexander* 25). It was, I suggest, upon this medical foundation—with help, of course, from their physical resemblance—that the corporate merger of Chnoumis and Glycon took place. That it took place is beyond doubt, for whether or not on a coin of Abonouteichos minted under Geta (A.D. 211-212) Glycon possesses Chnoumis' lion's head or only a dog's (dogs were common as healers in the cult of Asclepius), a gem exists whose obverse shows the lion-headed Chnoumis serpent, and in the field are clearly

---

the tutelary roles of the serpent in Greece and Egypt into one divinity. Hence Isis and Sarapis, as protectors, healers, saviors, givers of blessings, could readily graft themselves onto an essentially faceless but decidedly serpentine Agathodaimon. Note Sarapis-Agathodaimon, a human-headed serpent, on a gem Delatte-Derchain, *Les intailles magiques* #223, pp. 169-170, bearing the inscription ἡ χάρις τῶν φορούντις, of which, however uncouth its Greek, the meaning is quite clear. Agathodaimon himself, then, becomes human-headed: see Martin P. Nilsson, *Geschichte der griechische Religion* II. *Die hellenistische und römische Zeit* (HAW 5.2; 2nd ed.; München: Beck, 1961) 213-218; Ganschinietz, "Agathodaimon," PWSup 3.57.59-58.2, and generally the whole article for the other points raised here. Given the morphological and functional similarities (and the astrological basis of the latter will be made clear later) between Chnoumis and Agathodaimon, and given the association of Nechepso (whose interest in Chnoumis is already attested by Galen and will be further elucidated later) with the tradition, the Κνοῦφις equated with ʾΑγαθὸς Δαίμων by the thirteenth century Byzantine scholar Michael Italikos' source in ὅσα Κνοῦφις ὁ παρ' ἐκείνοις ʾΑγαθὸς Δαίμων παρέδωκε καὶ ὁ τούτου μαθητὴς ἐφιλοσόφησεν ῎Οσιρις (Ernestus Riess, *Nechepsonis et Petosiridis Fragmenta Magica; Philologus,* Supplementband 6; Bonn: Georgi, 1890; Testimonia #11, p. 32) may refer not to the ram-headed god Chnum (whose name does occur in Greek and earlier in a Meroitic inscription in this form) as Drexler, "Knuphis" 1250.9-20; Jacoby, "Ein Berliner Chnoubisamulett" 271; and Reitzenstein, *Poimandres* 125-126, 132-134, give grounds for thinking but rather to our Chnoumis.

inscribed XNOYBIΣ ΓΛΥΚΩΝΑ ΙΑΩ together with the familiar Chnoumis symbol.[51]

But where did this lion-headed serpent Chnoumis come from in the first place? Two texts ascribed to the authorship of Hermes Trismegistos, that great impresario of Egyptian mysteries for the Graeco-Roman world, reveal that Chnoumis' original home is in the Egyptian astrological tradition; specifically, he is the first decan of the constellation Leo. The first tract, which is superscribed Τοῦ 'Ερμοῦ πρὸς 'Ασκλήπιον ἡ λεγομένη ἱερὰ βίβλος, has the following entry for this decan:[52]

---

[51] For this gem see Delatte-Derchain, *Les intailles magiques* #82, pp. 67-68, as well as the literature on Alexander of Abonouteichos, of which the following are the most important: E. Babelon, "Le faux prophète Alexandre d'Abonotichos," *RNum* 4 (1900) 1-30 with pl. 1 (valuable for its treatment of the coins); Franz Cumont, *Alexandre d'Abonotichos. Un épisode de l'histoire de paganisme au IIe siècle de notre ère* (MCARB 40; Bruxelles: Académie Royale de Belgique, 1887); "Glykon," PW 7.1468-1469; Samson Eitrem, *Orakel und Mysterien am Ausgang der Antike* (Zürich: Rhein, 1947) 73-86 (Chapter VIII: "Der Orakelgründer in Paphlagonien"); A. D. Nock, "Alexander of Abonuteichos," *CQ* 22 (1928) 160-162; Marcel Caster, *Études sur Alexandre, ou le faux prophète, de Lucien* (Paris: "Belles Lettres," 1938), the best full study with a good translation and copious notes; W. Drexler, "Glykon," Roscher 1.1692-1693; Arthur Stein, "Zu Lukians Alexandros," *Strena Buliciana. Commentationes gratulatoriae Francisco Bulić . . . oblatae a discipulis et amicis* (Zagreb/Split: Narodnih novina, 1924) 257-265; Otto Weinreich, "Alexandros der Lügenprophet und seine Stellung in der Religiosität des II. Jahrhunderts nach Christus," *NJbb* 47 (1912) 129-151, reprinted in his *Ausgewählte Schriften* I, #90 (ed. G. Wille; Amsterdam: Grüner, 1969) 520-551, especially interesting because it alone addresses the question of predecessors for Glycon as a human-headed snake and finds them in Alexandrian portraits of Isis, Sarapis, Agathodaimon, and others (*Ausgewählte Schriften* I, 539-540). What may be another sculptured portrait of Glycon has been discovered in excavation of ancient Tomis in Pontus, not far from Abonouteichos: reproduced in Ramsay MacMullen, *Paganism in the Roman Empire* (New Haven and London: Yale University Press, 1981) 120-121.

[52] Joannes Baptista Cardinalis Pitra, *Analecta sacra spicilegio Solesmensi parata* V.2 (Farnborough: Gregg, 1967 [1888]) 287; better C.-É. Ruelle, "Hermès Trismégiste, Le livre sacré sur les décans. Texte, variantes et traduction française," *RPh* 32 (1908) 260.104-109 with translation p. 261. Wilhelm Gundel prints a German translation in his *Dekane und Dekansternbilder. Ein Beitrag zur Geschichte der Sternbilder der Kulturvölker* (2nd ed.; Darmstadt: Wissenschaftliche Buchgesellschaft,

This decan has the name Chnoumos. Its shape comprises the
face of a lion with solar rays, and its whole body is that of a
serpent, coiling (*v.l.* fiery-looking), standing erect. It rules
diseases which afflict the area of the heart. Engrave this
decan on agate stone, set it in whatever setting you choose
with (a piece of) the "lion-foot" plant underneath it, and wear
it while abstaining from hens' (?) eggs.

The second text, preserved only in Latin, offers this description at the
appropriate juncture:[53]

The first decan of Leo has the face of Saturn. Its name is
Zaloias. It rules the stomach. It is a big serpent in the form of
a lion; it (the serpent) has solar rays around its head.

Not only do the name preserved by the Greek text and both descriptions
of the decan precisely match that of the figure on the gem amulets, but
the region of the body over which they exercise control is identical with
that served by Chnoumis on the gems. That the Greek text centers on
καρδία is no matter; at a time when the function and relationships of the
internal organs of the human body were little known, distinctions are hazy
at best, and Greek medicine called gastric distress "heartburn" (καρδι-
αλγία), just as we still do.

Furthermore, the Hermetic texts reveal the source of the tradition
ascribing curative powers to Chnoumis: the Hellenistic Egyptian decanal
melothesia. In late Egyptian astrology the decans became ἄγγελοι of a
ruthless Εἱμαρμένη; they are called κοσμοκράτορες and φύλακες ἀκριβεῖς

1969) 376 with 160 (#13). Note that in this Hermetic text the third decan
of Cancer, that which immediately precedes the first of Leo, bears the
name Χνοῦφος and rules the spleen. For medical reasons (Cancer and Leo
both governed the same general area of the body: see further n. 55 below)
and for other reasons to be discussed later (surrounding the similarity of
their names) the two decans were closely enough related to collapse into
one; hence, in part at least, the variant ΧΝΟΥΦΙΣ on the extant amulets.
Note too on the Greek Hermetic tract Drexler, "Knuphis" 1262.14-35;
A.-J. Festugière, *La révélation d'Hermès Trismégiste* I. *L'astrologie et les
sciences occultes* (3rd ed.; Paris: Gabalda, 1950) 139-143.

[53] Wilhelm Gundel, *Neue astrologische Texte des Hermes Trismegistos.
Funde und Forschungen auf dem Gebeit der antiken Astronomie und
Astrologie* (*ABAW.PH* 12 [1936]) 21.1-3 with pp. 115-123; translation in
Dekane und Dekansternbilder 381 with p. 160 (#13).

καὶ ἐπίσκοποι τοῦ παντός dishing out good or evil fortune to men.[54] In conjunction with the distribution among the decans (as parts of the zodiacal constellations) of lordship over sections of the human frame from head to toe (and cp. CG II, *1 Apoc. John* 15 [63].29-18 [66].2), this development assigned to these astral dictators the power either to afflict or to heal (to cease to afflict) the parts of the body over which they exercised individual control.[55]

The great Hellenistic manual of decan therapeutics, upon which Galen relied and to which the two Hermetic works cited above are somehow related, was foisted upon king Nechepso, the last native monarch of Egypt, and his priest Petosiris, but the work is probably to be dated to the second century B.C. In it, according to Firmicus Maternus (*Instruction*

---

[54](W.) Gundel, *Dekane und Dekansternbilder* 27-28, 227-229 citing the *Testament of Solomon* (whose archetype Gundel dates to the first century B.C. and whose dependence on old tradition he establishes: *Dekane und Dekansternbilder* 49 with the stemmata pp. 45 and 92) and Hermetica preserved by Stobaeus, and generally pp. 299-305, 313-324; further his "Dekane," PWSup 7.117.29-34, 118.39-50. On the melothesia generally see, e.g., Bouché-Leclercq, *L'astrologie grecque* 319-325; Otto Neugebauer, "Melothesia and Dodecatemoria," *Studia Biblica et Orientalia* III (*Oriens Antiquus*) (AnBib 12; Roma: Pontificio Istituto Biblico, 1959) 270-275.

[55]Bouché-Leclercq, *L'astrologie grecque* 319, 323 n. 3, 438 n. 2; (H.) Gundel, "Zodiakos" 579.28-582.64 (note Firmicus Maternus, *Instruction* 2.24, cited 580.62 allotting *pectus et stomachus* to Leo); Drexler, "Knuphis" 1261.41-1262.14 citing the Theban astrologer Hephaestion, for whom χνουμις is the third decan of Cancer and χαρχνουμις the first of Leo (more on this later): Cancer rules the breast and the sides; those born under its third decan will be προγάστωρ and will have πόνους . . . περὶ τὰ σπλάγχμα; Leo rules the heart and the area around it; its first decan causes ἐμπνευμάτωσις (flatulence? lung trouble?) in its natives; and "Knuphis" 1262.35-1263.6 referring to Celsus in Origen, *Against Celsus* 8.58 (274.23-31 Koetschau; H. Chadwick, *Origen, Contra Celsum* 496: "They [the Egyptians] say that the body of man has been put under the charge of thirty-six daemons, or ethereal gods of some sort, who divide it between them, ... And they know the names of the daemons in the local dialect, such as Chnoumen, Chnachoumen [χνουμην, χναχουμην], ... And by invoking these they heal the sufferings of the various parts."), to Firmicus Maternus, and to the medical texts. Further (W.) Gundel, "Leo" 1990.27-56; "Dekane" 120.11-61; *Dekane und Dekansternbilder* 43, the stemmata 45 and 92, and especially 231-233, 262-277 with the tables pp. 286-287 and translations pp. 373-374, 409-411.

4.22.2), Nechepso maintained that the decans possess "great authority and power" and that "by them all fortunate and unfortunate events are decreed"; the monarch accordingly was gracious enough to provide mankind with a compendium detailing which decan by what means could be made to effect the cure of the part of the body that belonged to him.

Galen and the two Hermetic astrological texts securely place the lion-headed serpent Chnoumis in the setting of Hellenistic Egyptian iatro-mathematical science.[56] But how Chnoumis acquired this form is something of a puzzle; it certainly was not his (hers?) from the beginning. The *Salmeschoiniaka*, a yet earlier Egyptian seasonal calendar prognosticating the events—mostly catastrophes both personal (including illness) and social—caused by each decan's successive hegemony, a work upon which Nechepso-Petosiris seems to have drawn for its medical purposes, may

---

[56](W.) Gundel, *Dekane und Dekansternbilder* 48, 238, 269. The decans frequently figure in the Greek magical papyri fron Egypt, in part exactly because the magicians to whom the grimoires belonged were, as controllers of demonic powers, practitioners hired to exorcize them and so to relieve the ailments which their agents the decans inflicted upon the magicians' clients. Hence in *PGM* II P 50 recto 7-9 one reads of the first decan of Leo (in the form of its name which Hephaestion registers) καὶ εἰς τὸν κλῆρον / τόνδε πι χαι ρχι ν ιού ιμεος ι / ὁ περὶ φαρμακείας πίπτων τάδε ὅμοια / ἐνεργήσει; for the restoration see Karl Preisendanz's review of Gundel's *Dekane und Dekansternbilder* in *GGA* 201 (1939) 140 supporting Karl Schmidt; Hans Georg Gundel, *Weltbild und Astrologie in den griechischen Zauberpapyri* (München: Beck, 1968) 21. Another reference to the lion-headed decan probably underlies a common incantatory sequence, where an identification with Horus is assumed: Ἀρουῆρ (i.e., "Horus the Elder") Χνουφ at *PGM* I P 4.1576 and, more usually, the ἁρπον χνουφι or χνουφι formula: see (H.) Gundel, *Weltbild und Astrologie* 21; (W.) Gundel, *Dekane und Dekansternbilder* 288-289; Delatte, "Amulettes inédites" 69, noting in *PGM* I P 4.2199 the word division αρ πενχνουβι; Paul Perdrizet, " ΒΡΙΝΤΑΤΗΝΩΦΡΙΣ: l'un des noms magiques du dieu Chnum," *Mélanges Maspero* II. *Orient grec, romain et byzantin* (Le Caire: IFAO, 1934-1937) 137-144; Jacoby, "Ein Berliner Chnubisamulett" 271 with notes; Reitzenstein, *Poimandres* 143; and lately Delatte-Derchain, *Les intailles magiques* #89bis, pp. 72-73, citing Perdrizet; Dierk Wortmann, "Kosmogonie und Nilflut. Studien zu einigen Typen magischer Gemmen griechisch-römischer Zeit aus Ägypten," *BJbb* 166 (1966) 87-88. Scholars are largely in agreement that in all these cases—including the gems—the Egyptian god Chnum is meant, but this is at best only possibly and even then marginally accurate. I will return to the subject later.

have been the source of Nechepso-Petosiris's and Hermes Trismegistos'
description of Chnoumis' looks, but there is no way to be sure, as the
miserable remains of the only fragment (POxy 465) do not include the
month involving Leo, and, what is more, the *Salmeschoiniaka*'s descriptions which do survive (from Aquarius and Pisces) do not match very
closely, if at all, the decans subsumed under these zodiacal signs in the
Hermetic texts.[57]

In any case, the classical Egyptian predecessor of the lion-headed,
serpentine decan of Nechepso-Petosiris and the astrological Hermetica is
not so formed. The integration of the early Egyptian star-groups, which
measured the hours of the night, into the zodiacal signs as "decans" is a
late development, and, in truth, the original star-group which later
became the Chnoumis-Charchnoumis decans, its native Egyptian name
being *Knm.(t)*,[58] cannot be identified in terms of the animal it

---

[57](W.) Gundel, *Dekane und Dekansternbilder* 45 and 92 (the stemmata),
96-97, 229-230, 267-268, 302, with a translation of POxy #465 on pp. 413-
414. For the text with an English translation and notes see the original
edition by B. P. Grenfell and A. S. Hunt, *The Oxyrhynchus Papyri* III
(London: Oxford University Press, 1903) 126-137. The "remarkable degree"
of correspondence which Grenfell and Hunt (p. 137) discern between the
Salmeschoiniaka's decans and those of the Greek Hermetic text is not at
all remarkable; Gundel is more cautious. Gundel (*Dekane und
Dekansternbilder* 96) does remark upon the *Salmeschoiniaka*'s attribution
of "a tongue and a face that is fire" to what seems to have been its third
decan of Aquarius, adding (p. 96 n. 1): "Das Feueratmen und das feurige
Gesicht sind typische Attribute der hellenistischen Gestirngötter." *Apoc.
John*'s endowment of its Chnoumis-demiurge with eyes that shoot
lightning is thus possibly a reminiscence of his astral roots, just as is also
the case with the constant association of the leonine demiurge with fire in
Gnostic texts (and recall Rev 9:17 in a patently astrological context). The
Testament of Solomon, whose decans are correctly θηριοπρόσωπα, δρα-
κοντόμορφα, attests early Jewish assimilation of this decanal attribute:
the decans are also πυροειδῆ (*Test. Sol.* 18.1 in McCown's manuscript N,
p. 119 of his edition), with which one may compare the identical *varia
lectio* in the Greek Hermetic text translated just now. On the λεοντοπρό-
σωπος deity which the *Salmeschoiniaka* (line 162 of the papyrus) associates
with Pisces see Gundel, *Dekane und Dekansternbilder* 97.

[58]With *Knm.(t)* were anciently associated other stars or star-groups
identified by their position with respect to it (they are even grouped
together on some lists): for example, *tpy-ᶜ Knm.(t)*, "(the one) before
Knm.(t)," which eventually lost its separate existence, and *ḥry
(ḫpd) Knm.(t)*, "(the one) under (the hind part of) *Knm.(t)*," which survived

represented, but whatever it was, it was not a lion-headed serpent.[59]

---

into the Greek tradition as χαρχνουμις (Hephaestion), χναχουμην (Origen), χαρχνουμης (Kamateros), χραχνουβις and χολχνουβις (on gem-amulets). On the Greek attempts to transcribe *ḫry (ḫpd) Knm.(t)* see (W.) Gundel, "Leo" 1989.27-43; *Dekane und Dekansternbilder* 77, 79 (#13 in the tables of the names of the decans); Bonner, *Studies in Magical Amulets* 55, 59; on the original Egyptian complex around *Knm.(t)* see O. Neugebauer and Richard A. Parker, *Egyptian Astronomical Texts* I. *The Early Decans* (Providence, RI: Brown University Press, and London: Humphries, 1960) 25 on ##31a-34; *Egyptian Astronomical Texts* III. *Decans, Planets, Constellations and Zodiacs* (Providence, RI: Brown University Press, and London: Humphries, 1969) 106-107, 119, 129 (all ##1-3), 135 (##3-4), 14 (##1-2), 157 and 160 (##1-4). If in some Greek decan lists and on some gems the first of Leo is χαρ-χνουμις and the like it is because *ḫry (ḫpd) Knm.(t)*—with the noun *ḫpd* omitted as in the Tanis list of decans (Neugebauer-Parker, *Egyptian Astronomical Texts* III, 142 [#2], 169-170), a list which greatly influenced the Greek tradition—survived as a separate decan. Still, the decan *Knm.(t)* itself seems to have been recognized, as indeed it actually is, for the core of the cluster, since in a horoscope on a papyrus of the first century A.D. *ḫry (ḫpd) Knm.(t)* is absorbed by or subsumed under *Knm.(t)* in the form χνουμε ḫραχνουμ: (W.) Gundel, *Dekane und Dekansternbilder* 46, 77 (in the decan table), and translation pp. 408-409; Neugebauer-Parker, *Egyptian Astronomical Texts* III, 171—especially the latter work, as the readings which Gundel prints are imperfect and contradictory. Hence the prominence of the name Χνουμις (and variants) on the gems.

[59]Neugebauer-Parker, *Egyptian Astronomical Texts* I, 25; S. Schott in (W.) Gundel, *Dekane und Dekansternbilder* 4. The feminine ending *.t*, which disappears in Graeco-Roman times, indicates what its sex originally was. One element, at least, of the native Egyptian tradition for representation of the *Knm.(t)* decan was assiduously if somewhat crudely preserved by the gem-amulets of later times, and that is the symbol which regularly accompanies the Chnoumis-serpent; as Drexler already rightly observed ("Knuphis" 1264.5-29), on Ptolemaic temples at Dendera, Edfu and Philae *Knm.(t)* is represented by a serpent standing on its tail, its body crossed by three smaller serpents (my pl. 6b, with which cp. pl. 5e): Neugebauer-Parker, *Egyptian Astronomical Texts* III, monuments 49, 50a, 53 and 59 with pp. 135 (#3), 157 and 160 (#2) with pls. 30A (Edfu), 33 and 41 (Dendera), and 57 (Philae). A. A. Barb, in his review of Delatte-Derchain, *Les intailles magiques* (*Gnomon* 41 [1969] 302), goes astray when he explains the Chnoumis-symbol as "die kursive Form desselben semitischen N . . . , durchstrichen, um das SSS (ebenso wie auch oft das griechische Z auf diesen Steinen) nicht als Buchstaben, sondern als Siegel

Indeed, uncertainty about the identity of *Knm.(t)* must have been at least partially responsible for the adoption of a totally new body for the decan when the iatromathematical tradition made its depiction a necessity.

So where did the lion-headed serpent come from? Many features of Egyptian astrology certainly favored this new form. There is first the fact that when in the Hellenistic period the integration of the ancient Egyptian decans into the zodiacal signs took place, the *Knm.(t)* group, as originally leading off the series,[60] became part of Leo as beginning the Egyptian year,[61] and so it was natural that the first decan of Leo might acquire a

---

zu charakterisieren." There is no question, then, about the gems' Chnoumis being in name and in symbol a direct descendant of the *Knm.(t)* decan. Another interesting feature of Neugebauer-Parker's Seti I B family of decans, a feature which, together with the Chnoumis symbol and a peculiarity of the Dendera F list about to be mentioned, further suggests that it was chiefly from Ptolemaic examples of this family that Nechepso-Petosiris, the Hermetica, and eventually the gem-amulets drew their information, is the coordination of the decans with particular minerals in "sympathy" with them: *Egyptian Astronomical Texts* III, 134 (Dendera A and D), 135 (#3) with *Knm.(t)* given, according to Neugebauer-Parker, the garnet; Drexler, "Knuphis" 1264.29-46, citing an older generation of scholars (Brugsch, Lepsius, and Wendel) who think the mineral intended is red jasper or amethyst, precisely the stone (or the color stone) used in the majority of surviving Chnoumis amulets. See n. 49 for the problems connected with this matter.

[60]Neugebauer-Parker, *Egyptian Astronomical Texts* I, 37-42, on a cosmological papyrus of the second century A.D., 47-48 for a translation of the relevant section of the text, and generally 95-97; *Egyptian Astronomical Texts* III, 106-107, 119, 129, and 141-142 for the earlier texts in which the *Knm.(t)* group heads the list, with pp. 168-174 on the decans as parts of the zodiac. Origen, *Against Celsus* 8.58, is following good tradition when his enumeration begins χνουμην, χναχουμην.

[61]See note 29 and further Wortmann, "Kosmogonie und Nilflut" 80-82 with notes and the primary source material cited there. Wortmann (p. 86 with n. 155) correctly explains the confusion evident in assignment of *Knm.(t)/ḥry (ḥpd) Knm.(t)* to the last decan of Cancer/first decan of Leo (see nn. 52 and 55 above) as precisely due to fluctuation of fixing the beginning of the year, since the Nile-flood actually began when the sun was in Cancer, but it was traditionally linked to the heliacal rising of Sothis/Sirius, which occurred very soon after the sun's entry into Leo. In the Chnoumis-amulets Wortmann (p. 90) sees reference to the Nile-flood and its life-renewing powers, then, but, insofar as this thesis neglects the decan-melothesia and the iatromathematical science it supported, it is

lion's head. What is more, the deity which accompanies or represents *ḥry*
(ḥpd) Knm.(t) in two groups of decan lists (19th Dynasty) is Sekhmet, a
lion-headed goddess (her importance will become more apparent later),
and in Neugebauer-Parker's Seti I B family of decans (that whose depiction of *Knm.(t)* is the ancestor of the gems' Chnoumis symbol) by a similarly lion-headed goddess (Sekhmet again probably) with the uraeus-
serpent on her head.[62] Lion-headed gods or goddesses and serpents are, in
fact—and again particularly in the Seti I B family of decans—so frequently the deities associated with the decans that in one list of this
family (Dendera F, Roman period) every one of twelve pairs of decans is
associated with a cat- (or is it a lion-?) headed serpent (pl. 6c), which has
thus become a figure for all decans generally.[63] Finally, there are Hellenistic Egyptian portraits of Leo itself, which, as I have already pointed out
(in conjunction with pl. 4d, and cp. pl. 10b), is regularly shown in close
conjunction with a serpent.[64]

All of these motifs must have had a hand in influencing the selection of
a body for Chnoumis.[65] But the *Knm.(t)* group's patron goddess Sekhmet is

---

misleading. De Wit, *Le rôle et le sens du lion* 396-399, and Bonneau, *La
crue du Nil* 303-305, list ancient Egyptian associations of the flooding of
the Nile with the lion, associations which are not astrologically based but
which must have favored Leo when later the Babylonian zodiac was integrated into the tradition.

[62] Neugebauer-Parker, *Egyptian Astronomical Texts* III, 107 (#3), 129
(#3), 135 (#4), 155: Sekhmet under her title "Pre-eminent-in-Khas."
Depictions of Sekhmet: Lanzone, *Dizionario di mitologia egizia* 1098-1107
with pls. 363-364.

[63] S. Schott in (W.) Gundel, *Dekane und Dekansternbilder* 13; De Wit, *Le
Rôle et le sens du lion* 391-393; Neugebauer-Parker, *Egyptian Astronomical Texts* III, 2, 134-139 with pls. 30A, 33, 57; Dendera F: pp. 84-85 and
134 ("Only Dendera F uses a conventional figure, for pairs of decans,
made up of a cat head on a rearing serpent") with pl. 38B.

[64] Neugebauer-Parker, *Egyptian Astronomical Texts* III, 203-204 generally and 209 for Leo specifically. The Egyptians already knew a constellation Lion (my pl. 5a) long before, in later times, they adopted the Babylonian zodiacal system (Neugebauer-Parker, *Egyptian Astronomical Texts*
III, 183, 192-193 with figs. 27-31; [W.] Gundel, *Dekane und Dekansternbilder* 333). Its name, *nṯr-rw*, "god-lion," "lion-god," or *rw-nṯry*, "divine
lion," bears comparison with what was said earlier of אַרְיֵאל though influence from the Egyptian astrological tradition is doubtful.

[65] (W.) Gundel, "Leo" 1989.58-68; "Sternbilder, Sternglaube und Sternsymbolik" 954.59-61, holds that its body is the uraeus-serpent and that its

the real source of the new depiction. There is another very closely related realm to be reckoned with here, one in which the lion-headed serpent was common, and that is the world of magic, especially as it was applied to healing. It stands to reason that this powerful force in Egyptian culture should have exerted a great influence upon Nechepso-Petosiris and the Hermetic texts of its ilk because as ἰατρομαθηματικοί, their authors were, in effect, wedding the new astrology to the ancient Egyptian art of popular, magically oriented medicine. Here the useful characteristics of the lion and the serpent lay in their capacity to frighten off, to repel; the very things which made them so terrifying could, if controlled, be put to good use as weapons against inimical powers.[66]

The serpent uraeus (identified with the goddess Wadjet) had served this function since time immemorial in Egypt, spitting her venomous fire from Pharaoh's brow against his enemies; she had been gratefully granted the title wr.t ḥk3w "Great in magic," for her protective role. And the lion had served this function too. As sphinx the lion-king mauled his foes, a motif

---

head was borrowed from the feline of whose sign the decan became a part. The fact that Chnoumis' head is always radiate (rays or flames) assures, at least partially, a solar connection for the leonine element, Leo being the house of the sun and the fire sign *par excellence*: so Delatte, "Sphère magique du Musée d'Athènes" 262-263, noting as well the solar significance of the serpent ouroboros, which, I might add, also appears on amulets with the head of a lion: Mouterde, "Le Glaive de Dardanos" 72, with ʼΙάω πάντων δεσπότης inscribed inside it (my pl. 7a); Delatte-Derchain, *Les intailles magiques* #500, p. 330, also inscribed ΙΑΩ.

[66]Hopfner, "Der Tierkult der alten Ägypter" 42-43, states this point well: ". . . der Kult des Löwen ging bei der Urbevölkerung Ägyptens . . . sicherlich nur auf die Furcht und das Entsetzen zurück, das der König der Tiere überall bei seinem Erscheinen einflösste und das ihn als furchtbaren Dämon erscheinen liess . . . . Fürchtete man einerseits die ungeheure tödliche Kraft, die dem Tierdämon innewohnte, und suchte man sie von sich selbst abzuwenden, so hat man andererseits sicherlich den Wunsch gehegt, diesen gewaltigen Dämon für sich zu gewinnen und seine Kraft und Macht gegen Feinde wenden zu können. So bildete sich die Anschauung heraus, dass im Löwen auch ein schützender Dämon wohnen könne." The lion, like all powerful forces, is of ambivalent value; one's attitude toward it depends on whither its force is directed. What made the lion and the serpent perfect embodiments of demonic powers or symbols of more human enemies for the Psalmists of the Old Testament and for the chain of tradition they spawned is exactly what made these animals favorites of Egyptian sorcerers.

in the New Kingdom widely employed, in what may be taken to be magical contexts, for the purpose of conjuring a royal victory. The lion's awesome power made it an indispensable element in other classical Egyptian circles, official and more humble as well, where magic was applied, whether as a weapon to wield or a threat to avert.[67] From the uraeus-

---

[67] King as lion (in addition to more general references in n. 27): Hopfner, "Der Tierkult der alten Ägypter" 46; "Löwe," *RÄRG* 428-429; E. Hornung, "Die Bedeutung des Tieres im alten Ägypten," *StGen* 20 (1967) 76-78; Hermann Kees, *Die Götterglaube im alten Ägypten* (3rd ed.; Berlin: Akademie-Verlag, 1977) 4-6, 110; Schweitzer, *Löwe und Sphinx* 18-21, 32-36, 41-45, 58-63, 70-71 with pls. 9.5, 10.1-8, 15.1-6, and fig. 2; de Wit, *Le rôle et le sens du lion* 16-34, 39-56. Egyptian personal names can include the lion for the same reasons as those outlined for other cultures earlier in this chapter; in Egypt they refer either to the king or to a god: Hermann Ranke, "Tiernamen als Personennamen bei den Ägyptern," *ZÄS* 60 (1925) 77. The motif of Pharaoh as a sphinx trampling the enemies of Egypt begins with the great conquerors of the 18th Dynasty: Schweitzer, *Löwe und Sphinx* 61-62; de Wit, *Le rôle et le sens du lion* 43-51. The lion trampling the enemy in magical or quasi-magical contexts: de Wit, *Le rôle et le sens du lion* 34-36, 413; Lanzone, *Dizionario di mitologia egizia* 653.4 on a scarab; and thence down into the late antique magical tradition, where the prostrate man whom the lion is trampling (my pl. 7b-d) must simply be whatever it is that is threatening or opposing the possessor, or represent the vengeance carried out against his enemies: Bonner, *Studies in Magical Amulets* ##212-213 (pl. 10, pp. 288-289), 225 (pl. 11, p. 291), 241 (pl. 11, p. 293), and generally p. 151, where Bonner calls the prostrate body a mummy, which it is not; Delatte-Derchain, *Les intailles magiques* ##122-124, pp. 98-99, with p. 93 for an explanation, and also ##257-260, pp. 194-196, where it is Nemesis—inescapable retribution—who does the trampling (see pp. 193-194 in introduction to these gems); A. Merlin, "Note sur une intaille gnostique," *BCTH* (1919) 216-218, inscribed ΙΑΩ ΣΑΒΑΩ ΑΛΩΝΕ; A. Delatte, "Études sur la magie grecque III. Amulettes mithriaques," *MB* 18 (1914) 13-14, noting that in an ἀγωγή-spell, *PGM* I P 4.2130-2136, the magician recommends making a ring with just such an engraving on it: ". . . a ring, upon which you are to inscribe a headless lion . . . and he is to be trampling with his paws a skeleton, in such a way that his right (front) paw tramples the skull of the skeleton . . ."; "Amulettes inédites" 43 and n. 1, where, although Delatte flatly says: "Le sens de ces représentations est resté obscur," he astutely observes: "ce cadavre doit être l'image d'une maladie vaincue par le dieu." Wortmann, "Kosmogonie und Nilflut" 83, sees in the group Helios-Horus overcoming the enemies of Osiris. Amulets showing a lion with his front paw on what appears to be the skull of an animal are probably to be interpreted along the same lines,

goddess and in part for the similarity of their apotropaic function, the lion and many leonine deities (particularly Sekhmet) acquired fiery looks or fiery breaths (cp. pls. 5b, 7d) as expressions of their vengeful anger, the ferocious punishment which burnt the reprobate to a cinder.[68]

Naturally, then, an intimate relationship developed between the lioness Sekhmet and the serpentine Wadjet; the two goddesses (and others related to them) either share attributes, become kin (Sekhmet, for example, is

---

since, as I noted earlier, the lion as an image of Death is common in similar pose in contemporary sepulchral art; for such amulets see Bonner, *Studies in Magical Amulets* ##73-75 (pl. 4, pp. 256-266—#74 is inscribed κρατῶ σε, ἔχω σε), 226 (pl. 11, p. 291) with p. 36 on the type; Delatte-Derchain, *Les intailles magiques* #319, pp. 230-231. The lion in other classical Egyptian magical contexts, often medical (e.g., against migraine): de Wit, *Le rôle et le sens du lion* 412-417.

[68]De Wit, "Les inscriptions des lions-gargouilles" 29-45; and *Le rôle et le sens du lion* 5, 84-90, for the fiery eyes and faces of the lion-spouts on the roofs of the Ptolemaic temples at Edfu and Dendera (see n. 29 above)—-the very temples where the decan lists most influential for the Hellenistic iatromathematical tradition are found. The texts describe the lions in the following terms: "Je suis le lion au visage de feu, et dont l'oeil est une flamme (contre les ennemis)" (*Le rôle et le sens du lion* 86); "Il est celui au visage terrible, aux yeux de sang, lui qui est satisfait en mettant dans la flamme ceux qui commettent le crime en son endroit, leur place est le feu" ("Les inscriptions des lions-gargouilles" 35). The lion-headed deities which also served as guardians of these same temples are named, among other things, "La flamme dont on muert de peur" (*Le rôle et le sens du lion* 382). The tradition is far older than the Hellenistic period: note *Le rôle et le sens du lion* 141: "lion redoutable, aux yeux fulgurants, maître de la flamme contre ses ennemis" in a papyrus of the New Kingdom, and p. 372 noting in the book of *What is in the Netherworld* a lion-headed goddess spitting fire into a pit filled with the damned. This lion-headed goddess is likely to be Sekhmet, the furious lioness, who was from the late Bronze Age called "mistress of flame" and given a breath of fire with which she destroyed her enemies: de Wit, *Le rôle et le sens du lion* 28, 312-322; Roeder, "Sechmet," Roscher 4.581.6-11; 584.50-55, 60-62; 585.5-12, 41-45; and especially 585.58-586.3; "Sachmet," *RÄRG* 644-645. Certain amulets of the Graeco-Roman period remember this ancient Egyptian attribute of the lion: Bonner, *Studies in Magical Amulets* ##211 (pl. 10, p. 288), where the lion's tail ends in a cobra (my pl. 7d), and 233 (pl. 11, p. 292). When astrology entered the picture and the lion became a celestial Leo, this motif was naturally given solar significance, as the gems and Horapollo, *Hieroglyphics* 1.17 (pp. 49-50 Sbordone; 58-59 van de Walle-Vergote), show.

given a son *Wr ḥk3w*), or get identified altogether, the culmination of the process being incorporation of the two mistresses of magic into a single embodiment of fury boasting Sekhmet's fire-belching head and Wadjet's cobra body (pl. 7e).[69] The lion-headed serpent continued to be a popular figure in Egyptian magic of the Hellenistic period because it was the quintessence of power; it makes appearances in conjunction with gods of the conglomerate "pantheos" type and with the stelae of "Horus on the crocodiles"—stelae whose purpose was medical in the sense that they were designed to bring healing to those who, like Horus, had been stung by noxious insects or mauled by predatory beasts and been healed by Isis' magic.[70]

---

[69]Roeder, "Sechmet" 581.42-45; 584.20-25; 586.45-587.26; 592.35-51; 592.54-593.7; "Sachmet," *RÄRG* 644-645; "Hike," *RÄRG* 301-302; "Urthekau," *RÄRG* 848; "Uto," *RÄRG* 853-854; Lanzone, *Dizionario di mitologia egizia* 172-175 with pl. 56; de Wit, *Le rôle et le sens du lion* 213-214, 243, 312, 332-333, 336-338, 348-350, 358-359, 376 and 384 (lion-headed serpents at Dendera and at Edfu), 388, 425 (Buto, the Delta cult center of Wadjet, called Leontopolis in late antiquity, because of her assimilation to Sekhmet; see also Kees, "Λεοντούπολις," PW 12.2056.63-2057.6); Schweitzer, *Löwe und Sphinx* 22 with pl. 4.1-2 (on the snake-necked lions already on the Narmer palette), 49. François Lexa, *La magie dans l'Égypte antique de l'ancien empire jusqu'à l'époque copte* I-III (Paris: Geuthner, 1925) is of no help with this detail. A lion-headed serpent is shown over the head of an otherwise fully human goddess at Philae (my pl. 8a), and the text which accompanies her portrait reads: "(Words spoken by) Wepeset, Herrin der Flamme . . . die die Feinde ihres Vaters . . . niederwirft, die ihren Flammenhauch wider die Bösen sendet: (to the king [Ptolemy XII]) Ich gebe dir die Feinde, verbrannt zu Asche und sende (meinen) Schrecken gegen deine Widersachen" (Hermann Junker und Erich Winter, *Das Geburtshaus des Tempels der Isis in Philä* [Graz-Wien-Köln: Böhlaus, 1965] 216 and 217, 11-16).

[70]De Wit, *Le rôle et le sens du lion* 219; and Lanzone, *Dizionario di mitologia egizia* 46-47 with pl. 24 (an Amun-Re "pantheos" with a lion's paws for legs and on the top of whose plumed headdress are perched lion-headed serpents spewing flame); de Wit, *Le rôle et le sens du lion* 376; and A. Moret, "Horus sauveur," *RHR* 72 (1915) pl. 6 register 29, for the lion-headed serpent on the right side of the Metternich stele, the most famous of the stelae "Horus on the crocodiles" (now in the New York Metropolitan Museum of Art: see Nora E. Scott, "The Metternich Stela," *BMMA* 9 [1951] 201-217 with excellent photographs). Moret's article (pp. 213-287); Keith C. Seele, "Horus on the Crocodiles," *JNES* 6 (1947) 43-52 with pls. 1-3; and P. Lacau, "Les statues 'guérisseuses' dans l'ancienne Égypte,"

The ultimate repositories of apotropaic grotesquerie are the Bes and sphinx "pantheos" figures which I just mentioned, and in the wild aggregation of bellicose attributes that make them up the lion is, as it always was, naturally a characteristic part of their make-up, the sphinx type essentially leonine anyway, and Bes often given leonine attributes: a lion's paws for feet, greaves of lion-masks for his knees, and even a face— already wearing a frightful grimace and maned with a heavy beard—made even more distinctly leonine by the addition of a pair of lion's ears (cp. pl. 8b).[71]

MMFP 25 (1921-1922) 189-209 with pls. 15-16, are good introductions to the subject; G. Daressy, *Catalogue général des antiquités égyptiennes du Musée de Caire, N*[OS] *9401-9499. Textes et dessins magiques* (Le Caire: IFAO, 1903) illustrates and discusses many examples of these stelae; E. Jelínková-Reymond, *Les inscriptions de la statue guérisseuse de Djed-Her-le-Sauveur* (Le Caire: IFAO, 1956), studies one in detail. One of the noxious beasts which these stelae invariably represent Horus holding by the tail is the lion (see my pl. 8b); in this case the lion's power is injurious because it is directed *against* the magician/healer (alias the god Horus) and his patient, not directed *by* him. Amulets designed to allow the wearer, dead or alive, either to fend off marauding lions or to avail himself magically of the lion's power were understandably very popular: see Adolf Erman, *Die Religion der Ägypter. Ihr Werden und Vergehen in vier Jahrtausenden* (Berlin and Leipzig: de Gruyter, 1934) 148 with fig. 58; "Löwe," *RÄRG* 429; "Amulett," *RÄRG* 29; Hopfner, "Der Tierkult der alten Ägypter" 45-46; Sir W. M. Flinders Petrie, *Amulets* (Warminster, Wiltshire: Aris & Phillips, 1975 [1914]) 41-42 (##192, 194-196, pls. 34-36), 45 (##219-222, pls. 38-39). The lion's most famous protective role for the classical Egyptian deceased is in the shape of the mummy's bier, a role that survives into the late antique magical tradition: Bonner, *Studies in Magical Amulets* ##8-10 (pl. 1, pp. 254-255; my pl. 8c) and generally pp. 25-26; "A Miscellany of Engraved Stones" #31 (pl. 35, p. 146); "Amulets chiefly in the British Museum" #5 (pl. 96, p. 321); Delatte-Derchain, *Les intailles magiques* ##120-123bis, pp. 97-99, with pp. 90-94 in introduction —in many of these gems the lion on whose back the mummy rides is also depicted trampling a prostrate man, its protective value being thereby effectively doubled; Wortmann, "Kosmogonie und Nilflut" 82, interpreting the type as the Nile flood (Osiris) brought by Leo; "Neue magische Gemmen" #8 (p. 69). Lion-headed serpents as guardians/repellers of evil: e.g., François Daumas, *Les mammisis de Dendara* (Le Caire: IFAO, 1959) pl. 57 with pp. 97-98 for their names, pls. 61-61bis with pp. 139-142 (cp. my pl. 7e).

[71]See de Wit, *Le rôle et le sens du lion* 226-229, 415; "Bes," *RÄRG* 101-

Given the enormous popularity of these "pantheos" figures in Ptolemaic and Roman Egyptian religion and with the demi-monde of magic everywhere, it would not be surprising if they too, like the lion-headed serpent their next of kin, had had some influence on the Gnostic tradition. This is especially true of the sphinx "pantheos," representing a deity which in Egyptian texts is named *Twtw* (with many variants), rendered with Τιθοης or Τοτοης by Greek-speaking Egyptians, among whom (and even in Greece itself as well, so it seems) the god enjoyed great favor; onomastics and

---

109, especially 102-103 on the god's leonine characteristics, and note p. 107: "Die Löwen, die ihn geleiten oder auf denen er gar nach Art vorderasiatischer Götter steht . . . sind ihm . . . als Genossen verbunden, denn auch sie"—like Bes in a variety of forms—"schützen den Sonnengott. . . . An ihre Stelle treten gelegentlich Sphingen, die gleichfalls dem Sonnengott heilig sind; zuweilen hat man ihnen sogar einen B.-kopf gegeben. . . ." These latter figures connect him with the sphinx "pantheos" and also explain the connection. Note further A. Piankoff, "Sur une statuette de Bès," *BIFAO* 37 (1937) 29-33 with pl.; Sethe, "Besas," PW 3.324-326; Alice Grenfell, "The Iconography of Bes, and of Phoenician Bes-Hand Scarabs," *PSBA* 24 (1902) 21-40; and lately Henri-Charles Puech, "Le dieu Bésa et la magie hellénistique," *Documents* 7 (1930) 415-425. The Bes "pantheos" in part developed from stelae of "Horus on the crocodiles," for on most examples of the latter a protective Bes' head is shown over that of Horus and grows gradually more and more enormous: see Daressy, *Textes et dessins magiques* pl. 1-10, ##9401, 9405-9410, 9412-9415, 9417-9425, 9428-9429 (the latter two Bes "pantheos" figures), with pp. 1-3, 15-37; "Bes," *RÄRG* 105-106, especially 106 on the Bes-Horus theocrasy. Bes' apotropaic connection with the lion as a sign of protection is ancient (see Schweitzer, *Löwe und Sphinx* 49, for example, on Tutankhamun's Bes-lion unguent jar, and generally "Bes," *RÄRG* 104); it continued to be crucial on Graeco-Egyptian amulets: Bonner, *Studies in Magical Amulets* #378 (pl. 21, p. 317; my pl. 8d-e), showing on the obverse a "pantheos" with lion-mask greaves, holding in one of its hands a lion and a scorpion by the tail (as on the stelae "Horus on the crocodiles"), and on the reverse the cock-headed anguipede over a lion, the group surrounded by the inscription λέων ἐμί, λέοντα φορῶ, Διός ἐμι οἰκητήριον (with pp. 246-248 for Bonner's interpretation, and Wortmann, "Kosmogonie und Nilflut" 84-85, for other suggestions), and #395 (pl. 21, p. 321), showing a "pantheos" riding a lion; Delatte-Derchain, *Les intailles magiques* ##166-177, pp. 131-138, with excellent general introduction pp. 126-131. The leonine Bes, knife-wielding lions, and fantastic griffons (early sphinxes "pantheos") already appear on magic ivory knives from the Middle Kingdom: Daressy, *Textes et dessins magiques* pls. 11-12, ##9433-9440, with pp. 43-48.

Alexandrian coins minted under Trajan and Hadrian show as much(pls. 8f-g, 9a-c, 10a-b, 11a). He owed this favor in part to identification with the similarly sphinx-like γρύψ which represented Nemesis (cp. pls. 8g, 9a-b, where the γρύψ is on *Twtw*'s back), itself possessing ancient Egyptian ancestors and good connections with the *mafiosi* of the underworld of Egyptian magic.[72] The lion-god *Twtw*-Τιθοης is obviously a direct

---

[72]Consult particularly Adolf Rusch, "Tithoes," PW 6A.1512.14-53; Höfer, "Tithoes," Roscher 5.1021.17-27; Preisendanz, "Totoës," Roscher 5.1084.59-1085.3; "Sphinx," *RÄRG* 747-748; Lanzone, *Dizionario di mitologia egizia* 1283-1287 with pl. 407; de Wit, *Le rôle et le sens du lion* 269-273; Delatte-Derchain, *Les intailles magiques* 129-130; Henri Gauthier, "Le Dieu *Twt*," *Kêmi* 1 (1928) 115-122; Octave Guéraud, "Notes gréco-romaines II. Sphinx composites au Musée du Caire," *ASAE* 35 (1935) 4-24; Henri Seyrig, "Tithoës, Totoës et le sphinx panthée," *ASAE* 35 (1935) 197-202; Jean Yoyotte, "Une étude sur l'anthroponymie gréco-égyptienne du nome prosôpite," *BIFAO* 55 (1955) 135-138; and especially Ch. Picard, "La sphinge tricéphale, dite 'panthée,' d'Amphipolis et la démonologie égypto-alexandrine," *MMFP* 50 (1958) 49-84 with pl. 8 (its body encased in the coils of a serpent); and Serge Sauneron, "Le nouveau sphinx composite du Brooklyn Museum et le rôle du dieu Toutou-Tithoès," *JNES* 19 (1960) 269-287 with pls. 8-16; Ladislas Kákosy, "Reflexions sur le problème de Totoès," *BMHBA* 24 (1964) 9-16; for the coins Reginald Stuart Poole, *Catalogue of the Coins of Alexandria and the Nomes* (Bologna: Forni, [no date]) ##335 (p. 40), 460 (p. 56 with pl. 17), 506 (p. 61), 852-853 (p. 99 with pl. 26) for *Twtw*-Τιθοης and ##845, 850, 852 (where the γρύψ is on *Twtw*'s back) (p. 99 with pl. 26) for Nemesis' griffin. Lately note Jan Quaegebeur, "Tithoes, dieu oraculaire?" *Enchoria* 7 (1977) 103-108. On the γρύψ as associated with Nemesis and its connection with *Twtw*-Τιθοης the sphinx "pantheos," and magic see Paul Perdrizet, "L'ex-voto à Némésis du duplicaire Flavis," *ASAE* 31 (1931) 25-31 with the pl.; J. Leibovitch, "Le Griffon d'Erez et le sens mythologique de Némésis," *IEJ* 8 (1958) 141-148 with pls. 25-29; Elizabeth Riefstahl, "Nemesis and the Wheel of Fate," *BBM* 17 (1956) 1-7; Paul Perdrizet, "Némésis," *BCH* 36 (1912) 248-274 with pls. 1-2 (pl. 1 shows her trampling a human being, as on certain gems—see n. 67 above—an example of "Le type de Némésis foulant aux pieds le crime," pp. 250-255); Hans Volkmann, "Studien zum Nemesiskult," *ARW* 26 (1928) 296-321, especially pp. 297-312 for the popularity of her cult in Egypt, and especially at Alexandria, with astrological, particularly solar, associations—I shall say more about this later; "Neue Beiträge zum Nemesiskult," *ARW* 31 (1934) 57-76, especially pp. 63-72 for Egypt; Henri Seyrig, "Antiquités syriennes 4. Monuments syriens du culte de Némésis," *Syria* 13 (1932) 50-64, for Syria; H. Herter, "Nemesis," PW 16.2338-2380 (2354.23-2356.12 on her cult in Alexandria and 2370.32-2371.68 in magic);

descendant of the enemy-trampling sphinxes of earlier times (cp. pl. 9c, where *Twtw* holds a double axe with which he is about to smite an enemy whom he holds by the hair). If Bes occasionally appears in his company (pl. 11a), it is because the two deities are related in function as either beneficent or maleficent (depending on one's status as victim or beneficiary) repellers/destroyers of their enemies public or private, human or demonic. Hence *Twtw* is addressed, for example, as "grand de vaillance, ... qui détruit le messager funeste," but also as "le fils de Neith, le chef des émissaires de Sekhmet et des génies-errants de Bastet."[73] They are also related in form through possession of attributes borrowed from the most fearful, apotropaically effective beasts, lion and serpent (*Twtw*-Τιθοης' tail is often an uraeus cobra [pls. 8f-g, 9a-c, 10b, 11a], a feature which also crops up on the magic gems).

If the short recension of *Apoc. John* can secondarily bestow Chnoumis' two faces upon Yaldabaoth, or indeed a whole "multitude of forms," the Bes and sphinx "pantheos" figures may well have served as one of the models that underscored the feasibility or even the necessity of such a move, though the primary motive, as I suggested earlier, may have been to reconcile two discordant traditions and the initial impetus may have been provided by the solar pantheism that typified late antiquity. What is even more interesting, however, is the fact that, as a sphinx, *Twtw* is essentially human-headed (though occasionally he is fully leonine), and his

---

"Gryps," Roscher 1.1742-1777; Ziegler, "Gryps," PW 7.1902-1929. The sphinx "pantheos" was one of the ancestors of Sarapis' "Cerberus," the god's occasionally dog-, lion-, and jackal- (wolf-?) headed companion, whose body is frequently wrapped in the coils of a serpent or whose tail is serpentine: Guéraud, "Sphinx composites" 10-11; Picard, "La sphinge tricéphale" 53-55, 66-67; Willibald Kirfel, *Die dreiköpfige Gottheit. Archäologisch-ethnologischer Streifzug durch die Ikonographie der Religionen* (Bonn: Dümmler, 1948) 129-131 with pls. 42-43, figs. 118-122; de Wit, *Le rôle et le sens du lion* 273; Isidore Lévy, "Sarapis V. La statue mystérieuse," *RHR* 63 (1911) 139-141; Hornbostel, *Sarapis* 91-95 with pls. 4-8, 14-18, especially 25-30, and many other representations. R. Pettazzoni, "Il 'Cerbero' di Sarapide," *Mélanges Charles Picard* II, 803-809, though he appreciates Macrobius' speculative method, follows the Neo-Platonist's interpretation of the beast (*Saturnalia* 1.20.13-15) so far as to tie it to the Alexandrian cult of the Aion. Note that the Greek Sphinx can also have a serpent's tail: Fortwängler, *Die antiken Gemmen* I pl. 46 #23 with II 222.

[73]Sauneron, "Le nouveau sphinx composite" 270-271. For Bes in these roles see "Bes," *RÄRG* 103-105.

adventitious heads, regularly the same in number and in type—lion, bull, crocodile, baboon, jackal, hare, and Seth-animal—were originally affixed to an independent coterie of seven (*nota bene*) or seven groups of knife-wielding exacters of retribution (pl. 11a, upper left, b-c) of the type to which *Twtw* himself belonged, as a good śon of a pestilential Neith, and to which I referred generally earlier. If these seven murderous deities are, like *Twtw* their occasional chief, "messengers" of Sekhmet or some other ferocious goddess and their job is to afflict with disease and sudden death or to mete out punishment for crime,[74] as intermediaries of greater

---

[74]On these deadly "messengers" of Egyptian gods and goddesses see Otto Firchow, "Die Boten der Götter," *Ägyptologische Studien Hermann Grapow zum 70. Geburtstag gewidmet* (ed. O. Firchow; Berlin: Akademie-Verlag, 1955) 85-92; Zandee, *Death as an Enemy* 202-203; Sauneron, "Le nouveau sphinx composite" 278-283; Philippe Derchain, "La mort ravisseuse," *CEg* 33 (1958) 29-32; and especially Ém. Suys, "Les messa-geurs des dieux," *EgR* 2 (1934) 123-139. Sauneron's Table 1 ("Le nouveau sphinx composite" 281) registers the monuments on which the messengers are depicted, in the order and according to the head-type in which they appear; all six series evince a degree of uniformity which suggests a common tradition. It is as agents of Osiris in judgment of the dead that they are chastising demons: Firchow, "Die Boten der Götter" 87-89; the animal heads which they later acquire are in effect new embodiments of the horrible hybrid monster, part lion, part crocodile, part hippopotamus, that sat waiting to devour the souls of the damned at the tribunal of Osiris (de Wit, *Le rôle et le sens du lion* 371-372, in later times *totally* leonine), animals all supremely suitable exemplifications of an insatiable maw, a mythologem I have already traced from ancient Semitic texts into the Judaeo-Christian tradition. L. Kákosy, "Gnosis und ägyptische Reli-gion" 239, appreciates the broad relevance of these "messengers" to Gnosticism, but he does not explore the subject. Certain Bes-types, some in a manner similar to the "pantheos" figures bicephalic, and moreover armed with knives, belong to gods of this punishing "messenger" category: see Piankoff, "Sur une statuette de Bès" 31, citing as examples a vignette from a New Kingdom copy of the *Book of the Dead* which shows a Bes of this type "agenouillé devant un dieu à face léonine tenant un couteau," doubtless a relative of Sekhmet, and noting cases where Bes appears "dans le cortège des divinités terribles de l'au-delà égyptien"; "Bes," *RÄRG* 109. This fact helps account for Bes' popularity with magicians and his appear-ance in the company of *Twtw*, to whom he is, in this respect too, related. Hence Piankoff, "Sur une statuette de Bès" 32, rightly concludes of Bes that the god, like Sekhmet and *Twtw*, "nous apparait, dans la mythologie égyptienne, sous son double aspect de protecteur de l'homme et de démon

divinities they, like their Mesopotamian counterparts, are tailor-made for
assimilation to the Gnostic intermediaries Yahweh and his planetary seven
angelic ministers, especially for those to whom he was strictly a vengeful
god, a god of retributory justice, whose punishment is in the vast majority
of cases to strike down with illness or death. That the heads both of the
Egyptian and the Mesopotamian seven do not exactly match those of
Yaldabaoth and his archons is no matter since, as I pointed out earlier,
Ezekiel's חַיּוֹת had naturally to be adapted to the scheme, and personal
preference might tip the balance in favor of one beast or another; it is the
number (not, it seems, of astrological significance in its original Egyptian
or Mesopotamian contexts) and function that count.

In a fashion parallel to the Mesopotamian exorcism plaques depicting
the explusion of Pazuzu and Lamashtu, the multitude of stelae representing Twtw-Τιθοης are likely to be either propitiatory in intent, an appeal
to the god as chief of those death-dealing divine "emissaries" to deflect
their malignant power, or ex-votos for the *fait accompli*. Mesopotamian
and Egyptian medical and other texts show that magical means were
employed to avert illnesses whose unpredictability or inexplicability
assigned them to the agency of the messengers of Mesopotamian demon-
divinities or of Sekhmet who, as a lioness, was a goddess of the desert
wasteland and, in this respect like Seth, of storms and the *khamsin,* the
violent, scorching winds from the Sahara—similarly called "messengers,"
as Mesopotamians made demons of their storm winds—which brought

---

infernal at dangereux," adding interesting material for the god's survival
in the latter, demonic form into Coptic Christianity. For specifically lion-
headed, knife-wielding avengers or guardians of the Netherworld see de
Wit, *Le rôle et le sens du lion* 371-379. It is interesting that these seven,
theriomorphic, death-dealing Egyptian messengers have Mesopotamian
counterparts (see my pl. 3a, second register, where the seven animal
heads are, from the right, serpent, bird of prey, ram, sheep, wolf, lion,
and panther), one member of whom (though not the leader) is lion-headed
(so too in a Sumerian text that describes the seven, cited by Langdon, *The
Mythology of All Races* V 372-373). For other depictions and descriptions
of the seven see Thureau-Dangin, "Ritvel et amulettes contre Labartu" pl.
1, #1 reverse and #2 obverse with pp. 173, 175, 176-177; Frank, *Babylonische Beschwörungsreliefs* pls. 3B and 4G with pp. 11-36 ("Die Dämonen-
reihe"); R. Campbell Thompson, *The Devils and Evil Spirits of Babylonia* I.
"Evil Spirits" (London: Luzac, 1903) 88-103.

famine and plague in their wake.[75] This situation is strictly parallel to that of Chnoumis and the other decans as both inflicters and relievers of disease. Since, in fact, $Twtw$'s coterie is illustrated and their appeasement invoked on the very same late Egyptian temples (Edfu, Dendera, and Philae) whose decanal tradition played such a key role in the development of Egyptian iatromathematical science, Sauneron is justified in querying: "On peut se demander si les décans, tels qu'ils figurent sur les plafonds astronomiques des temples gréco-romains, n'ont pas, dans une certaine mesure, été associés aux 'messagers divins.'"[76] As I have pointed out, the decans were, after all, by astrological necessity the "angels" of Fate in administering good or evil fortune to men. $Twtw$'s assimilation to the γρύψ of Nemesis with its paw on Tyche's wheel gave the lion-god precisely the kind of astrological connection his coterie's work implied, if it did not already possess it outright.

One further point. That $Twtw$, as a son of the aggressive goddess Neith and particularly at Saïs in the Delta, one of the centers of her cult, was assigned leadership of the band of seven sanguinary emissaries of her "sister" Sekhmet, but that elsewhere the seven, originally not connected with him but functionally related, occur without him nicely parallels *Apoc. John*'s (in both recensions) elevation of Yaldabaoth out of the rank of the seven archons to a fully commanding position as an eighth independent of them. If Sekhmet's band of seven (and, in other contexts, Pazuzu's and Lamashtu's?) served as the prototype for the seven theriomorphic Gnostic archons to begin with, once $Twtw$'s popularity at their head began to make itself felt late in the first century and most strongly under the

---

[75]Firchow, "Die Boten der Götter" 86-87. If Sekhmet and her agents inflict disease, life and health are consequently equally in their keeping: see Gustave Lefebvre, "Prêtres de Sekhmet," *ArOr* 20 (1952) 57-64 with pls. 1-2; "Sachmet," *RÄRG* 564-646; Kees, *Der Götterglaube im alten Ägypten* 8: "Der Löwin als Gebieterin der Wüste schrieb man ähnlich wie dem Sethtier die Herrschaft über die Unwetter und Regenfälle zu, die aus ihrem Bereich kommen, ebenso die Sendung der 'jährlichen Seuche,' die mit den heissen Wüstenwinden im Sommer das Land überzieht. Auf diese Weise trat insbesondere Sachmet in Beziehung zu den Heilkünstlern. Die ägyptischen Ärzte nannten sich gern 'Spendepriester (Wêb) der Sachmet,' um die unheilspendende Göttin zu begütigen." Kees (p. 8 n. 4) connects the lion-spouts on Egyptian temples (see nn. 29 and 68) with storms as a feature of the lion's natural desert habitat. The lion's role as guardian manifestly played a part in this architectural tradition.

[76]"Le nouveau sphinx composite" 282 n. 82.

Severi a century or so later,[77] the appointment of a chief for the seven archons—and a polycephalic chief on the model of $Twtw$-Τιθοης, as in the short recension of *Apoc. John*, for reasons that will be discussed later— became a much more tempting proposition.

The short recension of *Apoc. John* may well have been influenced by $Twtw$ and his "pantheos" kin to endow Yahweh/Yaldabaoth with a plurality of heads. $Twtw$-Τιθοης shared Chnoumis' astrological and magical associations to so great an extent that it required no imaginative leap for the short recension to shift its attention from the latter to the former. The long recension, however, earlier lighted upon Chnoumis. That it could do so at all was assured by the homogeneity of function that I just noted between Sekhmet's troupe and the decans, by the troupe's acquisition of astrological connections (if it did not already have them), and by all the alluring associations of the celestial Leo that I discussed in the preceding section. It is significant that two of the three (out of a total of six) illustrated lists of Sekhmet's Furies which do *not* show $Twtw$ at their head are again precisely among the same Ptolemaic Egyptian temples (Edfu and Dendera) whose decans weighed so heavily upon the iatromathematical tradition in which Chnoumis had his roots, and, furthermore, that Sekhmet or her equivalent is a patron deity of—and *only* of—the *Knm.(t)* group of decans in the Seti I B family, of which Edfu's and Dendera's lists are members. In stricter accord with the archons' astral natures, then, and needing a single-headed, animal-headed being to suit his comrades, the long recension of *Apoc. John* turned to the decans as known to it through the iatromathematical tradition and chose *their* leader Chnoumis, already possessed of an impressive dossier of leonine associations, as the new identity for Yahweh/Yaldabaoth as the leader of his group. Why and in what setting Yahweh should have become a lion-headed man in the first place (when still one of the seven) is a subject that will be taken up in the next section, but it is further remarkable for the present that two (and possibly three, since the nature of Dendera's first figure can no longer be ascertained) of the six lists of Sekhmet's emissaries start the series off with a lion-headed man (Edfu and the Naos of Domitian). As servants of a lion-headed goddess this fact is not very astonishing; indeed, as I shall urge, it was exactly this son of Sekhmet who prompted Yahweh's strange metamorphosis in the first place.

But the questions which now remain to be answered are: When and

---

[77] Sauneron, "Le nouveau sphinx composite" 285-287; Guéraud, "Sphinx composites" 6.

above all why exactly did the Gnostic tradition represented by the long
recension of *Apoc. John* light upon Chnoumis as a new embodiment for
Yahweh/Yaldabaoth? Beyond the obvious reasons that I have already
suggested, that the decan, like Yaldabaoth in the older system exemplified by Celsus and Origen wherein he is still one of the seven, is also lion-
headed, and moreover that Chnoumis is the only decan in the iatromathematical tradition as preserved by the two Hermetic documents to be so
capitate, a number of other considerations may have exerted themselves
in the selection of Chnoumis.

One possibility deserves particular mention because it has received so
much attention and been the occasion for so much confusion. On the basis
of equivalence evident in the *Greek* forms of their names many
researchers have maintained that even if they were not originally identical at the native Egyptian level (an impossible view given Chnoumis' life
story) then at least in Greek-speaking circles a fusion took place between
Chnoumis and Chnum, the ram-headed Egyptian god of Elephantine and
other locales. A somewhat acrimonious debate has centered around this
issue, and a great deal of scholarly ingenuity has been exercised in an
effort to discover connections between the two aside from the similarity
of their names as transcribed into Greek, but the fact remains that
Chnum is never portrayed either lion-headed or as a lion-headed serpent;
Chnoumis and Chnum are in form quite distinct. If a rapprochement
between the two divinities ever was made, it can only have been founded
upon the homophony and perhaps additionally upon some attributes which
they secondarily shared through ties which made them cousins twice or
thrice removed.[78] But assuming that the identification of Chnoumis with

---

[78]Chnum's name, in Egyptian *Ḥnm(w)* and therefore not the same as
that of the decan *Knm.(t)*, is nevertheless transcribed into Greek with
Χνουβις, Χνουμις, and Κνουφις (the consonantal shift μ-β-φ is attested
in late Egyptian): Steuding, "Chnubis," Roscher 1.897.23-52; Drexler,
"Knuphis" 1250.9-29; Sethe, "Chnubis," PW 3.2349.53-2350.13. E. A. Wallis
Budge, *Egyptian Magic* (New York: Dover, 1971 [1901]) 180, takes the
identity of the gems' Chnoumis with Chnum for granted, though he notes
that Chnum never has a lion's head. A perusal of Ahmad Badawi's thorough
study *Der Gott Chnum* (Glückstadt, Hamburg, and New York: Augustin,
1937) confirms this fact. After discussion of Chnoumis' astrological
origins Drexler, "Knuphis" 1260.25-32, concludes: "In Wirklichkeit ist der
Chnumis dieser Gemmen nicht der alte kosmogonische Gott Chnum,
sondern vielmehr eine ägyptische *Dekangottheit*," and the Egyptologist
Sethe ("Chnubis" 2352.45-51) affirms on the basis of Chnoumis' looks that
the lion-headed serpent "also mit dem altägyptischen Gotte Ch. keinerlie

Chnum did take place, Chnum's role as a fashioner of man and for that

---

Ähnlichkeit zeigt." But Reitzenstein, *Poimandres* 132-134, takes Sethe to task for this judgment (on very tenuous grounds), and many others agree with him in persisting to take Chnoumis for Chnum or to see a connection (as already noted in nn. 50 and 56), mostly on a solar foundation—namely, Chnum's identification with the sun-gods Re or Horus (Sethe, "Chnubis" 2351.8-20; Drexler, "Knuphis" 1252.60-1253.9; "Chnum," *RÄRG* 138; Badawi, *Der Gott Chnum* 29, 31, 46-48; de Wit, *Le rôle et le sens du lion* 203-204, 248-253) and Chnoumis' solar associations as a decan of Leo: for example, Delatte, "Sphère magique" 262; "Amulettes inédites" 69; Wortmann, "Kosmogonie und Nilflut" 63, 81, 85-88. Bonner, *Studies in Magical Amulets* 25, stresses the connection without supporting argument; he goes so far as to aver, quite erroneously, that "adoption of the name Chnoumis for a decan may be a secondary development." Delatte-Derchain, *Les intailles magiques* 54-57, also stress the connection and reprimand Drexler with: "En realité, le dieu Khnoum . . . a cédé certains de ses attributs au Chnoumis/Chnoubis de la magie" and conclude: "Il faut donc admettre dès le départ la confusion des deux entités divines égyptiennes dans la personne du dieu des magiciens" (p. 55), but what these "attributes" are they do not make very clear. Apparently they mean Chnoumis' serpentine body, for, unable to account for it in any other manner (they say nothing of the native Egyptian traditions from which, in my view, both his head and his body derive), they resort to Doresse's claim ("Images des dieux gnostiques" 365) that Chnoumis is not Chnum but the serpentine (though not lion-headed) divinity *Km 3t.f* ("He who completes his time") of the Theban cosmogony (on whom see "Kematef," *RÄRG* 373-374) known to Porphyry (as cited by Eusebius, *Preparation for the Gospel* 3.11, 115a) as Κνηφ, and go on to cite *PGM I P 4.1636-1715 where* Κμηφ (1705) is a giant serpent (1637-1643) for proof that he, in turn, was identified with Chnum, although what the passage seems to be doing is depicting *Km 3t.f* as a giant ouroboros snake in the sky, i.e., the zodiacal circle through which the sun travels; Plutarch's characterization of Κνηφ as ἀγέννητος and ἀθάνατος (*On Isis and Osiris* 21 [*Moralia* 359D]) hints at the same thing. That Delatte-Derchain follow Doresse only succeeds in further bolloxing things up, since Doresse's statement that, besides the names Chnoubis and Chnouphis, the gems also give the lion-headed serpent "parfois aussi ceux d'Abrasax de Ialdabaoth ou de Sacla" is wrong, knowing which Delatte-Derchain assume Doresse is referring to astrological texts, though in fact for the latter two he can only be thinking of *Apoc. John.* Although I do not believe with Delatte-Derchain that Chnoumis acquired his *shape* through this triple merger, I second the learned editors' observation that theocrasy through nominal homophony is a standard and ancient Egyptian method, and therefore assimilation of

reason a deity eventually saddled with creation of the whole cosmos[79] would invite his and in turn Chnoumis' union with Yahweh/Yaldabaoth as creator of the world.

What makes this an even more attractive hypothesis is the possibility

---

Chnoumis to Chnum cannot be ruled out. And the physician-magicians who prescribed the gems certainly knew the god Chnum: Delatte-Derchain ##359-361, pp. 255-256, on uterine amulets where in other examples Chnoumis appears; possibly Bonner, *Studies in Magical Amulets* #52 (pl. 3, pp. 261-262 and 24); "Amulets chiefly in the British Museum" #15 (pl. 96, p. 324), though neither of these is certainly Chnum. In support of his thesis that Chnoumis is Chnum and following a suggestion of Carl Schmidt, Philippe Derchain has offered a solution to the words ΝΑΑΒΙΣ ΒΙΕΝΝΟΥΘ often accompanying Chnoumis' name on the gems which finds their derivation in the cult of Chnum: "Intailles magiques du Musée de Numismatique d'Athènes," *CEg* 39 (1964) 179-181 on #5. On this gem Chnoumis is not lion-headed but merely a bearded serpent, a fact which leads Derchain to see Agathodaimon in him (see n. 50) and to complete the circle by noting Philo of Byblos' statement (cited by Eusebius, *Preparation for the Gospel* 1.10.48) that the Phoenicians call the serpent Agathodaimon, whereas Egyptians name it Κνηφ. On Kneph see Roeder, "Kneph," PW 11.910-913; "Kneph," *RÄRG* 378-379; and "Kematef," *RÄRG* 374. This already murky situation is rendered even more turbid by the entry of yet another cosmogonic deity (or, more properly, the cosmogonic title of many deities)—this one self-created—into the amalgam of homophonies: *K3 mwt.f* ("Bull of his mother")—Καμηφις, particularly as a title of the ithyphallic god Min (see Roeder, "Kamephis," PW 10.1832-1836; "Kamutef," *RÄRG* 364-365) and by the proposal that Κνηφ/Κμηφ might also represent ḳm3.f, "'sein eigener Erzeuger'" or "'Selbstgeschaffener:'" so Karl Fr. W. Schmidt in his review of *PGM* I, *GGA* 193 (1931) 449, and of *PGM* II, *GGA* 196 (1934) 177, commenting on *PGM* I P 3.142, 471; 4.1705, 2094; *PGM* II P 7.583.

[79] Sethe, "Chnubis" 2350.43-55; 2351.43-59; Drexler, "Knuphis" 1253.51-1256.35; "Chnum," *RÄRG* 137-138; Badawi, *Der Gott Chnum* 13-14, 18-19, 36-40, 47-48, 52-58. It is in the Ptolemaic period that Chnum's demiurgic task is widened to include the whole world; his temple at Esna (Latopolis), where, incidentally, Chnum is brought into relationship with Shu, Tefnut and Menhit, lion-headed deities, and through them with *Twtw* (de Wit, *Le rôle et le sens du lion* 107-122, 198-212, 270, 324-332, 353-356; Badawi, *Der Gott Chnum* 31-33; Sethe, "Chnubis" 2352.2-29), preserves hymns of the most splendid grandeur celebrating his creation of all that exists. If the Theban serpent *Km 3t.f*-Κνηφ/Κμηφ is admitted to this muddle of associations through assimilation by homophony and ophidian nature to Chnoumis/Chnouphis the demiurgic complex is further strengthened.

that the existence in the fifth century B.C. (and earlier?) of a Jewish community on Chnum's home island of Elephantine led to syncretism between the two gods at this early date.[80] It remains only a possibility, however, for while Jeremiah berates all Egyptian Jewry for adoring the "Queen of Heaven" (Jer 44:1-30) and while the worship of the Jewish colony at Elephantine was likewise heterodox in marrying Yahweh off (so it seems) to ᶜAnat, so far as I know there is no direct evidence for a Chnum-Yahweh synthesis. It is true that there was intimate social contact between Jews and Egyptians at Elephantine, that Jews possessed Egyptian slaves, freely fraternized with and wed Egyptians, swore by Chnum's consort Sati, and had close relationships, some of them familial, with individuals bearing theophorous names in Chnum (e.g., Pachnum "He belongs to Chnum," and Tachnum "She belongs to Chnum"),[81] but none of this implies a syncretism, not even an ostracon in which (if correctly restored) in a single breath a blessing is pronounced in the names of Yahu and Chnum.[82] However that may be, the mere existence of a temple of Yahweh on Chnum's island provided an atmosphere in which Egyptians, following normal procedure, would have been provided sufficient cause to make the equation, but given the unfriendly actions—whatever motivated them—of the priests of Chnum, who managed to have their Persian masters order the colony's temple destroyed, it is doubtful that the priesthood of the god of the First Cataract would have encouraged the connection, even after the Jews' temple was restored, if it was.[83] The Chnum-Chnoumis-Yahweh combination could, of course, have been quite independent of any prod from an earlier tradition, and so it does not hinge upon the syncretistic leanings of the Jews at Elephantine.

But a much less complicated explanation can be arrived at on the astrological grounds that I mentioned earlier, grounds which the decans

---

[80]So A. A. Barb, "Abraxas-studien," *Hommages à Waldemar Deonna* (ColLat 28; Bruxelles-Berchem: Latomus, 1975) 75, in an effort to explain the presence of Chnoumis on early Christian armband-phylacteries.

[81]Arthur Ungnad, *Aramäische Papyrus aus Elephantine* (Leipzig: Hinrichs, 1911) ##1.5, 11.7, 12.2, 16.2, 22.5, 26.5 and elsewhere; Bezalel Porten, *Archives from Elephantine. The Life of an Ancient Jewish Military Colony* (Berkeley and Los Angeles: University of California Press, 1968) 33-34, 71, 149, 233, 251, 273, and generally 151-186.

[82]A. Dupont-Sommer, "'Yahô' et 'Yahô-Seba ʾôt' sur les ostraca araméens inédits d'Éléphantine," *CRAI* (1947) #23 (pp. 177-178).

[83]Porten, *Archives from Elephantine* 284-298; Badawi, *Der Gott Chnum* 25.

and Yahweh/Yaldabaoth shared aplenty. And why Chnoumis out of all the thirty-six? Like the original Yaldabaoth, seventh of seven, for whom he was selected as a new embodiment, Chnoumis is lion-headed, yes, but what is more: (1) Chnoumis suited Yahweh/Yaldabaoth because, like the latter as head of his band even while still a member of it (Origen, *Against Celsus* 6.31 "You, Yaldabaoth, first and seventh"[84]), the decan led its troupe, both originally as the *Knm.(t)* group and later as the third of Cancer/first of Leo at the beginning of the Egyptian year; and (2) as the decan which opened the Egyptian year and brought the Nile-flood with the sun's entry into its domain Chnoumis shared in the whole cosmogonic complex of associations which this position of his entailed and which made him a prime candidate for assimilation to the archontic world-creator; any further demiurgic tie of Chnoumis with Chnum is merely icing on the cake.

A further boost was given Chnoumis' candidacy by the Egyptian astrological doctrine of πρόσωπα. Just as each sign of the zodiac is home ground for a particular planet considered especially compatible with its nature, so each decan, as now part of the belt of signs, must be the πρόσωπον of a specific planet, the medium through which that planet's dignity is characteristically expressed and revealed.[85] The Latin Hermetic iatromathematical text cited above shows that the first decan of Leo was a πρόσωπον for Saturn, and if Yaldabaoth's original position as lord of the seventh sphere (counting outward from the earth) meant that Saturn was his planet (φασὶ δὲ τῷ λεοντοειδεῖ ἄρχοντι συμπαθεῖν ἄστρον τὸν Φαίνοντα Origen, *Against Celsus* 6.31; 101.10-11 Koetschau)[86] then a

---

[84]The word "first" here means foremost in prominence, not number one in the ordinal series. Origen's document begins with Yaldabaoth as chief archon, but he is seventh in order counting out from the earth—the natural order of enumeration since it is that which the soul necessarily follows in its ascent through the spheres in ecstasy or at death. The passwords show that it is the *ascent* which is of concern here, not the descent.

[85](W.) Gundel, "Dekane" 121.66-122.57; *Dekane und Dekansternbilder* 30-36, 248-256, and the table p. 81.

[86]See Bousset, *Hauptprobleme der Gnosis* 351-355; and "Der Gott Aion," *Religionsgeschichtliche Studien. Aufsätze zur Religionsgeschichte des hellenistischen Zeitalters* (ed. Anthonie F. Verheule; NovTSup 50; Leiden: Brill, 1979) 225-228. In accord with his view of the Syrian origins of Gnosticism, Bousset constructs a "Phoenician" heritage for

decan serving as πρόσωπον for Saturn was a natural if not a necessary choice. Generally speaking, moreover, that *Apoc. John* endows with "faces" the powers which the planetary archons create for themselves is in and of itself a clue that its author was quite familiar with this astrological doctrine and drew this idea, as well as that for Chnoumis, from it. Incidentally, if interpreted literally πρόσωπον as a technical astrological term would lend itself to confusion about the decan Chnoumis' actual

---

Yaldabaoth's looks on the basis of the Κρόνος–Χρόνος–Αἰών synthesis in conjunction with the Mithraic leontocephaline and a personified Time in late Orphic cosmogony (both of these topics will be taken up later), of Kronos-Saturn's affiliation with the lion (solar, as I will show later), and especially of the supposed cult of a leonine Gennaios—whom Bousset supposes to have been lion-headed because lion-masks appear on statues of Jupiter Heliopolitanus—which the passage from Damascius' *Life of Isidorus* places in Heliopolis. This is nonsense. The essential point in what Syria contributed to Gnostic speculation regarding the creator is not Yaldabaoth's leonine form but rather Yahweh's equation with astrologized Jupiters and Saturns through their underlying Syrian and Perso-Babylonian equivalents and, specifically, for the context here, what Tacitus (*Histories* 5.4) in the first century A.D. attests as a standard feature of the Roman aristocracy's knowledge about Judaism: the identification of the god of the Jews with Κρόνος-Saturn, both as divinity of Greek myth and as planet, the former in connection with the Idaean (*Idaei//Iudaei*) Dactyls (cp. *Histories* 5.2) as companions of Kronos in exile founders of the Jewish race and source of their religious traditions, the latter because the Jewish Sabbath is Saturn's day and because of all the planets Saturn moves "in the highest orb and exercises extraordinary power" over mankind, a reference on the one hand to the baleful, cataclysmic influence with which astrologers endowed the planet and on the other hand to Yahweh's well-touted claim to world supremacy and to ultimate authority over all other powers that be. What is more, Saturn suited Yahweh because, like his own, the planet's baleful influence centered precisely around retribution for wrong-doing; hence Saturn is in Egypt called "the star of Nemesis" (Bouché-Leclercq, *L'astrologie grecque* 94 n. 1, 307, 321 n. 2). It was, as I argued earlier, in part on the basis of their common retributory functions that Yahweh/ Yaldabaoth was assimilated to Τwtw-Τιθοης, the sphinx "pantheos," and the γρύψ of Nemesis. The identification of the planet with Nemesis is of native Egyptian origin: Volkmann, "Studien zum Nemesiskult" 309-310 (more on this latter); for Nemesis is a goddess of rebribution see Herter, "Nemesis" 2365.68-2370.31.

physiognomy, with which *à la rigueur* it has nothing to do. The Latin text well illustrates this possibility, for given that the first decan of Leo has the face (*habet faciem*) of Saturn, what then does *serpens est magnus forma leonis* say about the decan's looks? The liberties which the short recension of *Apoc. John* takes with Chnoumis' looks may well have been helped along by this kind of ambiguity.

The context in which the choice landed upon Chnoumis was clearly also conditioned by how greatly Judaism had influenced the Graeco-Egyptian magical tradition and, conversely also, as the *Testament of Solomon* indicates, the extent to which the latter had influenced the former. It is well known how saturated the magic papyri are with Jewish names, ideas, and references; the gem-amulets are no exception, ιλω being of extremely frequent occurrence on every type, including that of Chnoumis.[87] One of the major reasons, surely, is that Jewish medicine, like its Egyptian counterpart, was marked by strong if not exclusive belief in demonic pathogenesis and consequently relied heavily upon magic and thaumaturgic technique to heal. A notorious example is Eleazar (Josephus, *Ant.* 8.2.5 §§42-49) who, learned in Solomon's wisdom in such matters— and it surpassed even that of the Egyptians—in the presence of Vespasian exorcised a demon with the help of a ring under whose seal (i.e., seal-bearing gem) a certain root had been placed, with which one may compare *Jub.* 10:10-14; Josephus, *J.W.* 7.6.3 §§180-185; and the prescription in the Greek Hermetic text quoted earlier. Josephus claims the Essenes for outstanding adepts at this science (*J.W.* 2.8.6 §136), and texts from Qumran (1QapGen XX, 12-29; 4QPrNab) bear him out.[88] Jesus is another such example.[89] Moreover, Jewish interest in the oracular properties of stones is attested, for example, by Josephus, *Ant.* 3.7.5 §§162-171, on the ephod. In sum, the Egyptian iatromathematical tradition and Jewish exorcistic

---

[87] In addition to the gems referred to in nn. 48, 51, 65 and 67, Bonner, *Studies in Magical Amulets* #98 (pl. 5, p. 269); Delatte, "Amulettes inédites" 40.

[88] A. Dupont-Sommer, "Exorcismes et guérisons dans les écrits de Quomrân," *Congress Volume of the International Organization for the Study of the Old Testament* (VTSup 7; Leiden: Brill, 1960) 246-261.

[89] Whether or not (W.) Gundel, *Dekane und dekansternbilder* 277, is right to conclude of Matt 17:14-21 "dass wir . . . auf diese Glaubens-normen der hellenistischen Dekanreligion (viz., the specific methods recommended by the *Testament of Solomon* for exorcising affliction-causing decan-demons) stossen" is a moot point, but in principle he is quite correct.

medicine were bound to cross-fertilize each other for being generically identical; that they did so in the case of Chnoumis is indicated by the presence of ιλω on some gems and by Chnoumis' absorption of Yahweh's gigantomachy. Hence Chnoumis, the sorcerers' delight as a fusion of the fury of Sekhmet and Wadjet, the lord of the decans, their master healer, might with perfect justification be picked as a new form for Yahweh, in whose hands the power of life and death, of illness and rejuvenation resides (ἐγὼ ἀποκτεινῶ καὶ ζῆν ποιήσω, πατάξω κἀγὼ ἰάσομαι Deut 32:32 LXX). The theocrasy between Yahweh and Chnoumis may even have existed in magical-medical circles before the Gnostics behind *Apoc. John* took it up.

When, finally, did *Apoc. John* as represented by the long recension settle upon this choice? Unfortunately, the tradition as known to Irenaeus is of no help in answering this question. But if I am right in holding the short recension secondary and if the temporal background against which its changes are best understood is late in the second or rather early in the third century, then a date from mid- to late second century for the choice of Chnoumis as a new embodiment of Yahweh/Yaldabaoth is as likely as any to be correct, especially as it is also true that *Apoc. John*, at least in some respects, is dependent on a more primitive system exemplified by the documents which lay before Celsus and Origen. This period suits such a development, furthermore, because imperial patronage had by then begun to endow astrology with the all-pervasive influence in Mediterranean religion which it long thereafter continued to enjoy, and Chnoumis was riding the wave of favor accorded Egyptian iatromathematics to the pinnacle of stardom. The skein of medical, magical and astrological associations linking Yahweh and Chnoumis in the practice of Jewish and Egyptian healers is certainly older (first century B.C. to mid-first century A.D.) than *Apoc. John*'s choice and largely contributed to make it a natural step to take.

3.5   Yahweh, Mios, and the Two Cities Leontopolis

But who, then, was Yahweh/Yaldabaoth in his earliest Gnostic avatar as a lion-headed man? If the lion-headed god as leader of Sekhmet's band of astral emissaries was the prototype for Yahweh/ Yaldabaoth as leader of the planetary seven (Yahweh having already been coordinated with Saturn god and star in Syria), this still does not explain who the lion-headed Egyptian troop commander is and on what basis he was chosen for the Jewish creator. As a point of departure the Brummer gem discussed earlier and Origen's remark about the name Yaldabaoth in the "Ophite" system, that it is a name the sorcerers use (*Against Celsus* 6.32; 102.19 Koetschau)[90] lead once again into the world of late Egyptian magic and religion. A. A. Barb's sure instincts guided him aright when, commenting upon a magic armband from Syria, he refers in passing to the leonine deities of Egyptian religion and with forgivable exaggeration compares their number with the "countless" lion-headed divinities of the magic gems.[91]

Amulets depicting leontocephalic human beings (pls. 5m; 12a-f) are in fact relatively rare and the traits with which they are endowed not of great variety. Generally speaking they all mark the creature as (1) Egyptian or mixed Greek and Egyptian in origin, (2) a solar divinity, and (3) a form of the god Horus. The facts upon which these judgments are founded are: the figure regularly wears Greek (the chlamys) or, more commonly, Egyptian dress (as on the Brummer gem); invariably boasts solar rays, or nimbus and rays, or solar disk and rays, about his head (as is also true of Chnoumis); extends a finger of his right hand to his mouth; holds a whip in

---

[90]Origen knew whereof he spoke: note 'Αλδαβ<ι>αειμ as the demiurge 'Ιάω/Yahweh's name αἰγυπτιστί in *PGM* II P 13.84, 153, 462, 596 and the incantation which begins (with some variation) ιαλδαζαω βλαθαμ μαχωρ, similarly secret names of the Jewish creator (and so followed by κόσμου κτίστα . . . Μαρμαριώ 'Ιάω . . . ὁ κτίσας θεοὺς καὶ ἀρχαγγέλους καὶ δεκανούς *PGM* I P 4.1200-1203), in *PGM* I P 1.203-205; 4.1195-1199; II P 13.971-974 quoted by the magician on the authority of Moses ἐν τῇ 'Αρχαγγελικῇ. On these passages see Dieterich, *Abraxas* 45-46. With the papyri's 'Αλδαβαειμ compare the spelling ⲁⲗⲁⲃⲗⲱⲑ in CG II, *1 Apoc. John* 23[71].36, though it may simply be an error here. The variation in Semitic plurals (ם־/ן־) is not without precedent elsewhere in magic literature. The name itself has resisted decipherment; for a critique of previous solutions and a new attempt see Gershom Scholem, "Jaldabaoth Reconsidered," *Mélanges d'histoire des religions offerts à Henri-Charles Puech* (Paris: Presses Universitaires de France, 1974) 405-421. Wolfgang Fauth, "Seth-Typhon, Onoel und der eselsköpfige Sabaoth. Zur Theriomorphie der ophitisch-barbelognostischen Archonten," *OrChr* 57 (1973) 91 n. 75, agrees with Scholem "dass es sich . . . um eine der zahlreichen durch 'Sabaoth' angeregten Bildungen auf-aoth, abaoth handelt," adding what seems to me as good an explanation as any: "Vielleicht is der vordere Bestandteil des Namens nach magischem Usus aus Elementen von Jao, Elohim und Adonai zusammengesetzt."

[91]Alphonse A. Barb, "Magica varia IV. Ein magischer Armreif," *Syria* 49 (1972) 362-367. The reference alluded to appears on p. 365.

one hand and an orb in the other; clutches a serpent, a tall staff sometimes wrapped seven or more times around by a serpent, a situla (as on
the Brummer gem), an ʿnḫ.[92] These features, some of them standard
iconographic attributes of Helios and Horus, are enough to secure the
identity of the figures which possess them, but a passage from a magical
papyrus, *PGM* I P 1.142-148, which prescribes the manufacture of one
such type of gem-amulet, places the matter beyond doubt. The passage
occurs in the course of a spell to acquire a δαίμων πάρεδρος and runs as
follows:

> This [what immediately precedes] is the incantation to
> be spoken seven times seven times to the sun. The image
> that must be engraved on the stone

---

[92]Bonner, *Studies in Magical Amulets* ##98 (pl. 5, p. 269), 102? (pl. 5,
pp. 269-270), 149 (pl. 7, p. 277), 229-236 (pl. 11, pp. 291-293), and
generally pp. 19-20, 112-113, 150-153; "Amulets chiefly in the British
Museum" #13 (pl. 96, p. 323); Delatte-Derchain, *Les intailles magiques*
##302-308, pp. 222-226 with the introduction pp. 221-222; Delatte, "Amu-
lettes inédites" ##A36-37, pp. 88-90. As I already pointed out, Bonner
##99-101 illustrate the union of Abraxas and Chnoumis; the type repre-
sented by Delatte-Derchain ##306-307, showing the lion-headed man with
sword and head of Medusa, attest by inscriptions which they bear assimilation of this figure too to Chnoumis (#306 with a *vox magica* on its
obverse common on Chnoumis-gems and #307 with στάμαχε πέπτε), no
doubt in part because, as an ancestor of the healer Podaleirius, Perseus
was connected with medicine, and his butchery of the demonic Medusa
was obviously of superb apotropaic power. Bonner, "A Miscellany of
Engraved Stones" #42 (pl. 36, pp. 154-157), showing Medusa's head and
inscribed, among other things, **XNOYBI,** belongs to the same class.
Alexander of Abonouteichos exploited the same set of associations
(Lucian, *Alexander* 11), a fact which further links him to Chnoumis.
Bonner, *Studies in Magical Amulets* 152, knows an example in which the
serpent that the lion-headed deity holds is Chnoumis; the link between
Horus/Harpocrates and Chnoumis is also evident on the gem-type which
normally shows Harpocrates surrounded by animal groups but which on
occasion puts Helios or Chnoumis in his place: Bonner #391 (pl. 21, p. 320
with pp. 142-43); "Amulets chiefly in the British Museum" ##65-68 (pls.
99-100, pp. 339-340 with pp. 307-309); Delatte-Derchain, *Les intailles
magiques* #87, p. 71. The substitution therefore has a solar basis. The connection is in the third place manifest in the ἁρπον χνουφι formula (see n.
56).

—no stone is mentioned in the foregoing context; the necessity for one seems to be simply knowledge taken for granted by the magician—

> is that of Helioros ('Ἡλίωρος "Helios-Horus"), a lion-faced man holding in his left hand a globe of the heavens and <in his right> a whip, with a serpent biting its tail in a circle around him. On the reverse side of the stone inscribe this name (keep it secret): [a *vox magica* follows]; string the stone with cord of Anubis and wear it around your neck.

A passage from another papyrus, *PGM* I P 4.2111-2117 in a spell of the same sort, describes a figure obviously related to another type from the extant gems, but gives the figure no name:[93]

> The figure which must be drawn on the hide (of the ass) [mentioned earlier in lines 2014-2016] is as follows: a lion-faced man, girded about the waist, holding in his right hand a staff on which there is to be a serpent. About the whole of his left hand an asp is to be coiling, and from the mouth of the lion fire is to be breathing.

---

[93]On these two passages from *PGM* see Delatte, "Sphère magique" 259, 261; Dieterich, *Abraxas* 52-54, who pronounces the god in each of them a "Sonnen- und Feuergott," approves their reference to Aion and to Mithras, and interprets the Mithraic leontocephaline in their light. This is a subject I reserve for another section; for now I will simply follow out the connection with Horus which the one text and other, iconographical details suggest. (H.) Gundel, *Weltbild und Astrologie* 23-24, remarks of the second passage: "In einem Zusammenhang ist auf den ersten Blick eine typisch synkretistische Gottheit wie etwa der Zeitgott Aion-Zervan-Kronos-Saturn u.ä. zu erkennen; darüber hinaus aber scheint gerade hier in astraler Deutung das Sternbild des *Ophiouchos*, in dekanologischer einer seiner Dekane fassbar zu sein" and of the first: "Auch eine andere leontokephale Figur stellt sich bei näherer Prüfung als ein Dekan heraus und zwar als Knum-Chnum-*Chnubis*. ... Gewiss: auch hier ist zunächst das Aion-Bild bestimmend, wie wir es aus zahlreichen Darstellungen kennen." By "Aion-Zervan-Kronos-Saturn" and "Aion-Bild" Gundel means the Mithraic leontocephaline, underwriting thereby the conjectures of his predecessors, but he adds a new dimension to the creature's identity. Although the leonto-cephalic Helios-Horus which the passages describe does have decanological connections, as Gundel goes on to remark of Chnoumis as a lion-headed decan of Leo, and for other reasons I will point out later, this is clearly not the primary referent here.

That the lion-headed figures with whip and orb (symbolizing universal dominion) should represent Helios comes as no shock, considering the close astrological ties that bound the sun to Leo, ties which I have already repeatedly mentioned.[94] If the figure is a Helios-*Horus,* Horus had, thanks to the Heliopolitan priesthood, since ancient times in Egypt been given forms which absorbed him into the solar cultus as Harakhty (*Ḥr 3ḥty* "Horus the Horizon Dweller"). From the New Kingdom on the Heliopolitan Horus' permanent association with the lion was assured by the worship of the Great Sphinx at Gizeh as Harmachis (*Ḥr m 3ḥ.t* "Horus in the Horizon").[95] The gems' lion-headed figure sucking its finger is yet another

---

[94]Helios-Horus, human-headed, is often depicted riding, either seated or standing, upon a solar lion (Leo) (see my pl. 7b, d): Bonner, *Studies in Magical Amulets* ##211-213 (pl. 10, pp. 288-289), 225-226 (pl. 11, p. 291) with pp. 144, 150; Delatte-Derchain, *Les intailles magiques* ##312-314, pp. 227-228. Other gems simply show a lion, occasionally radiate, with star or star and meniscus in the field, symbols which patently give this lion too an astrological significance: Bonner ##73-75 (pl. 4, pp. 265-266), 237-239, 242-243 (pl. 11, p. 293) with pp. 35-36, 150-151; Delatte-Derchain ##317-321 (#318 human-headed), pp. 229-231; Delatte, "Amulettes inédites" #B11, pp. 93-94; Wortmann, "Kosmogonie und Nilflut" 83. Bonner is rightly suspicious of the traditional label of this type as "Mithraic." On the lion's solar alliance in Egypt see (in addition to the literature cited in the notes to section 3.3) Hani, *La religion égyptienne dans la pensée de Plutarque* 404-406; Neugebauer-Parker, *Egyptian Astronomical Texts* III, 192 (Petosiris called Leo the *3str n Rˁ,* "the constellation [ἀστήρ!] of Re"); Theodor Hopfner, *Griechisch-ägyptischer Offenbarungszauber* I (Amsterdam: Hakkert, 1974 [1921]) §§394, 428, 439, 461 (citing Proclus); Delatte, "Sphère magique" 259-260 (citing *PGM* I P 3.511-512 and 4. 1667-1668); and Theodor Hopfner, "Der religionsgeschichtliche Gehalt des grossen demotischen Zauberpapyrus," *ArOr* 7 (1935) 105, 120; "Orientalisch-Religionsgeschichtliches aus den griechischen Zauberpapyri Aegyptens" 143, 145-146; Schmidt's review of *PGM* II, *GGA* 196 (1934) 176-177; de Wit, *Le rôle et le sens du lion* 143-145—all on the same and other passages from the magic literature.

[95]Schweitzer, *Löwe und Sphinx* 34; de Wit, *Le rôle et le sens du lion* 56-67, 237-238, and 138-147 generally on the lion as an animal associated with solar divinities; "Sphinx," *RÄRG* 746-747; Hopfner, "Der Tierkult der alten Ägypter" 40; "Löwe," *RÄRG* 427. The Heliopolitan gods Shu and Tefnut are similarly portrayed as lions or lion-headed: de Wit, *Le rôle et le sens du lion* 107-122; Hopfner, "Der Tierkult der alten Ägypter" 41-42; "Löwe," *RÄRG* 427. The lion with sun disk becomes a frequent theme on Egyptian amulets in the 26th (Saite) Dynasty (Schweitzer, *Löwe und*

such solar Horus, Harpocrates (Hr $p3$ hrd "Horus the Child"), who enjoyed enormous popularity in the Hellenistic and Roman periods and is a frequent subject for portrayal on amulets in his more familiar lotus-sitting form.[96]

But the passages from the magical papyri and the Egyptian traditions just discussed do not pinpoint the specific cultic setting from which this lion-headed Horus with solar associations was taken up into the sorcerers' handbag of powerful numina; they still do not, that is, closely enough identify the divinity involved. Luckily, a red jasper amulet originally of the Abbott collection fills this lack (pl. 12g). The obverse shows a lion-headed god in Egyptian dress, solar disk encircled by the uraeus on his head, who holds in one hand an ʿnh and in the other a tall staff (topped by an indistinct object which Bonner takes for a lion's head but Lévy and Fröhner for a serpent's), attributes precisely matching those of some of the other gems' lion-headed deities. The long, unique inscription on the Abbott gem, covering the reverse, continuing on the edge, and ending with the god's names cut around him on the obverse, reads (if the corrections are all secure):[97]

Sphinx 71 with n. 449; de Wit, *Le rôle et le sens du lion* 30), perhaps in part because of the successful expulsion of the Assyrians, the lion being, as I have mentioned, intimately connected with the power to destroy the enemy.

[96]Bonner, *Studies in Magical Amulets* ##34-35, 46, 141, 189-194 (pls. 2, 3, 7, 9; pp. 258-260, 275, 285-286), among others, with pp. 140-146 and 151; Delatte-Derchain, *Les intailles magiques* ##130-162, pp. 104-123; Derchain, "Intailles magiques de Musée de Numismatique" #13 reverse, pp. 185-186, with lion, star and meniscus on the obverse. Harpocrates is shown in native Egyptian contexts seated on a throne supported by lions (de Wit, *Le rôle et le sens du lion* 265; Hopfner, "Der Tierkult der alten Ägypter" 41); hence, again with somewhat confused justice, Horapollo (*Hieroglyphics* 1.17; pp. 50-51 Sbordone with excellent notes on Horus as a solar and a leonine god; pp. 58-59 van de Walle-Vergote) says that the lion's "face is round, and in imitation of the sun the hair all about it is shaped like rays, which is why they place Horus' throne on lions, to show the symbolic resemblance which the animal bears to the god," that is, to the sun. Generally note too "Harpocrates," *RÄRG* 273-275.

[97]Bonner, *Studies in Magical Amulets* #283 (pl. 13, p. 300) with pp. 183-185, including a new reading and a translation; Lévy, "La statue mystérieuse" 141-143, who adduces it and the cult it presupposes to explain the lion as a constituent of Sarapis' "Cerberus"; Friedrich Preisigke, *Sammelbuch griechischer Urkunden aus Ägypten* I (Strassburg:

Reverse: Hear me, thou whose heritage is residence in
Leontopolis, thou whose image stands in the holy shrine,
lightener, thunderer, of stormy gloom and winds the lord,
thou to whom belongs the eternal power of celestial
Necessity.

Edge: You are the god who acts swiftly, the god who hearkens
to prayer, the god in lion form, great of glory. Your name is:

Obverse: Mios, Miosis, Horus-Mios, Osiris-Mios, Phre, son of
Miephe (?), the great god, light, fire, flame (μιως μιωσι
αρμιως ουσιρμιως φρη σι μιεφε φνουτο φῶς πῦρ φλόξ). Be
gracious to Ammonius.

Like the lion-headed gods on other gems the god of the Abbott amulet
is a form of Horus ('Αρμιως) and a solar divinity (Φρη "the Sun": φῶς, πῦρ,
φλόξ point in the same direction). What is particularly interesting, however, is that it attests a living cult at a place appropriately named Leontopolis and records the god's "proper" name, Μιως. The lion cult at Leontopolis is in fact repeatedly mentioned by classical authors, by Strabo
(17.1.40), for example, and by Diodorus Siculus (1.84.4) in the first century
B.C., and later by Philostratus (*Life of Apollonius of Tyana* 5.42, already
referred to in chapter 2) and by Porphyry (*On Abstinence from Animal
Food* 4.9), the latter of whom guarantees its survival well into the third
century A.D. The city was of major importance in the area and grew so
large as to become—possibly true already for the later Ptolemaic period—
the metropolis of a Leontopolite nome.

There can be no doubt that this Leontopolis was situated at the

---

Trübner, 1915) #5620, p. 599, reproducing the inscription and registering
the improvements of Wilhelm Fröhner, *Mélanges d'épigraphie et d'archéologie* I (Paris: Detaille, 1873-1875) 1-6. A better reproduction of the
obverse is offered by Paul Perdrizet, "Antiquités de Léontopolis," *MMFP*
25 (1921-1922) 357, fig. 2; the inscription is discussed p. 359. Eduard
Norden, *Agnostos Theos. Untersuchungen zur Formengeschichte religiöser
Rede* (Leipzig and Berlin: Teubner, 1913) 227-228, cites the inscription (in
part) as a good example of Greek invocatory style, remarking appositely:
"Hier ist zwar das Bestreben nach griechischer Stilisierung . . . ersicht-
lich. . . . Aber mit dieser stilistischen Ambition kreuzt sich das in Inhalt
und in den Partizipialkonstruktionen hervortretende Orientalische." Pieper
("Die Abraxasgemmen" 134) equates the god of the Abbott gem and
Chnoumis and then complains about the "tolle Durcheinander" of figures
on gems generally.

present-day site of Tel Moqdam in the eastern Delta (see map, pl. 12h); the sheer number of objects of every description discovered there which portray the lion-headed god or his leonine incarnations (pls. 13, 14, 15a) and which illustrate every facet of the cult is such that the fellahin largely responsible for their discovery christened the locale "Tell of the Lion(s)." The monuments confirm the god's solar character. They also confirm his conjunction with Osiris (the Abbott gem's Ούσιρμιως), a fact which would appear to indicate that, like all good souls, at death the living lions of Horus-Mios were united with the lord of the dead, yet, despite the mention on a stele from Leontopolis (pl. 15a) of an οἰκία τῆς ταφῆς τῶν λεόντων ἱερά, no mummified lions have ever been disinterred there.[98]

---

[98]Perdrizet, "Antiquités de Léontopolis" 349-385 with pls. 24-25; Edouard Naville, *Ahnas el Medineh (Heracleopolis Magna) with Chapters on Mendes, the Nome of Thoth, and Leontopolis* (Memoirs of the Egypt Exploration Fund 11; London: Egypt Exploration Fund, 1894) 27-31; Ahmed-Bey Kamal, "Notes sur quelques localités de la Basse-Égypte," *RTPE* 28 (1906) 22-25 (§1: "Tell-Mokdam"); Georges Daressy, "Léontopolis, métropole du XIXe nome de la Basse-Égypte," *BIFAO* 30 (1931) 625-649 with the plate; Jean Yoyotte, "La ville de 'Taremou' (Tell el-Muqdâm)," *BIFAO* 52 (1953) 179-192; "Leontopolis," *RÄRG* 423; H. Kees, "Λεοντόπολις," *PW* 12.2054.28-2055.55; Pierre Montet, *Géographie de l'Égypte ancienne* I. *La Basse Égypte* (Paris: Imprimerie Nationale, and Klincksieck, 1957) 130-133; Bertha Porter and Rosalind L. B. Moss, *Topographical Bibliography of Ancient Egyptian Hieroglyphic Texts, Reliefs, and Paintings* IV (Oxford: Clarendon Press, 1934) 37-39; de Wit, *Le rôle et le sens du lion* 423-425. Among the monuments from Leontopolis are bronze thrones of Horus which match Horapollo's description in that they are supported by a pair of lions (see n. 96); with Horus and the lion involved it is not suprising that Bes is also often present: Perdrizet, "Antiquités de Léontopolis" 361-364 with fig. 3, 370 with fig. 6 and n. 3. To judge from a long and impressive inscription published by Marcus W. Tod, "An Ephebic Inscription from Memphis," *JEA* 37 (1951) 86-99 with pl. 8, and expertly commented upon by Jeanne and Louis Robert in the "Bulletin épigraphique," *REG* 65 (1952) 190-197 (#180), Leontopolis was in the time of Elagabalus populous and important enough to institute (A.D. 220) an ephebic ἀγών in his honor, the divine sponsor being ῞Ηλειος Λεόντιος, i.e., the solarized Mios. The two Roberts doubt the reported provenance of the stone from Memphis or Sakkarah, though Sakkarah was evidently the actual find-site of the Abbott gem. The list of ἔφηβοι not surprisingly contains a large number of different names formed from λέων. Further portraits of Mios: Georges Daressy, *Catalogue général des antiquités*

Though the service of Horus-Mios at Leontopolis seems to have been established by Pharaohs (Osorkon I and II) of the 22nd Dynasty from their capital at Bubastis a few kilometers to the southwest (Bastet was reckoned the mother of Mios), in later times the cult owed its enormous popularity to the patronage of the Ptolemies. The vast majority of finds from Tel Moqdam date from this period, the period at which Leontopolis was made the chief city of a nome bearing its name. Some dozen dedicatory stelae from Leontopolis/Tel Moqdam (pls. 14 and 15a being two examples) show a Ptolemy in the act of venerating Horus-Mios in his leonine or lion-headed human form—or both—and at times of proffering the god the gift of a domain in the symbolic form of the hieroglyph *sḫt*. The most significant of these carries an inscription which bears witness to the construction of a new temple at Leontopolis at some time within a few years of 190 B.C. by order of Ptolemy V Epiphanes, whose beneficence to the animal cults of Egypt the famous Rosetta stone similarly celebrates. The inscription reads:[99]

> To king Ptolemy, Theos Epiphanes and Eucharistos, and to queen Cleopatra, Apollonius, the son of Antipater, scribe of Ornumenes, who founded on their behalf the temple of the Lion and all the appurtenances of the temple, (dedicates this stele).

égyptiennes du Musée du Caire N^{os} *38001-39384. Statues de divinités* I (Le Caire: IFAO, 1906) ##38574-38587 (pp. 150-152) with II (1905) pl. 32.

[99] On these stelae generally and that of Ptolemy V Epiphanes in particular see de Wit, *Le rôle et le sens du lion* 276-280; Daressy, "Léontopolis" 630-631, 646; Paul Perdrizet, "Une fondation du temps de Ptolémée Épiphane: le temple du dieu Lion, à Léontopolis," *CRAI* (1922) 320-323; "Antiquités de Léontopolis" 368, 372 fig. 7, 376 fig. 10; Kees, "Λεοντόπο-λις" 2055.33-39; Max L. Strack, "Inschriften aus ptolemäischer Zeit III," *APF* 3 (1906) 127 (#3); Wilhelm Spiegelberg, "Ein Denkstein aus Leontopolis," *RTPE* 36 (1914) 174-176 with pl. 8. On Spiegelberg's stele (my pl. 14) the god is represented both as a lion with sun-disk on his head and as a lion-headed man wearing the *3tf*-crown typical of Osiris and holding an *ᶜnḫ* in one hand and a *w3s*-scepter in the other. The solar disk of the animal and the hand-held attributes of the lion-headed figure are exactly those of the god on the Abbott and other gems. It is obviously from such Leontopolitan cult-reliefs that the gems derived their portraits, stressing what elements they chose; the serpentine (?) head on the god's staff on the Abbott gem is an adaptation of the *w3s*-scepter, it seems.

Perdrizet plausibly ascribes the necessity of reconstruction to the devastation that must have been widespread in the Delta as a result of the violent native Egyptian insurrection centered there which followed within a year of the battle of Raphia (217 B.C.) fought by his father Ptolemy IV Philopator, insurrections which became chronic thereafter.[100]

Ptolemy had good reason to patronize the cult at Leontopolis, and that on more than one account. Not only did it form part of what became his policy of appeasement toward the Egyptian priesthood, around whom the uprisings swirled, but the divine recipient of his largesse was a natural ally to invoke for aid against his Seleucid rivals. Horus-Mios of Leontopolis, in a manner true to his animal acolyte and like the other leonine deities already discussed—Sekhmet, Bes, *Twtw*, his sphinx ancestors, and the lion-headed members of his coterie, not to mention Yaldabaoth himself—was an aggressive god, ferocious, fearsome, at once a dispeller and a dispenser of evil. Perdrizet makes the attractive proposal that by calling himself γραμματεὺς 'Ορνυμένους Ptolemy's minister meant, not that he was the secretary of one Ornumenes, but rather that he was a sacerdotal functionary of the god Lion who "rushes at" or "springs upon" his prey, a title fully consonant with Horus-Mios' character.[101]

---

[100]Perdrizet, "Une fondation du temps de Ptolémée Épiphane" 321-323. For a concise history of the events involved M. Rostovtzeff and W. W. Tarn in *CAH* 7.150-152, 726-731; Maurice Holleaux in *CAH* 8.185-188; and Edwyn Bevan, *The House of Ptolemy. A History of Egypt under the Ptolemaic Dynasty* (Chicago: Argonaut, 1968 [revised reprint of the 1927 edition]), 224-232, 236-241, 388-392, offer readable narratives. The Rosetta decree of the coalition of Egyptian priests (196 B.C.), translated and discussed by Bevan (*The House of Ptolemy* 262-268), shows that insurrection in the Delta had continued into the reign of Ptolemy V, had centered around Lycopolis not far northwest of Leontopolis, had been suppressed by the king and had caused great damage to the temples of the whole area, damage which Ptolemy spared no effort or expense to restore. The rebellion dragged on, however, and was not quashed (and even then only for the moment) until 184-183 B.C. (Bevan pp. 275-276), *after* the restoration of Leontopolis.

[101]Perdrizet, "Une fondation du temps de Ptolémée Épiphane" 322-323. Perdrizet makes the equally attractive proposal that since this title is attested for the Milesian cult of the (originally pre-Greek) Didymaean Apollo, where the lion was also from ancient times a symbol and an incarnation of the god and where Apollo, like the Egyptian, was—certainly in Hellenistic times if not from the beginning—similarly a solar deity, it was conferred upon Horus-Mios by his royal cultists under the influence of

Mios' violent temperament was his from the beginning. The god's name was originally only an epithet, *m3i ḥs3* "the fierce lion," applied, already in texts of the Old Kingdom but with inceasing regularity by the great conquerers of the Middle and New Kingdoms, to the Pharaoh as savagely victorious over Egypt's enemies. It is thus a poetic description of the artistic convention, already discussed, of representing the king as a sphinx mauling a defeated foe and of the various 19th Dynasty Pharaohs Rameses of showing themselves accompanied into battle by pet lions which mangle the "wretched Asiatics" (pl. 15b, a Ptolemaic descendant). It was natural, then, that Mios should gradually assume independent existence as a martial deity who protected Egypt's borders and crushed its invaders; titles are heaped upon him which stress his guardian role and his warlike spirit: "lord of carnage," "great in courage" or "in power" among others of far more ferocious temper, particularly in later times, as, for example, in conjunction with the protective lion-gargoyles which adorn Ptolemaic temples.[102]

Mios quite logically gets identified or affiliated with gods and goddesses of comparable character. The assimilation to Horus attested by the Abbott gem—an assimilation which assured him solar and, with that, astrological ties—was based precisely on the bellicose side of Horus' nature, that side which Horus as the sphinx-king Harmachis exemplifies. Its mythological underpinning was the rich cycle of stories describing the conflict of Horus with Seth: one of the forms which Horus assumed in the course of the fight was that of a lion. In reflection of this myth Horus-

---

Naucratis in the Delta not far from Leontopolis, a city founded with a strong contingent, if not exclusively, from Miletus and the inhabitants of which may already have made the identification of Horus-Mios with Apollo. The old equation Horus = Apollo would certainly have helped them along. On the lion in the cult of Didymaean and many other Apollos: Keller, *Die antike Tierwelt* 47, 52-53; Bürchner, "Didyma," PW 5.437.60-64; 438.7-17; Barclay V. Head and Reginald Stuard Poole, *A Catalogue of the Greek Coins in the British Museum. Ionia* (Bologna: Forni, 1964 [1877]) 183-190 (Miletus; note #64, p. 190, showing on the obverse the head of Apollo and on the reverse a lion standing looking back at a star, with the inscription OPNYMENOΣ); and especially Herbert A. Cahn, "Die Löwen des Apollon," *MH* 7 (1950) 185-199, with pp. 187, 188-189, 191 on Didyma, and 195-198 on Apollo as a solar diety.

[102]De Wit, *Le rôle et le sens du lion* 16-34, 71-82, 85-90, 230-234; "Les inscriptions des lions-gargouilles" 29-45; Perdrizet, "Antiquités de Léontopolis" 357-358; "Miysis," *RÄRG* 468; Lanzone, *Dizionario di mitologia egizia* 81-84 with pl. 34, 269-273 with pl. 106.

Mios of Hebenu in Upper Egypt, portrayed lion-headed, armed with the curved knife, slaughters the Sethian oryx, and Leo trampling a serpent on the Dendera zodiac (as elsewhere) can be interpreted as Horus overcoming Seth.[103]

More important in the present context, however, is the cult of Horus of Mesen, an ancient frontier fortress in the eastern Delta not far northeast of Leontopolis, carried on not only at Mesen but also at many other border outposts, where Horus, like Horus-Mios of Leontopolis, was worshiped as a lion or a lion-headed man because the beast represented the god's power to guard the Delta against incursion by Semite nomads. It was precisely due to the vulnerability of the eastern Delta that lion-cults—and that of Wadjet as uraeus as well, who seems to have shared worship with Mios at Leontopolis and with his mother Bastet at Bubastis nearby—are numerous in the area. It was for their common animal and its martial function, then, that Horus and Mios were identified at Leontopolis; and it was because Ptolemy V, like his father and so many Egyptian monarchs before him, needed all the help he could get to counter the Syrian threat (in this case the Seleucids)—and internal rebellion too—that he showered attention upon Mios there.

Down to late antiquity Horus continued to be revered as a god who granted victory, appearing, like other Egyptian gods, in Roman military dress. As for Mios: (1) early taken up into the Heliopolitan embrace as a similarly leonine Shu and in turn identified with another fighter, Onuris (equated by the Greeks with Ares), he appears on Leontopolite nome-coins outfitted as a warrior, holding a lion, and (2) Mars (Horus) is made his planet.[104]

---

[103]Philippe Derchain, *Rites égyptiens* I. *Le sacrifice de l'oryx* (Bruxelles: Fondation Égyptologique Reine Élisabeth, 1962) 13-22; H. de Meulenaere, "Horus de Hebenou et son prophète," *Religions en Égypte hellénistique et romaine. Colloque de Stasbourg 16-18 mai 1967* (Paris: Presses Universitaires de France, 1969) 21-29; Georges Daressy, "L'Égypte céleste," *BIFAO* 12 (1916) 11; (W.) Gundel, *Dekane und Dekansternbilder* 331.

[104]De Wit, *Le rôle et le sens du lion* 32, 76-77, 87-88, 238-248, 395, and note 434-440 for a lengthy list of lion cults in the Delta; Schweitzer, *Löwe und Sphinx* 49 with pl. 12.1; Hopfner, "Der Tierkult der alten Ägypter" 41, 45; Daressy, "Léontopolis" 626-628, 642-648; Kees, "Λεοντόπολις" 2054.54-64; 2055.27-31; Perdrizet, "Antiquités de Léontopolis" 366; Montet, *Géographie de l'Égypte ancienne* I, 176, 188-191; "Löwe," *RÄRG* 427; "Horus," *RÄRG* 312-314 with fig. 79; Lanzone, *Dizionario di mitolo-*

Mios was accounted the son of two lion-headed goddesses: of Sekhmet, the consort of Ptah in Memphis and an extremely powerful goddess in the Delta, and of Bastet, who, though originally a tamer, cat-headed goddess, was early assimilated to her wilder and politically stronger neighbor Sekhmet and was revered with her son at Leontopolis.[105] Hence Mios is to be seen lurking behind the lion-headed leader of his mother Sekhmet's deadly emissaries (cp. pl. 16, where a Ptolemaic king makes offering to a series of lion-headed, knife-wielding relatives of Mios, protectors of his realm and exacters of his vengeance), and he is to be regarded as first counsin to *Twtw*, son of Neith and worshiped at Saïs not far to the west of Leontopolis. With such a family, as an avatar of Horus, and moreover because in general, like the others, he was a figure of enormous apotropaic power, Mios possessed, like them, intimate ties to the astrological and magical traditions. His solar and martial connections I have already mentioned. Through the mediation of his identity with Horus, their common solar associations and partially identical animal form, Mios was closely related to Chnoumis, whose head is Sekhmet (or actually, indeed, it might just as well be Mios as *Wr ḥk3w*) and whose body is Wadjet, both intimates of Mios. It must have been at least partially on the basis of this intimacy that Chnoumis could be chosen as a new embodiment for Yahweh/Yaldabaoth, whereas older tradition linked him to Mios (as I shall argue). I have already shown that Horus/Harpocrates and Chnoumis are related or interchangeable on certain gems; if that is so, it is so because the Tanis family of decans (like the Seti I B family also represented at Dendera) gives the *Knm.(t)* and *ḥry (ḥpd) Knm.(t)* decans Horus for a

---

gia egizia 668-678 with pls. 243-244. Like Mios, *Twtw* was also identified with Horus (Gauthier, "Le dieu *Twt*" 117) and for the same military reasons. Coins: Poole, *Catalogue of the Coins of Alexandria and the Nomes* 344 ##14 (Hadrian), 16 (Antoninus Pius).

[105]Perdrizet, "Antiquités de Léontopolis" 364-365; Hopfner, "Der Tierkult der alten Ägypter" 42; "Leontopolis," *RÄRG* 423; "Bastet," *RÄRG* 80-82; Kees, *Der Götterglaube im alten Ägypten* 7, 82-83, 137; Montet, *Géographie de l'Égypte ancienne* I, 173-178; de Wit, *Le rôle et le sens du lion* 292-298; Lanzone, *Dizionario di mitologia egizia* 223-231 with pls. 82-83. Horus-Mios was worshiped with his mother Bastet at Bubastis as Horus Hekenu: "Hor-Hekenu," *RÄRG* 306. The famous "Litany of Isis," POxy 1380.58-59, informs us that Isis too was worshiped at Leontopolis, as an ἀσπίς (Bernard P. Grenfell and Arthur S. Hunt, *The Oxyrhynchus Papyri* XI; London: Hart, 1915; 197); she too may have served as mother to Horus-Mios.

patron deity. Moreover, a text at Kom Ombo, in a temple whose construction was also initiated by Ptolemy V, identifies the Horus as Ḥr wr "Horus the Elder" of Letopolis in the Delta, a god who, through association with the Heliopolitan lion-pair Shu and Tefnut and with the Memphite Sekhmet was from ancient times also worshiped as a lion. This leonine Horus as patron god of Knm.(t) must also have had a hand in giving Chnoumis a lion's head, especially as Wadjet also played a role in the cult at Letopolis.[106]

Identified with Horus and made a dutiful son of Sekhmet or Bastet her virtual double, for all the reasons that these goddesses did, Mios cut an attractive figure for Egyptian healer-magicians. Aside from making him a son of Sekhmet his coalescence with Nefertem, the third member of the Memphite family trinity, helped in its own right. Naturally Nefertem acquired a lion's head for his trouble. At the eastern Delta frontier outpost now called Saft el-Henneh (and elsewhere too), in the beautiful shrine of Nectanebo II who, like other kings of the 30th Dynasty, had to contend with the Persian invasion, he takes on the ferocious form of a lion gnawing on the head of a prisoner whose hands are hog-tied behind his back. But in the bargain Mios acquired Nefertem's association with fragrant unguents and their medical and magical effectiveness against every noxious, evil influence. Not surprisingly, as a divine protector against harm Nefertem regularly appears near Horus on the apotropaic stelae "Horus on the Crocodiles."[107]

Horus-Mios was already, as I said, a magically potent figure for his ancient role as a raging destroyer of Egypt's enemies; his affiliation with

---

[106]Neugebauer-Parker, *Egyptian Astronomical Texts* III, 141-142, 154; de Wit, *Le rôle et le sens du lion* 248-253, 391; Montet, *Géographie de l'Égypte ancienne* I, 51-53; "Haroeris," *RÄRG* 270-272.

[107]De Wit, *Le rôle et le sens du lion* 235-237, 238; Edouard Naville, *The Shrine of Saft el Henneh and the Land of Goshen* (Memoirs of the Egypt Exploration Fund 5; London: Trübner, 1887) 1-13 with the plates; "Löwe," *RÄRG* 428; "Nefertem," *RÄRG* 508-510; Kees, *Der Götterglaube im alten Ägypten* 90 with n. 3, 286-288; Lanzone, *Dizionario di mitologia egizia* 385-389 with pls. 147-148; and especially Alexandre Piankoff, "Nefer-Toum et Mahes," *EgR* 1 (1933) 99-105. Befitting its station as a Delta guardpost and the ferocious cult of Mios-Nefertem and Sopdu carried on there, whose victorious might is celebrated in hymns on the shrine of Nectanebo, Saft el-Henneh knows the decans as ruthless apportioners of disasters to men: see Schott in (W.) Gundel, *Dekane und Dekansternbilder* 14-17.

Nefertem only made him all the more so. The very name *m3i ḥs3* seems to have conveyed the bewitching power of an angry lion's gaze to transfix anyone who stared him in the eyes and to strike the heart with terror. Aelian (*On the Characteristics of Animals* 12.7) preserves the memory of this tradition in his comments about the cult at Leontopolis:

> As the lions eat they (the priests) chant songs in the Egyptian tongue to them. And the theme of the song is: "Do not bewitch (βασκήνητε) anyone who looks at you." You might say that the chant serves the function of amulets.

Mios' gaze was like the evil eye; it needed to be defended against.[108] This spell-binding property of Mios' look underlies the ascription of fiery eyes to the lion-gargoyles, who represent Mios, to decans, and, eventually, to Yaldabaoth in Gnostic texts. So attractive a god was Horus-Mios for magicians, then—the Abbott gem is merely one outstanding instance— that he survived into the grimoires of late antiquity: as ʼΑρμιουθ in *PGM* II P 7.361, for example, and in the demotic magical papyrus of London and Leiden 9.21-22.[109]

It was Mios who originally instigated Yahweh's metamorphosis into a lion-headed god. There was material enough in all the magical, medical, astrological and cosmogonical contexts to serve to link the two divinities, material which I have already discussed in connection with Chnoumis and in the preceding paragraphs. Lead curse tablets from Cyprus show that

---

[108] On the name *m3i ḥs3*, translations of which often reflect the fascinating allure of Mios' fierce nature, and the passage from Aelian: de Wit, *Le rôle et le sens du lion* 17-18, 448-449, 456; Perdrizet, "Antiquités de Léontopolis" 359-361; Hopfner, "Der Tierkult der alten Ägypter" 43-44. With *ḥs3* denoting the transfixing glare of a lion's eye stalking its prey one might compare the classical Greek epithet χαροπός ("flashing-eyed"?) often applied to lions (Homer, *Odyssey* 11.611; Hesiod, *Theogony* 321).

[109] See Schmidt's review of *PGM* II, *GGA* 196 (1934) 172-174; Hopfner, "Der religionsgeschichtliche Gehalt des grossen demotischen Zauber-papyrus" 113-114, 119-120; F. Ll. Griffith and Herbert Thompson, *The Leyden Papyrus. An Egyptian Magical Book* (New York: Dover, 1974 [originally published as *The Demotic Magical Papyrus of London and Leiden*, 1904]) 70-73: "Mihos, mighty one, shall send out a lion of the sons of Mihos under compulsion to fetch them to me (*bis*) the souls of god, the souls of man, the souls of the Underworld, the souls of the horizon, the spirits, the dead, so that they tell me the truth to-day concerning that after which I am inquiring. . . ."

the identification indeed was made, for a recurrent formula in them runs: ὁ ἐν τῷ οὐρανῷ ἔχων τὸ ἐθέριον βασίλιον Μιωθιλαμψ ἐν οὐρανῷ Ιαω κὲ ὑπὸ γῆν Σαμβληνια Ιαω,[110] wherein "Mios shining in heaven"—as a solar Leo, no doubt—is Yahweh's heavenly form.

The tablets' ὁ ἐν τῷ οὐρανῷ ἔχων τὸ ἐθέριον βασίλιον reminds one of the Abbott gem's description of Mios ὁ τὴν ἐνουράνιον τῆς αἰωνίου φύσεως κεκληρωμένος ἀνάγκην. The former, based on Old Testament commonplaces filtered through the Septuagint, lent itself to astrological elaboration, evident in the latter. On a yet more primitive level the two gods shared a heavenly realm: Mios, as a leonine son of Sekhmet and like Seth, was a god of thunderstorms and the famine and plague which, in Egypt, regularly accompanied their season (hence he is called "lord of heaven"),[111] but then so, primevally so, was Yahweh. If the Abbott gem calls Mios ὁ ἀστράπτων καὶ βροντῶν καὶ γνόφου καὶ ἀνέμων κύριος and φῶς, πῦρ, φλόξ, one is hard-pressed to decide whether this is "purely" Egyptian or whether it too attests a synthesis of Mios and Yahweh on the basis of a multitude of Old Testament theophanies and passages like Pss 17:11-16; 96:3-5; and 103:2-4 LXX.[112]

But it was Mios' ancient military function as guardian of Egypt against invasion, a function which he continued to fulfill for Ptolemy V, as I have shown, that initially prompted the Mios-Yahweh theocrasy.[113] One may

---

[110]Augustus Audollent, *Defixionum Tabellae quotquot innotuerunt tam in graecis orientis quam in totius occidentis partibus praeter atticas in Corpore Inscriptionum Atticarum editas* (Frankfurt am Main: Minerva, 1967 [1904]) ##22.46-47 (p. 41), 24.27-28 (p. 45), 26.33-34 (p. 48), 29.31-32 (p. 53), 30.37-39 (p. 55), 31.30-31 (p. 57), 32.32-33 (p. 60), 33.35-37 (p. 65); Preisendanz, "Miôthilamps," PW 15.2028.25-45.

[111]De Wit, *Le rôle et le sens du lion* 230.

[112]Barb experiences the same difficulty here: "Ein magischer Armreif" 366 n. 4.

[113]Here again Jean Doresse glimpsed the truth but in the wrong context (he applies it to Yahweh/Yaldabaoth as Chnoumis) and without understanding all the ramifications of the subject: *Des hiéroglyphes à la croix. Ce que le passé pharaonique a légué au christianisme* (İstanbul: Nederlands historisch-archaeologisch Instituut in het Nabije Oosten, 1960) 47: "Il faut cependant noter qu'un autre dieu égyptien qu'Osiris a pu—du point de vue iconographique—contributer à la création par la Gnose de sa figure de dieu Ialdabaôth-Saclas, décrit ordinairement comme un monstreux serpent à tête de lion rayonnant: il s'agit du dieu Mahès, de Léontopolis, tel que l'invoque une agate gravée, d'époque romaine . . .," meaning the Abbott gem.

well ask why in heaven's name, in spite of all the contexts in which similarities between the two existed, Yahweh should have been identified with
a god like Mios; why not rather Ptah, or Re in all his forms, or Chnum? In
fact the scenario can be reconstructed and the social and political forces
which motivated the union can be delineated with enough precision to
make as good a case as circumstantial evidence will allow. That no literary record of the wedding survives, beyond the tablets of Cypriot sorcerers and the systems of Gnostics, both of the Roman period, need
occasion no surprise, since the Egyptian setting in which it took place
disappeared with the last of the Ptolemies. The Jewish group which was
responsible for causing it was a very special and isolated one; its activities and its worship cannot have met with universal approval from other
Jews, and they did not themselves much outlast the Macedonian masters
whom they served so well.

There is one more piece of the puzzle that needs to be outlined before
the picture is complete. There was yet another Leontopolis in the eastern
Delta, thirty kilometers or so southwest of Leontopolis/Tel Moqdam,
Bubastis, and Saft el-Henneh. It too must have been the center of a lion
cult, early drawn, like that at Letopolis, into the powerful Heliopolitan
circle of gods, in whose nome the town was situated, the nome capital
lying a scant eighteen kilometers to the south of it. Judging from the way
the name is mostly preserved (Λεόντων πόλις) it has been surmised that a
pair of lions was worshiped there and that they were held embodiments of
the Heliopolitan pair Shu and Tefnut, who were elsewhere too revered in
leonine form (at Letopolis, for instance).[114] However that may be, it was
at this Leontopolis that, on Josephus' evidence, Onias IV (and not his
father Onias III, as *J.W.* 1.1.1 §§31-32 and 7.10.2 §423 seem to have it, for
a number of good reasons an impossibility), deprived of the high priesthood in favor of a Hellenizing lackey of the Seleucid government, founded
probably within a decade or so of his flight to Egypt around 162 B.C., a
temple of Yahweh. It lasted until about A.D. 73 when, not long after the
Roman reduction of Judaea, prompted by the activities of Jewish extremists in Egypt and by the fear that the temple would become a rallying

---

[114]Kees, "Λεόντων πόλις," PW 12.2055.56-2056.4; *Der Götterglaube
im alten Ägypten* 154, 214, 220-221; Montet, *Géographie de l'Égypte
ancienne* I, 168-169; "Löwe," *RÄRG* 427; de Wit, *Le rôle et le sens du lion*
198-212, 324-332, 423; Lanzone, *Dizionario di mitologia egizia* 1234-1240
with pls. 395-396.

point for a fresh outbreak of rebellion, Vespasian ordered it closed and its rites abolished (*J.W.* 7.10.2, 4 §§420-421, 433-436).[115]

Beyond almost every shadow of a doubt the location of this temple was at the present Tel el-Yahoudieh 26 kilometers northeast of Cairo (see map, pl. 12h). Not only does its position in the Heliopolitan nome and its distance from the nome capital square well with the information provided by Josephus, but extensive exploration of the site for well nigh on a century has shown that, true to its Arabic name, in Ptolemaic and early

---

[115]The literature is vast; good general treatments are those of Emil Schürer, *Geschichte des jüdischen Volkes* III (4th ed.; Leipzig: Hinrichs, 1909) 42-43, 144-148; S. Krauss, "Leontopolis," *Jewish Encyclopedia* VIII (New York and London: Funk and Wagnalls, 1904) 7-8; Kees, "Λεόντων πόλις," 2055.56-2056.62; "'Ονίου," PW 18.477.47-479.47; A. Barucq, "Léontopolis," *DBSup* 5.359-372; Victor Tcherikover, *Hellenistic Civilization and the Jews* (trans. S. Applebaum; New York: Atheneum, 1959) 275-281, 392-397; the same scholar's "Prolegomena" in *CPJ* I.2, 44-46; and most recently M. Delcor, "Le temple d'Onias en Égypte," *RB* 75 (1968) 188-203 with a *"Post-scriptum"* by R. de Vaux, pp. 204-205; Martin Hengel, *Judaism and Hellenism. Studies in their Encounter in Palestine during the Early Hellenistic Period* I (Philadelphia: Fortress, 1974) 16 and n. 88 (vol. II, 12), 100 and n. 338 (II, 69) with 267-283 and notes on the Oniads; Robert Hayward, "The Jewish Temple at Leontopolis: A Reconsideration," *JJS* 33 (1982) 429-443, providing further references. John J. Collins, *The Sibylline Oracles of Egyptian Judaism* (SBLDS 13; Missoula: University of Montana, 1974) 49-53, discusses the possibility of reference to the Leontopolitan temple in *Sib. Or.* 3. The whole issue of a rival temple in Egypt has raised hackles: S.A. Hirsch, "The Temple of Onias," *Jews' College Jubilee Volume* (London: Luzac, 1906) 39-80. Even though it is generally acknowledged that Josephus' account of the Oniad succession is a mess, Hirsch's thesis (pp. 70-77 in particular), seconded in this respect at least by M. A. Beek, "Relations entre Jérusalem et la diaspora égyptienne au 2e siècle avant J.-C.," *OTS* 2 (1943) 119-143, especially 121-132, that the historian's figure for the duration of the temple (343 years, *J.W.* 7.10.4 §436) is correct and that the foundation is therefore to be ascribed to *circa* 270 B.C. and to Onias II (Beek: foundation by "Onias" is strictly legendary) has not met with approval, but, if the number is not simply an error—as so many numbers in Josephus are—it might represent an alternate tradition which sought to make out a more impressive lineage for the temple by tracing it to the time of Ptolemy II Philadelphus, legendary for his interest in Jewish matters. Pieper ("Die Abraxasgemmen" 130) mistakenly identifies the Leontopolis of the Abbott gem with Leontopolis/Tel el-Yahoudieh.

Roman times it was home to a large Jewish settlement. The necropolis has yielded a huge number of inscriptions in Greek, many of them of quite accomplished epigrammatic style, though no unimpeachable remains of Onias' temple itself have been uncovered, despite Petrie's claims to the contrary. What is more, a monument found at Tel el-Yahoudieh, dedicated by an admiral of the Bubastite 26th Dynasty, who shows himself holding a shrine in which the goddess Bastet is standing, furnishes evidence that supports Josephus' source in *Ant.* 13.3.1, 2 §§66, 70 when it informs us that in fact Onias refurbished a deserted temple of "Bastet the Wild"—i.e., Bastet as identified with Sekhmet and not in her tamer mode. Along with other finds, the admiral's monument shows that this Leontopolis, like that to its north and other cities of the eastern Delta, was a military outpost (Josephus' source explicitly calls it a fortress) whose lion-cult was a part of Egypt's religious Maginot line of defense against Semite invasion. The major difficulty standing in the way of firm establishment of Onias' Leontopolis at Tel el-Yahoudieh is the fact that, like their ancestors, Jews had settled in many different places in the Delta under the Ptolemies, one of them being a site near Bilbes, a dozen or so kilometers to the northeast of Tel el-Yahoudieh and once known by the same Arabic name (see map, pl. 12h), but it has yielded little, and it is not in the Heliopolitan nome. What is interesting is that the military nature of these Jewish settlements in the Delta is evident from the names under which they are preserved: (1) *Castra Judaeorum,* which may be a later name for Onias' Leontopolis (Josephus refers to what had been Leontopolis as ἡ 'Ονίου χώρα: *J.W.* 1.9.4 §190; 7.10.2 §421; *Ant.* 13.10.4 §287; 14.8.1 §131), and (2) τὸ καλούμενον 'Ιουδαίων στρατόπεδον, *not* identical with the Latin *Castra Judaeorum* or with Onias' Leontopolis, though often assumed to be. It is also evident from the information that we have about them, for the Greek-named "Camp of the Jews" (Josephus, *J.W.* 1.9.4 §191; *Ant.* 14.8.2 §133), near Letopolis and so it too in close association with a defensive Egyptian lion-cult, was the scene of a battle in Julius Caesar's Alexandrian War (48-47 B.C.).[116]

---

[116]Roeder, "Sechmet" 588.36-40; 589.20-24; 590.59-62; Kees, "Λεόντων πόλις" 2056.4-62; "'Ονίου" 477.47-478.15, 25-61; 479.15-47; *Der Götterglaube im alten Ägypten* 9; Porter-Moss, *Topographical Bibliography* IV, 56-58; Barucq, "Léontopolis" 360, 362-366; Tcherikover, "Prolegomena" 2-4, 8, 28; Schürer, *Geschichte des jüdischen Volkes* III, 42-43 (noting yet another Jewish colony at Athribis about midway between the two cities Leontopolis), 144-146; W. M. Flinders Petrie, *Hyksos and Israelite Cities* (London: University College, and Quaritch, 1906) 19-27 ("The Temple of

That being so, Onias' occupation of the site with its surrounding territory so graciously granted him by Ptolemy VI Philometor, and his rededi-
cation of the temple of Bastet there represented no disruption as far as
the function of the place in Egypt's strategic defense was concerned, for
it too was a military colony. The temple which Onias built at Leontopolis,
whether or not it resembled that at Jerusalem (Josephus' statements *J.W.*
1.1.1 §33; 7.10.3 §§427-430; *Ant.* 12.9.7 §388; 13.3.1, 3 §§63, 72-73;
20.10.3 §236 are conflicting), was, like its Egyptian predecessor there,
heavily fortified (*J.W.* 7.10.3 §427). We do not know what Onias' precise
motives may have been in fleeing Judaea and how he may have justified
erection of a rival sanctuary in defiance of Deuteronomic ordinance—
logically enough, though, on the basis of Isa 19:18-19 with its mention of
the "City of the Sun" (presuming that, with 1QIsa[a], to be the original
reading) in the context of an oracle promising the existence of an altar to
Yahweh in the land of Egypt (so Josephus *J.W.* 7.10.3 §432; *Ant.* 13.3.1, 2
§§64, 71; *b. Menaḥ* 109b-110a).[117] But his reasons for establishing it are

---

Onias") with pls. 15 and 20, and pp. 17, 18-19; Edouard Naville, *The Mount
of the Jew and the City of Onias. Belbeis, Samanood, Abusir, Tukh el
Karmus* (Memoirs of the Egypt Exploration Fund 7; London: Kegan Paul,
Trench, Trübner, 1890) 5-21 on our Tel el-Yahoudieh, and 22-23 on that
near Bilbes, with F. Ll. Griffith, *The Antiquities of Tell el Yahûdîyeh* (in
the same volume) 38-53, 58-59, and pls. 10.7-10, 16:2-4, 15-16 (scarabs
graphically illustrating the cult of Mios in conjunction with the military
function of the place). Le Comte du Mesnil du Buisson, "Compte rendu
sommaire d'une mission à Tell el-Yahoudiyé," *BIFAO* 29 (1929) 155-178;
"Le temple d'Onias et le camp Hyksôs à Tell el-Yahoudiyé," 35 (1935) 59-
71 with the plate, reports his—the most recent—exploration of the site.
The inscriptions from the necropolis at Tel el-Yahoudieh are in *CII* II,
##1451-1530, pp. 382-438, with pp. 378-381 in introduction, and in *CPJ*
III, 145-163.

[117]On this question and the possibility that the LXX's πόλις ασεδεκ at
Isa 19:18 may represent pro-Leontopolitan propaganda (from Isa 1:26) in
the face of hostility from other contemporary Egyptian (non-military)
Jewish circles (not to mention those in Judaea) see Delcor, "Le temple
d'Onias" 199-202; Barucq, "Léontopolis" 366-370; Hayward, "The Jewish
Temple at Leontopolis" 438-440; George Buchanan Gray, *A Critical and
Exegetical Commentary on the Book of Isaiah I-XXVII* (ICC; Edinburgh: T.
& T. Clark, 1912) 332-340; Kaiser, *Der Prophet Jesaja* 87-89; André
Feuillet, "Un sommet religieux de l'Ancien Testament. L'oracle d'Isaïe, xix
(vv. 16-25) sur la conversion de l'Égypte," *RSR* 39 (1951-1952) 65-87,
especially pp. 70-73; I. L. Seeligmann, *The Septuagint Version of Isaiah. A
Discussion of its Problems* (Leiden: Brill, 1948) 68, 91-94; Arie van der

(as a hostile Josephus nevertheless accurately surmises: *J.W.* 7.10.2, 3 §§423-425, 431; *Ant.* 13.3.1 §§62-63, 67) likely to have been (1) to unify the various Jewish military bases in the Delta, formerly indisposed to each other through possession each of its own house of prayer, by providing them with a central shrine at which to worship; (2) to serve Ptolemy's interests thereby, by strengthening Jewish allegiance to each other and to his cause, supporting the anti-Seleucid coalition among Onias' countrymen, and encouraging Jewish immigration to Egypt; and (3) perhaps too, where self-aggrandizement and other more personal reasons may have played a role, to preserve the legitimate Zadokite high priesthood which had come to an end with the murder of his father by founding a rival temple in which, in his own person, it might continue.

But his motives were first and foremost military because he was in the service of his royal patron. Well might Ptolemy VI Philometor welcome so politically valuable an asset as Onias, however young and untried he may have been upon arrival, and welcome too the huge band (to hear Jerome tell it) which accompanied him into Egypt, for the Ptolemies had, partially because native Egyptians had become habitually seditious (another uprising occurred during Philometor's reign), by this time come to be more and more dependent on mercenaries, and the mercenaries of choice against their Seleucid enemies were naturally the Jews, especially as handily settled on Egyptian soil. Moreover, Ptolemy had his hands full and desperately needed the alliance with Onias: the struggle with his ambitious younger brother, the future Ptolemy VII Euergetes II (Physkon) went on his whole life long, and the war with Seleucid Syria, having heated up again in the late 170s and culminating with Antiochus IV Epiphanes' invasion of Egypt (169 B.C.), in which Philometor himself was taken prisoner, occupied him to his death. And Onias served him well, as his letter to Philometor, together with the reply, both cooked up by a Hellenistic (Alexandrian?) Jew none too well-disposed toward the Leontopolitan temple but familiar enough with the facts of the garrison's service to Ptolemy, maintains in no uncertain terms (*Ant.* 13.3.1 §65). A papyrus letter of 164 B.C. (*CPJ* I, #132), if the "Onias" to whom it is addressed is correctly read and represents the same Onias (the early date is problematic), testifies to his having, even from his very arrival at Philometor's court, been accorded high standing; Onias may not have been as green as

---

Kooij, *Die alten Textzeugen des Jesajabuches. Ein Beitrag zur Textgeschichte des Alten Testaments* (OBO 35; Freiburg: Universitätsverlag, and Göttingen: Vandenhoeck & Ruprecht, 1981) 52-55.

is generally assumed. In the course of his career as commanding officer of the Jewish forces of the Delta, at any rate, Onias fought bravely for Philometor and, after the monarch's death in 145 B.C., marched to the defense of his widow Cleopatra II and her son against Physkon (Josephus, *Ag. Ap.* 2.5 §§49-56). The Jewish garrison at Leontopolis continued to be a force to reckon with for at least a century thereafter, since Onias' sons faithfully served Philometor's daughter Cleopatra III in her fight (roughly 107-101 B.C.) with her son Ptolemy VIII Soter II Lathyrus over the succession (Josephus, *Ant.* 13.10.4 §§284-287, quoting Strabo; 13.13.1-2 §§348-355) and, during Julius Caesar's Alexandrian War, held up the advance of an auxiliary force, allowing it to pass through its territory only after Antipater had negotiated their allegiance to Caesar's cause (*J.W.* 1.9.4 §190; *Ant.* 14.8.1 §§131-132).[118]

What must the native Egyptian priesthood have made of the Jewish garrisons of the Delta and their temple in what had once been a sanctuary of Bastet/Sekhmet? They can have cared little for whatever *interpretationes graecae* of Yahweh their Ptolemaic masters and the Greek intelligentsia were bandying about, still less for the lucubrations of Hellenized Jews in Alexandria. With Onias' and his successors' army serving in armed defense of the realm and with the shrine of their god set up in a place holy to the mother of Mios, one may well ask how they could have *avoided* the identification of Yahweh with Mios. That the god whom the Jews worshiped in *their* Leontopolis not far away from Leontopolis/Tel Moqdam was merely a continuation of the cult indigenous there and that their god was just as ferociously leonine were, after all, fair assumptions for them to make.

It was these assumptions, as old as the second half of the second century B.C., which eventually led to Gnostic portrayal of Yahweh as a lion-headed god. The astrological, magical and iatromathematical traditions which have been discussed must have helped to fix and to preserve the picture of Yahweh as leontocephalic in the Hellenistic Egyptian cultural

---

[118]Tcherikover, *Hellenistic Civilization and the Jews* 275-284; "Prolegomena" 11-15, 17, 19-25; Hengel, *Judaism and Hellenism* 15-18; Delcor, "Le temple d'Onias" 189, 191-195. For the history consult Bevan, *The House of Ptolemy* 282-305, 306-325, 326-331; and his contribution to *CAH* 8.495-526. The thesis advanced by S. H. Steckoll, "The Qumran Sect in relation to the Temple of Leontopolis," *RdQ* 6 (1967) 55-69, that Zadokite priests from Leontopolis established at Qumran, around 137 B.C., a schismatic cultus modeled on their own in Egypt has rightly met with criticism from Delcor and de Vaux, "Le temple d'Onias" 196-199, 204-205.

contexts in which those traditions were sacred lore, contexts upon which Gnosticism drew so heavily for its view of Yahweh/Yaldabaoth and his fellow archons. The emerging "Sethian" or "Ophite" strain of Gnosticism seized upon this Egyptian tradition, perhaps through the intermediary of proto-Gnostic Samaritan sorcerers like Simon Magus or Dositheus, both reputed to be well-schooled in Egyptian magic, or through the intermediary of the anti-Jewish polemic which became rife in late Ptolemaic and early Roman Egypt, or both. They fastened upon it, anyway, because, as an essentially military tradition to begin with, it fit so nicely with their concept of Yahweh as a planetary power (Saturn) and, true to Saturn's astrological nature, a repressive, vindictive, ruthlessly punitive god. Mios' associations with Egyptian astrological and magical science obviously helped, the former because Yahweh had already been identified in Syria with Saturn and with Helios, and the latter because the people who took up the Egyptian tradition into a proto-Gnostic setting were magicians. If they were also Samaritans, this fact might help to explain why the Rabbis chose כּוּתִים as a derogatory name for the Samaritan sect, for the Cuthite Nergal was as devilishly leonine as the Yahweh-Mios that Samaritan sorcerers like Simon Magus (and the stir he caused is obvious from Acts 8:9-11) had imported from Egypt. It was the members of these proto-Gnostic conventicles or their immediate descendants that pressed into supportive service the savage leonine imagery of the Old Testament, itself already typologically parallel to that in Egypt which had given rise to the equation of Yahweh with Mios in the first place, and, later, among their Christianized brethren, similar passages in the New Testament.

As many scholars are quick to point out, the influence exerted by Onias' temple at Leontopolis can only have been very limited—limited, in fact, to Jews in the Ptolemies' military employ—and must have petered out when Rome supplanted the Ptolemies as lords of Egypt. Though it continued to exist until the early 70s A.D., the history of the settlement and its shrine during the century and a quarter from Caesar's Egyptian campaign to its final dissolution is a total blank. But even in its heyday Jews of Alexandria and other metropolitan centers in Egypt can have known nothing of the implications of Onias' temple for native Egyptian religion, much less cared. It was the black sheep of the family; it is significant that Philo ignores it completely, for given his apologetic purposes, had he regarded it as a proper example of Jewish piety one would expect him to have held it up to pagan admiration as he does with the Therapeutae. It is no wonder that Jewish literature, and Greek literature about the Jews, preserves nothing of such a theocrasy, then. If it survived on Cyprus, that is doubtless because the island was, for the most part

continuously from its conquest by Ptolemy I Soter in 313 B.C., a Ptolemaic possession, and it was precisely Ptolemy VI Philometor who resided
there briefly in 163 B.C. and then later took the island by storm from his
conniving brother Physkon in 154. Onias or his mercenary army is likely to
have fought for Philometor there, and it was either at that time that the
Yahweh-Mios synthesis penetrated this bastion of the Ptolemaic domain,
or perhaps later when soldiers from Leontopolis were certain to have been
embroiled in fighting on Cyprus by Philometor's daughter Cleopatra III,
whom Onias' sons faithfully served, in her effort to have her son Ptolemy
IX Alexander, resident there, succeed to the throne.[119] If it was Jewish
mercenaries from Leontopolis who were responsible for importing the idea
into Cyprus, they must obviously themselves have known of it and con-
doned it. That is not unthinkable, for they may readily have fostered the
analogy for patriotic, diplomatic or social reasons without going so far as
to plant Mios' lion's head on their god. It was only others—Egyptians,
Samaritan sorcerers and their Gnostic successors—who took that fateful
step.

3.6   The Orphic Cosmology

Two other traditions involving partially or wholly lion-headed
deities must now be briefly discussed because they both have been implicated in the creation of a leontocephalic mien for Yahweh/Yaldabaoth.
The first is the Orphic cosmogony in two of its late antique forms. As I
noted earlier, Gilles Quispel sought to derive the lion-headed, serpentine
form of the creator in *Apoc. John,* from this quarter.[120]
To begin with, the problem of dating is crucial here, for the authors in
whose works these cosmogonies are imbedded are later than, or at best
coeval with, the Greek originals represented by the recensions of *Apoc.
John,* and so the thorny problem as to the age of the traditions they
contain imposes itself. Quispel, as others have done, ascribes the grosser

---

[119]Bevan, *The House of Ptolemy* 23-27, 37, 286, 291, 299-302, 328-331;
CAH 7.78 (W. W. Tarn), 126-127 (M. Rostovtzeff: Cyprus under a military
governor in command of a contingent of troops from the Ptolemies' Egyptian army stationed there); 8.284 (P. V. M. Benecke), 506-507 (Bevan).
[120]"The Demiurge in the Apocryphon of John" 1-32, in particular pp. 6,
10, 15-23. J. van Amersfoort, "Traces of an Alexandrian Orphic Theogony
in the Pseudo-Clementines" in the *Studies in Gnosticism and Hellenistic
Religions presented to Gilles Quispel* 13-30, follows up on Quispel's
article.

polymorphic descriptions in these myths to remote antiquity for their crudity, in this case to the Bronze Age. While such an early date may accurately reflect their roots, it need not accurately fix the time of the entry of such details into their present contexts nor take into account the possibility of their embellishment with elements totally alien to them originally. The fact is that myth-making was still very much alive and well in late Roman society, and "crude" mythological forms were even then still being creatively welded into new cosmogonic structures. The *Chaldean Oracles* and the various Gnostic systems are prime examples.

The two Orphic cosmogonies are (1) that which was known to Damascius under the names of Hieronymos and Hellanikos, who (Damascius supposes) may be one and the same person, but about whom, anyway, absolutely nothing certain is known, and (2) that which is commonly called the *Rhapsodic Theogony*.[121] For the details in which we are interested the earliest witness to the first is the apologist Athenagoras (if the Orphic cosmogony known to him was indeed essentially identical with that of

---

[121]See Otto Kern's introductions to *Orphicorum Fragmenta* (Dublin and Zürich: Weidmann, 1972 [1922]) 130, 140-143; Arthur Bernard Cook, *Zeus. A Study in Ancient Religion* II (New York: Biblo and Tannen, 1965 [1914-1940]) 1019-1054; F. Jacoby, "Hieronymos," PW 7.1560.62-1561.2; Gudeman, "Hieronymos," PW 7.1564.28-41 (who points out that "Hellanikos" may, as many think, be a pseudepigraphic reference to the Lesbian historigrapher, a contemporary of Herodotus, and who brands the common identification of Hieronymos with a Hieronymos cited by Josephus as the author of a Φοινικικὴ ἀρχαιολογία as "eine völlig in der Luft schwebende Vermutung"); Konrat Ziegler, "Orphische Dichtung," PW 18.1346.10-1347.13; 1349.5-1355.45; Karl Preisendanz, "Phanes," PW 19.1761.34-1774.4; Otto Gruppe, *Die griechischen Culte und Mythen in ihren Beziehungen zu den orientalischen Religionen* (Hildesheim and New York: Olms, 1973 [1887]) 612-675; "Phanes," Roscher 3.2248.51-2271.11; Seeliger, "Weltschöpfung," Roscher 6.474.1-494.68; Robert Eisler, *Weltenmantel und Himmelszelt. Religionsgeschichtliche Untersuchungen zur Urgeschichte des antiken Weltbildes* II (München: Beck, 1910) 382-399 with p. 393 n. 1 for his views on the identity of Hieronymos and Hellanikos; G. S. Kirk and J. E. Raven, *The Presocratic Philosophers. A Critical History with a Selection of Texts* (Cambridge: University Press, 1973 [1963]) 37-48; and especially W. K. C. Guthrie, *Orpheus and Greek Religion. A Study of the Orphic Movement* (2nd ed.; New York: Norton, 1966 [1952]) 69-107, 137-142, who summarizes the work of earlier scholars; lately Larry J. Alderink, *Creation and Salvation in Ancient Orphism* (Chico: Scholars Press, 1981) 38-39, 43-48.

Damascius' Hieronymos and Hellanikos, as it appears to have been). His *Embassy* or *Plea for the Christians,* addressed to Marcus Aurelius and Commodus, can be securely dated to the period A.D. 176-180. According to the apologist (Kern fr 57) Orpheus taught that water and slime were the original principles and that

> from the two of them was born a living creature, a dragon
> with the head of a lion growing from it, and between them
> was the face of a god. Its name was Heracles, and Time.

Though the obscurity of Athenagoras' summary has prompted gratuitous emendation, it seems to be making Chronos-Heracles tricephalic—snake, lion, and man. The continuation of the story (Kern fr 58) adds, among a wealth of other theriomorphic detail, that Phanes, who was hatched from the egg which Chronos-Heracles laid and (according to Athenagoras) was, like his dad, serpent-bodied or -shaped (ἢ σῶμα ἢ σχῆμα . . . δρά-κοντος), bore Echidna whose face was beautifully human but the rest of her a serpent.

Damascius' account (Kern fr 54) is somewhat different (Chronos-Heracles now has wings, for example) and likely represents a more developed tradition. From water and earth were born, in the version he knew,

> a dragon . . . with the heads of a bull and a lion growing from
> it, and between them was the face of a god. It had wings on
> its shoulders, and its name was unaging Time, and Heracles
> likewise.

It is from this description that the temptation to emend Athenagoras sprang, for the animal heads that flank the god's are by the Neo-Platonist made out to be those of a bull and a lion. Since a later Christian source cites Athenagoras' text as we have it, it is more in accord with the evidence to assume that the lack of specificity in the Orphic poem as known to Athenagoras concerning the nature of the third (serpent's) head allowed the substitution of a bull's (the serpent being only body now?) in the recension Damascius read. There was a reason, by now familiar, for the bull's being the animal of choice, and I will return to that momentarily. Damascius adds, at any rate, that in union with Orpheus' Chronos were Ἀνάγκη and incorporeal Ἀδράστεια whose reach spans the whole world. The god hatched from the egg, here called Πρωτόγονος, had

> golden wings on his shoulders. From his sides he had the heads

of bulls growing, and on his head he had a prodigious dragon
that assumed the forms of a great variety of beasts.

This cosmogony named Zeus, who, according to Athenagoras, devoured
Phanes so as to become infinite (ἀχώρητος) and so *is* Phanes, the πάντων
διατάκτωρ, and Pan.

In the *Rhapsodic Theogony,* on the other hand, Time is himself the
original principle, and he seems to have lacked the bestial characteristics
bestowed upon him by Hieronymos/Hellanikos. But the golden-winged
(Kern fr 78) hermaphrodite Phanes (*alias* Protogonos *alias* Metis *alias*
Phaeton *alias* Eros *alias* Dionysos: Kern frs 60, 64, 73, 74, 83, 85, 170),
who emerges as before from Time's egg, is once again an animal-
conglomerate; he has four eyes, four horns, and four faces (Kern frs 76,
77), and somehow additionally the four heads of a ram, a bull, a lion, and a
dragon (fr 81). In a line that Proclus actually cites (instead of summariz-
ing) to illustrate the polycephalic nature of the god, Orpheus (fr 79) says
that Phanes

uttered the bellow of bulls, and the roar of a flashing-eyed
lion.

These features of the god are also adumbrated in ταυροβόας and πολύμορφος as applied to Phanes Protogonos by *Orphic Hymns* 6.3 and 14.1.
Phanes went on to create a world for gods and men (frs 89-94), but, in this
account too, he is swallowed up by Zeus so that, as creator himself, he
may absorb Phanes' power and include within himself all that existed
before him (fr 167). As having engulfed Phanes Zeus too is pantheistically
described in some of the same theriomorphic (not to mention hermaphro-
ditic) terms that his predecessor is: the famous fr 168 (from Porphyry),
lines 3, 11-16, 24-26, makes him male and female, gives him wings to fly
everywhere with, and endows his head, which reflects the καλὰ πρόσωπα
οὐρανὸς αἰγλήεις, with sun and moon for eyes and two sets of bull's
horns to signify sunrise and sunset. Along with everything else Zeus, like
Chronos-Heracles in the Hieronymos/Hellanikos account and in accord
with his Stoic equation with Fate, also takes on the forces of Necessity:
"he was nursed by Adrasteia, mated with Ananke, and sired Heimarmene"
(fr 162).

Both Orphic cosmogonies are heavily indebted, as they were bound to
be, to Hesiod's canonical *Theogony,* in particular for elements that I have

not summarized here (the Ouranos-Kronos-Zeus succession).[122] While Phanes is alien to Hesiod, the animal features with which the Orphic cosmogonies, especially the *Rhapsodic Theogony,* endow him (and Chronos-Heracles in the Hieronymos/Hellanikos account) are, in part at least, of Hesiodic inspiration. If Athenagoras' Phanes is the father of Echidna, and she, true to the Boeotian's description (*Theogony* 298-299), is half beauty and half snake, this parentage links Phanes to a whole family of animal polymorphs. Not only are Echidna's children Lernaean Hydra and Chimaera many-headed gargoyles compounded of several of the same animals as Orpheus' deities—serpent, lion, and dragon (*Theogony* 308-324, lines 323-324 perhaps from Homer, *Iliad* 6.181-182)—but her husband Typhaon/Typhoeus (*Theogony* 306-307) also resembles her Orphic father rather closely in looks, if not in character. Typhaon is said to have springing from his shoulders (in addition to his human head) "a hundred heads of a serpent, a frightful dragon," but the voices which these heads utter are of every animal kind imaginable, a trait which bears close comparison with the line that Proclus cites of Phanes' animal cries. Explicitly mentioned by Hesiod are the voices of a god, a bull, a lion, and a snake (*Theogony* 820-835), again those creatures principally involved in the two Orphic cosmogonies. Like Phanes (and Damascius' Chronos-Heracles), moreover, Typhon is later said to be winged (Apollodorus, *Library* 1.6.3). These circumstances provided a classical Greek precedent for Phanes' and his father's forms in the Orphic cosmogonies, a precedent which, as literature pseudepigraphically attributed to an ancient bard, they desperately needed even if that precedent was not totally suitable; Typhaon/Typhoeus' resemblance to Phanes—and to Chronos-Heracles—ends with their animal heads and voices.

Yet another possibly Hesiodic reminiscence underlies Orpheus' Zeus' swallowing Phanes. It is not Phanes *qua* Hesiod's Typhaon (whom Zeus blasts with his thunderbolt in Hesiod, *Theogony* 836-68) who suffers this, but of course Phanes *qua* the Boeotian's Metis (*Theogony* 886-900). Earlier Orphic sources must also have made their mark: Phanes' wings probably directly derive from his equation with Eros who, in the ornithogony preserved by Aristophanes and commonly considered Orphic in inspiration,

---

[122]Ziegler, "Orphische Dichtung" 1355.46-1357.20; Kirk and Raven, *The Presocratic Philosophers* 38, 43, 46-47; Guthrie, *Orpheus and Greek Religion* 83-84. Note the list of entries from Hesiod in Kern's Index V. *Epici ab orphicis adhibiti* (p. 398).

hatches from a primal egg and is similarly endowed (*Birds* 693-703; Kern fr 1). An intimately bestial and infamously changeable Dionysos may also have contributed a share to Phanes' complicated physique (cp., for example, Nonnos, *Dionysiaca* 6.163-205, of Zagreus when attacked by the Titans).

But the two Orphic cosmogonies just reviewed are patently, in their present forms, heterogeneous complications. Their polycephalic, theriomorphic beings may owe something to Hesiod, but they obviously represent considerable remodeling under the impact of other traditions. Especially as applied to a body of pseudepigraphic literature, the process of redaction which the Orphic cosmogony underwent is not likely ever to have stopped, but rather to have continued right down to the age of the Antonines when Oriental cosmogonical elements (including those of the Jews, whose hermaphrodite Adam and talking serpent sparked a great deal of interest) were still being blended with Greek to gain acceptance and respectability for the cultures they represented.[123] What Athenagoras holds up to imperial scrutiny could just as well be the latest rage in cosmogonies as an Orphic bible of hoary antiquity, and if the picture of Chronos-Heracles as known to Damascius represents a development of that presented by the apologist, the redactional process did not stop in the second century either.

The two cosmogonies themselves illustrate this redactional process. Their relationship to each other as a whole in terms of temporal priority and dependence can hardly be decided on this basis alone, but, on the evidence I am considering, the *Rhapsodic Theogony* is the earlier of the

---

[123]On the problems of dating and Oriental influence see Ziegler, "Orphische Dichtung" 1349.27-30; Gruppe, "Phanes" 2263.64-2271.11; Kirk and Raven, *The Presocratic Philosophers* 39-40, 43; Guthrie, *Orpheus and Greek Religion* 84-92. Like many others M. L. West, "Graeco-Oriental Orphism in the Third Century B.C.," *Assimilation et résistance à la culture gréco-romaine dans le monde ancien. Travaux du VIe Congrès International d'Etudes Classiques (Madrid, Septembre 1974)* (ed. D. M. Pippidi; Bucharest: Editure Academiei, and Paris: "Belles Lettres," 1976) 221-226, dates both works to the early Hellenistic period. To concede this dating correct—and the reasons on which the *terminus ante quem* is based are extremely shaky—still does not exclude the possibility that further redaction was imposed upon the poems between their own Hellenistic redactions and the forms in which they reached the authors who have preserved them for us.

two. Whatever his source of inspiration, Pherekydes of Syros guarantees the entry—in however unsophisticated a fashion—of Χρόνος as a philosophical abstraction into Greek cosmogony by the sixth century B.C., and Aristotle's pupil Eudemos of Rhodes its possession of equally abstract Iranian associations by the end of the fourth;[124] the *Rhapsodic Theogony* is therefore more conservative in keeping its Chronos nondescript. Hieronymos/Hellanikos' Phanes is likely to have suffered some kind of redactional operation too; at least their use of the verb προσφύειν (translated by "growing from") in the description of both figures points in this direction. If so, then the bull's head which Damascius' Chronos-Heracles has lately sprouted and the likewise bovine heads which grow from Phanes' sides were grafted on to the deities, who previously lacked them, in the case of the former in the period between the different redactions of Hieronymos/Hellanikos—themselves perhaps one the epitomator of the other—read by Athenagoras and Damascius, and in the case of the latter either at the same time or earlier and serving as a model for his father's new head.

   The strange and clearly secondary application of the name Heracles to Chronos, lacking in the *Rhapsodic Theogony*, is in any case the key to Chronos' acquisition of theriomorphic characteristics for Hieronymos/Hellanikos, because Chronos' new bestial form makes him an astrological divinity, a transformation which followed naturally from the fact that Time is measured by the revolutions of heavens swarming with animal powers. A parallel development is Phanes, as Phaeton, turned Helios—suggested, no doubt, by the lines which Hermias cites in Kern fr 86 and supported by word play on his name. Chronos' union with the female forces of Fate is a dead giveaway of his astrological metamorphosis. His multiplicity of animal forms on a serpentine trunk, like the kindred protean serpent which Hieronymos/Hellanikos put on Phanes' head, without a doubt signifies Time's (Chronos) and the sun's (Phanes) passage through the zodiacal signs and all their animal-headed and/or animal-bodied affiliates. Prime examples of the cosmology underlying these portraits are the decans as πρόσωπα for the planets (most importantly the sun), discussed earlier, and the tradition that during the course of a day the sun successively takes on the forms of all the animals of an Egyptian δωδεκάωρος,

---

[124]Kirk and Raven, *The Presocratic Philosophers* 37-39, 48-72; M. L. West, *Early Greek Philosophy and the Orient* (Oxford: Clarendon Press, 1971).

including the bull, lion, and serpent, the standard astrological trio (*PGM* I P 3.499-536, and especially 4.1636-1695 where before the litany of transformations begins the sun's essential form is said to be μέγας ʼΟφις). It is precisely on this basis that *Corpus Hermeticum* 11.15-16 calls the cosmos (primarily, that is, the heavens) παντόμορφος, as *Orphic Hymn* 14.1 uses πολύμορφος of Phanes, and that the *Asclepius* 19 (similarly 35) names the οὐσιάρχης of the thirty-six decans Παντόμορφον *vel omniformem . . . qui diversis speciebus diversas formas facit.* (No wonder that magicians claim to know the secret of the sun's "true," hidden form!) The pantheistic description of Zeus in Kern fr 168, a description the god earned *qua* Phanes, shows why it was natural, in an Orphic context, for Chronos-Heracles (and the *Rhapsodic Theogony*'s Phanes as well) to acquire many heads, for if the cosmic Zeus' head is the sky and his head shows forth the καλὰ πρόσωπα οὐρανὸς αἰγλήεις, he might as well have all the heads of the different beasts that dwell there growing from his shoulders.

Heracles is the key to this development for Chronos because, as a result of the hero's old association with solarized Egyptian and, in particular, Syrian gods like the Tyrian Melqart as identified with Helios (Nonnos, *Dionysiaca* 40.369-391) he was, like so many other gods in late antiquity, merged into Helios. From these associations, particularly that with Nergal, Heracles inherited an ancient Near Eastern leonine iconography to match that which he already possessed in Greek art. His twelve labors, some involving readily adaptable figures (the Nemean lion as Leo, for example) and aided by catasterization, were consequently interpreted mystically of the twelve zodiacal signs through which the sun must pass to mark the passage of time through the seasons of the year.

The *tertium quid* in the equation of Heracles with Chronos, then, is Helios. In Orphic literatire the *Orphic Hymn* 12 (*to Heracles*).1 addresses the hero ἄλκιμε Τιτάν, v 3 αἰολόμορφε (naturally!) and χρόνου πάτερ, with vv 11-12 referring to his zodiacal "labors"; *Hymn* 8 (*to Helios*).13 addresses the sun χρόνου πάτερ.[125] If the Orphic hymn makes Heracles

---

[125]Preisendanz, "Phanes" 1763.11-1764.2; 1770.4-32; 1773.8-1774.4; Gruppe, "Phanes" 2255.31-2256.9; Seeliger, "Weltschöpfung" 478.35-66; Eisler, *Weltenmantel und Himmelszelt* II, 387-388, 394 and n. 1; Bouché-Leclercq, *L'astrologie grecque* 137 n. 1, 576-577 with notes; West, "Graeco-Oriental Orphism" 224-225; Gruppe, "Herakles," PWSup 3.981.25-984.13 (with 984.14-26 on Heracles in the Gnostic system of Justin); 986.42-988.19; and especially 1103.45-1105.42; Seyrig, "Héraclès-Nergal"

the father of Time instead of his equivalent as in the Hieronymos/
Hellanikos cosmogony, it matters little, for Time and the sun are so
intimately bound up with each other that their relationship can be
expressed in whatever way the context demands. (Another reason, entail-
ing the Κρόνος-Χρόνος equation, will be taken up momentarily.) The
aminals whose heads Chronos-Heracles sprouts (and those of Phanes in the
Rhapsodic Theogony as well, whose non-Typhonic ram suggests that he too
has suffered secondary astrologization) are either astral zodia themselves
or possess major astrological connections; if snake is the major component
of Chronos-Heracles' body and the primary form of the creature that
graces Phanes' head for Hieronymos/Hellanikos, one reason is surely that
the serpent οὐροβόρος was the standard late Egyptian symbol for the
course of the sun and the eternal cycle of time (see Servius, *Commentary
on Vergil's Aeneid* 5.85; Horapollo, *Hieroglyphics* 1.1-2). If it owes something to Typhaon/Typhoeus' and to Phanes' possession of a human head,
Chronos-Heracles' human head is doubtless also a concession to Heracles;
the great hero (even as Melqart) cannot, in an Orphic context with preten-
sions to classical Greek antiquity, lose a human head. Chronos-Heracles'
serpentine body also had the advantage of neatly serving both the con-
straints of the myth and the Greek thirst for rationality, since only a
reptile can lay a cosmic egg, a human being logically cannot.

With due consideration given to these motivations, it seems to me a
distinct possibility that here again Chnoumis was a prime mover in
Chronos' acquisition of theriomorphic form. As first and lord of the
decans at the top of the astrological ladder and with solid solar qualifica-
tions he was a natural basic model for Chronos' body. His lion's head,
pushed aside to give the human Heracles good Greek top billing, was an
added plus because Leo well suited Heracles' new solar function and
because the lion was a major link in the hero's union with his Semitic
counterparts, who either had lions as acolytes or were "Masters of Animals" with lions in their grasp, like Gilgamesh. Even standard Greek
iconography helped because the skin of the Nemean lion which he regularly wears with its head on his head is for all intents and purposes an
adventitious head.

Chronos-Heracles' polycephalism is, then, strictly parallel to Yahweh/
Yaldabaoth-as-Chnoumis' multi-headed transformation in the short

---

62-80; Dussaud, "Melqart" 205-230. The Phoenician cult of Nergal discussed early in chapter 2 is due to the equation of Melqart with Nergal.

recension of *Apoc. John,* and the factors which motivated it were identical: the necessity for the κοσμοκράτωρ, the director of Time, the master of Fate, to sum up in himself all the multifarious forms of the astral zodia under his command. Polycephalism is in both instances a response to the need to unify a temporal sequence of incorporations in a single spatial representation, and the result is montage. But the essential feature underlying it is the sun's prosopographical transformation in its passage through the zodia and their decans: Yahweh/Yaldabaoth's capacity to "present himself in whatever form he wished," as the short recension of *Apoc. John* put it with handy assimilation of Ezekiel's הַיּוֹת and the capacity of the serpent on Phanes' head to "assume the forms of a great variety of beasts."

Despite Athenagoras' claim that Phanes had ἤ σῶμα ἤ σχῆμα of a serpent—the apologist may be purposely twisting the facts of the Hieronymos/Hellanikos representation to suit his ends, namely, to hold pagan worship of animalistic gods up to ridicule—Phanes, unlike his sire, is in both Orphic cosmogonies essentially human, not serpent-bodied. Bull's heads may grow from his sides, the prodigious mutable serpent may rest on his head, as hermaphrodite he may have more than one face (like Aristophanes' primal hermaphrodite human in Plato's *Symposium* 189D-190A), but he is still primarily human.[126] This obviously original human

---

[126]This is well illustrated by the famous relief at Modena (*CIMRM* ##695-696 with fig 197; my pl. 17a), if, as seems probable, it represents Phanes, though a Mithraic synthesis is confirmed by the inscription *Felix pater* which accompanies the figure. Standing in a niche surrounded by an oval frame whose twelve compartments contain the signs of the zodiac is a young male figure who holds a scepter and thunderbolt; he has the hooves of a bull (as Dionysos) or of a goat (as Pan), and from his shoulders springs a magnificent pair of wings. The god stands on an inverted cone from which fire is shooting, and a similar cone, open downwards, is over his head; they clearly represent the two halves of the egg from which he has just emerged. His whole body is wound round several times by a huge serpent whose head rests on the cone over his head; on his chest is the face of a lion, and from his flanks project the heads of a ram and a goat. The sickle of the moon is visible over his shoulders, and solar rays emanate from his head. See Eisler, *Weltenmantel und Himmelszelt* II, 399-407; Guthrie, *Orpheus and Greek Religion* 254-255, 278 with pl. 12; Doro Levi, "Aion," *Hesp* 13 (1944) 299-301; Franz Cumont, "Mithra et l'orphisme," *RHR* 109 (1934) 63-72 with pl. 1, in the context of a discussion of an

conception of Phanes exists somewhat uneasily side by side with the astrological, which, taking its cue from the god's multi-faceted physiognomy, from his association with light, and from the fact that Orphic cosmogony combined in his person all the Greek divinities associated with creation in any way, secondarily made him a solar *Allgott* somehow additionally provisioned, like his father and now virtual double Chronos-Heracles, with the faces of the whole sidereal bestiary.

But the two cosmogonies effected this astrological transformation in different ways. Like the Modena Phanes' similarly placed ram's and goat's heads the Hieronymos/Hellanikos cosmogony attached zodiacal bull's heads to his sides and, again like the Modena Phanes, put a giant self-transforming serpent on his head. Indeed, Athenagoras had *some* grounds for saying that Phanes' had the shape of a serpent, for the serpent *is* Phanes' new astrological form, only it is not as fully integrated with his old form as the apologist suggests, but literally superimposed upon it. The *Rhapsodic Theogony* seems to have faced a special problem in that Phanes was earlier already endowed with four human faces (a trait which Hieronymos/Hellanikos naturally pass over in silence), like the Janus *quadrifrons* installed in a temple at Rome in the mid-third century B.C. and readily interpretable himself as a four-dimensional Aion (Servius, *Commentary on Vergil's Aeneid* 7.607; 12.198; Macrobius, *Saturnalia* 1.9.13-14;

---

inscription to Zeus-Helios-Mithras-Phanes (*CIMRM* #475) and of the links between Mithras and Phanes which made the theocrasy logical; Ugo Bianchi, "Protogonos. Aspetti dell'idea di dio nelle religioni esoteriche dell'antichità," *SMSR* 28 (1957) 115-117; and especially Martin P. Nilsson, "The Syncretistic Relief at Modena," *SO* 24 (1945) 1-7. The identity of Mithras with Phanes is also illustrated by a sculpture (*TMMM* #273d with fig. 315; *CIMRM* #860 with fig. 226; Guthrie, *Orpheus and Greek Religion* pl. 13) from Borcovicium (Housesteads, England) which shows Mithras hatching from an egg within the circle of the zodiac. The debate over the identity of the Modena figure—Phanes, Mithras, Aion—merely illustrates their mutual solar equivalence. The same debate has centered around similar late antique representations of youths in zodiacal circles: see Levi, "Aion," 269-314, in particular pp. 284-301. The winged serpent coiled around the omphalos of the famous Orphic alabaster bowl may represent Phanes as R. Delbrueck and W. Vollgraff, "An Orphic Bowl," *JHS* 54 (1934) 129-139 with pls. 3-5, especially p. 135, think it does, or it could be Chronos-Heracles.

John Lydus, *On the Months* 4.1-2).[127] Like Typhaon/Typhoeus and as embodying all life Phanes could, however, even then utter animal cries (Kern fr 79); there was, as I said, Hesiodic precedent for thus far associating animals with the god. But the redactor of the *Rhapsodic Theogony* under astrological inspiration was not content to let the matter rest there, could not allow the animal heads to remain invisible, and yet he did not want to (or could not, because it was hallowed tradition) get rid of Phanes' many-faced human head either, because it was of appropriately cosmic significance. His solution was simply to attach the animal heads

---

[127]See Reitzenstein, *Poimandres* 274; *Das iranische Erlösungsmysterium* (Bonn: Marcus & Weber, 1921) 210-212; Bousset, "Der Gott Aion" 192; Cook, *Zeus* II, 373-374. Bousset offers many interesting parallels and intelligent commentary on the whole subject we are discussing here, but his explanation (p. 218) for Chronos-Heracles' animal heads is hardly convincing: "Sollte es zu kühn sein, diese Schilderung des Gottes mit der Tatsache zu verbinden, dass er als mann-weiblich erscheint und dass in vorderasiatischer Kultur die männliche Hauptgottheit als Stier, die weibliche als Löwe erscheint." The situation is certainly complicated by the possibility of influence on the Orphic cosmogony from the Phoenician as it was transmitted in Hellenized form for Hellenistic and Roman audiences (and here too Hesiodic influence needs to be considered); that Heracles has a Phoenician counterpart is by no means the only circumstance that suggests a Phoenician-Orphic connection: see West, "Graeco-Oriental Orphism" 226; Bianchi, "Protogonos" 118-122. But while Philo of Byblos has Taautos devise four wings and four eyes as a sign of royalty for El-Kronos (Eusebius, *Preparation for the Gospel* 1.10.36-37) and this bears some resemblance to the *Rhapsodic Theogony*'s Phanes, it does not help explain either his or his father's theriomorphic characteristics. As James Barr, "Philo of Byblos and his 'Phoenician History,'" *BJRL* 57 (1974) 59-60, points out, however, this feature of Philo's narrative may, like others, stem from knowledge of the Old Testament (Isa 6:2 or Ezekiel in this case) and so it is possible that the "Phoenician" accounts contained the proper theriomorphic descriptions and that the Seraphim and the Cerubim, through "Phoenician" intermediaries, helped give Phanes and his father animal heads. For Philo there is now Albert I. Baumgarten, *The* Phoenician History *of Philo of Byblos.* A Commentary (EPRO 89; Leiden: Brill, 1981); worth reading further are Otto Eissfeldt, "Phönikische und griechische Kosmogonie," and Hans Schwabl, "Die griechischen Theogonien und der Orient," both in *Éléments orientaux dans la religion grecque ancienne. Colloque de Strasbourg 22-24 mai 1958* (Paris: Presses Universitaires de France, 1960) 1-15 and 39-56; P. Walcot, *Hesiod and the Near East* (Cardiff: University of Wales, 1966).

adventitiously around his already existent head, a situation parallel to Hieronymos/Hellanikos use of προσφύειν in attaching heads to its Chronos-Heracles and bull's heads to its Phanes; Proclus' actual words in fr 81 are καὶ ὁλικώτατον ζῷον ὁ θεολόγος ἀναπλάττει κριοῦ καὶ ταύρου καὶ λέοντος καὶ δράκοντος αὐτῷ <u>περιτιθεὶς</u> κεφαλάς. It is interesting to note that in late antiquity Hesiod's Typhaon/Typhoeus underwent a similar treatment to that of Phanes, for if in Hesiod his snaky heads have animal throats only, for Nonnos (Dionysiaca 1.156-162) the monster has acquired the animal heads themselves.

If Typhaon/Typhoeus[128] helped shape the theriomorphic depiction of Orpheus' Phanes because Hesiodic inspiration was so desirable, the same is yet more glaringly true of the Gnostics' Yaldabaoth. There is no denying that Typhaon/Typhoeus bears a suspicious resemblance to the Gnostic creator. Beside the fact that his own looks and those of his many polymorphous children (Hydra and Chimaera, already mentioned; Orthus, Cerberus, the Sphinx, the dragon with a hundred heads that guarded the apples of the Hesperides, and the eagle that devoured the liver of Prometheus: Hesiod, Theogony 308-312; Apollodorus, Library 2.5.11; 3.5.8) suited his service as a model for transforming Phanes and Yaldabaoth into astrological pantheoi, there was another aspect of him that made his attractiveness more than merely skin deep. What made him an unsuitable model for Chronos-Heracles or for Phanes was precisely what made him a supremely fitting character to Gnostics: his ugly temperament. He is, like the Gnostic demiurge, the consummate rebel against the divine order beyond him; born of Tartarus, Typhaon/Typhoeus is, like Yaldabaoth, "savage and arrogant and lawless" (Hesiod, Theogony 307; cp. 821-822). Like Yahweh/Yaldabaoth he is a fiery god; his eyes are incandescent (like Yaldabaoth's in Apoc. John) and his mouth vomits fire (Hesiod, Theogony 826-827, 845, 859-867; Apollodorus, Library 1.6.3).

What is even more significant is the story of his birth as related by Homeric Hymn 3 (to Pythian Apollo).305-355, the circumstances of which

---

[128]The identity of Typhaon with Typhoeus is presupposed by Homeric Hymn 3 (to Pythian Apollo).306, 352, 367. On him see M. L. West's edition of Hesiod's Theogony (Oxford: Clarendon Press, 1971) 252, 379-383, whose commentary on all aspects of his story is excellent; and Francis Vian, "Le mythe de Typhée et le problème de ses origines orientales," Éléments orientaux dans la religion grecque ancienne 17-37, especially pp. 24-26 on "L'aspect de Typhée dans la littérature et dans l'art"; snake-footed depictions of Typhaon were the source of the magic gems' anguipede, which are frequently identified as Iao/Yahweh.

too closely match those of Yaldabaoth's childhood to be coincidental. Like Sophia Hera (his mother in this branch of the tradition) bore her hideous son apart from intercourse with her husband (334-352) and reared him secretly, away from the ken of her peers (305-306, 353-354). Moreover, CG II, *4 Hyp. Arch.* 95 [143].11-13 has Yaldabaoth suffer ejection into Tartarus, just as Hesiod does with Typhaon/Typhoeus (*Theogony* 868).

Voracious appetite is yet another trait which Yaldabaoth need not only have inherited from the Hesiodic and earlier Orphic cosmogonies but which is a distinctive feature of both of them and which is therefore *a priori* likely to have had some impact on his mythology. The truth is that this feature of the Greek cosmogonies enjoyed an embarrassingly vociferous popularity with a public for whom its lurid and revolting details held a special fascination. Voracity, as I pointed out earlier, is something to which lions were noted for being prone, and the ancient Near Eastern mythological traditions which for this reason adopted the lion's insatiable maw as a metaphor for the demonic powers of Death and the Underworld as well as for human prosecutors helped to secure Yaldabaoth's lion-head on his shoulders. It is quite understandable, then, that, as in the *Pistis Sophia* and in logion 7 of *Gos. Thom.* behind whose lion the chief archon is lurking, Yaldabaoth should be a devourer. But the act of devouring as a persistent aspect of the dynastic succession in the Hesiodic and especially the Orphic cosmogonies is too attractive a mythologem to have failed to have had some influence upon a voracious, leonine Yahweh/Yaldabaoth. All the more so as Kronos, the most infamous perpetrator of this terrible deed (Hesiod, *Theogony* 453-506; the *Rhapsodic Theogony*, Kern frs 80, 146-148; *Orphic Hymn* 13 [to Kronos].3), was, as I pointed out earlier, already known to Tacitus as an *alias* of the Jews' god, and this fact, in combination with Yaldabaoth's coordination with the planet Saturn, could only encourage his mythological acquisition of the gluttonous habits of Hesiod's and Orpheus' Kronos. In the Gnostic myth it is naturally pleromatic elements which Yaldabaoth must try to engulf, not his own children, who, after all, are mere hypostases of his own being.

But to return to Quispel's thesis. Chronos-Heracles is certainly a much better candidate for comparison with *Apoc. John*'s similarly shaped Yaldabaoth than is a more human Phanes. It is particularly, as I just suggested, the short recension's polycephalic version that is most applicable in the present situation. Whether or not Hieronymos/Hellanikos' Chronos-Heracles derived his primary form from Chnoumis as the short recension of *Apoc. John* derived its two-headed serpent from the long recension's Chnoumis-Yahweh/Yaldabaoth, the polycephalism they both present is a parallel development in response to the same set of astrological pressures.

I am inclined, then, to see this feature of the Hieronymos/Hellanikos cosmogony as roughly contemporary with the short recension of *Apoc. John* in this respect and consequently to hold that the document which Athenagoras knew was an Orphic account of the creation related (as having common sources) to that contained in the *Rhapsodic Theogony* but one which, like the latter, had been updated under the influence of mixed Hellenistic "Chaldean" and Egyptian astrological lore with its concomitant solar pantheism and of deities like Chnoumis and the polycephalic Bes and sphinx "pantheos" figures, who served as plastic prototypes. Athenagoras was no fool; his plea is not founded on favorable comparison of Christianity with outmoded pagan religious forms, but concentrated on the very latest and most cherished aspects of the Empire's cultural synthesis. If the short recension of *Apoc. John*'s Yahweh/Yaldabaoth and Hieronymos/Hellanikos' Chronos-Heracles are contemporary experiments in polycephalism, as I think they are, it is impossible to say whether one influenced the other—they could just as well be independent developments—and, if dependence existed, to say which way it went.

Phanes' acquisition of animal heads in the *Rhapsodic Theogony* as known to Damascius is, as I said, likely to be part of the same phenomenon. That the same thing happened to Yahweh/Yaldabaoth is much less surprising than that it happened to Phanes; there were many more reasons for it to. The old Greek etymology Κρόνος-Χρόνος and Chronos' early rise to prominence in Greek cosmogony[129] clearly helped Yaldabaoth (and Chronos-Heracles) acquire the many-headed form with which the short recension of *Apoc. John* endowed him. In late antiquity the Κρόνος-Χρόνος equation gained a significance which far transcended its catchiness as a

---

[129]Waser, "Chronos," PW 3.2481.25-2482.53; Roscher, "Chronos," Roscher 1.899.14-900.14; Ziegler, "Orphische Dichtung" 1324.10-14; 1326.23-27; Seeliger, "Weltschöpfung" 474.1-479.42; Maximilian Mayer, "Kronos," Roscher 2.1546.38-1548.48; Pohlenz, "Kronos," PW 11.1986.49-66; Eisler, *Weltenmantel und Himmelszelt* II, 382-387; Jean Pépin, *Mythe et Allégorie. Les origines grecques et les contestations judéo-chrétiennes* (2nd ed.; Paris: Études Augustiniennes, 1976) 126, 157, 328-335. The Kronos-Chronos synthesis meant that the god Kronos could be represented with the serpent οὐροβόρος which symbolized the cyclicality of the celestial wheels of Time: see W. Deonna, "La descendance du Saturne à l'ouroboros de Martianus Capella," *SO* 31 (1955) 170-189; and Jean-G. Préaux, "Saturne à l'ouroboros," *Hommages à Waldemar Deonna* 394-410, both commenting on Martianus Capella, *The Marriage of Philology and Mercury* 1.70.

nice play on words. The ever-growing influence of an astrological cosmology, aided by Stoic, Neo-Platonic and Neo-Pythagorean philosophers, brought into increasing prominence the mighty Power, the celestial Eternity, which had originated and which now controlled the whole vast clockwork mechanism of the cosmos and, with that, the fortunes, the births and the deaths of men. Like Αἰών, which late antique Orphics (if it is they whom Damascius means by οἱ θεολόγοι) seem to have used in the plural, like the Gnostics, as a general term for their πολυμόρφους θεούς (*Problems and Solutions concerning First Principles* 151; II, 33.25-26 Ruelle, not in Kern), Χρόνος was a good abstract name for this something less than personal godhead.[130] Time was not now a mere philosophical abstraction, however, but the culminating principle of a whole astrological hierarchy. The Orphic cosmogonists could well feel the need to flesh him out and Gnostics to include him in their accounts of the origin of things.

The Κρόνος–Χρόνος equation, furthermore, meant that Saturn, as the highest, farthest, slowest planet, was the ultimate embodiment of Time. When Damascius reports of the Phoenicians that they believe the Hebdomad to be the special and primary property of Kronos and that their myths have him seven-headed (*Problems and Solutions concerning First Principles* 265 and 266; II, 131.13; 132.29-133.1), it seems that our old Ugaritic friend the seven-headed serpent, equated with Kronos (as overcome by Baᶜal-Zeus), was a natural symbol for Kronos-Chronos' astrological transformation into a polycephalic Aion. On a slightly more personal level that other heavenly body which could logically be regarded as the outstanding vehicle of this Power, Helios as the most powerful of heavenly bodies and the source of all life, was singled out for special reverence as the demiurge, a δεύτερος θεός, a role which he had from time immemorial played in Egypt anyway. And even the two of them were not

---

[130]On Αἰών see particularly Wernicke, "Aion," PW 1.1042-1043; but better Lackheit, "Aion," PWSup 3.64.49-68.62; Bousset, "Der Gott Aion" 192-230; Reitzenstein, *Poimandres* 256-291; *Das iranische Erlösungsmysterium* 151-250 ("Aion und ewige Stadt"); Max Zepf, "Der Gott Αἰών in der hellenistischen Theologie," *ARW* 25 (1927) 225-244; Festugière, *La révélation d'Hermès Trismégiste* IV. *Le dieu inconnu et la Gnose* 152-199; "Le sens philosophique du mot ΑΙΩΝ. À propos d'Aristote, de Caelo I 9," *PP* 2 (1947) 172-189; A. D. Nock, "A Vision of Mandulis Aion," *HTR* 27 (1934) 78-99; Levi, "Aion," 269-314. If Nonnos (*Dionysiaca* 36.422-423) pictures Αἰών rolling the wheel of time it is analogous to the γρύψ of Nemesis with the wheel of Τύχη.

totally distinct, for the close link which the "Chaldeans" forged between Saturn and the sun (Diodorus Siculus 2.30.3, for example), because the god Kronos had been equated with solarized Semitic gods so that Saturn/ Kronos was the planet of the god Helios, meant that the two great cosmic powers were intimately related. Older gods were caught up by this new development and assimilated to one of its protégés, particularly Helios, whence eventually the "solar monotheism" that comes to dominate Roman religion in late antiquity.[131]

Yahweh was certainly not exempt from these cultural pressures, for he had been subject to them in his eastern homeland for a lot longer than more western divinities were. Syria and Phoenicia were early hotbeds of this astrolatrous revolution, and the proximity of Israel, the policies of the Seleucids (not to mention close ties with Ptolemaic Egypt), the ouranological speculations of post-Exilic Jewish apocalyptic, and Ezekiel's חֵיּוֹת if not themselves astral zodia of Perso-Babylonian syncretism then readily to be interpreted in its light, all combined to bring the forces of astrological transmogrification strongly to bear against him. Under its influence, in the course of the Hellenistic period—the time during which Yahweh was being equated with a solar Mios—the Jewish creator was sucked down into the astrological maelstrom of the Seleucid empire and became yet another god Ὕψιστος (so in Asia Minor), a שמם בעל, a Zeus Οὐράνιος, a *Jupiter summus exsuperantissimus,* a *Caelus aeternus.* This development is already implicit in Hecataeus of Abdera's statement (*FGH* #264 fr 6; similarly Juvenal, *Satire* 6.545) around 300 B.C. that the Jews worship Heaven as the only god and lord of all things. If Yahweh was known to Tacitus as the god Kronos and the planet Saturn, then, it was precisely on this astrological basis, as the lord of the highest heaven, backed up by Jewish apocalyptic and by real or supposed Syrian and Babylonian equations like El= or Bel=Kronos and El= or Bel=Helios (Philo of Byblos in Eusebius, *Preparation for the Gospel* 1.10.16, 20, 29, 4.16.11; Servius, *Commentary on Vergil's Aeneid* 1.642, 729; Damascius, *Life of Isidorus,* in Photius, *Library* 343b), the latter of which makes the giant

---

[131]Classic expositions are those by Franz Cumont, "La théologie solaire du paganisme romain," *MAI* 12 (1913) 447-479; *Les religions orientales dans le paganisme romain* 190-210; *Astrology and Religion among the Greeks and Romans* (New York: Dover, 1960 [1912]), especially 57-76; and Gressmann, *Die hellenistische Gestirnreligion.* More recently see Nilsson, *Geschichte der griechischen Religion* II^2, 268-281, 486-510, 569-578; Jean Gagé, "Le paganisme impérial à la recherche d'une théologie vers le milieu du IIIe siècle," *AAWLM.G* (1972) 587-604; Gaston H. Halsberghe, *The Cult of Sol Invictus* (Leiden: Brill, 1972).

serpent that Bel and the Dragon 23-27 ascribes to the worship of Bel the counterpart of the dragons of late Orphic and other astrologically influenced cosmogonies.[132]

Against this syncretistic Syrian, "Chaldean," and Egyptian astrological background it was natural for Yahweh to be affiliated both with Saturn and with the sun. As part and parcel of the same astrological syndrome in Graeco-Syrian dress, the equation of Yahweh with Zeus, discussed earlier, far from hindering these alternative equations, in fact aided them (through solarized Syrian Jupiters) or even presupposes them. The Syrian-based identification of Yahweh with Kronos as god (Yahweh is El-Kronos or בעל שמם) and as planet (Yahweh dwells in the highest heaven, Saturn's orb) gave Yaldabaoth his position as first of the seven in Celsus' and Origen's sources and made Saturn his star. But his solar associations, helped by the "Chaldean" Saturn-sun connection, by the solarized Syrian Jupiters, and by his role as creator, along with his lion's head, must have derived—the latter certainly—from the Egyptian Mios-theocrasy, and it was Yahweh's acquired solar character which paved the way for his eventual transformation into a polycephalic deity whose different heads represented the sun's trip through the zodia.

If to Gnostics Yahweh/Yaldabaoth is the enemy, then, it is not (or not only) that he is the god of the Jews that mattered, but that he is the creator of this world, chief of the planets (Saturn-Kronos, warlike, ruthless, cold, maleficent), or ruler of the decans, Sekhmet's deadly messengers (Chnoumis, Twtw-Τιθοης), in any case lord of Fate. Suitably savage passages by the multitude, helped by the lion-persecutor tradition, were dredged up from the Old Testament to support this view of him. Christianized Gnostics expanded this view by adapting the popular Platonic belief in a transcendent, wholly immaterial, wholly good, wholly one GOD to the revelation of Jesus, superimposed this pure spiritual realm beyond Fate upon the astrologically conditioned Creator's, and made the

---

[132]Pohlenz, "Kronos" 2000.9-65; Mayer, "Kronos" 1498.40-1500.13; F. Boll, "Kronos-Helios," *ARW* 19 (1916-1919) 342-346; *Sphaera* 313 n. 3; Franz Cumont, "Jupiter summus exsuperantissimus," *ARW* 9 (1906) 323-336; "Le Jupiter héliopolitain et les divinités des planètes" 45 and n. 31 Hajjar, *La triade d'Héliopolis-Baalbek* I, 49, 293-294 (noting the lion as the representative of the African Saturnus); Gressmann, *Die hellenistische Gestirnreligion* 19-20, 26-28; Arthur Darby Nock, Colin Roberts, Theodore C. Skeat, "The Gild of Zeus Hypsistos," *HTR* 29 (1936) 39-88; Otto Eissfeldt, "Ba'alšamēm und Jahwe," *ZAW* 57 (1939) 1-31; Hengel, *Judaism and Hellenism* I, 296-298 with notes II, 198-201.

Jews' god (and anti-Judaism certainly was a factor here) seem all the darker by comparison. In a little known article Hugo Gressmann hits the nail on the head, it seems to me, when he says: "Die doppelte Kampfrichtung der christlichen Gnosis (i.e., neben der antijüdischen eine antichaldäische) wird verständlich, sobald man voraussetzt, dass es schon vorher eine judenheidnische Religion gab, in der Jao bereits wie einst der chaldäische Bel zum Herrn der Planeten geworden war; dann musste notwendig der Kampf gegen die Planetengötter auch ein solcher gegen Jahwe werden."[133] But as I said the widespread and by then old hatred of the Jews contributed its ugly share to this development.

3.7   The Mithraic Leontocephaline

Finally, the Mithraic tradition needs to be examined because it too has been implicated in the formation of the Gnostic leontomorphic creator. Leisegang suggests a relationship—what exactly he does not say—between Origen's (and Celsus') lion-headed Yaldabaoth and the Mithraic leontocephaline (pls. 17b, 18a-c),[134] and the nature of this relationship, if it exists, needs to be assessed.

One thing can be confidently denied. The new tack upon which Leipoldt embarks after abandoning the exegesis of *Gos. Thom.*'s seventh logion as involving the doctrine of the transmigration of souls is equally inadmissible. Behind the man's eating the lion and the lion's assimilation to man (2b-c) lies, he thought, reference to a Gnostic sacrament; the lion is a "Deckname" for a god whom believers ceremonially ate. Leipoldt refers by way of analogy to "den sog. Aion" of the Mithraists, meaning the leontocephaline. "Es handelt sich aber," he goes on to concede, "in der Gnosis wohl nicht um ein wirkliches Essen (obwohl das vorkommt, z. B. bei Herakleon), sondern nur um ein geistig gedachtes wie bei Philon, wenn er davon spricht, dass die Frommen den Logos geniessen."[135] To see a sort

---

[133]"Die Aufgaben der Wissenschaft des nachbiblischen Judentums," *ZAW* 43 (1925) 23-24.

[134]Leisegang, *Die Gnosis* 173, also claiming the Mithraic leontocephaline modeled "nach dem Vorbild eines orphischen Mythos."

[135]*Evangelium nach Thomas* 57. Utterly ridiculous is the view that Robert Grant once proposed—and I include it here merely for completeness—that 2b refers to the consumption of lion-meat for medicinal purposes: "Notes on the Gospel of Thomas," *VC* 13 (1959) 170, appealing to passages from Galen and the elder Pliny cited by Steier, "Löwe" 982.12-36. This was only a stab in the dark, and Grant does not repeat it in later work (*Secret Sayings* 126).

of eucharistic background for the logion is an interesting suggestion, but
it does not explain the leonine character of the host in the present circumstances, not even in a Mithraic context.[136] Whatever the leontocephaline was, Mithraic initiates certainly did not eat it, however symbolically, in their communion-banquets.[137]

A lively debate still swirls around the identity and origin of the iconography of the Mithraic leontocephaline. The classic view to which all
studies respond, whether pro or con, is that of Franz Cumont. In accord
with his theory that Mithraism in the Roman world was pretty much
directly of Iranian extraction the great Belgian historian of religions held
that the leontocephaline represented Αἰών or Χρόνος as Κρόνος, though in
fact these names were but western equivalents for the creature's true
identity as *Zurvān akarāna*, or endless Time, and that, as in the Zurvanite
system from which it was directly derived, the leontocephaline was the
supreme god of the Mithraic pantheon.[138] Cumont's view of the leontocephaline's Zurvanite origin and its supreme status in Mithraism has been
subjected to a good deal of criticism as arbitrary and unfounded on hard
evidence.[139]

There are, in fact, three interlocking problems involved here: (1) what
the leontocephaline was named, (2) what it represented, and (3) whence its
iconographic features—which are by no means uniformly the same in all
examples—stemmed. As far as the first is concerned, what may have been
a leontocephaline (its head is missing and its body is not wrapped round by
the usual serpent) found at York (*CIMRM* #833) is the only example (if it

---

[136]If by his remark ("Theology of the Gospel of Thomas" 94) that
Doresse's interpretation of the lion as Christ "would at best cover half the
saying" Turner meant that 2a-c are to be taken eucharistically, that is as
impossible as referring it to the second half of the logion, for the lion is
not a Paschal lamb.

[137]A good up-to-date discussion is that by J. P. Kane, "The Mithraic
cult meal in its Greek and Roman environment," *Mithraic Studies. Proceedings of the First International Congress of Mithraic Studies* II (ed.
John R. Hinnells; Manchester: Manchester University Press, 1975) 313-
351.

[138]Franz Cumont, *TMMM* I (1899) 74-85; "Aion," PWSup 1.38.63-68;
The Mysteries of Mithra (trans. T. McCormack; New York: Dover, 1956
[1903]) 105-110; and most recently "The Dura Mithraeum," published
posthumously (trans. and ed. E. D. Francis) in *Mithraic Studies* I, 169-206,
especially pp. 170-171.

[139]See particularly R. L. Gordon, "Franz Cumont and the doctrines of
Mithraism," *Mithraic Studies* I, 215-248, especially pp. 217, 221-224.

is one) out of several dozens[140] to bear a dedicatory inscription (*CIMRM* #834) that identifies its subject (*if* indeed it does so, since there is uncertainty whether the word in question should be restored as a nominative or as an accusative—a dative is evidently impossible). On the provisos that the statue represents a leontocephaline (it does have the usual wings and keys), that the crucial word is correctly restored, and that it identifies the statue itself, the being's name was Arimanius, that is Ahriman, the great Evil One of the Iranian pantheon, who is known to have figured as a *deus* in the Mithraic cult (*CIMRM* ##369, 1773 with fig 461, 1775) and to have been concretely represented by a statue (*signum Arimanium*: *CIMRM* #222).

Those who stress this identification either discover that the Mithraists were Iranian heretics who worshiped the Devil after all or are forced to deny the leontocephaline the supreme status in the Mithraic order which Cumont accorded him, since Ahriman could by no stretch of a Zurvanite imagination be *Zurvān akarāna* itself. Some nevertheless press themselves hard to explain how Ahriman might have acquired a somewhat sweeter disposition and might have become affiliated with cosmic periodicity, both of which are alien to the Iranian deity but which are clearly implied by the iconography of the leontocephaline. This Ahriman-hypothesis follows Cumont to the extent that it assumes a direct Iranian derivation for Mithraism and therefore tends to labor under the illusion that the leontocephaline as Ahriman must necessarily be an evil being, even though this is quite untenable because Ahriman must surely have meant something different to the Mithraists from the Evil One of Zoroastrian and Zurvanite contexts and because, as I said, the iconography often makes it quite plain that the leontocephaline was not an utterly evil soul.[141] At

---

[140]One may find an analysis of the iconographic features of all existing leontocephalines together with a survey of the debate up to that point and sensible conclusions in John R. Hinnells, "Reflections on the Lion-headed Figure in Mithraism," *Monumentum H. S. Nyberg* I (AI 4; Téhéran-Liège: Bibliothèque Pahlavi, 1975) 333-369.

[141]F. Legge, "The Lion-headed God of the Mithraic Mysteries," *PSBA* 34 (1912) 125-142 with pls. 13-19; 37 (1915) 151-162 with pls. 18-19; *Forerunners and Rivals of Christianity from 330 B.C. to 330 A.D.* (New Hyde Park, NY: University Books, 1964 [1915]) 254-255; Jacques Duchesne-Guillemin, "Ahriman et le dieu suprême dans les mystères de Mithra," *Numen* 2 (1955) 190-195; "Aiōn et le Léontocéphale, Mithra et Ahriman," *NC* 10 (1958-1960) 91-98; *Symbols and Values in Zoroastrianism. Their Survival and Renewal* (New York: Harper and Row, 1966) 111-

times his lion-head is distinctly benign (for instance *CIMRM* #1134 with
fig 295); and at other times the figure has, like the Modena relief, a
beautiful human face, young (*CIMRM* #777 with fig 211, again like the
Modena relief in having a lion-mask on its chest) or old (*CIMRM* #1326
with fig 350 with the lion standing behind him as with the youth *CIMRM*
#775 with fig 209)—these examples being, strictly speaking, not leonto-
cephalines but identifiable as belonging to the genre by the presence of
one or more of the other most typical attributes (serpent-entwined body,
wings, clutched keys). But those who insist on his malevolent nature for
his identity with Ahriman and for his sometimes horrific leonine visage
derive his looks from Babylonian and Assyrian portraits of Nergal and his
lion-headed demons.[142]

117; R. C. Zaehner, *Zurvan. A Zoroastrian Dilemma* (Oxford: Oxford
University Press, 1955) 19 with the retraction in the preface, pp. viii-ix;
"Postscript to *Zurvan*," *BSOAS* 17 (1955) 237-243; *The Dawn and Twilight
of Zoroastrianism* (New York: Putnam, 1961) 129-130. The attempt made
by Zaehner to derive the iconography of the leontocephaline from Iranian
or Iranian-influenced sources (as for example Mani's description of Satan
as preserved by al-Nadim, a description already compared with the Mithraic leontocephaline by Heinrich Junker, "Über iranische Quellen der
hellenistischen Aion-Vorstellung," *VBW* [1921-1922] 147) cannot be
pronounced successful. On the York statue and for a critique of this whole
tack see Mary Boyce, "Some Reflections on Zurvanism," *BSOAS* 19 (1957)
314-316; and, defending Cumont's Zurvan hypothesis, Geo Widengren, "The
Mithraic Mysteries in the Greco-Roman World With Special Regard to
their Iranian Background," *La Persia e il mondo greco-romano* (*AANL.P* 76
[1966]) 441-442; *Die Religionen Irans* (Stuttgart: Kohlhammer, 1965) 230-
232—this remark, p. 232, is, it seems to me, especially apposite: "Zu der
Behauptung, der löwenartige Charakter der Gottheit kennzeichne diese als
böse, ist übrigens ganz grundsätzlich zu sagen, dass es mehr als eigenartig
ist, hier eine Identifizierung mit einem bösen Gotte auf der Löwen-
Eigenschaft aufbauen zu wollen," because the Mithraic grade *leo* and the
use of the lion in other iconographic contexts makes this unthinkable;
Gordon, "Franz Cumont and the doctrines of Mithraism" 221-223;
Hinnells, "Reflections on the Lion-headed Figure" 335-343; Hubertus von
Gall, "The Lion-headed and the Human-headed God in the Mithraic Mysteries," *Études Mithriaques. Actes du 2ᵉ Congrès International, Téhéran,
du 1ᵉ au 8 septembre 1975* (AI 17; Téhéran-Liège: Bibliothèque Pahlavi,
1978) 511-525 with pls. 29-32, in particular pp. 518-520. Cumont (*TMMM*
II, #474) naturally read the crucial name of the York inscription as a
nominative because to him the leontocephaline was *Zurvān akarāna*.

[142]For example A. D. H. Bivar, "Mithra and Mesopotamia," *Mithraic*

Whether or not the leontocephaline was named Arimanius, there is general agreement among scholars that the attributes which the deity possesses suffice to identify it as a χρονοκράτωρ, a κοσμοκράτωρ, an embodiment, that is, of the world-ruling Power generated by the endless revolution of all the wheels of the celestial dynamo, familiar enough now from the last section. This inference based on the actual iconography of the figure is far more solid than extrapolations from its identity with an Iranian Ahriman. The early identification of the figure by Georg Zoega as Αἰών, if not correct as the name by which Mithraists knew the deity, certainly correctly expresses his essence.[143] These attributes are not the wings and the lion-head (to which I will return momentarily) so obviously as (1) the second most distinctive feature of these figures, the snake which winds their bodies (less often their wings) round in its coils,[144]

Studies II, 275-289 with pls. 7-9, especially pp. 277-279, 282-285; von Gall, "The Lion-headed and the Human-headed God" 515; and H. J. W. Drijvers, "Mithra at Hatra? Some remarks on the problem of the Irano-Mesopotamian Syncretism," *Études Mithriaques* 151-186 with pl. 12, on the lion-headed Nergal relief from Hatra on which Bivar bases part of his argument. Already Cumont held to an Assyrian genealogy for the leonto-cephaline because to him too the figures are "toujours repoussants" (*TMMM* I, 75) and because the lion-head "ne rappelait sans doute plus aux initiés que le pouvoir destructeur du Temps qui dévore toutes choses" (*TMMM* I, 79), a view shared by M. J. Vermaseren, *Mithras, the Secret God* (London: Chatto & Windus, 1963) 121-122 (with help from Arnobius' sensationalizing description, *Against the Heathen Nations* 6.10), and which stems from the lion's reputation as a devourer and from the contribution of Kronos (who devoured his children)-Chronos as Aion to the leontoceph-aline's symbolic make-up. Those who endorse the leontocephaline's evil nature extrapolate from its position at Heddernheim a theory about its exclusion from general view—a theory which cannot be sustained: Hinnells, "Reflections on the Lion-headed Figure" 348-349.

[143]Levi, "Aion" 276, 292-297; Ernest Will, *Le relief cultuel gréco-romain. Contribution à l'histoire de l'art de l'empire romain* (Paris: de Boccard, 1955) 186-188; Hinnells, "Reflections on the Lion-headed Figure" 356-358, 364-367; Vermaseren, *Mithras, the Secret God* 117; Duchesne-Guillemin, "Aiōn et le Léontocéphale" 95; Leroy A. Campbell, *Mithraic Iconography and Ideology* (EPRO 11; Leiden: Brill, 1968) 298, 348, who calls it *Deus aeternus*, by which he means Αἰών (this work must be used with some caution).

[144]For serpent-enwrapment and its cosmic, especially solar, asso-ciations with celestial circles and cycles, with life and death, note Macro-bius, *Saturnalia* 1.17.58-59, 67 with his interpretation 69; the snake

(2) the zodiacal signs which appear between the coils of the serpent on some occasions (*CIMRM* ##545 with fig 153, 879 with fig 227; my pl. 17b) or, as with the Modena Phanes, on others in close conjunction with which the leontocephaline is portrayed (*CIMRM* #390 with fig 112 in a position suggesting his mastery of them), (3) the scepter which the god regularly

---

entwined representations of Sarapis' "Cerberus" and *Twtw* as "pantheos" (see n. 72); the related motifs of the serpent οὐροβόρος (as in the case of the cave of Time described by Claudian, *On the Consulship of Stilicho* 2.424-430, and of the gem showing a lion-headed Helios-Horus recommended for manufacture by *PGM* I P 1 discussed earlier) on which the Bes "pantheos" often stands, and of the snake-encircled staff of the leonto-cephalic Helios-Horus on extant gems (Delatte-Derchain, *Les intailles magiques* ##303-304, p. 223); Eisler, *Weltenmantel und Himmelszelt* II, 437-439; Gressmann, *Die hellenistische Gestirnreligion* 24-25 with fig. 6, in the context of a discussion of the Mithraic leontocephaline (pp. 23-26 with figs. 3-5), on the mummiform statuette (what god exactly it represents is unknown) found in the sanctuary of the Syrian gods on the Janiculum (note, e.g., Volkmar von Graeve, "Tempel und Kult der syrischen Götter am Janiculum," *JDAI* 87 [1972] 314-347, especially figs. 1-2 [p. 315] and pp. 335-338, 347; Marcel Leglay, "Sur les dieux syriens du Janicule," *MEFR* 60 [1948] 129-151, especially pl. 1 [p. 133] and pp. 130-139); Delatte-Derchain, *Les intailles magiques* ## 90-91, p. 76 (on #91 the serpent may have a lion's head and is thus conceivably but not surprisingly Chnoumis), and #172, pp. 134-135 (beside a lion-headed deity), with pp. 73-75 in introduction, for mummiform figures (Osiris or Sarapis) similarly serpent-entwined (like Sarapis' "Cerberus") on gems; Richard Wünsch, *Sethianische Verfluchungstafeln aus Rom* (Leipzig: Teubner, 1898) #16, pp. 14-16; #17, pp. 19-20; #18, pp. 20-21; #23, p. 34; #34, p. 45; and Bonner, *Studies in Magical Amulets* #148 (pl. 7, p. 277) illustrating similar themes; B. H. Stricker, "Een egyptisch Cultusbeeld uit grieksch-romeinischen Tijd," *OMRO* 24 (1943) 1-10 with pls. 1-2; L. Kákosy, "Osi-ris-Aion," *OrAnt* 3 (1964) 15-25 with pl. 41; Franz Cumont, "Une représentation du dieu alexandrin du Temps," *CRAI* (1928) 274-282 with the plate, on an Egyptian or Egyptianizing relief found at Rome which depicts a man (headless now) with a two-headed (one on each shoulder) serpent wrapping itself around his body (included in *CIMRM* #419 with fig. 116 as Mithraic, but the figure lacks all the other common attributes of the explicitly Mithraic leontocephalines); and M. J. Vermaseren, "A Magical Time God," *Mithraic Studies* II, 446-455 with pl. 16, on the snake-enwrapped male in stiff posture on a magical (the figure is labeled, among other standard *voces magicae*, ΙΑΩ ΑΛΩΝΑΕΙ) gold leaf found at Ciciliano, similarly listed in *CIMRM* (#168), but (though the figure does hold a key) again nothing identifies it as specifically Mithraic.

holds (pl. 18a), (4) the cosmic globe, sometimes girdled by the two bands of the ecliptic and the Milky Way, on which he stands (*CIMRM* ##382, 390, 543 with fig 152, 551 with fig 157, 1051, 1705 with fig 444, 2320 with fig 643, restored in ##545 with fig 153 and 665 with fig 188; my pls. 17b, 18a). There is, finally, (5) the key or keys that he constantly clutches to his breast (pl. 18a) and that are logically to be interpreted as opening (or locking) the zodiacal and planetary gates through which the soul descends into embodiment (Hades on earth in astral mysticism) and ascends out of it, as Celsus, quoted by Origen (*Against Celsus* 6.22), and other Mithraic evidence suggests.[145] If Nonnos' description (*Dionysiaca* 7.23) of Αἰών as ποικιλόμορφος, ἔχων κληῖδα γενέθλης, did not have exclusively the Mithraic leontocephaline in mind, the key which Aion's Mithraic counterpart holds nevertheless has a function identical with that assigned to it by Nonnos.

The Mithraic leontocephaline represents what Kronos-Chronos-Heracles-Helios-Aion and all the other abstractions and astrologized deities represented for late antique minds. This explains why some of the

---

[145]Eisler, *Weltenmantel und Himmelszelt* II, 440-442; Hinnells, "Reflections on the Lion-headed Figure" 356-357 with n. 83; Legge, *Forerunners and Rivals of Christianity* 254; and Cumont, *TMMM* I, 84-85 on Janus as *claviger*. Von Gall, "The Lion-headed and the Human-headed God" 517-518, takes the keys to be properly "the figural expression of his character as a guardian and tutelary god of the temples" and thus only generally to refer to the mysteries, but this is less in accord with the meaning of the whole figure itself. Gressmann, *Die hellenistische Gestirnreligion* 24, rightfully sees in the vision described Rev 1:13-18 of a man whose face shines like the sun, whose eyes radiate fire, who holds seven stars and the keys of death and Hades, and who is First and Last, a κοσμοκράτωρ, however earlier and Jewish-Christian, of the sort (and with many of the same features with related symbolic significance) that we have been discussing in somewhat later Orphic and Mithraic contexts. For keys to the gates of celestial realms note Plutarch, *On Socrates' Daimonion* 22 (*Moralia* 591B); *PGM* I P 3.541-542; 4.340-342 Ἀνούβιδι κραταιῷ . . . τῷ τὰς κλεῖδας ἔχοντι τῶν καθ' Ἅιδου with Delatte-Derchain, *Les intailles magiques* ##115 (p. 95, labeled ΙΑΚΩ and ΙΑΩ), 294 (pp. 215-217) for representations of Anubis holding the key, and further Siegfried Morenz, "Anubis mit dem Schlüssel," *WZ(L).GS* 1 (1953-1954) 79-83 with figs. 1-5, for others, including Bes, functioning in this respect as Anubis. On the passage Origen, *Against Celsus* 6.22, see Robert Turcan, *Mithras Platonicus. Recherches sur l'hellénisation philosophique de Mithra* (EPRO 47; Leiden: Brill, 1975) 44-61.

Mithraic figures can be human- (either young or old) and others lion-headed. In the hodge-podge of theocrasies which symbolized celestial Eternity, two basic astral bodies stand out, as I pointed out in the last section, figures which were both natural candidates for the job and between which a "Chaldean" relationship existed close enough to guarantee that they could merge Aionic symbolism at the same time as they might also retain their individual status and iconographic peculiarities. In the Orphic cosmogony of Hieronymos/Hellanikos there are two Aion-figures—(Kronos-)Chronos-Heracles and Phanes, corresponding to Saturn and the sun, respectively—but the coalescence of the two exemplars is apparent, as I showed, even here. Chronos-Heracles is not simply Saturn, for the astral Heracles fell as much on the solar side of the line as, in Semitic contexts, on the Saturnine.

The same confusion is equally evident in the case of the Mithraic Aion-figures, especially as there are not, as in the Orphic cosmogonies, two fully distinct personages between which the prototypes might be chiefly apportioned, but only one. No hard and fast rules can be applied in attributing specific Mithraic figures to one prototype or the other; those with a youthful human head might surely in this respect be taken to be Helios iconographically (as the Modena Phanes is also Helios-Mithras), but those with a lion's head are not (as with the old man of *CIMRM* #1326, of Nonnos' *Dionysiaca* 7.24-25, 41-44; 41.179-182, and of Claudian's cave of Time, *On the Consulship of Stilicho* 2.433-440) therefore automatically Saturn as Chronos as Aion since, as ought to be clear by now, the lion, insofar as it is an astrological symbol (Leo), is a solar, not a Kronian emblem, not even in a Semitic setting. The fluidity evident in the Mithraic iconography is obviously, then, due to the overarching concern to convey to the viewer what the figure *symbolizes,* not what particular deity is represents. In fact, even if its Mithraic name was Arimanius it still represents no one single particular deity, but rather an astrological concept to which many deities had been assimilated; Mithraic artists purposely and "pantheistically" conglomerated iconographic traits from the host of deities that had been identified in one way or another and for one reason or another with Helios and/or Saturn as the two great representatives of celestial Eternity. The choice between a leonine or a human head, in sum, was not governed by any essential difference in the identity of the Power symbolized by the figure as a whole but rather only, if anything, by the particular aspect of the exercise of that Power being stressed and by the setting in which the figure was to be placed and used, distinctions which do not allow the division to be made simply along benevolent/malevolent lines.[146] I will enlarge upon this later.

Yet that in Mithraism the two astrological representatives of Αἰών were still distinct enough, as in the Hieronymos/Hellanikos Orphic cosmogony, to warrant occasionally separate portraiture in nevertheless all but identical iconographic form is illustrated by the drawing which survives of the mostly lost monument of Ottaviano Zeno (*CIMRM* #335). On it two nude, snake-enwrapped, human-headed figures are shown, one winged and holding a staff, the other lacking these attributes, the former flanked on either side by a series of three and four blazing altars, which symbolize the planets, the other standing at the end of the series of three. The winged figure with scepter in the middle of the planet-altars is Helios-Aion, a normal position of the sun; the other, who looks distinctly but unreliably older, is Kronos-Chronos-Aion.[147] It means nothing that Saturn and the sun are, in effect, represented twice, once by an altar and

---

[146]On the human- as opposed to the lion-headed leontocephalines, with gratuitous theories (stemming from Cumont, *TMMM* I, 75-76) as to the development of one type out of the other, note Levi, "Aion" 284-291, 305-306; René Dussaud, "Le dieu mithriaque léontocéphale," *Syria* 27 (1950) 253-260, particularly p. 255 (for Dussaud's fantastic view of the origin of the leontocephaline's lion-head see his "Anciens bronzes du Louristan et cultes iraniens," *Syria* 26 [1949] 223-225); R. D. Barnett, "A Mithraic figure from Beirut," *Mithraic Studies* II, 466-469 with pl. 32a-b; and especially von Gall, "The Lion-headed and the Human-headed God" 519-525. Ugo Bianchi, "Prolegomena. The Religio-historical Question of the Mysteries of Mithra," *Mysteria Mithrae. Atti del seminario internazionale su 'La specificità storico-religiosa dei Misteri di Mithra, con particolare riferimento alle fonti documentarie di Roma e Ostia' Roma e Ostia 28-31 Marzo 1978* (ed. Ugo Bianchi; EPRO 80; Leiden: Brill, 1979) 39-40 (similarly pp. 41, 44-45) contrasts the "'noble'" human-headed type with the "ontologically inferior" leontocephaline proper, whose name was Arimanius and is only a doorkeeper.

[147]M. J. Vermaseren, *Mithiaca IV. Le monument d'Ottaviano Zeno et le culte de Mithra sur le Célius* (EPRO 16; Leiden: Brill, 1978) 50-53 with pls. 11-17. Zoega, as cited by Vermaseren (p. 52), thought the two figures were TIme and his son Aion, which is essentially correct; Vermaseren points out, however, that "en tout cas il semble certain que l'artiste a voulu représenter deux figures différentes du même dieu, en qui nous sommes habitués à voir le dieu du Temps éternel." Von Gall's comments, "The Lion-headed and the Human-headed God" 523-524, are not very helpful.

again by an Aion-figure (Helios is actually represented three times, since Sol and Luna in their chariots form the borders of the scene, Sol next to Kronos-Aion, suggesting the sun's "Chaldean" affiliation with Saturn—so too *CIMRM* ##693, 1727—and Luna at the other end). It means nothing because the figures are first and foremost what they symbolize, not the heavenly bodies or deities which had thrust themselves forward as exemplars of this symbology. Equally useless, in this light, is the objection that the leontocephaline cannot be Kronos as Chronos as Aion because the god Kronos-Saturnos frequently figures on Mithraic monuments.

Granted, then, that an understanding of what the Mithraic leontocephaline generally stood for may be garnered from the attributes which it most commonly possesses, one may rightfully demand the source and significance of the commonest feature of all, the creature's lion-head. One tack has been to resort to the Orphic texts discussed in the last section, for the interpenetration of Orphism and Mithraism is evident both from the Modena Phanes in the inscription which accompanies it as well as from the relief itself and from the Borcovicium monument. A relationship between their respective Aion-figures (on the Orphic side not Phanes so much as Hieronymos/Hellanikos' Chronos-Heracles) was already posited by Cumont and continues to be posited, with influence flowing from Orphism to Mithraism.[148] Cumont's argument is based on a passage in the fourteenth century *Third Vatican Mythographer* (text: *TMMM* II, 53-54) which describes the god Saturnus as holding in his right hand a *draconem . . . fammivomum qui caudae suae ultima devorat,* symbolizing the year, and as himself an old man who can also be portrayed as a boy because every year his body grows old in winter but young again in spring. "He is also represented," the text goes on,

---

[148]Cumont, *TMMM* I, 75 and n. 5; Nock, "A Vision of Mandulis Aion" 79 n. 78; Bianchi, "Protogonos" 115-133; Eisler, *Weltenmantel und Himmelszelt* II, 405-448 and beyond; Vermaseren, *Mithras, the Secret God* 123-125, on the Modena relief (proposing that the Felix who dedicated it was first a member of an Orphic conventicle and later, as a Mithraic *pater*, rededicated it to Mithras) and its likeness to the Mithraic leontocephaline; Dussaud, "Le dieu mithriaque léontocéphale" 254; and especially Stig Wikander, *Études sur les mystères de Mithras* (Lund, Gleerup, 1950) 33-36. On Mithras and Phanes as gods of light and the Zeus-Helios-Mithras-Phanes inscription note further Margherita Guarducci, "Il graffito *natus prima luce* nel mitreo di Santa Prisca," *Mysteria Mithrae* 160-162.

at one time with the face of a serpent because of the excessive cold, now with the gaping jaws of a lion because the heat
is so exceedingly fierce, and then again with crests in the
form of a boar's tusks because of the frequent inclemency of
the elements, which, as everyone knows, all (successively)
assert themselves as the seasons change.

Suppressing the third element in this passage, Cumont maintained that the
Mithraic leontocephaline was originally bicephalic, snake and lion, and
hence comparable to (he does not quite say derivable from) Damascius'
Chronos-Heracles.

This really does not help much. The passage just translated from the
Third Vatican Mythographer represents what is evidently a correctly
seasonal exegesis (with the explanatory clauses added) of the description
which Martianus Capella (fifth century A.D.) offers of Saturnus in *The
Marriage of Philology and Mercury* 2.197.[149] It is clear from both sources
that Saturnus' heads do not subsist on his shoulders all at once but follow
one upon the other in that they represent the change of seasons (the most
transparent of which is the lion as a mid-summer Leo) and correspond to
father Time's rejuvenation. While the Ἥλιος–Κρόνος–Χρόνος equations
underlie this portrait of Saturnus just as they do the Orphic Chronos-
Heracles and Phanes and the Mithraic leontocephaline, Martianus
Capella's attribution of a multiplicity of heads to Saturnus, though it
involves some of the same animals for the same astrological reasons,
expresses a different aspect of the situation (seasonal change) than do his
figure's Orphic and Mithraic counterparts, and even disregarding his boar's
tusks does not make him look exactly like any one of the others. While
they are comparable for symbolizing identical concepts, whatever his
sources were, Martianus Capella's Saturnus is not likely to have been the
model either for the Orphic Chronos-Heracles or the Mithraic leontoceph-

---

[149]In addition to the literature cited at the end of n. 129 see Waldemar
Deonna, "Le Saturne à l'ouroboros de Martianus Capella," *MSNAF* (1954)
103-107; William Harris Stahl, Richard Johnson, and E. L. Burge,
Martianus Capella and the Seven Liberal Arts II (New York: Columbia
University Press, 1977) 60. Eisler, *Weltenmantel und Himmelszelt* II, 389
n. 2, refuses the passage from the *Third Vatican Mythographer* any Mithraic connection, restricting its reference to the Orphic Chronos. The
seasonal reference of Saturnus here (Kronos-Chronos = Annus) explains
why he is now old, now young (see Macrobius, *Saturnalia* 1.18.10); it stems
from Saturnus' old connection with agricultural products.

aline, but, if anything, they for him. Wikander's express effort to derive
the Mithraic leontocephaline from the Orphic Chronos-Heracles by ridding
the latter of his bull's head as an error of Damascius is no less arbitrary
than Cumont's suppression of Saturnus' boar's tusks in the *Third Vatican
Mythographer*. Even then the Mithraic figure's features still differ too
much from those of Chronos-Heracles (and from those of Phanes as well)
to be directly derivable from Orphic sources.

One thing, at any rate, follows pretty clearly from the comparison of
the Mithraic leontocephaline with Martianus Capella's Saturnus and the
Orphic deities, and that is that the Mithraic leontocephaline's lion-head,
like that of Yahweh/Yaldabaoth both as Mios and as Chnoumis, is at least
partially to be explained as representing the zodiacal Leo, the house of
Helios whose eternal world-ruling, world-creating course through the
heavens the Mithraic figure as a whole, like all of its kin, symbolically
represents by its welter of iconographic attributes. The many late antique
contexts in which the lion occurs as a solar emblem make it very unlikely
that the Mithraic leontocephaline's lion-head is an exception, especially as
astrological symbolism plays such an important role in Mithraism. The
Oxyrhynchus leontocephaline (*CIMRM* #103 with fig 36) actually shows
the lion-head surrounded by a nimbus and rays and between its wings on
the left side the lion with a star over its head familiar from the magic
gems, giving the lion—in this example, at least—unmistakably solar
associations. The lion's importance for the Mithraic Aion-figures and its
emblematic character in conjunction with them are both even apparent
from the human-headed "leontocephalines," for, as is true of the Modena
Phanes, the youth-headed figure from Merida (*CIMRM* #777 with fig 211)
has a large lion-mask on his chest (the lion-headed figure from Castel
Gandolfo, *CIMRM* #326 with figs 89-90, has similar masks on its midriff
and its knees), whereas the bearded old man from Argentoratum (*CIMRM*
#1326 with fig 350) has a great lion standing behind him.

In spite of the paucity of Mithraic monuments from Egypt (mostly
Memphis and Oxyrhynchus, though Alexandria is known from literary
sources to have possessed two Mithraea and, moreover, a flourishing cult
of Aion), attention has been directed there as a source for many of the
iconographic features displayed by Mithraic leontocephalines, in particular by Raffaele Pettazzoni.[150] Though attested in Syrian contexts, the

---

[150]"La figura mostruosa del Tempo nella religione mitriaca," *AnCl* 18
(1949) 265-277 with pls. 1-7, also published in *AANL.P* 15 (1950) 6-16 with
pls. 1-7. An English translation of most of the article appeared as "The

serpent-entwinement, along with the figure's often noted stiff, hieratic posture, is likely to be of Egyptian origin. Many individual leontocephalines evince unmistakably Egyptian or Egyptianizing elements; the Egyptian loincloth has been noted on *CIMRM* #1326, for example, and the fact that, in addition to his hieratic pose, the Sidonian leontocephaline (*CIMRM* #78 with figs 29a-b; my pl. 18b-c) is unusual in holding his keys, as Egyptian gods do their ankhs, which the keys here resemble, in hands on arms hanging stiffly along his flanks. Pettazzoni himself focuses his argument principally upon the Castel Gandolfo leontocephaline (*CIMRM* #326 with figs 89-90). Like many a Bes "pantheos," whom Pettazzoni considers to have exerted great influence upon the iconography of the Mithraic leontocephaline, the Castel Gandolfo figure has four wings, four arms, an eye on his chest, and lion-masks on his knees;[151] beside him sits the (in this case) dog-, lion-, and jackal- (wolf-?) headed "Cerberus" of Sarapis, a not unnatural companion for the Mithraic Aion-figure since the equations Sarapis=Helios=Aion were common, for which reason Macrobius (*Saturnalia* 1.20.13-15) can logically impose a learned temporal interpretation upon his pet.[152]

Monstrous Figure of Time in Mithraism," *Essays on the History of Religions* (trans. H. J. Rose; SHR [NumenSup] 1; Leiden: Brill, 1954) 180-192 with pls. 6-12. Dussaud, "Le dieu mithriaque léontocéphale" 256-257, and von Gall, "The Lion-headed and the Human-headed God" 516, are too superficially critical of this view. On Egyptian influence note further Will, *Le relief cultuel gréco-romain* 189-192; Cumont, "Une représentation du dieu alexandrin du Temps" 277-278; Vermaseren, *Mithras, the Secret God* 125-127; Hinnells, "Reflections on the Lion-headed Figure" 365, in an attempt to account for the prominence of leontocephalines at Rome: "The iconographic connections were such as to attract the lovers of esoteric teachings and ritual with the deliberate attempt to recall the Egyptian or Egyptianizing monuments so well known in Rome."

[151]On this last attribute note the essay by A.-J. Festugière, "Les cinq sceaux de l'Aiôn alexandrin," reprinted in *Études de religion grecque et hellénistique* (Paris: Vrin, 1972) 201-209 with pl. 3 and added notes by E. Coche de la Ferté and J. Vandier.

[152]For Egyptian connections of the Mithraic leontocephaline Pettazzoni's article "Kronos-Chronos in Egitto," *Hommages à Joseph Bidez et à Franz Cumont* (ColLat 2; Bruxelles: Latomus, 1949) 245-256, is of interest in discussing (1) Kronos' identification with Anubis, whose keys, mentioned earlier, then become even more comparable to those held by the Mithraic leontocephaline, (2) Saturn's being called in Egypt the "star of Nemesis," a fact which nicely puts Kronos-Chronos on a par with

As far as the Mithraic figure's lion-head is concerned, Pettazzoni points to descriptions of Mios as a lion-headed man,[153] and given the leontocephaline's other iconographic connections with Egypt, Mios' solar associations, and, through Nemesis, Kronos' (and Helios') affiliation with partially leonine sphinx "pantheos" figures (Sarapis' "Cerberus" being a parallel development), this is a very plausible hypothesis, especially since, unless one accepts the Ahrimanian nature of the Mithraic figure and derives its lion-head from Babylonian and Assyrian demons, there is no other suitable prototype to be found. All the more is Mios an attractive source as, like $Twtw$-Τιθοης as boss of the messengers of Sekhmet, and like Yahweh himself, he was a god who dispensed retribution (whence his popularity with magicians); his leadership of his lion-headed mother's emissaries, through their coalescence with functionally related astrological figures like the planets and the decans, guaranteed that Kronos, as "star of Nemesis" and intimately involved in retribution, could well acquire, in his Chronos-Aion synthesis, the iconography of the god of Leontopolis. The lion as a solar emblem (zodiacal Leo), already involved in Mios' cult, also fit in well with the contribution of Helios to the Aion-format, a fact which, as I said, accounts for the lion's presence in the makeup of the Mithraic leontocephaline's Orphic counterparts. Cumont is quite justified, then, in saying that the lion-headed man that the great Paris magical papyrus (*PGM* I P 4.2111-2117, discussed earlier) recommends representing girded about the waist, holding a staff in one hand and with a serpent coiling around the other, "rapelle absolument" the Mithraic leontocephalines;[154] if anything, he does not go far enough. The fire

---

Nemesis' γρύψ and $Twtw$-Τιθοης (as I pointed out earlier: n. 86) and brings him iconographically into contact with the lion, and (3) Egyptian knowledge of the "Chaldean" Saturn-sun connection in the context of Nemesis' solar associations through the ancient tradition of the sun, like Yahweh (cp. Mal 3:20-21), as a god πανεπόπτης and righter of wrongs. Kronos' identification with Anubis is due to his confinement to Tartarus and his consequent lordship of the realm of the dead, a realm which for Kronos as the planet Saturn means the whole world: see Dieterich, *Abraxas* 76-83; S. Eitrem, "Kronos in der Magie," *Mélanges Bidez* (Annuaire de l'Institut de Philologie et d'Histoire Orientales 2; Bruxelles: Secrétariat de l'Institut, 1934) 351-360, commenting on *PGM* I P 4.2315-2317, 3087-3124, and other passages.

[153]"La figura mostruosa del Tempo," *AnCl* 18 (1949) 269, followed by Will, *Le relief cultuel gréco-romain* 189.

[154]*TMMM* II, 57. So too Dieterich, *Abraxas* 53-54, remarking: "Es kann kaum eine bessere Interpretation dieser Bildwerke (i.e., the Mithraic leon-

which the magician further ordains his leontocephaline to have breathing from its mouth and which ties his figure to Mios and his mother Sekhmet is also a frequent feature of the Mithraic leontocephalines. This attribute is actually depicted on *CIMRM* #383 with fig 109, where the leontocephalic figure's breath kindles the flame of an altar (my pl. 19a); the same may be implied in #902 with fig 230. It is implied by the similar function which the holes that often pierce the figure through to the gaping mouth (*CIMRM* ##78 with figs 29a-b, 543 with fig 152, 544 with *TMMM* II, #40 and fig 47, and 954 with fig 258E and *TMMM* II, #361g; my pl. 18c) seem to have served, whether it was air or somehow fire that blew through the aperture.[155]

But the origin of the leontocephaline's lion-head is one thing and its full significance in a Mithraic form is another. To begin with, the lion appears in a wide variety of different settings in Mithraic art, and its symbolic meaning is just as varied and as complex as this chapter has demonstrated it to be in other, contemporary contexts. The lion figures often, for example, as a companion of Sol, in which case one is certainly justified in holding it to represent the zodiacal Leo, just as the leontocephaline's head partially does. But free-standing sculptures of a lion holding an animal's head between its paws are also of frequent occurrence, a motif familiar from Roman sepulchral art (and, with a somewhat different meaning, on magic gems), in which case the lion symbolizes, as I pointed out at the beginning of the chapter, the voracity of Death.[156] The lion is, then, in

---

tocephalines) geben als unsre Papyrusstellen . . . ," by which he means, in addition to the passage Cumont cites, that other, for example, from *PGM* I P 1 which concerns the leontocephalic Helios-Horus.

[155]Cumont, *TMMM* I, 80-81. Cumont connects the fiery breath which the Mithraic leontocephaline is shown spewing and may actually have spewed from its mouth with the fiery breath which, according to the Magi as reported by Dio Chrysostom, *Discourse* 36.47-48 with 43-44, once descended from the horse of elemental fire at the chariot of Zeus and consumed the world. In the posthumous report on "The Dura Mithraeum" 204-205 he refers this attribute of the leontocephaline to a Mithraic baptism of fire on the basis of graffito from that Mithraeum (*CIMRM* #63 as corrected in II, p. 14) which speaks of a πυρωτὸν (πυρωπὸν Cumont) ἄσθμα τὸ (for δ Cumont) καὶ μάγοις ᾧ (instead of ἤ) νίπτρον ὁσ‹σ›ίω[v], but, though it may presuppose an earthly ritual, this text is probably better seen as an eschatological reference to the River of Fire in which, according to Iranian apocalyptic, souls must bathe, and does not directly implicate the leontocephaline as dispenser of the νίπτρον.

[156]Hinnells, "Reflections on the Lion-headed Figure" 352-354; and

Mithraism as elsewhere, an ambivalent figure, and if, similarly, the leontocephaline's head is sometimes frightening and evil-looking yet at other times benign it is because the astral force he represents is a fatal power that oversees the subjugation of human souls to the contraints of embodiment and to the unpredictable ups and downs of Fortune dished out by its agents at the same time as the Mithraic figure's keys also guarantee the initiated soul escape into its solar eternity and universality.

There is no doubt that the leontocephaline had some bearing on the Mithraic mysteries, and specifically for the Mithraic grade *leo*; the portrait of the lion-headed human being who represents this grade on the Konjica relief (*CIMRM* #1896 with fig 491) discussed earlier can hardly be without some relevance to the leontocephaline. Besides the outward resemblance of the Konjica representative of the grade *leo* (pl. 4c) to the leontocephaline, the two also share, firstly, association with Zeus/Jupiter, the thunderbolt appearing both on or with the leontocephaline (*CIMRM* ##312 with fig 85, 665 with fig 188, 882bis) and as a symbol of the grade *leo* on the mosaic aisle of the Mithraeum of Felicissimus at Ostia (*CIMRM* #299 with fig 83; and note #480.4 *Nama l[e]on[i]b[us] tutela Iovis*), an association which doubtless stemmed from the assignment of the zodiacal constellation Leo to the tutelage of Zeus and, in the case of the leontocephaline, from the Syrian equation of Zeus with gods like בעל שמם as lord of the heavens. Secondly, the two share an associaton with fire, which is natural enough for the lion as a fiery animal. As regards the leontocephaline, I have already mentioned its fire-blowing or fire-kindling capabilities, and, similarly, with respect to the grade *leo*, there is, among other things, (1) the fire-shovel as its symbol in the Mithraeum of Felicissimus (*CIMRM* #299 with fig 83; with the leontocephaline: *CIMRM* #1123 with fig 291); (2) the literary evidence of Tertullian, *Against Marcion* 1.13 (*TMMM* II, 50), who says *aridae et ardentis naturae sacramenta leones Mithrae philosophantur*, and of Porphyry, *On the Cave of the Nymphs in the Odyssey* 15 (*TMMM* II, 40):

> When those who are being initiated into τὰ λεοντικά have honey instead of water poured out onto their hands [confirmed by *CIMRM* #2269 in *leo melichrisus*] to cleanse them with, (the officiators) exhort them to keep their hands pure from everything offensive, hurtful, and foul; because he is an initiate of fire, which purifies, they use a cleansing agent (for

---

earlier in "Reflections on the bull-slaying scene," *Mithraic Studies* II, 301-302.

his hands) which is related to it, rejecting water as inimical
to fire;

and (3) the famous lines from the Santa Prisca Mithraeum
accipe thuricremos, pater, accipe, sancte, leones,
per quos thuradamus, per quos consumimur ipsi,

which confirm that the Mithraic *leones* burned incense on behalf of the
other members of the community, whom, *pace* W. Vollgraff, the *leones,*
like good representatives of the voracious and fiery lion, by that act
purified—"consumed," as the fire the incense.[157]

If the leontocephalines as fire-breathers were not the fonts of some
fiery "baptism" for Mithraic *leones,* but rather both, as involving the lion,
automatically thereby embodied fire, the basis for the fiery and solar
connections between the lion-headed Mithraic cosmocrator and the grade
leo in specific relation to Mithraic initiation is evident from Porphyry's
(source's) statement in *On Abstinence from Animal Food* 4.16 (*TMMM* II,
42) that ὁ τε τὰ λεοντικὰ παραλαμβάνων περιτίθεται παντοδαπὰς ζῴων
μορφάς. One can hardly accept, as Cumont seems inclined to do,[158] the
validity for the Mithraic initiation itself of the explanation that Pallas (in
Porphyry) offers, namely, that the ritual taught that souls παντοδαποῖς
περιέχεσθαι σώμασι, i.e., the doctrine of transmigration. As his use of
αἰνίττεσθαι here and his contrast of it to the "common opinion" show,

---

[157]Hinnells, "Reflections on the Lion-headed Figure" 361-364;
Campbell, *Mithraic Iconography and Ideology* 264-266, 309-310 (on p. 264
n. 9 Campbell says of *Gos. Thom.*'s seventh logion: "This verse sounds very
much like a polemic directed against the Lion of Mithra"—not likely);
Turcan, *Mithras Platonicus* 69-70; M. J. Vermaseren and C. C. van Essen,
The Excavations in the Mithraeum of the Church of Santa Prisca in Rome
(Leiden: Brill, 1965) 156-157, 224-232 with fig. 70 (p. 215) and pl. 69.1; W.
Vollgraff, "Le rôle des Lions dans la communauté mithriaque," *Hommages
à Léon Herrmann* (ColLat 44; Bruxelles-Berchem: Latomus, 1960) 777-785;
Bianchi, "Prolegomena" 53-54; Concetta Aloe Spada, "Il *leo* nella
gerarchia dei gradi mitriaci," *Mysteria Mithrae* 642-643 on the Santa
Prisca verses and the connection between the grade *leo* and the leontocephaline (I concur with her judgment: "Anche se, a mio avviso, è forse
eccessivo vedere con Hinnells nel *leo* 'the earthly counterpart to the
cosmic being depicted with a lion's head,' non siamo distanti dal vero—ci
sembra—se affermiamo l'esistenza di un rapporto tra il personaggio a
volto leonino e il grado di *leo*" on the basis of the Konjica relief alone).
[158]Cumont, *TMMM* I, 40, 309 and n. 6, 315 and n. 5.

Pallas was well aware what the ritual meant for initiates themselves, but, as a good Neo-Pythagorean, felt obliged to offer what to him is the "true and accurate conception" that the philosophically minded must hold of it. The "common opinion" at which Pallas turned up his nose rightly referred it to the zodiacal circle, and, as should be clear by now, the ritual was designed to allow the initiate to join the sun, *Sol invictus* (= Mithras), and partake of his eternity and universality by sharing in his perpetual metamorphosis. The similarity of παντοδαπὰς ζῴων μορφάς with Hieronymos/Hellanikos' description of Phanes' serpent (//a polycephalic serpent Chronos-Heracles// Yahweh/Yaldabaoth in the short recension of *Apoc. John*) as παντοδαπαῖς μορφαῖς θηρίων ἰνδαλλόμενον is not accidental, but directly attributable to the sun's zodiacal transformations, whether as an Orphic Phanes or a Mithraic *leo*. The Mithraic *leo*'s initiation, then, made him the companion of Mithras as Helios, exactly as the lion is constantly shown with Mithras in the tauroctony, on the hunt, at the feast with Sol.

It is difficult to know what exactly περιτίθεται means in reference to the leontic initiation, but the verb clearly implies investiture of some kind. I doubt that it refers, as some seem to think, to mimetic action, to the wearing of animal masks (for the masks of the initiates in the Konjica relief are different grades), but rather incline to agree with Reitzenstein that it alludes to something like the *Olympiaca stola* of (in addition to?) the twelve initiate's robes (clearly zodiacal) with which Lucius was invested after his Isiac initiation in Aplueius, *Metamorphoses* 11.24, which was adorned with all sorts of animals, and which made him *ad instar Solis exornatus*.[159] But however that may be, in whatever respect the Mithraic leontocephaline was involved in the initiatory ritual for *leones*,[160] the

---

[159] Reitzenstein, *Das iranische Erlösungsmysterium* 167-169, who brands Pallas' opinions as "die Klügeleien eines theologischen Philosophasters" (p. 168); Campbell, *Mithraic Iconography and Ideology* 309; Turcan, *Mithras Platonicus* 36-38; Robert Eisler, *Orphisch-dionysische Mysteriengedanken in der christlichen Antike* (Hildesheim: Olms, 1966 [1925]) 316-328 in the context of a good, far-ranging discussion, accepts Pallas' transmigrational explanation as valid for the Mithraic mysteries themselves and interprets the leontic investiture as a successive donning of masks.

[160] If the *leonteum, cum signo et cetero cultu exornatum*, of which an unedited Mithraic inscription from San Gemini in Umbria (Umberto Ciotti, "Due iscrizioni mitriache inediti I," *Hommages à Maarten J. Vermaseren* I, 233-239 with pl. 28) commemorates the erection *a solo* by a group of

text from Porphyry shows that the figure represents that into knowledge

---

leones refers to a cult niche or shrine and the *signum* to a statue of the leontocephaline (as the leontocephaline *CIMRM* #1123 with fig 291 was found in a niche in Mithraeum III at Heddernheim), then some special connection between *leo* and leontocephaline is established. On this inscription note further Aloe Spada, "Il *leo* nella gerarchia mitriaci" 647-648. Note too that *CIMRM* #1773 is an altar dedicated *Deo Arimanio*, who may be the leontocephaline, and that Silvio Panciera, "LEONI SANCTO DEO PRAESENTI," *Mysteria Mithrae* 127-135, seeks to explain the inscription that forms the title of his paper (continued on the stone by A. CAECILI FAUSTINI) and which, though presently displayed at the entrance of the Barberini Mithraeum, is neither certainly from it nor certainly Mithraic, by its reference to some god-lion from the East: to Mios, or to the Heliopolitan god γενναῖος of Damascius' *Life of Isidorus*, or to the lion-god, whoever he or she is to whom, along with other gods (Σειμίῳ καὶ Συμβετύλῳ καὶ Λέοντι θεοῖς πατρῴοις), an inscription (dated A.D. 224) dedicates the construction of an olive press with funds from a second century sanctuary in a humble northern Syrian village now Kafr Nabo: on it see Milik, "Les papyrus araméens d'Hermoupolis et les cultes syro-phéniciens" 568-570; Hajjar, *La triade d'Héliopolis-Baalbek* 154-155; du Mesnil du Buisson, *Études sur les dieux phéniciens* 124-126; "Le groupe des dieux Él, Bétyle, Dagon et Atlas chez Philon de Byblos," *RHR* 169 (1966) 45-47; René Dussaud, "Temples et cultes de la triade héliopolitaine à Baᶜalbeck" 43-44; Wolfgang Fauth, "Simia," PWSup 14.689.15-690.31); H. J. W. Drijvers, *Cults and Beliefs at Edessa* (EPRO 82; Leiden: Brill, 1980) 100-101. Of those three Mios seems the best choice for his something more than strictly local popularity in late antiquity (recall, for example, the evidence presented at the end of n. 98), though any other evidence for the presence of his devotees at Rome is lacking. But Bianchi, "Prolegomena" 28-29 (and cp. pp. 54-55), considers the inscription Mithraic (a possibility which Panciera does not rule out: "Relazioni con il culto mitriaco, dopo quanto si e detto, come non possono essere provate, neppure vanno escluse," "LEONI SANCTO" 134) A. Caecilius Faustinus being a newly initiated *leo* and the *leo sanctus, deus praesens*, either another initiating *leo* in whom "a divine personage" is "incorporated" and "manifested" or else "the divine counterpart, the divine 'twin' or *genius* of the very neophyte lion himelf." Neither of these seems likely to me; if the inscription is Mithraic at all, I think what Bianchi barely suggests, namely, that the god-lion in question is the leontocephaline as patron of the leontic initiation, is the most reasonable solution. The adjective *praesens*, as applied to a *deus*, means here, as often, "present" in the sense of "aiding, favoring, propitious," and the Latin genitives, in my view, are to be explained as the result of the strict equivalence of

of which the candidates were being initiated, precisely as Mithras himself, the initiate's guide and savior, is frequently shown ascending, his demiurgic work completed, in Sol's chariot to heaven, where he is greeted by the snake-enwrapped representative of celestial Eternity (*CIMRM* ##1935 with fig 505, 1958 with fig 512, 1972 with fig 513, 2166, 2171 with fig 591, 2291 with fig 634b) who sired him in the first place (the rock from which Mithras *saxigenus* is born is constantly shown girdled by the coils of a serpent). If the Aion who greets *him* is always human-headed in these scenes, it is doubtless because a theriomorphic Aion was not appropriate to it, all the more as the figure is in the act of greeting the travelers, a human response accorded his equals, which human initiates properly are not. If, on the other hand, the vast majority of the Mithraic Aion-figures are leontocephaline it is likely to be due precisely to their connection with τὰ λεοντικά, with the rites that recapitulated this aspect of Mithras' experience, for human *leones*. The leontic mysteries were certainly (to judge from the literary evidence and the preponderance of inscriptional references to the grade *leo*) of key importance in the Mithraic pilgrim's progress toward celestial bliss, an importance which Porphyry's supposed division of the seven Mithraic grades into initiates μετέχοντες and initiates ὑπηρετοῦντες with the median *leo* the first of the former (*On Abstinence from Animal Food* 4.16) is held to underline.[161] This importance would explain why the leontocephaline was such an important figure in Mithraism.

If Cumont[162] is right in thinking that the Mithraic mysteries somehow reflected the doctrine attested in Neo-Pythagorean sources, discussed earlier, that souls begin their embodiment at Leo, the house of the sun, the source of Soul, then the leontocephaline's lion-head, as Leo, makes him, like Helios, all the more the lord of γένεσις. Porphyry's assignment to Mithras, γενέσεως δεσπότης, of a seat straddling the equinoxes with Cautes and Cautopates to his left and right presiding, torch up and torch down, over the ascent and the descent of souls, respectively (*On the Cave of the Nymphs in the Odyssey* 24)[163] and the position of an "eighth gate"

---

praesens (upon which they thus depend) with Greek ἐπήκοος which takes that case and of which the dedicant was actually thinking.

[161] On this two-fold division of the grades and the importance of *leo* see, for example, Aloe Spada, "Il *leo* nella gerarchia dei gradi mitriaci" 639-648; Scherling, "Leontika," PW 12.2041.20-39.

[162] *TMMM* I, 40 and n. 2.

[163] *TMMM* II, 41. Consult the revised text published as Arethusa Monographs I by the Department of Classics, State University of New

at the top of Celsus' κλίμαξ ἑπτάπυλος (Origen, *Against Celsus* 6.22) suggest that gates in the zodiac of fixed stars did form the outermost portals of the Mithraic cosmos. The leontocephalic Aion-figures are lion-headed, then, not simply because they somehow presided over τὰ λεον-τικά but because the lion as zodiacal Leo, both generally as the house of the sun, the source of all life, and specifically as that sign in which souls begin their descent into embodiment, oversaw the incarnation of human souls. The being who greets Mithras cannot, therefore, well be lion-headed.

As for Gnosticism and its lion-headed Yahweh/Yaldabaoth:[164] There can be no question of deriving the Gnostic archon's leonine looks from the Mithraic leontocephaline or *vice versa*; if anything, as with the Orphic Chronos-Heracles and Phanes, it is a matter of common Hellenistic Syrian and Egyptian sources for the iconography of beings who represented solar Eternity. But, especially in the case of Yahweh/Yaldabaoth as elevated by *Apoc. John* out of the ranks of the seven planetary rulers to the status of a full-fledged polymorphic or polycephalic Aion κοσμοκράτωρ—a development which I posited to have occurred at a time contemporary with the only datable Mithraic leontocephaline (*CIMRM* #312 with its inscription #313: A.D. 190 under Commodus)—the two figures shared a similar function for symbolizing the same world-ruling, world-ensouling Power. As the highest planetary archon at Saturn's sphere (Yahweh/Yaldabaoth being yet Kronos, whence the Kronos-Chronos equation aided his advancement to a solar Aion) Origen's Gnostics' Yaldabaoth, like the Mithraic leontocephaline with his keys, is chiefly overlord of the "gates of the rulers chained for eternity";

> And thou, Ialdabaoth, first and seventh, born to have power with boldness, . . . , I bear a symbol marked with a picture of life, and, having opened to the world the gate which thou didst close for thine eternity (αἰῶνι σῷ), I pass by thy power free again (Origen, *Against Celsus* 6.31).[165]

York at Buffalo, 1969; p. 24.9-15.

[164]Treated by Hinnells, "Reflections on the Lion-headed Figure" 358-360; Bianchi, "Protogonos" 126-129; and especially his "Mithraism and Gnosticism," *Mithraic Studies* II, 457-465, with a long and detailed discussion of the York monument, but otherwise somewhat confused and confusing.

[165]Chadwick's translation, *Origen: Contra Celsum* 347.

But Hinnells wisely cautions against pressing the analogy too far; there is an important qualitative difference between the two figures in their respective settings that must not be overlooked. Gnosticism's world-view was certainly far more dualistic than Mithraism's can have been. For the former, as for extremists in the Judaeo-Christian tradition generally (cp. Eph 6:12), the planetary powers that rule this world (if they did not also create it—this step deriving from exegesis of Plato's lesser demiurges) are evil; the Gnostic mystic whose encounter with Yaldabaoth Origen preserves must use magical means to compel the opening of a gate locked by its guardian for the whole age of his ascendancy. The Gnostic's salvation comes from a realm beyond and in opposition to that overseen by Yaldabaoth and the rulers, whose order and willful oppression of the human spirits in their grip must be overthrown by the intervention of the Savior.

As I tried to show, this cannot have been true for the Mithraic leontocephaline. Because its Aionic κοσμοκράτωρ represented a fatal Power essentially identical with Yaldabaoth's in that it served to ensoul the cosmos and to subject all that lives to the laws of Τύχη and Εἱμαρμένη Mithraism, like many another late antique religion, cannot have been totally optimistic about just how beneficial that Power is for the human soul. As in Orphism confinement in a body somehow spells death for the soul, and hence the leontocephaline's face may often be frightening, its leonine head the symbol of that "death." But this does not mean that Mithraism was necessarily as totally pessimistic as Gnosticism was; documents like the *Kore Kosmou* show that the two attitudes toward cosmogenesis may well subsist, however unreconciled, side by side. The fact that the Mithraic initiatory grades are under the tutelage of deities long correlated with the planets and that links exist which connect the leontocephaline with the leontic initiation indicate that the planets, far from opposing the soul's quest for freedom, actively participated in it, and that the leontocephaline, as the distillation of celestial power, was not an irredeemably oppressive force but, as it embodied souls, so it might aid— by initiation and not by compulsion—in freeing them from that embodiment. This could be so for Mithraism because the leontocephaline has strong solar associations, if it may not be said to be a representation of the sun, and the sun, both as an independent figure and as an hypostasis of Mithras, is a fully divine being in the cult of the Iranian god, intimately involved in Mithraic soteriology. As solar the Mithraic leontocephaline simply cannot be evil through and through. In Gnosticism, on the other hand, the sun is, if anything, just another subordinate ruler and, so far as I know, except in Manichaeism is never endowed with a role in the process of salvation.

3.8   Summary

The process of Yahweh's transformation into a leontocephalic deity began with the foundation of a Jewish temple in the mid-second century B.C. at a site in the Egyptian Delta formerly devoted to the worship of the lion-headed goddesses Sekhmet and Bastet. This fact, together with the military nature of the Jewish colony there and the proximity of another Leontopolis to the north of it, prompted the identification of Yahweh with its god Mios, and lion-headed son of Sekhmet/Bastet and, like the Jewish colony's god, an aggressive defender of the Ptolemies' realm. Through this theocrasy Yahweh inherited Mios' position in command of his mother's band of seven ferocious emissaries, death-dealing angels of her wrath and, like the Gnostic Yahweh, subordinate agents of divine retribution. With astrological associations gained through its functional similarity to the Egyptian decans, this theriocephalic troupe, or perhaps, in contexts where Mesopotamian tradition predominated, that in the train of demons like Pazuzu and Lamashtu, served as the original prototype for the evolution of what became the seven Gnostic planetary archons made up of a lion-headed Yahweh/Yaldabaoth as chief and six additional hypostases of himself. The transitional intermediaries of this development were perhaps proto-Gnostic Samaritan sorcerers and healers who latched on to the Yahweh-Mios synthesis for its magical and medical usefulness, an asset it already possessed in its purely Egyptian setting.

Yahweh/Yaldabaoth's position as highest in a planetary hierarchy was guaranteed by his equation in Seleucid Syria, similarly beginning at least in the second century B.C., either with deities whose Greek equivalents were Kronos and who therefore assured Yahweh's coordination with the planet Saturn, a coordination reinforced in Egyptian soil by Saturn's association with retribution as the star of Nemesis, or with deities who, like Ba⁣ʿal Šamem, were lords of the heavens. The identification of the latter with Zeus and Zeus' tutelage of the zodiacal Leo (the lion being king of beasts as Zeus of gods) helped to fix Yahweh's affiliation with this animal. The ouranological speculations of Jewish apocalyptic, on the rise in the same time period, encouraged these Syrian theocrasies and the astrological associations which the popularity of the Chaldean science foisted upon them by setting Yahweh firmly in the highest heaven. Ezekiel's חַיּוֹת and the development of Merkabah mysticism, a visionary adjunct of apocalyptic, aided in giving theriomorphic faces to Yahweh's archontic hypostases by influencing the choice of animal forms, but was not itself the source of the Gnostic tradition.

Christian Gnostics of the second century supported the portrait of a leonine Yahweh/Yaldabaoth with all the suitably savage passages of the Old Testament in which Yahweh's vindictive fury, like Mios', expresses its ferocity as a lion. They availed themselves of a long-standing exegetical tradition which, beginning in Maccabean times, interpreted the "lions" of the Psalms, themselves already metaphors for oppressors both human and demonic, of tyrannical persecutors like Antiochus IV Epiphanes. The New Testatment attests this martyrological tradition and the incipience of its mythological translation to a cosmic plane. The virulent anti-Jewish sentiment widespread in early Christianity together with the facts that the earliest Christians read Jesus' Passion into Ps 22 [21] and that the Gnostics' enemies were the oppressive astral henchmen of Fate aided their application of the lion-persecutors of this martyrological tradition to an already leonine Yahweh/Yaldabaoth.

The new lion-headed serpentine form attested for Yahweh/Yaldabaoth by the long recension of *Apoc. John* derives from Chnoumis, the first decan of the Egyptian Leo. The transition from Mios to Chnoumis was made natural by the intimate link between the two figures' lion's head and by the functional homogeneity of Sekhmet's troupe with the decans, both apportioners of disastrous fates. Chnoumis as a new identity for Yahweh/Yaldabaoth commended itself (1) because Chnoumis was known all over the Roman world through the popularity of Egyptian iatromathematical science and the decanal melothesia and through assimilation to Alexander of Abonouteichos' Glycon, (2) because like the Gnostic archon and his model Mios Chnoumis was suitably leontocephalic and the head of his particular band, and (3) because Chnoumis, as the decan which presided over the world-renewing Nile-flood and possibly equated with Chnum, shared Yahweh's role as creator.

The primary impetus for the choice of a new embodiment for Yahweh/Yaldabaoth and the choice of Chnoumis specifically stemmed from the desire to represent the chief archon as a solar κοσμοκράτωρ, a representative of the one great world-creating, world-ruling celestial Power. This development accounts not only for the choice of Chnoumis—a decan of Leo, domicile of the sun, the lion and the serpent that comprise him being the prime exemplars of cosmogonic fire and the cyclical eternity of the heavens—but also for Yahweh/Yaldabaoth's concomitant elevation out of the ranks of the planetary rulers to a position independent of them to match his new, more exalted status. The temporal and cultural background against which these innovations in the Gnostic archontic hierarchy took place is the late second and early third century onset of the "solar monotheism" that typifies late Roman religion and which was due to the patronage by the Severi of solarized Syrian cults and the worship of Mithras.

The shift evident in the short recension of *Apoc. John* toward a polymorphic and, more specifically, a polycephalic portrait of Yahweh/Yaldabaoth is similarly a product of this solar revolution; it represents the attempt to depict the sun's transformations in the course of its passage through the decans and all the other bestial inhabitants of the Egyptian sky. The Bes and sphinx "pantheos" deities, the latter as Τωτω-Τιθοης who at this time appears as chief of Sekhmet's troupe of seven, both possessing strong solar associations and enjoying enormous popularity, helped effect the chief archon's promotion in rank and physical metamorphosis.

The Orphic figures Chronos-Heracles and Phanes and the Mithraic leontocephaline are contemporary responses to the same astrological pressures, though each adapted to its own particular setting. If they influenced the Gnostic tradition at all, it was to provide further impetus for the transformation to which the short recension of *Apoc. John* is witness. Yahweh/Yaldabaoth's mythology does share with Orphism considerable inspiration from Hesiod's *Theogony* and other early Greek cosmogonic tradition.

4

The Platonic Tradition

4.1   The Lion and the Passions

As I pointed out in the second chapter, there is yet a whole anthropological dimension to the Gnostic tradition of a leonine creator; logion 7 of the *Gospel of Thomas* makes it plain that the struggle carried on by the divine order to recover parts of itself lost to the cosmos and its rulers is played out on the battlefield of the human soul. In order fully to understand the logion and its origins it is not sufficient to restrict oneself to the leonine demiurge, for if he is lurking behind the "lion" of the logion, it is obviously not directly the creator himself whom the Man "devours" and by whom he is "devoured," but rather that part which the leontomorphic demiurge contributed to the formation of man as a spiritual being embodied in the material universe. It is to the task of addressing this more human aspect of the Gnostic tradition that the final chapter is directed.

Scholars are in accord that the general import of *Gos. Thom.*'s seventh logion must be the opposition between the worlds of matter and spirit and the struggle of each in man to overcome and absorb the other.[1] This

---

[1] Kasser, *L'Évangile selon Thomas* 38-39; Giversen, *Thomasevangeliet* 38-39; Turner, "Theology of the Gospel of Thomas" 93-94; Doresse, *Livres secrets* II, 134; Grant and Freedman, *Secret Sayings* 126; Ménard, *L'Évangile selon Thomas* 88; Gärtner, *The Theology of the Gospel according to Thomas* 159-171, whose whole exposition of the theme is full and clear; Grant, "Notes on the Gospel of Thomas" 173-179; H.-Ch. Puech, "The Gospel of Thomas," in Hennecke-Schneemelcher, *New Testament Apocrypha* I, 278-284; Y. Janssens, "L'Évangile selon Thomas et son caractère gnostique," *Le Muséon* 75 (1962) 305; William R. Schoedel, "Naassene Themes in the Coptic Gospel of Thomas," *VC* 14 (1960) 225-234, particularly pp.

follows from a comparison of the logion (1) with other sayings of the collection, especially saying 11 (34 [82].18-22) where it is a question of devouring what is dead and making it alive, and saying 60 (43 [91].16-22) where finding a place in ἀνάπαυσις is contrasted to becoming a corpse and being eaten, (2) with passages from the *Gospel of Truth* (CG I, 3; 25.10-19: man will attain unity by consuming matter within him like fire, darkness by light, death by life) and the *Gospel of Philip* (CG II, 3; 66 [114].4-6: those who love the flesh are swallowed up by it; and 73 [121].19-27: this world feeds on death; the truth feeds on life), and (3) with Naassene traditions ostensibly based in part on their use of a recension of *Gos. Thom.* (they knew logion 11: Hippolytus, *Refutation* 5.8.31-32; 95.1-4 Wendland). With occasional and sketchy reference to Gnostic sources, then, commentators explain the lion as symbolizing the body's ravenous appetites which threaten to devour the spiritual man and bury him in the material world. This is surely on the right track, for the Gnostic myths outlined in the last two chapters show that the leonine demiurge is regularly associated with the passions, with desire. Irenaeus reports from his "Barbeloite" source (*Refutation* 1.27.2; I, 226 Harvey) that the Protarchon, himself invariably the product of illicit desire, mated with his own feminine Arrogance to spawn a host of human passions (cp. CG II, *1 Apoc. John* 15 [63].23-19 [67].12). In the triple-tiered Gnostic universe the contribution of the world-ruling powers to the creation of man, who is a microcosmic composite of elements from all three macrocosmic tiers, is passionate soul, precisely that level of being (ψυχικός) of which the archons are themselves the celestial counterparts. It is this contribution which forms the bridge between man and archon.

The Gnostic tradition of a leontomorphic Yahweh/Yaldabaoth dovetailed nicely into the astrological doctrine of the world-rulers as the sources of passionate soul because the lion was in a number of ways closely associated with sexual desire and, as lord of the whole realm of γένεσις, a more fitting passion for the chief archon could scarcely be imagined. Sexuality is a pursuit in which felines are generally well known for proneness to excess, and the spectacular behavior of the greatest of cats in their mating rituals did not fail to attract the attention of ancient naturalists. The elder Pliny, for example, remarks the *magna . . . libido coitus* in lions and the competitive *ira* that males consequently express

---

226-228; E. M. J. M. Cornélis, "Quelques éléments pour une comparaison entre l'Évangile de Thomas et la notice d'Hippolyte sur les Naassènes," *VC* 15 (1961) 83-104, especially pp. 95-98.

over the females; the violence and lust of their courtship is such that lions, leopards, and panthers were held to cross-breed indiscriminately (*Natural History* 8.17.42).

The fact that under astrological impetus popular folklore had made the lion an animal the very marrow of whose bones was fire further helped the king of beasts become a symbol of desire, for the image of fiery passion and unquenchable ardor were as much hackneyed commonplaces in antiquity as they are banal clichés of modern love songs.[2] Hence those born under a fiery Leo were held to be εἰς πράγματα ἀφροδισιακὰ ἐκκεχυμένοι, μοιχοί, ἀναιδεῖς (Hippolytus, *Refutation* 4.19.2; 51.17-18 Wendland). The stress that the Gnostic accounts place upon the lion-headed god's fiery aspect at times palpably suggests this symbolic connection of the lion and of fire with sexual passion (CG II, *1 Apoc. John* 20 [68] .35-21 [69] .14 with 10 [58] .23-28 and 12[60].3-5, for example). The truth is that this symbolism had become so widespread that even Rabbinic Judaism put it to good haggadic use. A strange homily attributed by *b. Sanh.* 64a (a parallel account in *b. Yoma* 69b) to third century Amoraim relates how, in response to fasting and entreaty, the "Tempter to idolatry" issued from the Holy of Holies in the form of a fiery young lion (כגוריא דנורא), was captured and imprisoned. Impressed by their success, the people pray for the "Tempter to (sexual) sin" to be delivered over to them as well, but once that is done (in similarly leonine form?) all fertility ceases. The tale illustrates (and was meant to illustrate) just how closely related for Judaism were the lust for idolatry and that for illicit sexual relationships; both were expressions of יצר הרע and were still as interconnected for the audience at whom the Rabbis' tale was directed as it was for the Israelites seduced by the ministrants of Baal of Peor (Num 25).[3]

The final link, I might add, in this complex symbolic chain to which the passions have now been added is the equation of soul with fire. Schematically we have so far: fire as cosmogonic principle = Yahweh as creator (discussed in chapter 3.3); lion = fiery animal; zodiacal Leo = cause of psychogenesis (also discussed in chapter 3.3); Gnostic creator = passionate soul; Gnostic creator = lion; lion = sexual desire; fire = sexual desire (and

---

[2]For example note: in Hebrew Cant 8:6-7; in Greek Pindar, *Pythian Odes* 4.219; Aristophanes, *Lysistrata* 9-10; Plato, *Laws* 783A; and in Latin Vergil, *Eclogues* 4.68; *Georgics* 3.215-216; Horace, *Epistle* 1.2.13.

[3]On the two passages from the Babylonian Talmud see Ephriam E. Urbach, *The Sages, their Concepts and Beliefs* (trans. I. Abrahams; 2 vols., consecutively paginated; Jerusalem: Magnes, 1975) 474 and n. 24, p. 895, with the whole surrounding discussion.

note that Hippolytus' Simonian source makes this identification as well as that of cosmogonic fire with Yahweh as creator: *Refutation* 6.17.4-7, especially 6.17.4; 143.13-15 Wendland: πάντων, ὅσων γένεσίς ἐστιν, ἀπὸ πυρὸς ἡ ἀρχὴ τῆς ἐπιθυμίας τῆς γενέσεως γίνεται, justifying this opinion by reference to πυροῦσθαι in 1 Cor 7:9). Like the concept of cosmogonic fire the idea that the soul is fire was also disseminated in the Hellenistic period by Stoic philosophers, and for them it had quite sexual connotations. Note, for example, Zeno fr 98 (*SVF* I, 27.17-19) comparing the πρῶτον πῦρ to a σπέρμα because it contained the causal principles of all that exists, fr 120 (*SVF* I, 34.25-26) identifying the τεχνικὸν πῦρ with the φύσις and the ψυχή of living things, and fr 126 (*SVF* I, 35.31-32): *animalium semen ignis is, qui anima ac mens.*[4]

To return to the lion and the passions. Conventions of the Hellenistic and Roman iconography of two divinities enshrined the animal's erotic affiliations in the canons of the symbolism of the Gnostics' age and must have encouraged its application to new, literary contexts. In part motivated by his assimilation to Dionysos (both gods were λυσιμελής) and by his mother's ancient Near Eastern ancestors' possession of lions as acolytes, a favorite depiction of Eros (whose Orphic ties to Greek cosmogony cannot have encumbered a rapprochement with the Gnostic creator) in the post-classical period is astride the back of a lion. Lucian's parody of this motif (*Dialogues of the Gods* 12.1-2) shows that it was held to illustrate the irresistible power of Love to conquer and to tame even the strongest and fiercest heart; small wonder, then, that Eros (equated with Harpocrates) on lion-back was a subject of choice for amulets designed to relieve the pain of magicians' heartsick clients, many of whom were jilted lovers seeking redress. The equally popular representations of Eros vanquishing Heracles (Love was the only foe Heracles could not defeat) and of Eros regaled in Heracles' lion-skin and armed with his club were likewise meant to suggest the invincible might of Love, the lion being here again an ambivalent symbol since it is at once agent and patient of Love's power. When Theocritus (3.15-17) complains that Eros must have suckled the breasts of a lioness it is clear that the lion was as much his avatar as his victim.[5]

---

[4] For fire at the root of the Gnostic conception of passion see Jonas, *The Gnostic Religion* 189, 197-199; *Gnosis und spätantike Geist* II.1, 160 n. 3, citing Irenaeus, *Refutation* 1.1.10; I, 48-49 Harvey.

[5] Keller, *Die antike Tierwelt* I, 53-54 with n. 32, remarking (p. 54) of the lion's erotic symbolism: "Gewiss soll in allen obenerwähnten Fällen der Löwe nichts anderes besagen, als die unwiderstehliche Naturgewalt des

The second iconographic context in which the lion had erotic associations is specifically Egyptian, though the Hellenistic Eros may certainly have had a hand in fixing it as a standard element in its genre. Not the least bizarre feature of the invariably ithyphallic Bes "pantheos" figures is that its *glans penis* is regularly a lion's head. The purpose of this attribute is clearly allusion to the generative power of an aggressive sun as represented by lion-gods of solar character, for its ultimate source is leontocephalic depictions of the ithyphallic god Min of Coptos, who underwent an early identification with Re and whose lion-head similarly attests a solar theocrasy (with Horus-Mios?). That the lion-head later migrated to his penis is simply the result of the fact that another divinity—Bes in the case of the Bes "pantheos" figures—has taken its place on the shoulders.[6]

Gnosticism naturally took the lion's intimate association with sexual desire to its bosom, assimilating the idea to the uncomfortably immanent, demonic "lions" of the Psalms, who are, after all, in their Old Testament setting engaged in more immediate and perpetual persecution of mankind than the remoter leontomorphic demiurge might be. It is easy to see that if on the mythological level the Psalmists' "lions" stood for the world-ruling powers hounding the incorporeal primal Man into enslavement in embodiment, on an anthropological level they represented the passions, specifically sexual desire, the lust for γένεσις in the psyche of Everyman, that part of our make-up for which those powers are responsible and which ensures the continuance of that enslavement. Thus the Naassene sermon subjects the soul of the primal Man to two ordeals, one by water and the other by fire; that by water it discovers in Ps 29 [28] :3, 10 and that by fire in the references of Pss 21:21-22 LXX and 34:17 LXX to "lions," which it places as a desperate cry on the lips of Man trapped in the archons' world of Becoming (discussed at the end of chapter 3.1

---

erotischen Triebes"; Charbonneau-Lassay, *La bestiaire du Christ* 47-48 ("Le lion et l'amour"); A Furtwängler, "Eros," Roscher 1.1364.47-54; 1367.39-50; 1368.25-30; Waser, "Eros," PW 6.510.68-511.7; 512.21-50; 513.67-514.15; Furtwängler, *Die antiken Gemmen* I pl. 57 #1 with II 259; Bonner, *Studies in Magical Amulets* 144; Delatte, "Amulettes inédites" #A11, pp. 43-45; Campbell Bonner, "Eros and the Wounded Lion," *AJA* 49 (1945) 441-444 (see my pl. 19b-c, where Eros pulls the thorn of love from the lion's paw). See further n. 94 to chapter 3.

[6]"Löwe," *RARG* 428 with fig. 105; Hopfner, "Der Tierkult der alten Ägypter" 40; de Wit, *Le rôle et le sens du lion* 167, 219, 228, 234-235, 241. For further illustrations consult the works cited in n. 71 to chapter 3 and Daressy, *Statues de divinités* I #38850 (p. 211) with II pl. 43.

earlier). A pleromatic voice responds with Isa 43:2 LXX in answer to his prayer: ἐὰν διὰ ποταμῶν διέλθῃς, οὐ μή σε συγκλύσωσιν, ἐὰν διὰ πυρὸς διέλθῃς οὐ μή σε συγκαύσει, and by "rivers" in this passage, the Naassenes inform us, the prophet meant τὴν ὑγρὰν τῆς γενέσεως οὐσίαν, by "fire" τὴν ἐπὶ τὴν γένεσιν ὁρμὴν καὶ ἐπιθυμίαν (Hippolytus, *Refutation* 5.8.15-16; 92.1-10 Wendland). The equations operant here are precisely that the Psalmists' "lions" = Isaiah's "fire" = the lust and (sexual) desire for generation.

Mandaean and Manichaean sources show that this tradition took firm root in communities of ascetic bent, and that is surely to be expected, for the celibate's Devil is a demon that tempts with lust and all the other carnal desires to which flesh is heir. That the leonine and serpentine enemy are also in fact bestial parts of man, and not simply demonic agencies totally external to him is implicit in the Manichaean accounts of the primal Man's encounter with the world-ruling powers cited from the Coptic *Psalm-Book* in chapter 2.5: the Man purposely exhibits his soul to the lion and the dragon *in order that* she may infiltrate them (but not, however, be "swallowed" by them for that would imply defeat) and conquer them. It is a spiritual struggle that is afoot here, a battle in which man is a privileged combatant, his soul at once the secret weapon and the prize, and the outcome is: "she wormed her way into them and bound them all without their knowledge." The Mandaean counterpart is *Ginza*, Linker Teil, 3.1 (507.18-24 Lidzbarski): "O Seele, steh auf, geh hin, tritt in den Körper ein und lass dich im Palaste gefangen halten. Der grimme Löwe wird durch dich gefangen genommen werden, der grimme, grimmige Löwe. Der Drache wird durch dich gefangen genommen werden, der Böse wird an seinem Orte getötet werden." It is of this spiritual contest that the purpose ascribed to Sophia's descent by the *Pistis Sophia* (discussed at the end of chapter 2.3)—to swallow the lion-faced power—must be understood; the cosmic tragedy of soul's incorporation takes on a somewhat more positive and aggressive aspect when viewed through the abstinent eyes of those who had tasted triumph over the world's enticements, over the "lion" whose maw engulfs and whose belly entombs the soul in passion, over a Death itself now "swallowed up in victory" (1 Cor 15:54).

Some passages in Mandaean and Manichaean sources are quite vitriolically explicit that the Psalms' "lion" and "dragon" have become demons of desire, the fleshly drives with which the spiritual man must wrestle for mastery over himself, and not merely cosmic powers. In the *Ginza* it is the whole general defilement of embodiment that the two creatures signify: the House of the great Life sends his messenger to Adam to draw him up "aus dem schmutzigen, stinkenden, verzehrenden, verderblichen

Körper, dem reissenden Löwen, dem lodernden, verderblichen Feuer . . . , dem Drachen, der die Welt umkreist," the world that Ptahil and the seven planets have made (Linker Teil, 1.2; 430.12-21 Lidzbarski; similarly 433.32-434.1). Similarly, the Manichaean *Psalm of Heracleides* 284 celebrates the singer's liberation "from the galling bonds of the lion-faced flesh" (restoring ⲧⲥⲁⲣⲝ   ⲛ̄ⲋⲁ   ⲙ̄ⲙ[ⲟ]ⲩ̈ⲓ̈); when further on the psalmist rejoices: "the skins of the lion which clothe my limbs, I have stripped them off," a later hand has glossed ⲙ̄ⲙⲟⲩⲓ̈ with ⲛ̄ⲧⲋⲩⲗⲏ, "of matter," to make sure the reader gets the point (106.29-30 and 107.24-25 Allberry). At other times it is the more specific defilement of sexual passion, the drive which begets new embodiment, that the two beasts symbolize. So *Psalm to Jesus* 257 (69.20-21 Allberry): "This lion that is within me, I have strangled him; I have turned him out of my soul, him who ever defiles me." When, furthermore, in the *Wanderers' Psalms* (149.22-25 Allberry) fasting and virginity are the weapons recommended for overcoming the "lion that is always roaring" and "the serpent with seven heads," one is justified in concluding that they represent the desires, especially when in *Kephalaion* 5 (29.18-21 Polotsky-Böhlig) the King of Darkness is said to hunt down the soul with his net of fire and ἐπιθυμία (the lion = fire = sexual desire formula again) and when *Kephalaion* 100 (251.27-253.24 Böhlig) makes it clear that the seven heads of our old ophidian friend have been allegorized as the ἐνθύμησις of the body and as its channels the αἰσθητήρια, which had long been held to number seven. Clearest of all is another section of the *Wanderers' Psalms* (156.9-20 Allberry), which makes those whose "God is their belly," whose "glory is their shame" (Phil 3:19), become "lions by day through the fire which devours" (a reference to Deut 4:24 by way of Gnostic tradition, as I have shown) and some other beast "by night through desire (ἐπιθυμία)," and which is confident that "the pure Church, she it is will be victorious over them, the [fire and] the lust (ἡδονή), the dragon with the face of a lion" (another passage which confirms Manichaean knowledge of *Apoc. John*'s portrait of the creator).

The Naassene sermon and the Manichaean and Mandaean texts just discussed show that it is in the light of this hermeneutical tradition linking the Gnostic leontomorphic world-ruler and the "lions" of the Psalms to the flesh and its desires (particularly sexual) that the seventh logion of *Gos. Thom.* must be understood, especially as both Naassene and Manichaean familiarity with the logia-collection in one or another of its recensions is firmly supported by evidence.[7] All three groups share the same rabidly depreciatory attitude toward the body and its soul-polluting functions;[8] indeed, the seventh logion itself provides a clue that such is the milieu from which the saying emanates and such the context in which it must be interpreted: внт in 3a means "unclean," "foul," not "cursed" as the *editio princeps* and others have it, and is often specifically used of sexual defilement, either in reference to forbidden sexual relations or to the messiness of ordinary intercourse.[9] The ascetic communities which produced and used the *Gospel of Thomas* in something like its present form—that is, including extra-canonical sayings of Jesus strongly encratite in tone—during the course of the second half of the second century (and then beyond) must have been among those who spearheaded the establishment of the exegesis of the Psalms' "lions" along erotic lines, basing itself on the Gnostic mythologem of theriomorphic archons with a leontocephalic leader. That this leonine symbolism continued to have great appeal in monastic circles in Egypt (precisely those which enjoyed the Coptic version of the *Gospel of Thomas*) is indicated by an apophthegm of Poimen (first half of the fifth century, preserved by the

---

[7] The importance of the Naassene psychological exegesis of the "lions" of the Psalms for understanding logion 7 of *Gos. Thom.* is appreciated by Archie L. Nations, *A Critical Study of the Gospel according to Thomas*; Ph.D. dissertation, Vanderbilt University, 1960; 190. For Mani and his movement's use of the logia see Puech, "The Gospel of Thomas" 279, 283-284, with pp. 299-300 and 302 (on the prologue and logia 1, 4, 17 and 69); Ernst Hammerschmidt, "Das Thomasevangelium und die Manichäer," *OrChr* 46 (1962) 120-123.

[8] The *Gospel of Thomas* is generally so encratite in tendency that Gilles Quispel classified it under this rubric, refusing to label it "Gnostic": "Gnosticism and the New Testament," *The Bible in Modern Scholarship* 253-257.

[9] Rightly pointed out by Kasser, *L'Évangile selon Thomas* 39 n. 1; and by Nations, *A Critical Study of the Gospel according to Thomas* 190-191. The passage from the Manichaean *Psalm to Jesus* 257 cited just now ("him who ever defiles me," 69.21 Allberry) employs, not вωтє, but its synonym xωₐм. The same motif crops up in the *Second Book of Ieou* 43 in polemic against a libertine sect: Taricheas, who has the face of a pig and of a lion in back (animals exemplifying filthiness and lust) is the lord of those who eat menstrual blood and the semen of men. For the text see now *The Books of Jeu and the Untitled Text in the Bruce Codex* with Carl Schmidt's Coptic text and a translation by Violet MacDermot (NHS 13; Leiden: Brill, 1978) 100.18-101.3.

alphabetic series of the *Sayings of the Desert Fathers* (*PG* 65.365A, #178);[10] it runs as follows:

> Again he (Poimen) said: "David, when he fought the lion, held
> him by the throat and straightaway dispatched him. And if we
> too hold ourselves by the throat and by the belly [χοιλία,
> which covers the sexual organs], with the help of God we
> shall be victorious over the invisible lion."

If the tradition is here tied to the exploits of David (1 Sam 17:34-35) and not to his Psalms, it is because the monks naturally chose to stress the victorious battle and not the enemy's incessant harassment.

To recapitulate, then: In logion 7 of *Gos Thom.* the lion represents the roaring, ravenous appetites of the flesh, especially those for its genera-tion, that constantly threaten to devour the spiritual man, just as the world-ruling powers with their leontomorphic chieftain aboriginally used them to engulf the primal Man and enslave him to embodiment in the cosmos. The battle between the two forces is a battle now fought out on the plain of Virtue in the human soul and over its possession. Self-restraint is man's weapon for the fray; fiery, ferocious passion the lion's. For the man to triumph (2a-c of the logion) is a blessed estate, a godly life; for the lion to do so (3a-c) is a defilement for the soul, a life of unmuzzled license.

4.2   The Platonic Tradition

The problem is, however, that the Gnostic lion-headed creator is uniformly a hateful character, and his passions mean only defilement for the soul. How is it, then, that the blessing of 2a of the logion is pro-nounced, not upon the man, who would seem to be the one to deserve it, but upon the lion, and the curse of 3a not upon the lion, but upon the man? Turner, sensing the difficulty, remarks: "The lion seems to get the better of the bargain both ways."[11] The curse, at least, is not so troublesome

---

[10] A French translation is offered by Jean-Claude Guy, *Les Apoph-tegmes des Pères du Désert* (no publication information provided) 254 (#197).

[11] "The Theology of the Gospel of Thomas" 94. By interpreting the "lion" of the saying as a cipher for the Devil (*Het evangelie van Thomas* 66-67) Schippers runs afoul of the same difficulty, holding that the bless-ing conferred upon the Devil must mean that he has lost his devilish nature.

because one expects the censure to fall upon the man; his spiritual task is to hold his passions in check, and if he succumbs to them the blame is his to bear. But why then does the praise not equally devolve upon him when he succeeds; why did 2a-b of the logion not read "Blessed is the man who eats the lion"?

The answer is that in logion 7 of *Gos. Thom.* the influence of another, more optimistic tradition that has not yet been discussed is to be traced. That influence played a major role in the development of high Gnostic anthropology during the second century and in the psychological and soteriological applications of the essentially inhuman mythologem of the lion and the polycephalic serpent as cosmic agents of passion and desire. That tradition is Platonic, and the passage from which it ultimately stems is the famous parable in the ninth book of the *Republic* (588B-589B) where the human soul is likened to a trichotomous hybrid of different natural forces.

To refute the advocates of injustice Socrates suggests to Glaucon that they fashion[12]

> a symbolic image of the soul . . . , one of those natures that the ancient fables tell of . . . , as that of the Chimaera or Scylla or Cerberus, and the numerous other examples that are told of many forms grown together in one.

This particular one is to have three components: in a descending scale of size, first

> a manifold and many-headed beast that has a ring of heads of tame and wild beasts and can change them and cause to spring forth from itself all such growths,

second, a lion, and lastly, a man, whose likeness is to ensheath the others, so that, for all one can tell, he is all the creature is.

To the person who maintains that injustice pays Socrates urges that

> he is affirming nothing else than that it profits him to feast and make strong the multifarious beast and the lion and all that pertains to the lion, but to starve the man and so

---

[12]Translations of passages from the *Republic* are those of Paul Shorey for LCL ##237 and 276 (Cambridge: Harvard University Press, 1969-1970 [1930 and 1935]).

enfeeble him that he can be pulled about whithersoever either
of the others drag him, and not to familiarize or reconcile
with one another the two creatures but suffer them to bite
and fight and devour one another.

On the other hand, the man who holds that justice is the more profitable
pursuit

affirms that all our actions and words should tend to give the
man within us complete domination over the entire man and
make him take charge of the many-headed beast—like a
farmer who cherishes and trains the cultivated plants but
checks the growth of the wild—and he will make an ally of
the lion's nature, and caring for all the beasts alike will first
make them friendly to one another and to himself, and so
foster their growth.

The picture that Plato paints of the soul relies for its inspiration on the
fabulous monsters of Greek myth that Socrates offers as models at the
outset of his psychological fantasy. His many-headed beast earned its
polycephalicity from all three of the examples Socrates mentions by
name: Cerberus had fifty heads, according to the oldest literary tradition
(Hesiod, *Theogony* 311-312), Homer's Scylla six (*Odyssey* 12.85-92), [13] and
the fire-breathing Chimaera those of a lion, a dragon and a goat, with a
composite body (again like Plato's man) made up of all three of these
animals (Homer, *Iliad* 6.181-182; Hesiod, *Theogony* 319-324; Apollodorus,
Library 2.3.1).[14] Among the unnamed others referred to Plato must also

---

[13] The scholium on this passage in the *Republic* (588C: *Scholia Plato-
nica*; ed. William Chase Greene; Haverford, PA: American Philological
Association, 1938; 270) follows the tradition represented by Apollodorus,
giving Cerberus three dog's heads, the tail of a dragon, and the heads of
all sorts of snakes on his back (*Library* 2.5.12), and giving Scylla the
single, normal head of a woman, but with six dogs' heads attached to her
sides (*Epitome* 7.20; note attachment of heads to the flanks, as with
Phanes). Sir James George Frazer's notes on these passages in his translation of Apollodorus, LCL ##121 and 122 (Cambridge: Harvard University
Press, 1967 and 1970 [1921]) provide good nutshell summaries of the
various traditions regarding these monsters.

[14] On the Chimaera, its representations in art and their Oriental inspiration, note, for example, Anne Roes, "The Representation of the Chimaera," *JHS* 54 (1934) 21-25; "The Origin of the Chimaera," *Studies*

have had in mind Cerberus' and Chimaera's sibling the Hydra, many-headed with a vengeance, their mother the half-serpentine Echidna, and their polycephalic father Typhaon/Typhoeus, the last especially as his heads embodied the voices of every animal in existence (Hesiod specifies bull, lion, and snake), an attribute which made him a particularly suitable exemplar for Plato's beast, and as the *Phaedrus* (229D-230A) indicates that he was. There Socrates admits that he is hard pressed to explain his own nature, much less those of the teratological wonders of Greek myth—the Centaurs, the Chimaera, the Gorgons, or Pegasus—and jokingly suggests that he himself might be "a beast more complex and more savage than Typhon."[15]

I discussed in chapter 3.6 the role that these monsters seem to have played in the metamorphosis of the leontocephalic Gnostic Yahweh/Yaldabaoth into a polycephalic solar "pantheos" as in the formation of a similarly many-headed solar Phanes. On this basis alone it is logical *a priori* to assume that educated (or even not-so-educated) Gnostic circles must have felt an intense interest in the mythological dimensions of Socrates' parable; the capacity of its many-headed beast to change its heads was, like Homer's appropriately Egyptian god Proteus (*Odyssey* 4.385, 417-418, 455-458: lion, dragon, leopard and boar are among his animal guises), handily comparable to the sun's change of faces in its trip through the celestial Egyptian zoo, a mutability for this reason possessed by *Apoc. John*'s Yaldabaoth (cited in chapter 2.4).

The interest that Socrates' parable had for Gnosticism was not, however, primarily mythological; it was anthropological, for this passage from the *Republic*, along with others in Plato, was the ultimate and principal source of the Gnostic tradition making beasts the symbols of passion and theriomorphic planetary powers the donors of passionate soul to the

---

presented to David Moore Robinson on his Seventieth Birthday II (ed. George E. Mylonas and Doris Raymond; Saint Louis, MO: Washington University, 1953) 1155-1163; Pierre Amandry, "ΠΥΡΠΝΟΟΣ ΧΙΜΑΙΡΑ," *Mélanges Picard* I, 1-11. In her plastic forms as for Euripides also (*Electra* 472-475, where she is called a πύρπνοος λέαινα) more lion than anything else, the Chimaera's fiery breath and serpent-tail are attributes of ancient Near Eastern origin that she shares with a variety of other leonine beings in late antiquity of similar heritage, as I have pointed out.

[15]Paul Friedländer, *Platon* III (2nd ed.; Berlin: de Gruyter, 1960) 446 n. 54, refers to the passage from the *Phaedrus* and suggests that Typhon was the model for the many-headed beast of the parable.

human amalgam. The contribution that Plato made was the transformation of the myths upon which Socrates' parable is based by internalizing
them; the passage from the ninth book of the *Republic* is only a figurative
restatement of a psychology worked out in book four (436A-441C) where
agreement had already been reached as to a tripartition of the soul—at
least to the extent that affective functions are foisted upon it by embodiment—into faculties λογιστικόν, θυμοειδές, and ἐπιθυμητικόν.[16]
They correspond to the man, the lion and the many-headed beast, respectively, of the parable.

---

[16]For the thorny problems involved in the study of the development of
Plato's psychology and its relationship to his social philosophy consult Paul
Shorey, *The Unity of Plato's Thought* (Chicago: University of Chicago
Press, 1960 [1903]) 42-43; F. M. Cornford, "Psychology and Social Struc-
ture in the *Republic* of Plato," *CQ* 6 (1912) 246-265; "The Division of the
Soul," *HibJ* 28 (1929-1930) 206-219; R. Hackforth, "The Modification of
Plan in Plato's *Republic*," *CQ* 7 (1913) 265-272, answering Cornford's
article in the same journal; J. L. Stocks, "Plato and the Tripartite Soul,"
Mind 24 (1915) 207-221; Eduard Zeller, *Die Philosophie der Griechen in
ihrer geschichtlichen Entwicklung* II.1 (6th ed.; Hildesheim: Olms, 1968
[unchanged from the 5th ed., 1922]) 843-51; W. F. R. Hardie, *A Study in
Plato* (Oxford: Clarendon Press, 1936) §§99-103, pp. 138-146; N. R.
Murphy, *The Interpretation of Plato's Republic* (Oxford: Clarendon Press,
1951) 24-44 ("The Parts of the Soul"); Joseph Moreau, "Platon et la con-
naissance de l'âme," *REA* 55 (1953) 249-257; W. K. C. Guthrie, "Plato's
Views on the Nature of the Soul," *Recherches sur la tradition platonicienne* (EFH 3: Vandoeuvres-Genève, 1955; Verona: Valdonega, 1957) 3-19;
D. A. Rees, "Bipartition of the Soul in the Early Academy," *JHS* 77 (1957)
112-118; Robert W. Hall, "Ψυχή as Differentiated Unity in the Philosophy
of Plato," *Phronesis* 8 (1963) 63-82; Andreas Graeser, *Probleme der plato-
nischen Seelenteilungslehre. Überlegungen zur Frage der Kontinuität im
Denken Platons* (Zetemata 47; München: Beck, 1969); T. M. Robinson,
Plato's Psychology (Toronto: University of Toronto Press, 1970) 39-46,
119-125; Yvon Brès, *La psychologie de Platon* (Paris: Presses Universitaires de France, 1973) 308-319. The doxographical tradition, which some
accept because it invokes the weighty authority of Poseidonios, attributes
this three-part division of the soul to a pre-Platonic Pythagoras or Pytha-
goreans: see Stocks, "Plato and the Tripartite Soul" 209-210; John Burnet,
Plato's Phaedo (Oxford: Clarendon Press, 1972 [1911]) in his notes on
Phaedo 68C (p. 40); Walter Burkert, *Lore and Science in Ancient Pythago-
reanism* (trans. E. Minar, Jr.; Cambridge: Harvard University Press, 1972)
74 and nn. 133-136.

As the pseudo-Aristotelian tract *Magna Moralia* (1182a) and the doxo-graphical tradition (Aëtius 4.4.1) baldly state—as, indeed, Socrates' simili-tude itself as well as other passages in Plato suggests—this tripartition of the soul is actually the result of the subdivision of one member of an even more basic psychic bipartition into elements rational and irrational, the one human and the other animal. Schematically represented, the situation is this:

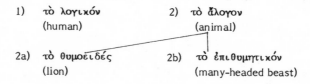

1)	τὸ λογικόν (human)	2)	τὸ ἄλογον (animal)
2a)	τὸ θυμοειδές (lion)	2b)	τὸ ἐπιθυμητικόν (many-headed beast)

The lion of the parable is still a beast, τὸ θυμοειδές essentially irra-tional, and in the soul of the man not in control of himself the lion is as nastily bestial as any head of the polycephalic monster—that is, is as appetitive as the rest of the appetites. It is only when the only truly human facet of the soul—cool, calm, calculated Reason—is in the driver's seat that the lion may be made an ally in controlling the Typhon of our natural drives, which, like its brother ὕβρις, is πολυμελές and πολυειδές (*Phaedrus* 238A), the insatiable beast of desires that live in the belly, the urges for food, drink and sex, and the lust for the money to gratify them with (*Timaeus* 70D-71A; *Republic* 439B, 442A, 580D-581A). As a potential executor of the will of Reason in subduing its fellow animals the *Timaeus* places the seat of θυμός in the heart, in a position apart from and some-what higher than the rest of its kin, but as the essentially irrational emotion of anger, for being "unappeasable," it is nevertheless part of the passionate mortal soul (consistently symbolized by animals) which the lesser demiurges create to house the immortal (human) soul created by their Father and which is as a whole separated from the latter, set in the head, by the isthmus of the neck (*Timaeus* 41C-D, 42D-E, 69C-71A).[17]

---

[17]On these passages see A. E. Taylor, *A Commentary on Plato's Timaeus* (Oxford: Clarendon Press, 1928) 252-253, 263-264, 493-505; Francis MacDonald Cornford, *Plato's Cosmology. The Timaeus of Plato translated with a running commentary* (New York: Harcourt, Brace, and London: Kegan Paul, Trench, Trubner, 1937) 139-143, 146-147, 279-286. In connection with the *Timaeus* placement of a leonine θυμός in the καρδία and with the influence of the whole Platonic tradition on Gnosticism, it is instructive to recall that in the decanal melothesia a partly leonine Chnoumis ruled the καρδία.

Even as an ally of Reason, then, the lion must still be tamed; he must be brought to accept the yoke of obedience to his human master (*Republic* 441E). What the lion represents—θυμός—is a passion that, unlike the others, when properly trained (subjected to Reason) can be ennobling; Plato goes so far as to aver that it is, in fact, *by nature* Reason's helper, "unless," of course, "it is corrupted by evil nurture" (*Republic* 441A). If θυμός is the heart of Plato's man and his lion has a redeemable nature it is because θυμός is the very heart of Homeric man, the seat and expression of his anger, his courage, his lust for victory, his ambition for honor and distinction. It was natural that Plato should choose this wild, amoral force in the breasts of ancient Greek heroes to exemplify the nobler aspects of passionate human nature; it was the epic use of θυμός as the source of manliest virtue—and additionally the fact that in Homer θυμός is a ratiocinative faculty as well as an emotional one (cp. *Iliad* 1.193; 16.646, for instance)—that suggested its intermediate status for Plato and prevented its staying merely another tentacle of the instinctual octopus. The problem is, of course, its very amorality; what sufficed to make Mycenaean warlords virtuous was hardly the same as that for the majority of fifth century Athenians: θυμός had to be civilized. And how is the boundless energy of θυμός to be harnessed so as to serve ethical ends and to bring out its finest qualities, the noble and honorable qualities that its cipher (again animal) the soul-charioteer's (Reason's) subservient white horse embodies (*Phaedrus* 246A-B, 253D)? Its high-spirited anger must be self-directed, its *élan* transmuted into moral indignation. To show that even the θυμός of Homeric heroes was capable of self-reproof Plato is fond of quoting *Odyssey* 20.17-18 where Odysseus' θυμός is stirred to anger and he debates with himself κατὰ θυμόν whether to slaughter the suitors, "his heart growling within him" (lines 9-13), but ends up chiding himself (the lines Plato cites) and telling himself to endure (*Republic* 390D, 441B-C; *Phaedo* 94D). This new and distinctively Platonic task for θυμός is well illustrated by the story of Leontios—his very name points forward to the representation of θυμός as a lion—who rebukes himself for being driven, against his will, by the ἐπιθυμία to see some corpses (*Republic* 439E-440A with the conclusions drawn 440A-441C as to the consequent isolation of internalized θυμός from the other ἐπιθυμίαι).

That Plato should employ the lion to symbolize θυμός followed equally directly from epic usage, for the Greeks formed no exception to the universal ancient Near Eastern regard for the lion as the archetype of ferocity, boldness, magnanimity and courage. Homeric similes compare him with the bravest of warriors (*Iliad* 18.161-164 of Hector; *Odyssey* 6.130-134 of Odysseus); so much was the lion the very soul of epic θυμός that θυμολέων, "lion-hearted," is a standard tag, applied, like the leonine similes, to paragons of manly virtue (*Iliad* 7.228 and Hesiod, *Theogony* 1007 of Achilles; *Odyssey* 4.724 of Odysseus; *Iliad* 5.639 and *Odyssey* 11.267 of Heracles). Not surprisingly, then, Tyrtaeus (cited by Galen, *On the Doctrines of Hippocrates and Plato* 3.3; V, 309 Kühn), the Spartan eulogizer of the martial spirit, may talk of someone αἴθωνος δὲ λέοντος ἔχων ἐν στήθεσι θυμόν and Aristotle, speaking of the characters of animals, may say that lions are ἐλευθέρια καὶ ἀνδρεῖα καὶ εὐγενῆ (*Study of Animals* 488b; similarly the pseudo-Aristotelian *Physiognomonica* 805b; 806b; 811a, b; 812a, b; 813a; and especially 809b). Hence, earlier in the *Republic* (341C) Plato has Socrates adduce the proverb about the danger of trying "to shave a lion" in connection with his grappling with a furious (and aptly named) Thrasymachus.

A passage in the *Gorgias* (482E-484B) is especially enlightening for the implications that the leonine imagery of Mycenaean θυμός possessed for Plato. A hostile Callicles is lecturing Socrates that "might makes right"; like Thrasymachus he falls decidedly on the φύσις side of the νόμος-φύσις controversy. Civilized society, Callicles argues, takes the young lions of its youth and bewitches them with its laws, which are but conventions concocted by weaklings, into giving up the lion's share of the spoils that is naturally theirs for the taking, but when a leader of sufficient force arises, he sweeps away these man-made laws and restores the law of nature to its rightful place. It is of such leaders that Aristotle (*Politics* 1284a) admits transcendance of law; they are a law unto themselves. It would be ridiculous, he says, to attempt to impose law upon them; they would only respond with the answer that, in Antisthenes' story, the lions gave the assembly of rabbits demanding equal rights: "Where are your teeth? Where are your claws?"[18]

Callicles' lion is, in effect, the wild Mycenaean lion brought to bay by the lawmakers of civilized society, truculently snarling at his captors and watching for the opportunity to turn upon them. No wonder, then, that Plato's leonine θυμός needs taming! Like the warrior class in the state, to which it fittingly corresponds, the lion-θυμός in the soul must be carefully

---

[18]On the passage from the *Gorgias* and its relationship to the *Republic* see Friedländer, *Platon* III, 112-123; and E. R. Dodds' commentary in his edition of the *Gorgias* (Oxford: Clarendon Press, 1959) 263-272.

groomed for the service of Reason (*Republic* 441E-442C), otherwise it will, like corrupt guardians, turn against its master the legislator and the laws of harmonious order to which it has pledged its allegiance, and overthrow them (*Republic* 415D-424E, 429B-430C). The urgency with which Plato alludes to the subversion of τὸ θυμοειδές, to its abandonment of the service of Reason and its pursuit of its own selfish, violent ends, shows how real and ever-present the danger is of recidivism, of reversion to the vices of its wild and bestial state (*Republic* 548C, 550B, 553B-D, 586C-D, 590B). Here again, as with the lion in Egyptian contexts, the lion is an ambivalent force; the mercurial emotion θυμός is an unreliable ally of rationality. Its raw, explosive force—anger—is morally neutral. It is only, as Plato explains the word in the *Cratylus* (419E)—on a sound etymological basis in the first instance—a θύσις, "raging," and a ζέσις, "seething," of the soul; the object against which it rages and seethes may be either λογισμός for its restraint or ἐπιθυμία for its constraint, the effect for ill or for good. The sad truth is that Plato seems to have grown less confident as time went on of the ability of Reason to maintain the grand alliance, to keep the lion in line; in the *Timaeus* θυμός is part of the mortal soul because it is essentially irrational, because it is, like Hesiod's lion with an ἀναιδέα θυμόν (*Theogony* 833), "unappeasable." In the *Laws* (863B), towards the end of his life, he even expresses uncertainty whether it is after all strictly a πάθος or really a distinct part of the soul because it is "innately an insuperably contentious thing" that "upsets everything with its irrational force." According to Plutarch (*On Moral Virtue* 3 [*Moralia* 442B]) Aristotle underwent a similar change of heart about the emotion, at first following the Platonic tripartition but then abandoning it to hold θυμός just another ἐπιθυμία as the "desire for revenge" (an implicit reference to Aristotle, *On the Soul* 403a30-31; cp. *Nicomachean Ethics* 1147a; *Eudemian Ethics* 1223a, b).

Later generations generally concurred in that judgment. When in Socrates' parable and then more allusively in other passages Plato metaphorically likened the appetitive and affective faculties of the soul to beasts, he bequeathed an heirloom to philosophy which, with astrological assistance, eventually became a commonplace of late antique thought. With its Homeric backing the lion naturally continued to be a popular symbol of θυμός as, for example, in Manilius 4.187, noting that the *ingenium* of those born under Leo is inclined *ad subitas iras*; Hippolytus, *Refutation* 4.19.2, similarly of those born under Leo: ὀργίλοι, θυμώδεις, καταφρονηταί, αὐθάδεις; Horace, *Odes* 1.16.13-16 in an apology for an outburst of anger:

'Tis said Prometheus, obliged to supplement the substrate earth with a tiny slice of every living thing, the lion's rabid fury positioned in our breast,

where the poet means passionate, "animal" soul; Clement of Alexandria, *Exhortation to the Greeks* 1.2.2: the "lions" whom Orpheus tamed were men θυμικούς; and Horapollo, *Hieroglyphics* 1.17:

When they (the Egyptians) wish to indicate anger (θυμόν) they draw a picture of a lion, for the animal has . . . fiery-colored pupils . . .,

the rest of the passage, cited earlier, being devoted to comparing the lion to the sun.[19] But in all these cases the lion is no courageous friend of

---

[19]The connection between anger and the lion, as that between the lion and the sun, is fire; the purely fanciful section 2.38 (159-160 Sbordone; *CEg* 36 [1943] 212-213 van de Walle-Vergote) shows that this is so: "If (they wish to indicate) uncontrolled anger, anger so great that the enraged person is feverish (πυρέττειν) as a result of it, they draw a lion crushing the bones of its own cubs—a lion because of the anger, cubs with their bones crushed because fire shoots out of the bones of lion-cubs when they are broken" (a tradition I cited earlier—in chapter 3.3—from Aelian and which stems ultimately from Aristotle, *Study of Animals* 516b). The lion was a perfect symbol for anger (in addition to love) not only because the association had epic underpinnings and furthermore because the animal is so easily riled and its roaring fury is so terrifying, but because the quintessentially fiery nature attributed to the lion by current zoology and astrology paralleled the fiery metaphors used in descriptions of anger—metaphors equally trite then as now and equally seminal as similar ones applied to Love in tying the lion to the passion. Examples of "burning" rage, "consuming" anger, and the like are Homer, *Iliad* 17.565; Vergil, *Aeneid* 2.575-576; 9.66. As with erotic passion the metaphor has a physiological ground: note Seneca's marvellously observant description, *On Anger* 1.1.4, beginning *flagrant ac micant oculi, multus ore toto rubor exaestuante . . . sanguine*. In the light of the lion's intimate association with θυμός it is quite logical that the reverse of one of the amulets showing a ferocious, lion-headed Horus-Mios on the obverse (Bonner, *Studies in Magical Amulets* #149 [pl. 7, p. 277] with pp. 103-106, arguing that Mouterde, "La Glaive de Dardanos" #11, pp. 77-80, is another example) is inscribed with a θυμοκάτοχον (after *voces magicae*: κατάσχες τοὺς θυμοὺς Τασοι), that is, a spell to restrain someone's anger. A good study of such spells is that by Theodor Hopfner, "Ein neues ΘΥΜΟΚΑΤΟΧΟΝ. Über

Reason, no noble voice of self-reproof, merely its base and bestial self, θυμός as anger, rage, fury. One can well imagine that this subsequent stress on vicious θυμός made the more unpleasant aspects of Plato's lion interesting information for Gnostics who already possessed a mythological tradition of theriomorphic archontic persecutors and who saw in their leonine leader Yahweh/Yaldabaoth a vengeful god whose fiery paroxysms of anger consumed his enemies. Aristotle's definition of θυμός as the desire for vengeance was well remembered; note, for instance, Plutarch—a near contemporary of the Gnostic masters—in his *Platonic Questions* 9.1 (*Moralia* 1008C). Like a lion, which, according to Democritus (D-K 68 [55] A 156), is the only animal born τρόπον τινὰ τεθυμωμένον, Yahweh burst onto the stage of history in a blaze of intimidating fire (Exod 3:1-6). All the more must Plato's insensate lion have been of interest for Gnostics as in the immediate sequel to Socrates' Parable (*Republic* 590A-B) Plato conjoins lion and snake in a typification of degenerate θυμός:

> And do we not censure self-will and irascibility when they foster and intensify disproportionately the element of the lion and the snake (τὸ λεοντῶδες τε καὶ ὀφεῶδες) in us?

Plato may have had the Chimaera in mind,[20] whose relevance for the

---

die sonstigen θυμοκάτοχα, κάτοχοι, ὑποτακτικὰ und φιμωτικὰ der griechischen Zauberpapyri in ihrem Verhältnis zu den Fluchtafeln," *AO* 10 (1938) 128-148. As the commentators point out (49 Sbordone; *CEg* 35 [1943] 59 van de Walle-Vergote) Horapollo is not wrong in declaring that the Egyptians conveyed the idea of anger with the lion, for late Egyptian usage did precisely that, as Coptic ⲗⲓⲃⲉ "to be mad," "to rave," "to rage," and ⲗⲁⲃⲟⲓ "lioness," reflect.

[20] So Shorey, LCL #276, p. 406 n. c, suggesting further, after Schleiermacher, that the serpentine element, newly introduced here, may have been included in τὰ περὶ τὸν λέοντα (rendered by Shorey, whose translation was cited earlier, with "all that pertains to the lion") referred to in 588E. There is no need to emend ὀφεῶδες to ὀργῶδες as Werner Jaeger, "A New Greek Word in Plato's Republic. The Medical Origin of the Theory of the θυμοειδές," *Eranos* 44 (1946) 123-130, reprinted in his *Scripta Minora* II (Roma: Edizioni di Storia e Letteratura, 1960) 309-316, proposes to do. For further reasons see James Adam in the note *ad loc.* in his edition *The Republic of Plato* II (2nd ed.; Cambridge: University Press, 1963) 365-366, refuting as well the emendation (ὀχλῶδες) proposed by Nettleship. Friedländer, *Platon* III, 114 and n. 52, similarly rejects Jaeger's alternation; his summary (einem Löwen, der von Schlangen umgeben ist") implies that τὰ

Gnostic mythological tradition I have touched on more than once, but the specific combination of lion and serpent here is an enticement to coalescence with similar conjunctions in other traditions—with the lion and dragon of Ps 91 [90] :13 and especially with Chnoumis whose lordship of the καρδία likewise connected him with Plato's lion-as-θυμός, for Chnoumis/Yaldabaoth (and Chnoumis originally as a son of Sekhmet and Wadjet) is, as I said, nothing if not θυμός at its worst. That it was an enticement which Gnosticism did not resist (and it may conceivably have played a part in the choice of Chnoumis as a new embodiment for Yahweh/Yaldabaoth) is perhaps to be seen in the fact that αὐθάδης is a persistent designation—and αὐθάδεια a regular hypostasis—of Yaldabaoth, for in the passage cited just above the two facets of the ugly side of θυμός are αὐθάδεια ("self-will" = τὸ λεοντῶδες: cp. *Republic* 548E) and δυσκολία ("irascibility" = τὸ ὀφεῶδες: cp. *Republic* 411C), whence the epithet derives, perhaps filtered through astrological genethlialogy, for, as the passage quoted earlier from Hippolytus indicates, it preserved αὐθάδεια as a characteristic of those born under Leo.

Those who, in the Hellenistic period, were responsible at once for the abandonment of any Platonic nobility in θυμός and for the preservation of Plato's likeness of affective states to beasts were the Stoics. To begin with, Stoic orthodoxy could not accept the Platonic idea of any functional partition of the soul. In its view *all* affective behaviors were excessive, pathological conditions of the soul's essentially rational self. Passion was the expression of a diseased soul, and θυμός was no exception to the rule;[21] they had passages like Euripides, *Medea* 1077-1080, to which to

---

περὶ τὸν λέοντα in reference to the serpent *could* be understood in a much more strictly local and, for late antique circles whose cosmology included snake-enwrapped Aion figures like the Mithraic leontocephaline, much more suggestive sense than Shorey's translation in terms of a general relation. John Hansman, "A Suggested Interpretation of the Mithraic Lion-man Figure," *Études Mithriaques* 215-227; and later in "Some Possible Classical Connections in Mithraic Speculation," *Mysteria Mithrae* 607-608, actually proposes that the Mithraic leontocephaline in all of its various forms is the visual reproduction of Socrates' parable, but that is extremely doubtful.

[21] Max Pohlenz, *Die Stoa. Geschichte einer geistigen Bewegung* I (Göttingen: Vandenhoeck & Ruprecht, 1948) 85-92, 141-153; II (1949) 76-83 (Erläuterungen); J. M. Rist, *Stoic Philosophy* (Cambridge-London-New York-Melbourne: Cambridge University Press, 1969) 22-36; Émile Brehier, *Chrysippe et l'ancien stoïcisme* (revised ed.; Paris: Presses Universitaires de France, 1951) 245-258.

appeal (Galen, *On the Doctrines of Hippocrates and Plato* 3.3 and 4.6; V, 306-307 and 408 Kühn, of Chrysippus). So when, for example, Cleanthes (fr 570; *SVF* I, 129.35-36) stages a little repartee between Λογισμός and Θυμός it goes like this:

> Reason: "What is it you want, Anger? Come, tell me."
> Anger: "I would have *you*, Reason, do everything I want you to!"

and when, again, Novatus remarks that those animals that show the most anger are also the most noble (doubtless with the lion—and Plato's leonine Θυμός—in mind), his respondent upbraids him and likens anger to the same hellish monsters that Plato based his many-headed beast upon (Seneca, *On Anger* 2.16.1; 2.35.5 *monstra . . . succincta serpentibus et igneo flatu*—the Chimaera become a serpent-entwined "pantheos"!). Naturally, then, the Stoics were only too glad to retain Plato's image of savage beasts as ciphers for—and only for—vices which devour sick souls or which turn them into beasts (and recall the Stoic and Cynic connections of the lion-tyrant in the maxim of the *Sentences of Sextus* discussed in chapter 3.1): so, for instance, in Epictetus 2.9.1-12; in the eclectic document (first century A.D.?) which goes under the name *Tablet of Cebes* 22.1-23.2 and 26.2, where seven vicious states are called τὰ μέγιστα θηρία over which the virtuous man triumphs in the greatest ἀγών of all and which formerly "devoured" him; and in the Stoic and Cynic convention that transformed Heracles into a paragon of virtue and the animal monsters he overcame into symbols of vice: Cornutus 31; pseudo-Heracleitus, *Homeric Questions* 33; Apion in pseudo-Clement, *Homilies* 6.16; Gnosticized by Justin (Hippolytus, *Refutation* 5.26.27-28) for whom the twelve labors (of which only the distinctly bestial Lion, Hydra and Boar are explicitly mentioned) are expressions of the ἐνεργεία of "the twelve wicked angels of creation" (= the zodiacal constellations, as I said earlier). Educated Christians put this Platonic and Stoic tradition to their own good use, discovering appropriate proof-texts for it in the Old Testament: Irenaeus (*Refutation* 5.8.1-2; II, 339-341 Harvey), for example, who cites Jer 5:8; Ps 49:20 [48:21]; and Lev 11:2-3, and—significantly enough—equates the feral individuals with Paul's ψυχικοί and σαρκικοί (1 Cor 2:14; 3:3); and Tertullian (*On the Soul* 32.8-10; 46.4-25 Waszink) who, similarly adducing Ps 49:20 [48:21], advocates the beast metaphor in an effort to refute the literal assimilation to animals inculcated by the doctrine of transmigration of souls. Origen shows that this tradition was also—and naturally enough—applied to Ps 91[90]:13, a development which paved the way for the specifically ascetic twist which the Manichaeans gave it (the "lion" = sexual passion, the lust for γένεσις); in his *Homilies on Luke* the Alexandrian Father internalizes the "lion" and the "dragon" of Ps 91[90] (*Homily* 31.6-7 on Luke 10:19), warning the reader: *Tu es* draco, *tu es* leo, and elsewhere (*Homily* 8.3 on Luke 1:46), in a characteristic digression supported by oblique references to Matt 23:33 and Deut 4:16-17, he remarks that human beings are capable of "putting on" the image of the Devil as well as that of God:

> Actually, to be sure, the Lord is neither diminished nor belittled; it is we who put on other images instead of the image of the Savior. Instead of the image of the Word, of Wisdom, of Justice and the other virtues we assume the form of the Devil, so that we may well be called "serpents," "a generation of vipers." And we also put on the mask (*personam*) of a lion, of a dragon and a fox when we are full of poison, violent, crafty, and of goats as well, when we are too inclined to lust,

a passage where Ps 91[90] was also obviously in his mind.

The man most instrumental in handing on this philosophical tradition to late antiquity was a Stoic, but yet one sufficiently enamoured of Plato to preserve some remnant of his tripartition of the soul. That man was Cicero's older contemporary and teacher Poseidonios, of whose tract *On Passions* Galen has preserved considerable fragments embedded in a long if somewhat biased treatment of the subject.[22] In order to preserve the possibility of internal conflict Poseidonios accepted Plato's operative tripartition in a much fuller sense than his predecessors were willing to do. But just how independent of τὸ ἐπιθυμητικόν he conceived τὸ θυμο-ειδές to be, that is, to what extent he thought it capable of the noble

---

[22]Isaak Heinemann, *Poseidonios' metaphysische Schriften* I (Hildesheim: Olms, 1968 [1921]) 55-63; Pohlenz, *Die Stoa* I, 208-238, especially pp. 224-226; II, 112-113; "Poseidonios' Affektenlehre und Psychologie," *NGWG.PH* (1922) 163-194, especially pp. 184 and 192-193; "Tierische und menschliche Intelligenz bei Poseidonios," *Hermes* 76 (1941) 1-13; Rist, *Stoic Philosophy* 201-218, 256-272; Georg Pfligersdorffer, "Studien zu Poseidonios," *SÖAW.PH* 232.5 (1959), in particular pp. 23-32; Marie Laffranque, *Poseidonios d'Apamée. Essai de mise au point* (Paris: Presses Universitaires de France, 1964) 369-448, especially pp. 394-399 and 424-427; I. G. Kidd, "Posidonius on Emotions," *Problems in Stoicism* (ed. A. A. Long; London: Athlone, 1971) 200-215.

alliance with Reason, is not very clear from Galen's account, but he certainly must have conceived it somehow, even though he also held to the more basic and similarly Platonic bipartition of the soul along rational and irrational lines as the famous citation of Galen (*On the Doctrines of Hippocrates and Plato* 5.6; V, 469 Kühn—Poseidonios fr. 187.4-9 Edelstein-Kidd) makes clear, in which Poseidonios says that the αἴτιον of the passions is not to be totally obedient to the δαίμων within us, which is of the same nature and kind as that which pervades the whole world, but always to be inclined to be dragged about by the meaner and brutish (ζῳώδης) one. To judge from Seneca's *Epistle* 92.8-10, which explicitly mentions Poseidonios and is likely to represent his thinking, the Apamean married Plato's tripartition as represented by Socrates' parable to Aristotle's (*Nicomachean Ethics* 1102a-1103a) and assigned to the faculty ἐπιθυμητικόν only the most vegetatively bovine of bodily functions. The passions themselves, though still part of irrational soul, are animals of a higher order; though hard to control, they are nevertheless inherently better and more worthy of a human being—a bit wild, but admirably spirited. Presumably, like Plato's lion they need only be tamed (and cp. Jas 3:7-8) to transmute them into virtues, their raw impulse harnessed to Reason's chariot and directed onto ennobling paths. Hence Philo, in probable dependence on Poseidonios and his successors, may dream of a time when the pacification of wild beasts, both those within us and those without us as prophesied by Isaiah (11:6-9; 62:25; note too Job 5:3; Hos 2:18 [20]), will become a reality, the latter shaming us into the former (*On Rewards and Punishments* 15-16 §§85-93).

No doubt Philo postponed to the end of time the appearance of a phenomenon that Poseidonios and his fellow Stoics held as rare as hen's teeth: a man fully in control of himself. In the present order of things Poseidonios and his followers seem to have concentrated on the reality of the bestial savagery of unbridled passions and consoled themselves by stressing their strictly adventitious character. They seem to have done so by accepting the invitation offered by the use of the animal-metaphor in both passages to join Socrates' parable with the image that Plato paints of the soul a little further on in the *Republic* (611B-612A): since the soul is immortal it cannot be essentially composite; it is only through communion with the body that its unity is destroyed; its mortal elements—all the passions and desires which render it πολυειδής—have attached themselves (προσπεφυκέναι, similarly *Timaeus* 42C-D of the body) to it like barnacles and seaweed to the sea-dwelling Glaukos, which mar his features and make him "look in every way much rather like a beast than what he actually is by nature," accretions which represent the πάθη and the εἴδη that the soul must suffer in human life. Seneca suggests that that is what they did by citing Vergil's description of Scylla (*Aeneid* 3.426-428) which gives her, like Plato's Glaukos (who resembled Scylla enough to woo her: Ovid, *Metamorphoses* 13.900-968 and beyond), a human heart (face and breast) with *fera animalia adiuncta* (*Epistle* 92.9) and by the argument of *Epistle* 13.

The Platonic tradition as channeled through men like Poseidonios exerted enormous influence on late antique philosophy and, with that, necessarily on Gnosticism. The tracks of the influence of Socrates' parable, for example, can be traced through Poseidonios to Plotinus (*Enneads* 1.1.7, 10)[23] and to many others after him.[24] But by the second century A.D. the tradition had been subtly altered by the steady encroachment of astrological speculation. Aside from that, Plato's bestial imagery for passionate, mortal soul begged for comparison with the zodiacal constellations in animal form (as Leo in Heracles' astrologized labors and in Numenius' related psychogony) or with the Gnostic theriomorphic planetary world-creators. But there was a much more solid basis for that comparison of Plato's animal-imagery with theriomorphic celestial agencies. Thanks to the astrological logic which tied them to Ἀνάγκη, Plato's Errant (planetary!) Cause (πλανωμένη αἰτία *Timaeus* 47E-48A), and to the heaven-governing, evil-working Soul of the *Laws* (896D-E; 906A), the lesser demiurges, to whom the *Timaeus* attributed creation of passionate, mortal soul, had early come to be equated with the divinities of the

---

[23]See, for example, Willy Theiler, "Plotin zwischen Platon und Stoa," *Les sources de Poltin* (EFH 5: Vandoeuvres-Genève, 1957; Genève: Kundig, 1960) 65-103, especially pp. 77-79 comparing the Plotinian passage with that from Seneca, *Epistle* 92; Philip Merlan, *From Platonism to Neoplatonism* (The Hague: Nijhoff, 1953) 30-52 ("Posidonius and Neoplatonism").

[24]In his edition of the *Republic* (*Platonis Opera Omnia* III.2; 2nd ed.; Gotha and Herford: Hennings, 1859) Gottfried Stallbaum notes (with his references updated) Themistios, *Oration* 13.169C; Synesios, *Dion* 14 (58B); *On Kingship* 10 (10A-B; 11A-B); and Iamblichus, *Exhortation to the Study of Philosophy* 3 (13.23-14.14 Pistelli) and 5 (31.19-32.5 and beyond) among others of less certain reference to the parable. Add Eusebius, *Preparation for the Gospel* 12.46.1-6 (615b-616c); Proclus, *Commentary on Plato's* Republic (ed. Kroll) I, 160.24-25; 225.16-18; 226.8-11; 227.24-27; 229.23-26; 292.28-293.2; II, 127.1 in their contexts; *Commentary on Plato's First Alcibiades* (ed. Westerink) 43.11-12; 160.2-3; 244.2-3; *On Providence and Fate* (ed. Cousin) 183.4-9; Julian, *Oration* 6.197A-B, and I'm sure the list is by no means exhaustive.

planets. Sufficient indication of this equation, helped along, no doubt, by
genethlialogical claims for the planets as sources of each individual's
personality traits and by the zoologically based physiognomonic science
which read them in the human face, is the astral psychogony's endowment
of the planetary powers with the investiture of souls descending into birth
each with its own individual, generally vicious, passion—Venus with sexual
desire, for example, Mars with anger and daring, and so forth: to cite but
the Hermetica note *Poimandres* 25 (the process in reverse); *Kore Kosmou*
27-29; and *Corpus Hermeticum* fr 29 (IV, 98-100 Nock-Festugière). The
investiture of souls with the passions even accommodated the Platonic
bifurcation of its lower (now planetary), irrational (passionate) aspect, as
Servius (*Commentary on Vergil's Aeneid* 6.439) shows in quoting as the
opinion of some (Stoics like Poseidonios) that *intra novem hos mundi
circulos inclusas esse virtutes, in quibus et iracundiae* (= τὸ θυμοειδές)
sunt et cupiditates (τὸ ἐπιθυμητικόν), though of course here again θυμός
has nothing good about it. If Gnostic texts invest a theriomorphic
Yahweh/Yaldabaoth and his planetry rulers with the same passionate,
animal soul-producing power, it is simply a parallel expression of a contemporary development that wedded Platonic, Stoic and Pythagorean
eclecticism to Oriental astrological speculation.[25]

That the Gnostic exponents of this theory interested themselves in the
two metaphors from Plato's *Republic* (combined, as I said, for their shared
animal imagery) which were in some part contributors to that theory is
evident from what Clement of Alexandria reports to us of the Basilidean
gnosis: Basilides' son Isidorus wrote a book περὶ προσφυοῦς ψυχῆς, echo-
ing προσπεφυκέναι of Glaukos' barnacle encrustation (*Republic* 611D);
generally they and their "school" held the passions to be "attachments" or
"appendages" that affix themselves adventitiously to the rational soul, and
about them, in turn, grow heterogeneous, alien spirits of animal form (=
the theriomorphic archons) whose business it is to assimilate the lusts
(ἐπιθυμίας) of the soul to the likeness of themselves—wolf, ape, lion, and
goat are specifically mentioned—even down to the vegetative level of
plants, a sort of living metempsychosis (*Miscellanies* 2.112.1-113.3).
Basilidean man, Clement remarks (not without a twinge of sarcasm), is

---

[25]The literature on all this is vast; profitable reading are, for
example, Willy Theiler, "Gott und Seele im kaiserzeitlichen Denken,"
Recherches sur la tradition platonicienne 65-91; Josef Kroll, *Die Lehren
des Hermes Trismegistos* (Münster: Aschendorffsche Verlagsbuch-
handlung, 1928) 264-289; Pierre Boyancé, "Dieu cosmique et dualisme. Les
archontes et Platon," *Le origini dello gnosticismo* 340-356.

like the famous wooden horse, "harboring as he does in one body such an army of different spirits," with which is to be compared the Stoic view, probably of Poseidonian origin, cited by Seneca, *Epistle* 113.3; *multa milia animalium habitent in his angustiis pectoris, et singuli multa simus animalia aut multa habeamus animalia.* It is this kind of adaptation of Plato's metaphors that, translated to a cosmological plane and embodied in creatures that represent the world-ruling sources of this level of soul, and with help from Oriental sources (solar gods "pantheos"), resulted in the late Orphic pictures of Phanes and Chronos-Heracles with their adventitious heads discussed in chapter 3.6; even the same verb προσφύειν is used in their description, as I noted then. But because they shared a far more pessimistic outlook, astrologically conditioned and dualistically expressed, on the cosmos and human life within it, the Gnostics, like their contemporary Numenius, veered far from the earlier Poseidonian adaptation of the Platonic tradition. Numenius (frs 43, 44, 52 des Places) made explicit what is clearly implied by the Basilidean psychology: the supposititious passionate soul(s) from the theriomorphic planetary world-creators is not simply inferior, but alien, totally other, a second soul, whether as world-soul or human soul.[26] Between the two there is a great gulf fixed; their mutual antagonism seems to have become irreconcilable.

But in truth it was not totally irreconcilable. As degraded as irrational soul might be for late antique minds, Plato still envisaged some hope for a part of it if only it would listen to reason. When one observes that the well-known Valentinian division not only of all humanity but as well the souls of individual human beings into elements πνευματικός, ψυχικός,

---

[26]Poseidonios' ideas (see pp. 196-197) did encourage the development; Philo, for example (*Questions and Answers on Exodus* 1.23), seems already more dualistic. On this subject note, e.g., Pierre Boyancé, "Les deux démons personnels dans l'antiquité grecque et latine," *RPh* (1935) 189-202. For Basilides, see Werner Foerster, "Das System des Basilides," *NTS* 9 (1963) 233-255, particularly pp. 254-255; Wolf-Dieter Hauschild, "Christologie und Humanismus bei dem 'Gnostiker' Basilides," *ZNW* 68 (1972) 67-92, particularly p. 88; Barbara Aland, "Gnosis und Kirchenväter. Ihre Auseinandersetzung um die Interpretation des Evangeliums," *Gnosis. Festschrift für Hans Jonas* 182-185. Clement goes on to attribute a similar doctrine of "appendages" to Valentinus: see G. C. Stead, "In Search of Valentinus," *The Rediscovery of Gnosticism. Proceedings of the International Conference on Gnosticism at Yale, New Haven, Connecticut, march 28-31, 1978* I. *The School of Valentinus* (ed. Bentley Layton; SHR [NumenSup] 41; Leiden: Brill, 1980) 79-80; E. R. Dodds, "Numenius and Ammonius," *Les sources de Plotin* 7-8.

and ὑλικός (or σαρκικός) (Irenaeus, *Refutation* 1.1.10-11; Clement of Alexandria, *Extracts from Theodotus* 51, 53-57), that this grouping neatly compares with the three facets of Plato's tripartition of the soul, even to the point of the ambivalence of allegiance for the element ψυχικός (= τὸ θυμοειδές), one is justified in suspecting that the Platonic tradition helped to shape the psychology of the most sophisticated and influential Gnostic systems of the second century, even though the terms in which the Gnostic tripartition is usually couched derive from Paul. The influence of the two parables of the *Republic* on the Basilideans is undeniable, and equally so the Platonic tripartition on Basilides' trichotomous sonship, the middle one "requiring purification" (Hippolytus, *Refutation* 7.22.7-16).[27] The media through which the Platonic stock reached its shareholders may——in many cases but by no means necessarily in all—have been subject to the distortions of astrological pollution, admixture of later philosophical elements (Stoic, through Poseidonios, for instance), and simplification in popularizing doxographical manuals, but reach them it did; it is interesting to find Ephraim indignantly reporting that even the Manichaeans, doubtless of the cultured, fully Hellenized breed know to Alexander of Lycopolis, ranked Plato on a par with Hermes Trismegistos and Jesus as envoys of illumination to this ignorant world of ours.[28] Plato's tamed lion, a passionate, bestial, but nevertheless redeemable part of mortal soul joined forces with the Old and New Testaments' insistence on salvation for the soul which repents and focuses its attention on the will of God (Plato's soul element λογικός, the Gnostics' πνευματικός) to soften and to humanize the harsh Gnostic mythology that roundly hated the savagely leonine creator Yahweh/Yaldabaoth with his theriomorphic cronies as agents of an oppressive Heimarmene. If the cruel Gnostic demiurge might clap the transmundane human spirit in the irons of his bestial passions,

---

[27] An excellent account of the intermediate status accorded to soul by late antique thought is provided by Hans Jonas, "The Soul in Gnosticism and Plotinus," *Le néoplatonisme* (Paris: Centre National de la Recherche Scientifique, 1971) 45-53. On the Gnostic tripartition see, for example, Stead, "In Search of Valentinus" 92-94; Birger Albert Pearson, *The Pneumatikos-Psychikos Terminology in 1 Corinthians. A Study in the Theology of the Corinthian Opponents of Paul and its Relation to Gnosticism* (SBLDS 12; Missoula: Scholars Press, 1973).

[28] C. W. Mitchell, *S. Ephraim's Prose Refutations of Mani, Marcion, and Bardaisan* II (London and Oxford: Williams and Norgate, 1921) xcviii-xcix and 208-209.

humanity might tame them and guarantee them (and him) some part in salvation (cp. Irenaeus, *Refutation* 1.1.12, for example).

It is the more forgiving, soteriologically conditioned Gnostic anthropology, shaped in part by the Platonic tradition, that informs the struggle of the lion and the man of the *Gospel of Thomas'* seventh logion to "devour" one another. One can well imagine that Socrates' parable might have held a special interest for the second-century ascetics who coined the logion on the basis of Gnostic recognition of Paul's wavering ψυχικοί in Plato's ambivalent lion; the results that Plato expects to follow from the alliance of Reason with the lion's nature (*Republic* 589A-B) is that ὁ ἐντὸς ἄνθρω- πος (where Christians cannot have failed to recall Rom 7:22-23; 2 Cor 4:16; Eph 3:16) will be ἐγκρατέστατος, a word and state with great appeal for late antique readers with abstemious frames of religious mind. In any case it was on the foundation of the kinder Gnostic psychology produced by the blend of the theriomorphic mythological tradition with the Pauline doctrine of redemption and the Platonic comparison of passionate soul to beasts (and perhaps too in this instance the subdued Platonic lion)[29] that

---

[29]One wonders whether the multitude of stories concerning the willing service paid to anchorites everywhere by lions (and other animals, but particularly lions), who abandon their wild nature and fawn upon their masters, did anything to increase the popularity of Socrates' parable and allow it to percolate down to such humbler circles. On such stories see Jacques Lacarrière, *Men Possessed by God. The Story of the Desert Monks of Ancient Christendom* (trans. R. Monkcom; Garden City, NY: Doubleday, 1964) 193-196; A.-J. Festugière, *Les moines d'Orient* I. *Culture ou sainteté* (Paris: Cerf, 1961) 53-57; Karl Heussi, *Der Ursprung des Mönchtums* (Tübingen: Mohr, 1936) 96-97, 174-175. Poimen knew the lion as a symbol of anger, as an apophthegm of his in the *Sayings of the Desert Fathers* (*PG* 65.351B, #115; Guy, *Les Apophtegmes des Pères du Désert* 241, #117; // Rufinus in *PL* 73.747C-D, #16 founded, like the other involving the lion, on reference to 1 Sam 17:34-35: see p. 183) shows: "A brother asked Abba Poimen: 'What shall I do, for I am being driven to lust and anger?' The old man replied: 'It was of this that David was speaking when he said "I smote the lion; I strangled the bear." He meant: I cut away anger, I squeezed out lust with hardships.'" A saying in the same collection has Hyperechios using the lion to represent moral strength (*PG* 65.430C, Hyperechios #1; Guy, *Les Apophtegmes des Pères du Désert* 309, #1; // Pelagius in *PL* 73.870C, #45; // M. Chaîne, *Le manuscrit de la version copte en dialecte sahidique des "Apophthegmata Patrum"* [Le Caire: IFAO, 1960] 2, 86 [#8]): "Abba Hyperechios said: 'Just as the wild asses fear the lion, so do desires (ἐπιθυμίας) the thoughts (λογισμοῖς) of

the well-behaved lion of 2a-c in the *Gospel of Thomas*' logion earned his blessing. When the passions are under control, "devoured" (an echo of the harsher mythological tradition) by the man, they may well be blessed because they have become human, and the aboriginal unity of man, upon which the *Gospel of Thomas* lays so much stress, is restored thereby. When the inner man is weak and the lion unruly—the situation of 3a-c— the man is "polluted" by the failure to bring the lion to heel.

The problematic wording of 3c is similarly understandable in the light of Gnostic anthropology as shaped by the Platonic tradition. It is to be noted that in Socrates' parable Plato does not have the lion—or the many-headed beast either, for that matter—devour the man not in control of himself, but rather each other. This is natural enough for an ebulliently rationalist thinker like Plato, who could not abide having the true, inner man, the immortal, rational soul, swallowed up by irrational passions. But the Gnostics groaned, as I said, under the weight of a far more oppressive cosmological burden in which the spiritual elements of man are engulfed, like Plato's Glaukos, by the tide of γένεσις, encrusted with and rendered unrecognizable by myriads of supposititious elements clinging to him. As I showed, in the hands of many interpreters the Platonic tradition grew more pessimistic as time went on, and Gnostics might well, therefore, have the lion devour the man, especially with their hearts set on an intractable leonine creator of the passionate "lion" in man and all the savage imagery from the Old Testament with which they bolstered this view of him. Still, on one point the Gnostics were in full accord with Plato: the Gnostic lion might "devour" the man and defile him, but the lion could never annihilate him. Though swallowed up and perhaps even deformed beyond recognition by the body and the passions in which the world-creating theriomorphic agents of Fate have trapped him, the primal Man is yet not totally absorbed by them, only perhaps lulled into obliviousness by them; his essential nature is unaltered because it is unalterable. Hence the logion's 3c *cannot* have said "the man shall become lion," and that for the same reason that in Plato's theory of the transmigration of souls a human soul may live the life of a beast, but it remains a *human* soul (cp. *Phaedrus* 249B, for example). In both 2c and 3c of the logion it is the lion that is made to undergo the transformation, then, not the man, even though in the latter set of circumstances he is the one consumed.

---

a tried monk.'" If these sayings attest the influence of the Platonic tradition (which they may or may not), it is obviously at some remove from the discussions, say, of their Neoplatonic contemporaries in Alexandria, Antioch, or Athens.

4.3   A Coptic Gnostic Version of the Parable

An astounding confirmation of the importance that Socrates' parable had for Gnostic mythology and anthropology has been provided by the fact that the passage from the ninth book of the *Republic* has turned up in a Coptic version at Nag Hammadi (CG VI, 5). To find the translation of a passage from Plato among the sacred books of a fourth-century monastic order is, to say the least, "something of a surprise,"[30] for Platonic influence is one thing, but a lengthy direct citation is another.[31] That the document's earliest editors did not recognize it for what it is is therefore quite understandable;[32] the credit for having realized its true provenance goes to Hans-Martin Schenke.[33]

------

[30]James Brashler in the preface to his translation in *The Nag Hammadi Library in English* 290; "eine grosse Überraschung" exclaims Carsten Colpe, "Heidnische, jüdische und christliche Überlieferung in den Schriften aus Nag Hammadi I," *JAC* 15 (1972) 14. It is even more of a surprise for Coptic literature generally; as Tito Orlandi aptly remarks: "chi ha familiarità con la letteratura copta, anche di traduzione, sa bene che l'esistenza di un testo di Platone ha del miracoloso" ("La traduzione copta di Platone, *Resp.* IX, 588b-589b: Problemi critici ed esegetici," *AANL.R* 8.32 (1977) 46.

[31]For treatments of Platonic influence on texts from Nag Hammadi see Birger A. Pearson, "The Tractate Marsanes (NHC X) and the Platonic Tradition," *Gnosis. Festschrift für Hans Jonas* 373-384; Alexander Böhlig, "Die griechische Schule und die Bibliothek von Nag Hammadi," *Zum Hellenismus in den Schriften von Nag Hammadi* (GOf 6.2; Wiesbaden: Harrassowitz, 1975) 9-53, particularly pp. 34-37. A short summary of this essay appears under the same title in *Les textes de Nag Hammadi* (ed. Jacques-É. Ménard; NHS 7; Leiden: Brill, 1975) 41-44.

[32]Martin Krause and Pahor Labib, *Gnostische und hermetische Schriften aus Codex II und Codex VI* (ADAI.K 2; Glückstadt: Augustin, 1971) 52-53, 166-169. They refer to the document simply as "titellose Schrift."

[33]"Zur Faksimile-Ausgabe der Nag-Hammadi-Schriften. Nag-Hammadi Codex VI," *OLZ* 69 (1974) 236-241. Schenke ("Nag-Hammadi-Codex VI" 236)—and all other scholars explicit in this regard as well—records *Republic* 588B-589B as the parameters of the Coptic excerpt, but this is technically an error that should be emended. The correct reference is actually 588*A*-589B as a comparison of the Coptic, whose beginning corresponds to Greek ἐπειδὴ ἐνταῦθα λόγου γεγόναμεν, with an edition of the *Republic* (that by Adam, for example [cited earlier: see n. 20] , p. 362, which Schenke cites, "Nag-Hammadi-Codex VI" 238) in which the section divisions are marked will show; 588B begins with γεγόναμεν. The

The passage in its Coptic form was obviously of sufficient interest to the men to whom the Nag Hammadi library belonged to warrant its retention and preservation. They, at least, may not have been aware that it stemmed ultimately from Plato; given the veneration accorded Plato by Hermetists, it is conceivable that the document came to them along with the three Hermetic tracts which follow it in Codex VI[34] and that they had no clue as to its Platonic origin, but the presumption of ignorance is dangerous, and the truth may well be that the parable had by this time acquired such notoriety from its integration into Gnostic anthropology that no introduction was necessary. It does not automatically follow, in any case, that the brethren who excerpted the passage, whether directly from the *Republic* or from some doxographical work,[35] and gnosticized it

---

erratic divisions are a convention adopted from the page numbers in Stephanus' edition of 1578 and are unfortunately not always exactly defined as to their limits in modern editions of Plato. They are not in John Burnet's edition (*Platonis Opera* IV; Oxford: Clarendon Press, 1962) which Brashler prints below the Coptic in his edition of the latter in *Nag Hammadi Codices V, 2-5 and VI with Papyrus Berolinensis 8502, 1 and 4* (NHS 11; Leiden: Brill, 1979) 328-338.

[34]So Schenke, "Nag-Hammadi-Codex VI" 238, citing a section of Zosimos of Panopolis (an early to mid-fourth century contemporary and compatriot of the Nag Hammadi library's community), *On the Letter Omega*. Note the Hermetic parallels to the tripartite psychology and other aspects of the excerpt cited by Orlandi, "La traduzione copta di Platone" 61.

[35]So Böhlig, *Zum Hellenismus in den Schriften von Nag Hammadi* 36-37 (*Les textes de Nag Hammadi* 43); Brashler, *The Nag Hammadi Library in English* 290; *Nag Hammadi Codices V, 2-5 and VI* 325-326; and Elias G. Matsagouras, *Plato Copticus. Republic 588B-589B. Translation and Commentary*; M. A. dissertation, Dalhousie University, 1976 (a summary of this work was published as "Plato Copticus" in Πλάτων. 'Εταιρεία ἑλλενῶν φιλολογῶν 29 [1977] 191-199), 96, who adduces Irenaeus, *Refutation* 2.18.2 for proof that Gnostics put together centos from Greek philosophers, but Irenaeus is actually only offering the routine heresiological charge of plagiarism from Hellenic philosophy to discredit his Gnostic opponents by depriving them of originality. I feel a good deal of reservation about this thesis of derivation from some anthology of edifying quotes or from some doxographical manual, firstly because no philosophical doxography known to me so much as mentions much less contains the parable, secondly because the excerpt is rather too lengthy and unwieldy to have come from such a source, and most importantly because the allusions in contemporary Neo-Platonists like Iamblichus and Proclus attest to its accessibility in the original and, as the work of men like Zosimos and Nonnos, both from Panopolis (Akhmim) not far from Nag

(to anticipate my argument) were followers of Hermes Trismegistos. Its position at the head of Hermetic tractates may be simply fortuitous (and it is preceded by Gnostic tractates), and besides, Egypt was full of world deniers who counted Plato among their number and who read each other's literature. Not the least of these were the Manichaeans, whose interest in beasts like the lion and the serpent as symbols of passion is plentifully attested to by the contemporary Coptic Manichaica and who therefore, like their predecessors the ascetics who coined *Gos. Thom.* logion 7, had every reason to take a special interest in Socrates' parable as the chief embodiment of the whole Platonic tradition discussed in the preceding section.

It is not out of the question that the group responsible for excerpting and adapting the parable were, in fact, identical with that which translated the document into Coptic, spiritual sons, in effect, of the late second-century ascetic community who took the Platonic tradition of beastly passionate soul as melded with the Gnostic tradition of a leonine creator and crystalized it in logion 7 of the *Gospel of Thomas.* Such a group was that which surrounded the early, native Egyptian anchorite Hierakas, of whom Epiphanius provides an extremely interesting but tantalizingly brief report (*Medicine Chest,* heresy 67, together with the *Life of Saint Epiphanius* 27, which records the bishop's acrimonious meeting with the man; when Epiphanius wrote Hierakas had already died, reputedly over ninety years of age; he must therefore have been born about A.D. 275 at the latest). To judge from the bishop's report, Hierakas was a man perfectly capable, like Origen his spiritual father, of reading Plato, excerpting and adapting Socrates' parable to suit his own ascetic purposes, and translating the result into Coptic; Epiphanius speaks somewhat grudgingly of his erudition in all branches of Greek and Egyptian learning, both humanistic and scientific, his equal mastery of the languages of both cultures, and his composition in both of them, especially what were to Epiphanius unorthodox, allegorical commentaries on the Hexaemeron, right up to the day he died.[36] Socrates' parable may, of

---

Hammadi, illustrate, Upper Egypt was not the cultural backwater it is commonly supposed to have been at this time.

[36]On Hierakas see Adolf Harnack's entry in RE^3 8.38-39 and his *Geschichte der altchristlichen Literatur bis Eusebius* II.2 (2nd ed.; Leipzig: Hinrichs, 1958) 83-84; Heussi, *Der Ursprung des Mönchtums* 58-65; Bernhard Lohse, *Askese und Mönchtum in der Antike und in der alten Kirche* (München and Wien: Oldenbourg, 1969) 179-181. One cannot dispose of Epiphanius' evidence simply by labeling it "einen gelehrten Traum" as does Johannes Leipoldt, "Geschichte der koptischen Literatur"

course, equally well have circulated in its gnosticized form in Greek long before translation into its present Coptic form. The adaptation may rather be due to Hierakas' severely ascetic predecessors and contemporaries the Manichaeans or even to the probably Syrian ascetics of the second century who coined the seventh logion of the *Gospel of Thomas* in partial dependence on the parable's imagery as seen through encratite eyes. But Hierakas' interest in the passage would be quite explicable, in any case, on the basis of the long Christian tradition which adapted Plato's beast-metaphor to the Gnostic mythologem of theriomorphic archons and their passionate images in man, and it is reasonable to conclude that if he and his followers, who continued in existence to the end of the fourth century, were not responsible for excerpting and adapting Socrates' parable it is likely to have been they who took an interest in it, translated it into Coptic, and forwarded it to their Pachomian brethren in the south.[37] Hierakas lived just outside Leontopolis (Tel Moqdam), whose lion-cult was evidently still intact at this time (Porphyry, *On Abstinence from Animal Food* 4.9, suggests it was); one can imagine that this proximity might stir his interest in Plato's lion as reflected in the ascetic tradition of the Gnostics who adapted Socrates' parable.

There can be no doubt that someone, whoever it was and whenever it was, has worked Socrates' parable over with a view to transforming its animal-metaphor into an exponent of the Gnostic theriomorphic mythology and its consequences for human psychogenesis. The parable's tripartite psychology couched in temptingly bestial imagery must have proved irresistibly attractive to those who made a Gnostic allegory of it, predisposed as they were to read into Plato's lion the leontomorphic demiurge and his reflections the "lions" of the Psalms who had come to symbolize—under the impact of the very same Platonic tradition of which Socrates' parable is the chief source—the passions, specifically the lust for γένε-σις.[38] Schenke is of the opinion that the excerpt does not represent a

---

in *Geschichte der christlichen Literaturen des Orients* (Leipzig: Amelang, 1907) 145. On Hierakas' position at the threshhold of the development of Coptic literature see Carl Schmidt, "Die Urschrift der Pistis Sophia," *ZNW* 24 (1925) 218-240, especially pp. 218-227.

[37] For speculation (and unfortunately that is all it is) regarding other possible connections between Hierakian monks and the Nag Hammadi codices see Frederik Wisse, "Gnosticism and Early Monasticism in Egypt," *Gnosis. Festschrift für Hans Jonas* 431-440, particularly pp. 438-440.

[38] Aland, "Gnosis und Kirchenväter" 184-185, adduces the Coptic excerpt for the similarity of its representation of the tripartite soul to the Basilidean, remarking (p. 185): "Hier ist ein direkter Beweis dafür

Gnostic reworking of the passage from Plato, that Socrates' parable has merely been "fürchterlich misshandelt durch die Übersetzung eines nicht nur in der Philosophie, sondern auch schon in der griechischen Sprache Unmündigen."[39] Brashler concurs in this judgment, though he rightly points out that on this account CG VI, 5 "represents an exception to the rest of the tractates in the Nag Hammadi codices, which generally have been translated from the Greek with considerable skill and understanding."[40] Orlandi and Matsagouras, on the other hand, argue for Gnostic redaction.[41]

---

gegeben, dass die Gnostiker Platon selbst studierten und benutzten" ("benutzten" yes, but not necessarily "studierten"). Matsagouras, *Plato Copticus* 64-71, also posits Valentinian and Basilidean psychology as the reason for Gnostic interest in the passage from Plato. Orlandi, "La traduzione copta di Platone" 59-60, refers to sections from Clement of Alexandria's *Extracts from Theodotus* (those cited on p. 201 above) in explication of the excerpt's psychology and compares *Extracts* 84 with its allusion to the "lions" of Pss 22:21 [21:22] and 35[34]:17 to VI, 5; 50.24-28 of the Coptic excerpt.

[39]"Nag-Hammadi-Codex VI" 236; so too col. 239: "NHC VI/5 . . . nichts anderes als eine unmögliche Platon-Übersetzung ist, und nicht etwa eine gnostische Bearbeitung des Platon-Textes." Schenke goes on to say: "An diesem Text war ja auch gar nichts gnostisch umzudeuten, weil sich die gnostische Daseinshaltung in ihm direkt wiedererkennen konnte," but that does not in itself constitute a discouragement to redaction, and, moreover, there are elements in Plato's version that did *not* accord well with the Gnostic view of things. A little further on, however, Schenke admits: "Wo er (the Coptic excerpt), abgesehen von offenkundigen Missverständnissen, von Platon abweicht, handelt es sich nur darum, dass etwa ein Ausdruck doppelt wiedergegeben wird, bzw. ein kurzschlüssiges und ratendes Umbiegen der grundsätzlichen und hypothetischen Aussagen des Textes ins Moralische oder ins Reale." In this "Umbiegen . . . ins Moralische" lies the rub, for the question then is: In what direction and to whose interest was this detour carried out?

[40]*The Nag Hammadi Library in English* 290; *Nag Hammadi Codices V, 2-5 and VI* 325-326. The citation is from the latter work, p. 325.

[41]Orlandi, "La traduzione copta di Platone" *passim*, but particularly p. 54: "C'è stato un intervento molto deciso da parte non di un traduttore, ma di un *redattore* che ha preso il brano platonico come puro pretesto per scrivere un vero e proprio brano gnostico"; Matsagouras, *Plato Copticus* 25, on the mention (unfortunately in a broken context) of "archon[s?]" in the Coptic at VI, 5; 49.6 where no such word exists in the corresponding text of the *Republic* (588C). Schenke's reasoning here ("Nag-Hammadi-Codex VI" 240) seems unnatural and oversubtle to me; to him the presence

It is not my purpose here to carry out a full and systematic comparative analysis of the Coptic and the Greek texts, but merely to show that CG VI, 5, like *Gos. Thom.* logion 7, is yet another example of the Gnostic assimilation of the Platonic tradition under review, one, in this case, that, willingly or no, went directly to the source. It is significant, in the first place, that the passage from the *Republic* as delimited by the excerpt has, even in its original state, nothing good to say about the lion; the excerpt breaks off precisely at the point where Plato is about to mention the lion for its beneficial function ("making an ally of the lion's nature"). By helping to shape Gnostic anthropology and soteriology the Platonic tradition may have softened the Gnostic mythology with its ruthless leonine cosmocrator, but no ascetic could go so far as to allow himself any alliance with the savagely bestial lion, whether representing Plato's θυμός, or lust, or any other passion.[42] The passionate "lion" might be blessed if he bowed to superior authority and let himself be swallowed up by the

---

of ⲁⲣⲭⲱⲛ in the Coptic has come about through a blunder: the translator's intention was to render παλαιός in the Greek text with ἀρχαῖος, but he (or a redactor) confused this word with ἄρχων. I do not deny that misreadings and mistranslations may lie behind some of the instances in which the Coptic varies from the Greek, but I do not think that error is exclusively and principally the cause of them; the "errors" are too often Gnostic in tendency. Arthur Hillary Armstrong, "Gnosis and Greek Philosophy," *Gnosis. Festschrift für Hans Jonas* 99, in the context of judicious remarks on Gnostic use of Greek philosophy ("Possible influences of Greek philosophy on the Gnosis," pp. 99-103), similarly argues for Gnostic adaptation. It is interesting to observe how handily the brief analysis of CG VI, 5 offered by the Berliner Arbeitskreis für koptisch-gnostische Schriften in "Die Bedeutung der Texte von Nag Hammadi für die moderne Gnosisforschung," *Gnosis und Neues Testament* (ed. Karl-Wolfgang Tröger; Berlin: Evangelische Verlagsanstalt, 1973) 52-53—written, as the final paragraph admits, before Schenke announced the passage's Platonic identity—interprets its content in the light of Gnostic theologoumena.

[42]Schenke, "Nag-Hammadi-Codex VI" 238, notes that Eusebius' verbatim excerpt of the same passage from the *Republic* (see n. 24 above) corresponds rather closely in its limits to those of the Coptic tractate. But the correspondence is not exact; the bishop's text includes ξύμμαχον ποιησάμενος τὴν τοῦ λέοντος φύσιν and the conciliatory words that follow. Eusebius' purpose in citing the passage is, interestingly enough, for comparison of its creatures with Ezekiel's הַיָּה.

man (*Gos. Thom.* logion 7, 2a-c)[43] and so take part in the inner man's salvation, but a mutual non-aggression pact—never! Thus what Plato does say about the lion within the confines of the excerpted section, wrenched as it is from its context, has in both cases been twisted to serve what is unmistakably a more pessimistic Gnostic interest. In the first instance (588D), where Socrates directs Glaucon to the final two stages of the process of constructing their fabulous man: "Then fashion one other form of a lion and one of a man," the Gnostic redactor (VI, 5; 49.33-35) has turned this simple directive into a contrast between the two natures: "For ... the image of the lion is one thing and the image of the man is another."[44]

The second mention of the lion in the setting of the Coptic excerpt is equally tendentious in its treatment of Plato. Socrates' presentation of what the advocate of the profitability of injustice is really advocating (588E-589A) is rendered (VI, 5; 50.24-51.1): "But ... what is profitable for him is this: that he cast down every image of the evil beast ... and trample them along with the images of the lion. But ... the man is in weakness in this regard. ... As a result ... he is drawn to the place where he spends the day with them at fi[rst]."[45] What Socrates makes the activity of the unjust man has been transformed by the Gnostic redactor into a recommendation to rid oneself of the lion and the beast, and the

---

[43]Matsagouras, *Plato Copticus* 72, mentions *Gos. Thom.* logion 7 in the course of his exposition; he appreciates the fact that the blessing pronounced upon the lion in 2a is the result of the animal's assimilation to a more human level of existence.

[44]Brashler, *Nag Hammadi Codices V, 2-5 and VI* 335, whose translation I follow here and in the next paragraph.

[45]Brashler, *Nag Hammadi Codices V, 2-5 and VI* 337, to which I have added "at fi[rst]" from the Coptic, presuming the restoration ⲛ̄ϣⲟ[ⲣⲡ̄] is correct. The last clause is somewhat problematic; ⲉⲡⲙⲁ ⲉⲧϥ̄ⲣ̄ ϩⲟⲟⲩ ⲉⲣⲟⲟⲩ ⲛ̄ϣⲟ[ⲣⲡ] might also be translated "to the place which does evil to them at first," although it is difficult to see how the world could do evil to the beasts and their images that are both quite at home there, but they are the only possible antecedent for ⲉⲣⲟⲟⲩ, unless the third person plural is a pronominal shift and refers to human beings. Krause and Labib, *Gnostische und hermetische Schriften* 169, choose this course in rendering the clause, offering "an den Ort, der ihnen Übles tut" with "Zu[erst]" beginning a new sentence, though [ⲁ]ⲩⲱ, which follows ⲛ̄ϣⲟ[ⲣⲡ] , shows that the latter phrase goes with what precedes. Orlandi's "nel luogo in cui (?) risiedeva prima" ("La traduzione copta di Platone" 53) seems to reflect the former alternative.

recommendation is couched in terms and circumstances suspiciously reminiscent of the Gnostic traditions encountered in the *Pistis Sophia* and the Coptic Manichaica. It is actually not the lion and the beast themselves which are to be rejected, but their "images," an expression which reflects the Gnostic mythologem of the infusion of the cosmos by the leonine creator and his bestial adjutants with a level of being fashioned in their own image (Gen 1:26-27 being at the root of this). The un-Platonic hostility that the Coptic excerpt breathes toward the lion and the beast is a reflection of the fact that the harsher Gnostic mythology has been allowed to override the more strictly anthropological dimensions of the passage in its Platonic context; in CG VI, 5 the lion and the beast are not facets of the soul (only their "images" are), but autonomous creatures fully independent of man. The motif of "trampling" the evil powers is similarly suggestive of the Gnostic mythological adaptation of Ps 91[90]:13 and Luke 10:18-19 that is evident in the *Pistis Sophia* (see chapter 2.3); the "place" to which the man in his weakness is drawn and "where he spends the day with them at first" is their lair, the cosmos, into which the Manichaean lion and serpent take their quarry the soul of the primal Man (see chapter 2.5). If it is only "at first" it is doubtless because, again as in the *Pistis Sophia* and the Manichaean texts, the Man eventually makes good his escape from their clutches through a holy life of continence.

But, unless it was merely a regrettable oversight, the Gnostic redactor has permitted something of Plato's more forgiving anthropology to stand. Although the oppressive leonine overlord of the material universe was primarily in his mind and the parts of man for which he is responsible are mere images of the creator's bestial self, although he has consequently altered what Plato says of the lion in the interest of its disparagement, he has nevertheless left Plato's injunction to feed and care for the *tame* beasts (*Republic* 589B) unaltered (VI, 5; 51.16-21). For him as for the composer of the seventh logion of the *Gospel of Thomas* the ferocity of the leontocephalic demiurge can be mollified by becoming part of man and by being coaxed into willing servitude (so Plato) or starved into submission by ἄσκησις (so the Christian ascetics). As an "image" in the human soul even the Coptic excerpt's lion still seems to have a hope of salvation.

4.4   Summary

There is a whole anthropological dimension to the astrologically conditioned Gnostic myth of a leonine creator and his theriomorphic helpers, and it centers around the contribution made by these astral powers to the makeup of the human soul, the contribution of that intermediate level of being of which they are themselves the cosmic representatives: the passions. As planetary agents of Fate the Gnostic archons shared the duty accorded the planets by late antique astral mysticism: to endow the immortal soul descending into birth in the world with the various affective states they typify; hence in Gnostic myth the demiurge is at once the product and the source of all passion.

The lion's mythological association with the lord of creation was especially well suited for this new facet of the tradition because for a variety of reasons—astrological, zoological and iconographic—the lion was intimately connected with sexual desire, and sexual passion is the quintessentially cosmogonic force. Beginning in the second century Gnostic texts, especially those from groups with strongly abstinent leanings, attest the linking of the lion with the lust for γένεσις.

The lion as a symbol of sexual desire for Gnostic ascetics is but a special application of a broader tradition that used beasts as metaphors of the πάθη. That tradition stems from the likeness that Plato has Socrates paint of the human soul in the ninth book of the *Republic*: the soul comprises an immortal, human element, a many-headed beast, who represents the basest of drives, and thirdly a lion, who is, for Plato, the potentially salvageable passion of θυμός, the sum of all that is spirited, aggressive and courageous in man. The Greek philosophical tradition, especially Stoics like Poseidonios, kept this Platonic metaphor alive, but under astrological impetus in its inevitable assimilation to the passionate, theriomorphic archons of Gnostic myth it was more and more pessimistically interpreted. It was only as assimilated to the tripartite Gnostic psychology, founded in part upon Plato's, reflected in Socrates' parable, and in part upon Paul's neatly parallel tripartite soteriology, that Plato's well-behaved lion retained any favor with men.

It is against this background that logion 7 of the *Gospel of Thomas* must be explained. Its lion is the summational representative of all passion, perhaps specifically sexual passion for the ascetics who coined the logion, and if it may be blessed it is not as the leontocephalic creator but rather as his element in man which may nevertheless be redeemed by being obedient to—"devoured" by—his more spiritual master. The enigmatic wording of the last clause of the saying is to be explained, not as an error, but as the expression of the equally Platonic and Gnostic impossibility of having the spiritual Man be totally absorbed when he is lost to the "lion."

This originally Platonic tradition using the lion and other animals as symbols of passion continued to be a standard feature of ascetic Christian exegesis, both in its more orthodox as well as in its Gnostic streams. The emergence of a gnosticized version of Socrates' parable in Coptic at Nag Hammadi attests, as it were, the return of the tradition to its source and its reinterpretation in the light of all the changes in outlook that six or seven hundred years of water under the bridge had wrought. The document's redactor was an ascetic of precisely the same mold as, and possibly indeed a member of, the second-century encratites who fashioned logion seven of *Gos. Thom.* and treasured the whole collection. Later candidates are the Manichaeans or even conceivably the early Origenist anchorite Hierakas, whose literary activity in Coptic makes him (or his followers) at any rate a prime candidate for the source of the Coptic version of the adapted parable which his Upper Egyptian monastic brethren chose to include in their library and then to ferret away to be discovered, with the cognate logion from the *Gospel of Thomas,* centuries afterwards.

Plate 1

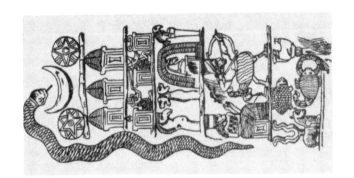

b

a

Plate 2

b

a

Plate 3

b

a

Plate 4

a

b

c

d

Plate 5

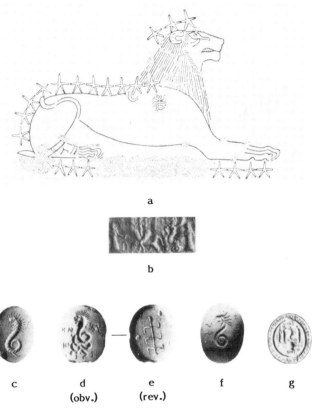

a

b

c   d   e   f   g

(obv.)   (rev.)

        l   m

h   i   j   k

(obv.) (rev.) (obv.) (rev.)

Plate 6

a

b

c

Plate 7

a

b

c

d

e

Plate 8

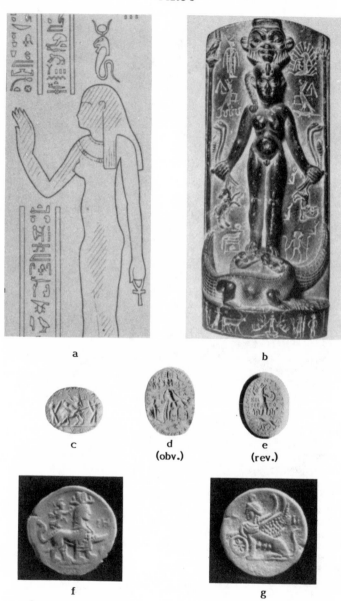

a

b

c

d
(obv.)

e
(rev.)

f

g

Plate 9

a

b

c

Plate 10

a

b

Plate 11

a

b

c

Plate 12

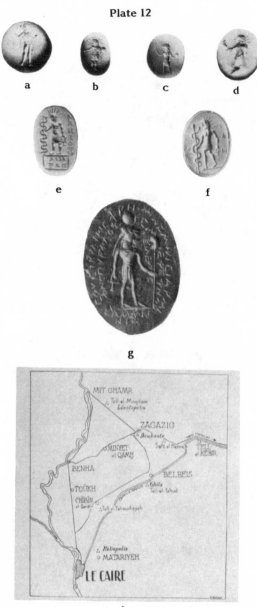

a   b   c   d

e   f

g

h

Plate 13

Plate 14

Plate 15

a

b

Plate 16

Plate 17

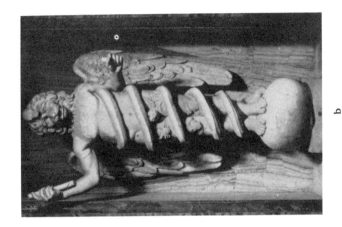

b

a

Plate 18

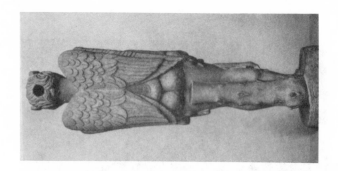

c

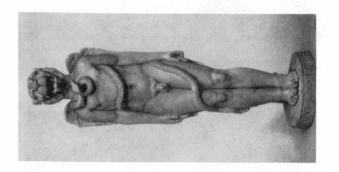

b

a

Plate 19

a

b   c